Dobermanns

A PRACTICAL GUIDE FOR OWNERS AND BREEDERS

Jay Horgan

THE CROWOOD PRESS

First published in 2017 by
The Crowood Press Ltd
Ramsbury, Marlborough
Wiltshire SN8 2HR

www.crowood.com

British Library Cataloguing-in-Publication Data
A catalogue record for this book is available from the British Library.

ISBN 978 1 78500 3080

Typeset by Jean Cussons Typesetting, Diss, Norfolk

Printed and bound in India by Parksons Graphics

CONTENTS

ACKNOWLEDGEMENTS

My gratitude to the many people who helped me with this book. I am indebted to all the photographers and people who donated images of their beloved dogs, which have been invaluable. The people who donated images of their beloved dogs have been invaluable to the success of the book, as have the friends who proofread the chapters for me. I have made every effort to be as accurate as possible, but inevitably there will be some errors which I hope you will forgive.

I am deeply indebted to my husband Martin, without whose support and indulgence I could not have had the time or resources to complete this task.

As any owner will tell you, the Dobermann is unique and I am lucky to share my life with all the great dogs we have owned who have taught me so much. I cannot imagine life without a Dobermann by my side.

1 THE HISTORY OF THE BREED

The Dobermann is by nature a protector, guardian and companion. Kept in a home and in intimate touch with people, he will display his inherently watchful, willing, obedient and brave character.

Phillip Gruenig

The Dobermann began life in Apolda, Thüringen, in central Germany in the late 1800s. Much of its history is based on hearsay and conjecture, which in part adds a touch of mystery and intrigue to the breed. The breed was named after its original creator Karl Louis Friedrich Dobermann, who was born in Apolda on 2 January 1834, where he remained resident until his death on 9 January 1884, at fifty years old.

During his lifetime Herr Dobermann had a variety of occupations, including working in the slaughterhouse as a skinner, being the local dog catcher, and some say acting as a police officer in the evening hours; but his most famous role was as municipal tax collector for the Niederossla-Apolda Chamber of Accounts. This was as unpopular a role then as it is today, and necessitated having a dog by his side that would be a disincentive to anyone who might cause him trouble on his rounds. In 1870 he owned such a dog, called Schnupp, described as a black male with red markings and a grey undercoat. (Schnuppe/Schnupps/Schnuppine was a very common name for dogs at that time, meaning grey.)

Although the dog seen at Herr Dobermann's feet was apparently this dog Schnupp, it was not the dog used in his breeding foundation, as it was castrated at nine months. Schnupp was remembered by Herr Dobermann's son, Unser Louis Dobermann, as 'a dog of such great intelligence as is seldom found. He was clever and fearless and knew how to bite. My father could not have chosen a better one.'

Dog breeding was very popular throughout Germany, and particularly in the Apolda region at that time. An annual dog market was held there at Whitsuntide from 1860, when about a hundred or more dogs would be on sale and on show, and would attract many buyers and sellers of dogs. Dogs would be classified as hunting breeds, butcher's dogs, ratters and terriers, guard dogs and small toy luxury dogs, and others. This market also included food stalls and music, and it became such an important event that it is officially recorded in the history of the city of Apolda.

The only known photograph of Herr Dobermann with friends and dogs.

Market square in Apolda with a sculpture of Dobermanns.

Herr Dobermann was a regular visitor to this dog market, because with his various occupations it provided him with the ideal opportunity to select dogs with the physique and character that particularly interested him for his breeding plans. From the outset his motivation was to breed dogs not just for the sake of it: his intention was to breed a dog that would be capable of reproducing itself – to create a new and particular breed.

In the early days of his ambitions he could only breed the occasional litter as his homes were too small to cope with the larger scale plans that he had; but in 1880 he finally moved to large enough premises to breed more litters. In the meantime he was fortunate to have had two colleagues,

night-watchman Herr Rabel and Herr Stegmann, who were eager to join him in his plans for the breed, and with whom he was able to place stud dogs and breeding bitches.

EARLY INFLUENCES

Herr Dobermann's vision was of a large, terrier-type dog, sturdy but agile, with a sharp mind – and most importantly it had to be an unparalleled personal guard dog of fearsome reputation. With the sources available to him, and with a selection of various dogs from other breeds in the region, he began to breed his ideal dog. This part of the history of the Dobermann is open to speculation, as no breeding records were kept;

consequently disagreement has always existed over the original types of dog used to create the breed.

Trying to place 'Dobermann's dogs' into any category at this time is quite impossible, as they were wholly different from the Dobermann of today. They were short (35–40cm/14–16in) and squat, and appeared more terrier-like than anything else. The consensus of opinion is that up to the first half of the 1900s the probable originators of the breed were a type of dog predominant in the region colloquially known as the 'German butcher's dog', the Thüringian Shepherd (a smaller herding breed than the model of the breed that we know today), the Thüringian (German) Pinscher, and the Beauceron (an old French hunting dog).

The 'butcher's dog' was the type of dog that accompanied Mr Stegmann on his journeys to Switzerland to buy in new stock. Butcher's dogs were not a uniform type, as the term seemed to refer to the divergent types of the Metzgerhund, the ancestor in type to the Rottweiler, including a larger, more ponderous animal used for draft work and in particular for pulling the butchers' meat carts, and a smaller, more agile type used mainly for herding. Although the butcher's dog is credited as being one of the originators of the Rottweiler, in 1925 Max Kuensler wrote that 'the sheep dog, the Weimaraner and the German Pinscher were involved, but certainly no Rottweilers or Terriers were known in Apolda at that time.'

The Thüringian Shepherd, which is now extinct as an individual breed, was known in the Apolda region before Herr Dobermann began breeding, and these were a cross between a type of Pinscher and a sheepdog. A German dog magazine article dated 1898 reads as follows:

> At the end of the 1860s, the owner of a gravel pit at Apolda called Dietsch had a blue-grey bitch, a sort of Pinscher, which he mated with a black butcher's dog. The sire already had the characteristic tan markings and was a cross between a sheepdog and a butcher's dog. Herr Dobermann, a skinner who unfortunately died too early, crossed the issue of these two dogs, which became good guard dogs, with German Pinschers. That is the origin of today's Dobermann.

Beaucerons dated back to the 1500s and were known to be in the region of Apolda at that time,

German Pinscher (Arco v.d. Lauter, 12 April 1912).

Prinz Lux v Rhein, born 1904 (Graf Belling v. Gronland × Lucca v. Braunsfeld).

Beauceron, also known as Bas Rouge (Red Stocking). Int/Ir Ch Jupiler du Regard Mordant, owned by Steve and Jackie Barnes.

having been left behind from the occupying forces of Napoleon's army. The Dobermann shares many similarities with the Beauceron in the shape of its head, body and working characteristics. Beaucerons are known for their unique double hind dewclaws, and these occasionally surface in Dobermanns. (A litter born to the author in 2006 contained three puppies, each with double hind dew claws.)

The town of Apolda is the capital of the Weimar region, and it is known that the Weimaraner hunting dog was in existence in the region from the 1600s. Certainly the shape, the close hair and the occasional (and highly undesirable) light eye in the Dobermann hold similarities. It is believed that the Weimaraner introduced the blue colouring to the breed, along with the blue Great Dane and the Beauceron.

The markings, colouring, shape and character of the various breeds have obviously drawn attention to their relationship with the Dober-

Great Dane 1890 (working type).

mann. The Thüringian Pinscher and Thüringian Shepherd both had a smooth black coat with red markings, and both were known to have an aggressive and sharp character.

The ancestor of the Rottweiler, the Metzgerhund, carried the same coat colour and markings as the Dobermann, although the coat was a lot thicker and wavier: this is still seen today, especially in dogs of Eastern European breeding. They were also the same height, but were solid in body, and had a much heavier head shape, with a shorter foreface-to-skull length: it is worth noting that head shape will readily revert to this proportion if breeders do not breed to keep the head as a blunt wedge instead of a triangular wedge.

The head shape of the French Beauceron resembles that of the Dobermann more closely than any other breed. Also in the varying colours all have the tan markings, with what were called Bas Rouge, or red stocking, which referred to the red rust leg markings. Beaucerons may also have a few white hairs on the chest, and although these are considered highly undesirable in Dobermann breed standards, they do still appear in Dobermanns worldwide.

The German Pinscher, the Beauceron and the greyhound all carry brown and tan, blue and tan, and fawn and tan in their genes. Phillip Gruenig and other references suggest that the English Black and Tan Terrier, which later became known as the Manchester Terrier, was used in the formation of the Dobermann, but breed authorities Otto Goeller and Herr Strebel both discount the use of them in the original formation of the breed because they were not known in the region of Thüringen until well after 1890, by which time the Dobermann was well established.

One cross breeding with a Black and Tan Terrier is recorded much later, in 1900, one cross breeding with the greyhound in 1906, and then some time later again with the Manchester Terrier. Karl Peter Umlauff, who was for many years President of the Dobermann Pinscher Club of Germany, bred Black and Tan Terriers for a short time in addition to his breed of choice, the Great Dane. His daughter Gerda was a noted breed authority in her own right.

Black and Tan Terrier, Zürich 1899.

The first dog show in Germany was held at Hamburg in 1863, but the first German Dog Stud Book was only established in 1876. In the 1882 issue it was noted that: 'In the German dog shows there is some confusion about the English Black and Tan Terrier, also known as The Manchester Terrier, and our shorthaired Pinscher.'

In 1901, Richard Strebel (a German authority on canine matters) wrote: 'It is doubtful if the Dobermann Pinscher is a true Pinscher; it should probably be classified more as a sheep dog.' In 1933 the ongoing question as to the origins of the breed was once again raised by the German Dobermann Club, and the opinions of many old breeders were sought, including those of Goswin Tischler, who knew Herr Dobermann personally, and Robert Dobermann, Herr Dobermann's youngest son.

The conclusion was that the German Pinscher was the main ancestor of the Dobermann. In 1947 Gruenig wrote that the Dobermann probably descended more from the Beauceron, as he did not believe it would have been possible to raise the shoulder height of the German Pinscher from 30cm to 70cm in only thirty years. Although Gruenig is an undoubted and unparalleled authority on the breed, this comment did come nearly seventy years after Herr Dobermann bred his first dogs, and a great deal may already have changed in this period.

The German Shepherd Dog (GSD) is also said to have a place in the history of the breed, but as a specific breed they themselves did not come into existence until 1899, well after Herr Dobermann's dogs became established.

Discuss this as we may, just as our forefathers did, the exact origins of our breed will all remain subject to conjecture, and in reality it is as difficult to confirm them as it is to confirm those of a crossbreed.

In 1863, at the age of just twenty-nine, Herr Dobermann presented his 'Dobermann Pinschers' at the dog market in Apolda, where they were received most enthusiastically. With Herr Dobermann as their leader, the three men – Herr Dobermann, Herr Rabel and Herr Stegmann – soon became renowned for the quality of their fierce guard dogs, which fetched high prices and were sold as fast as they could be bred.

The Dobermann at this time was virtually unrecognizable from today's dog in both character and looks. Ever alert, he was hair-trigger quick to react, with little or no bite restraint at the first hint of trouble, and over-keen to take on opponents, from other dogs to human aggressors. Responsive to the slightest provocation and with a high nerve threshold, this dog had become the ultimate deterrent to any attacker, and one that guarded his master without any thought for himself.

One of the most prominent bitches bred by Herr Dobermann was Bissart. She was originally named Bismarck, until a senior officer stated that it was unlawful to give a dog the same name as a great statesman (Count Otto von Bismarck lived in that time). Bissart was black with tan markings and a grey undercoat, and Herr Dobermann's son Louis reported that his father bred some quality puppies from her. Most were black with red markings, although two were mainly black with red and white markings. Bissart had a daughter named Pinko, who was a natural bobtail, and he subsequently bred her to a bobtailed stud, but there was only one bobtailed puppy in the litter. There were also blue puppies in that litter, which gives credence to the early influence of the other breeds mentioned that were known to carry this colour.

ESTABLISHING A BREED STANDARD

After Herr Dobermann's death in 1884 it was recognized that the development of the breed up until that time had been conducted in a very haphazard manner. Popular though it was, dog breeding was not highly regarded as a profession, and although there were by now several fanciers of the breed, the lack of any formal registration system impeded progress. Dogs that were bred or kept in their owners' name, usually changed names with subsequent ownership, so tracing the parentage of these dogs was often very difficult.

Herr Oskar Vorwerk of Hamburg encouraged several hobby breeders to join forces and establish a breed standard that could be recognized by the German National Kennel Club. Existing Dobermann owner and breeder Otto Göller and his wife were persuaded by Vorwerk to take up the task of developing what was still a very undeveloped and rough breed. Göller eventually became known as the architect of the breed, and he further substantiates the origins of the Dobermann when he wrote:

> I am quite convinced that it was principally the German Shepherd dog, the smooth-haired Pointer, the blue Great Dane, and the German smooth-haired Pinscher which played a remarkable part in the creation of this breed. Those dogs that I bought in the villages had no undercoat, or very little, red markings, short, absolutely black hair like hounds, little marked lips, and long toes. Those dogs which came from Apolda were more like German Shepherd dogs and Pinschers.

When the number of dogs overwhelmed their accommodation, they were often placed in suitable 'breeding homes', and this remains common practice in Germany and other countries.

Even by this stage the Dobermann was physically not particularly advanced in type, and a contemporary show report in that year describes them as being 'coarse and heavy-headed, inclined to be long and wavy-coated with thick grey undercoat and straw-yellow markings'. White spots on the chest were commonplace, and they generally appeared to look like a small Rottweiler.

Göller was already familiar with the exceptional intelligence of the Dobermann, but he also recognized that the dogs were too fierce and vicious, and although he wanted to retain its superb guard-dog characteristics, he knew that if these dogs were to be accepted into general ownership a more amenable temperament was required (though what we term as generally amenable, and what was the case at the turn of the century, were very different indeed!)

Otto Göller's breeding name was 'von Thüringen'. On 16 May 1896 he bred a litter by the sire Lord v. Thueringen (alias v. Dennstedt/v. Gröenland) out of the bitch Schnuppine v. Dennstedt; the male pups were Lux, Schnupp, Landgraf and Rambo, and the females Tilly1 NZ17, Helmtrude, Hertha and Elly. These dogs are among those that formed what is termed the 'germ cell' of the breed, as so many important lines descended from them.

Hertha v. Gröenland.

A founding breeder who bred closely with Herr Göller was Goswin Tischler, whose kennel was named 'von Gröenland'. In 1898 his black female Tilly 1 NZ17, bred by Otto Göller, was bred to Lux v. Gröenland (Nero × Ceres), and the resulting progeny were of such high quality that they were known as the 'five-star litter'. They included Greif DZ184, Tilly ll NZ28, Krone DZ2, Lottchen DZ8, and Graf Belling NZ1 (the last two were later known as Lottchen v. Thueringen and Graf Belling v. Thueringen, after they were bought by Otto Göller). It is impossible to choose just one particular dog from this litter as a breed example, as they were all fundamental to the creation of the breed, but what is of greater importance is how those early dogs were bred together to provide its foundations.

Graf Belling and Gerhilde v. Gröenland/v. Thüringen. Graf Belling v. Gröenland was the first Dobermann registered with the National Dobermannpinscher stud book, number NZDB1, in 1898.

We know that many of the dogs were mated very closely together to create a Dobermann type, as it is otherwise impossible to create a breed that produces itself to type in such a relatively short time from completely unrelated dogs. During these early years of breed development in the late 1800s, this very tight line-breeding would have consisted of matings between half and full siblings, and grandparents to grandchildren, to cement breed type and powers of heredity; thus the combination of the apparent quality

13

and hereditary powers of Göller's 1896 litter and Tischler's five-star litter resulted in dogs such as Hellegraf, who carried great hereditary powers. Although some of the bloodlines of these dogs have died out, many others of these early litters are still found throughout the world, and the progress of the breed would undoubtedly have been considerably slower without these incestuous breeding combinations.

REGISTRATION

In 1899 Otto Göller and his colleagues founded the National Dobermannpinscher Club, and the breed standard for the Dobermann became adopted by the German Kennel Club in 1900, requiring every breeding animal to be registered.

The German Kennel Club (DPZ) had for some years formalized pedigree dog breeding, and dogs were usually registered in one of the stud books that accorded to the locality in which they were born and the clubs of that area. The stud book prefix of NZ refers to the National Dobermannpinscher Stud Book. DZ was the stud book published by the Dobermannpinscher Club of Hamburg, the Dobermannpinscher Verien, and the Dobermannpinscher Verband, and the prefix 'DPZ' refers to the German Kennel Club.

Initially the colour of the Dobermann was listed solely as black and tan, but in 1901 the standard for colour was changed to include brown and tan, and blue and tan, and remains as this today.

The first Dobermann registered (retrospectively) with the German Kennel Club was Louis Dobermann's female Schuppine, who was registered as DPZ1 as a tribute to him. Graf Belling v. Gröenland (alias v. Thueringen) was the first Dobermann registered with the National Dobermannpinscher stud book, number NZDB1, in 1898.

The male Bosco born in 1893 and female Cäsi in 1894 were the oldest Dobermanns to be entered in the new Dobermann stud books. Although they were not initially registered themselves, they became registered when their most famous son Prinz Matzi von Gröenland was born and registered in 15 August 1895 DZ7. Prinz Matzi von Gröenland was shown in Berlin where he became

the first Dobermann Sieger. He was purchased by Otto Göller, and later given to Otto Vorwerk in Hamburg.

Matzi was not a perfect Dobermann even for those days: he was of a coarse type with long hair and thick undercoat, his eyes were too light and his skull was very heavy. He also had a very tough and sharp temperament, which he passed to his progeny. A story is told of the day of his arrival in Hamburg, where he attacked and apparently killed a Great Dane that Herr Vorwerk had just purchased for the great sum of DM 1100. Matzi was promptly returned to Otto Göller in Apolda with the message 'before I shoot him I want you to use him for breeding'. Otto Göller did indeed use him for breeding, but it seems he never was shot because after a few years he was sold as a stud to Frankfurt. He sired some good local dogs, such as Siegwart v. Hochheim, but after a few years there was no record of his progeny, and he was of no real importance in the founding of the breed.

Of particular value to the breed were the v. Ilm-Athen dogs of Herr G. Krumpholz from Wikkerstedt near Apolda. In 1899 his kennel marked the beginning of a very important turning point in the development of the breed, with a Dobermann female named Lady v. Ilm-Athen. Her parents were reputedly Bosko vom Hensdorf (himself sired by Bosco) and Ada v. Apolda, who were both unregistered, but Lady v. Ilm-Athen carried the blood of the Manchester Terrier, and her value to the breed in the whelping box was significant, providing a clean outline and dark markings.

When she was mated to Greif v. Gröenland (Lux × Tilly) they produced Prinz v. Ilm-Athen in 1901, who became a highly influential stud dog, benefitting the breed with new genetic input especially in terms of depth of colour and refinement of style. His progeny had a greatly improved shape, and bore what became the distinct and dark markings such as the thumbprint on the cheeks and feet. These traits were passed on through many of his descendants and are synonymous with the breed as we know it today. Prinz v. Ilm-Athen is behind the many great breeding and show dogs of the early twentieth century.

The previous two decades had brought particular kennel names to the fore, and in addition to the v. Thueringen and Ilm-Athen importance, Aprath, Isenburg, Burgwall and Luetzellinden were also significant.

(Landgraf) Sighart v. Thueringen, 14 November 1900, was of significant value to the emerging Dobermann breed and produced a very dominant male line: five distinct main bloodlines emanated from him. One of the most important Dobermanns of this time was his son 'Hellegraf von Thüringen' DZ172, born in 1904 out of Ulrichs Glocke v. Thueringen, whose dam Freya v. Thueringen NZ3 (bred by Herr Seifert of Weimar under the Thueringen name) was one of the great brood bitches. The famous Dobermann historian Philipp Gruenig later wrote of Hellegraf that 'he was a paragon of beauty, perfection and power. His was a degree of genuine "Adel" that will be difficult to surpass or even equal. Let the name be written in letters of fire'.

Hellegraf was brown, but from his sire Sighart's line he carried all four colours, so clearly the genes for all colours were already established by this time. Landgraf Sighart was known to be the carrier of colours, as his sons Hans and Hellegraf were both brown, and his grandson Gunzelin (Prinz v. Ilm-Athen × Suse v. Thueringen) was blue. Hellegraf was reportedly hard to fault in himself, but even more notable was his power to transmit breed quality. Ten main lines radiate from him, and many more minor lines.

A bitch which is often under-reported for her significance to the breed is Lady v. Calenberg: although unregistered (she was part – probably half – Manchester Terrier), she and her progeny became renowned for throwing close, smooth and short coats with great depth of colour. She is best known as the grand-dam (through her son Tell v. Kirchweyhe × Thina v. Aprath) of two important brown brothers, Fedor v. Aprath and Hans v. Aprath (later v. Walde). Both these males became known for contributing a great depth of dark brown coat colour with strong rust markings on their progeny, and had long, elegant and balanced heads influenced in part by the Manchester blood. Neither were big males, but both were said to have had particularly good front

angulation and sound conformation. Hans was sold to Switzerland, where he played a large part in establishing the breed there. The line was also noted for their high predatory inclination.

Fedor v. Aprath b.1906.

The Greyhound was introduced to the breed for speed and elegance, and although many breeders used Greyhounds or Greyhound blood in their breeding, it did not bring such positive benefits as the Manchester Terrier blood had done. Not everyone was pleased with these crosses, with many specialists warning that the working abilities of the Dobermann would be diluted by the prey drive of the Greyhound, and that physically the dogs were too slender and lacking in substance, with a narrow pigeon chest and arched back. The head type was also markedly different.

At a general meeting of the National Dobermannpinscher Club in Apolda in 1905, it is reported that Otto Göller warned against these crosses, and instructed judges of Dobermanns to withhold first prizes at shows from terrier-type dogs, those with heavy, coarse Dane and Rottweiler-type heads, and 'brindled' dogs. Herr Gruenig also later warned against further Manchester Terrier cross breeding, as the shoulder position caused restricted (terrier-like) movement, which impeded the 'free flowing movement of the

Dobermann, who must be able to gallop and move freely without being hampered by such construction'.

In 1906 a blue male, Gunzelin v. Altenburg, was born (Prinz v. Ilm-Athen), as was another in 1908 from almost pure v. Ilm-Athen lines, named Loni v.d. Wendendburg. The depth of colour in the markings was something that breeders were endeavouring to achieve on all colours at that time; in particular tan markings were more a faded yellow than the desired dark rust tan that had been introduced by Manchester Terrier breeding.

Nevertheless a recognizable and consistent physical type had begun to emerge, and a few individuals stood out as particularly good examples of the breed. Sturmfried v. Ilm-Athen, born in 1906 (Prinz v. Ilm-Athen × Betti 1 v. Ilm-Athen), was said to lean heavily to his grandsire, Greif v. Gröenland, on both sides of his pedigree, and he was renowned for throwing both great attitude and particularly deep colour in the black and red markings, notably from his grandmother's (Lady v. Ilm-Athen) Manchester Terrier blood. Sturm-field's many successful descendants, in particular his grandson Prinz Modern v. Ilm-Athen, have assured him of a place in the history books.

Greif v. Gröenland.

Lord v. Ried, born 1907, was from the sire Hellegraf to Nora v. Ried, whose pedigree carried dogs of very strong hereditary powers on both sides. Lord v. Ried inherited his imposing stature and 'Adel' from Hellegraf and his dam Nora, whose pedigree, as mentioned above, returns to dogs of great hereditary value, such as Graf Wedigo v. Gröenland. In this year Gruenig noted that the Dobermann had 'achieved an advanced degree of evolutionary development', and remarked how he well recalled the sensation created at the time when this novice was first exhibited at Frankfurt, where he won the Sieger title. Gruenig also observed that 'mere astonishment was heightened to dumb wonder when Helmuth v. Aprath and Annemarie v. Thueringen also appeared'.

Lord was a well used sire, with many of the show dogs of the 1930s being sired by him and his progeny, along with other dogs of high quality. Their influence was therefore now being spread over a wide geographical area, resulting in a rapid expansion of the gene pool of a renowned and recognizable type.

In 1908 a bitch called Stella was born from Max v. Kaisering/v. Isenburg × Flora v. Reid. There were various breeding experiments in the region at that time, and it was believed that her breeding included a black (English) Greyhound. Her daughter Sybille v. Langen was apparently 'visibly like a Greyhound'. Other references for the period demonstrate a clear line pedigree back to v. Reid, v. Ilm-Athen, and v. Thueringen breeding. Whichever was the case, Sybille became the foundation bitch of the Silbergberg kennels; the Blankenburg line also had a marked influence on the breed.

This was a great era for the breed, with an enthusiastic following of Dobermann fanciers, thriving clubs, many dog exhibitions, and breeders uniting to improve the breed. The reputation of the Dobermann was beginning to reach far beyond Germany.

It was also in 1908 that Dobermanns first arrived in America. Bertel v. Hohenstein and Hertha v. Hohenstein were imported by a Mr Jaeger, who with a partner named Mr W. Doberman (perhaps related to the original Herr L. F.

Dobermann) established their kennel which they called 'Doberman'. Of course no one would be permitted to register a kennel name with the name of a breed these days, but perhaps this is where the spelling with a single 'n' originated. Hertha became Hertha Doberman, and the following year a dog they bred called Doberman Dix became the first US Champion Dobermann.

From the earlier experimental matings that had been so denounced by pillars of the breed, a dog was born in Germany in 1909 that was to take the breed forward in a new direction. The dog was Prinz Modern Ilm-Athen, by Lux Edelblut v. Ilm-Athen out of Lotte v. Ilm-Athen, the bloodline returning through Edelblut to Hellegraf. Lotte was the daughter of the very prominent Sturmfried v. Ilm-Athen, who was a refined black dog of quality type, and transmitted the strong, clear markings from his paternal grand-dam Lady v. Ilm-Athen with her Manchester Terrier blood.

Prinz Modern v. Ilm-Athen.

The pedigree of Prinz Modern v. Ilm-Athen shows the practice of repeated incestuous breeding to stamp type. Very close incestuous matings were not uncommon in the formative years of the breed to create type. It is also noteworthy that almost a hundred years later, on 1 September 1997, full siblings Astor and Arielle d'Amour del Citone produced the world famous Gino Gomez del Citone.

Apart from his smaller stature, Prinz Modern v. Ilm-Athen had the breed type and shape of the Dobermann as we know it today, although his head was apparently too wide and heavy. Furthermore reliable references report that his character was cowardly, and according to Gruenig 'much damage was done to the breed by the spread of this character'. Nonetheless he was a very important sire.

Aside from the total lack of record keeping it is impossible to put together a factually correct pedigree from these formative years of breed history, so pedigrees from this era may contain inaccuracies. Names were frequently changed on ownership transfer, different birthdates were listed for the same dogs, and all the variations of Schnuppe were widely used, just as Max, Zeus and Apollo are these days. From 1912 to 1928 there are at least six Dobermanns listed with the name Lux, six Trolls, five Lords and six Lottes, not even counting the Prinzes. The subject of original pedigrees and significant dogs in this period of history requires so much investigatory detail that it merits a book to itself. (*See* Recommended Reading.)

THE WAR YEARS 1914–1918

Dogs have been used in war from ancient times, giving great advantage to their accompanying forces. The Germans had been developing formal training for dogs from the late 1800s onwards by encouraging people to attend village training schools, with regular competitions between clubs. Therefore by the time World War I broke out the Germans had literally thousands of dogs trained for a variety of roles, including for defence or attack, to act as sentries, and to search for prisoners – these alone saved more than 4,000 Germans who would otherwise have died or been taken prisoner. The British and Allied Forces had no formal dog-training programme for service work until at least 1910, so were way behind the Germans in the advantages of using dogs for war work.

However, not all dogs were trained in war work or ready for action, and for those that were not, times were very hard for any dog, let alone for pedigree dog breeding. As Phillip Gruenig observed:

> Most of the German breeders were at the front, and inescapable necessity compelled their remaining dependants to have their highly prized and dearly loved household pets put to a merciful death as the only alternative to starvation and suffering along with their owners. How deeply this cut into the heart of a true dog lover can be testified by me. On the second day of mobilization, the day on which I was ordered to the front, no less than eighteen half grown pups from my kennel fell victims to strychnine. It had to be, to safeguard them from the more horrible fate of death from slow starvation. In a moment of weakness induced by the hope of saving them, I retained two of my best dogs, Walhall v. Jaegerhof (a litter sister of Edelblut) and Ebbo v. Adalheim (a son of Marko v. Luetzellinden). They died miserably of malnutrition in 1916. Untold thousands suffered the same pain I did, for wives and children barely escaped the same fate of starvation. How wonderfully far has our much-touted civilization brought us!
>
> Phillip Gruenig

Dobermanns were used to advantage by the Germans in the war, particularly as messenger dogs, and dogs were both chosen from private owners and bred by the military. It therefore seems odd that so many potentially good dogs were destroyed when they could have made great use of such dogs for service. Despite having been shot through the bone, one extraordinarily good Dobermann male named Schreck von Peronne continued to deliver a message, finishing his task on three legs. Dogs were also used to carry cables, and another Dobermann called Hans carried a telephone line for more than half a mile in two minutes whilst under artillery and gunshot fire. Hans was apparently shown to Hitler on a formal visit as an example of the excellent German breed.

THE WAR YEARS

Many breeders managed to save their dogs' lives by sending them to neutral countries, and the loss of so many good dogs from Germany was often the gain of other countries.

Private breeding did still continue in some regions of Europe less affected by the battlefronts, and the stud dog Edelblut v. Jägerhof, 25 January 1913 (Prinz Modern v. Ilm-Athen × Tatjana v. Jägerhof) was advantageously placed in the relatively safe area of the Rhineland near to Holland, to be used widely at stud. By the time he died he had been bred to 104 females, and his name can be found on most important Dobermanns in the world today.

This preponderance of Edeblut's bloodline prompted Gruenig to make dire warnings about the dominance of one dog on the breed, par-ticularly with respect to transmitting not only their positive attributes, but also their negatives. Edelblut had few faults, but is reported to have had 'loose shoulders', which he passed on to all his progeny until, according to Gruenig, 'all of Western Germany has succumbed to its evil'.

World War I military Dobermanns.

Exactly the same problem was perpetuated with the over-use of Lux vd. Blankenburg. It was warned that by relying too largely on a leader dog at any time or in too tight a region, the leader's faults would be established to too great an extent to rid the breed of faults. Gruenig's warnings against oversaturation by any one blood, with its attendant faults, still hold true today.

The arrival of Dobermanns in other countries due to the war prompted a surge of interest by overseas breed fanciers, and German breeders began to rapidly re-establish the breed. In 1916 the brown male Salto v. Rottal settled in Czechoslovakia, where he helped found the breed; in 1919 the Austrian Dobermanpinscher Club was formed; and in Holland, Edelblut's brown progeny Urian and Undine v. Grammont were important for the breed.

Burschel v. Simmenan, b.1915 (Arno v. Glucksburg, down from Sturmfried, Prinz v. Ilm-athen, Stella and Lotte, x Gudrun v. Hornegg, down from Lord v. Ried, Hellegraf, and Betty) had survived the war and later became a Sieger winner. Burschel played a major role in re-establishing the breed in post-war Germany, and his son Lux vd. Blankenburg was one of the top sires ever in Germany.

Burschel v. Simmenau, 1915.

In 1921 the Dutch-bred brown male Favorit vd. Koningstad (Carlo vd. Koningstad × Angola v. Grammont) was born, and he had great success throughout Europe at shows and stud. Favorit was sold for a large sum to America. He was said to be the best sire to be seen yet in America, where he greatly increased the popularity of the breed.

Prinz Favorit vd. Koningstad, about whom Gruenig wrote 'a well built Dobermann with a perfect head, the desired goal for permanent head type'.

The twenties and thirties were boom times for the Dobermann, and the enthusiasm for pedigree dog breeding reflected the positive post-war mood of the era. Membership of the Dobermann clubs in Germany was around 3,000 members, and the breed thrived.

Post War

Just four years after the end of the war, in 1921, 119 high quality Dobermanns were shown at the Munich Sieger Show. The following year at the Sieger show in Berlin the quality was even better, with 233 Dobermans entered.

In that same year of 1921, the Doberman Pinscher Club of America (DPCA) was formed, and just two years later, in 1923, three German breed specialists were invited to judge in America.

Sgr Muck v. Brunia.

Ferry von Rauhfelsen.

Three generations of Sieger and BIS-winning dogs started with Sgr, Int. Ch. Muck v. Brunia b. 1929 (Luz v. Roedeltal × Hella vd. Winterberurg), who became a Sieger and was used to advantage in Europe before being sold in 1933.

Before he left Germany, Muck sired double World Sieger Troll vd. Engelsburg b.1933 × Adda v. Heek), whose bloodline lies behind many Russian dogs. Troll is also behind the founding dogs to the UK. One of Troll's best known sons was the male Ch. Ferry von Rauhfelsen (of Giralda). Ferry's dam was Ch. Jessy v. Sonnenhoehe b.1934, also from Germany, and was said by the DPCA to be the most important dam of her time.

THE WAR YEARS 1939–1945

In World War II times were again hard for both the individual and the breed. However, having already established military breeding and training centres in World War I, the Germans were well prepared for the use of dogs in service again. Dobermanns and other breeds were used for guarding prisoners in concentration camps, tracking escapees and helping to find wounded soldiers.

Chief of Staff of The German Army Dog Office was Dr Bruckner, who knew a great many dogs of all breeds. Dr Bruckner stated that:

Jessy v. Sonnenhoehe.

> The Dobermann usually follows a trail with his nose rather high, but is as sure a trailer as the breeds which work close to the ground. As a

Ferry von Rauhfelsen with owner Geraldine Rockerfeller-Dodge (Giraldo).

Dobermann in training to release his master in World War II.

result a Dobermann can follow the scent, especially when artificially laid, very fast. When in training the breed is inclined to be a trifle more headstrong than some other breeds, particularly the easily handled German Shepherd, however, he enjoys working and learns quickly, and in spite of a fondness for running, he is serious about his work and will always give satisfactory results when properly bred for working qualities.

Dobermanns in Service for the Americans

Before 1942 the Americans did not have a formal training programme for dogs in the military. However, although they did not become involved in the war in Europe until much later, they did need to regain and protect the Pacific islands, which had been occupied by Japanese forces.

Having seen the successful use of Dobermanns and German Shepherds by the Germans in World War I, it was felt that a dog unit was necessary, and in 1942 the Marine Corps War Dog Training Facility was established at Camp LeJeune, North Carolina.

The Dobermann Pinscher Club of America (DPCA) was approached to procure Dobes for the newly formed unit, and DPCA officials gave their own time and money to help find and assess suitable dogs for them. Many Dobermanns were offered by private owners and members of the DPCA, and an initial fourteen were chosen to go the Marine Corps under the direction of Captain Samuel T. Brick. The First Marine Dog Platoon and their Dobermanns landed on Bougainville, Solomon Islands on 1 November 1943.

First Marine Dog Platoon landing at Bougainville, South Pacific 1943.

in the liberation of the islands. The dogs were revered by their handlers who naturally became very close to them, and any injured dogs were carried on stretchers to be treated by camp doctors as carefully as any human soldier.

Soldier and his injured Dobermann with a captured Japanese flag at Okinawa.

The dogs were used in advance positions as sentries, and for searching out enemy combatants in caves and dugouts. Their incredible senses enabled them to detect the threat of danger, and on one occasion they detected the presence of Japanese troops half a mile away.

The Marine Dogs earned the nickname of 'Devil Dogs', and the people who lived through the Japanese occupation remember them with great awe and respect for their invaluable part

A DEEP BOND

Soldiers wrote home to their own families, and those of the dogs, and Dogs For Defence HQ in New York received a constant stream of letters home from the dogs to be forwarded to their owners. One such letter was from a Marine who wrote to the owners of his Doberman: 'During the past months, Judy and I have been through a lot together and I have become very fond of her. I would like to have her after the war. So if you can possibly see your way clear to part with her I would be forever grateful to you and although I am not a person of any wealth, I would be only too happy to pay any amount I could afford, if I could have her.' Owners understood the deep bond that their dogs now had with their handlers, and invariably agreed to the requests.

The 'Always Faithful' memorial statue in Guam was commissioned by the United Dobermann Club and sculpted by Susan Bahary. It is a permanent remembrance of the courageous Dobermanns that gave their lives in service to America and the US Marine Corps during World War II.

The Marine Corps and their Devil Dogs were officially credited with leading 350 patrols during the battles, accounting for over 300 enemy killed or captured.

THE POST-WAR YEARS

In October 1950 the German Dobermann Club were allowed to hold the first working dog trial since the war, and Dobermann breeding once again resumed.

The acquisition of so many of Europe's top Dobermanns by the Americans was the saving grace of the breed, as the six years of war took its toll on the breed in the homeland, where many Dobermanns and their breeders died. Most remaining breeders had lost their homes and had few, if any Dobermanns to start breeding again.

Meanwhile the Dobermann in America had been thriving, with some serious and dedicated sponsors including Mr Fleitmann (Westphalia), Mr Glenn Staines (Pontchartrain), and Mr Moore (White Gate). These gentlemen collectively imported many great dogs, and with George Earle III, were among the founding members of the DPCA. They gradually diverged in their view of the ideal Dobermann, and although they remained lifelong supporters and friends, their dogs became markedly different in style.

Pathfinder Dobermanns
In 1936 Glenn Staines had begun training Dobermanns as guide dogs for the blind under the

Four 'Leader' Dobermanns. Note the height of the breed.

23

name of 'Pathfinder'. He did not use the top winning dogs 'for fear of introducing undesirable character to his breeding'. He donated many dogs to blind people who simply couldn't afford to pay, and in 1945 donated dogs to blinded veterans. By 1951 over 1,000 Pathfinder Dobermanns had been placed with blind owners, and they were in demand right up to his death in 1951.

Joanna Walker of the world-famous Marks-Tey Dobermanns was one of the pioneers who promoted the popularity of Dobermanns in the early years. She was a passionate supporter of the 'seeing eye' Pilot Dobermann programme, which started in Ohio in the 1950s. That Dobermanns are used for so many service dogs in the USA is largely credited to the pioneering efforts of people such as Joanna Walker and Glenn Staines. It is a great shame that service dog organizations in the UK have a policy not to use guarding breeds.

Am. Ch. Marks-Tey Shawn CD and Joanna Walker. This dog's pedigree returned to Dictator v. Glenhugel and the old Damasyn lines famed for their heads, the quality of which is evident in this image.

Names of Influence

The 1940s were a golden era for the breed, with many great dogs. Peggy Adamson, who is considered to be one of the early architects of the Doberman in the USA and would become a fundamental part of US history, wrote of what she called 'Illena and the Seven Sires'. These seven dogs and one bitch each produced over ten champions. Their names were Ch. Dow's Illena of Marienland, Ch. Favoriet v. Franzhof, Ch. Westphalia's Uranus, Ch. Emperor of Marienland, Ch. Domossi of Marienland, Ch. Alcor v. Millsdod, and Ch. Dictator v. Glenhugel.

These dogs and the inter-marriages of their progeny collectively formed the backbone of a great and lasting legacy for the American Dobermann.

Damasyn: Peggy Adamson became world famous for her Damasyn kennels, established in 1945. Ch. Dictator v. Glenhugel b.1941 was bred by John Cholley and owned by Peggy, and where Ferry could not be touched, Dictator had a hugely beneficial effect on the perception of the breed by extending a gentle paw to greet children and being as elegant and dignified as his owner. He won a Group 1 at Westminster, and sired over fifty-two champion progeny and many more grandchildren champions.

Ch. Dictator v. Glenhugel.

All the Damasyn dogs were trained to a minimum of CD standard. Peggy's dogs were always expected to have excellent breed type and temperament, and the Damasyn head and character are still imprinted on the breed.

Ch. Rancho Dobe's Storm: In 1949 another all-time great dog, Ch. Rancho Dobe's Storm, was born from Ch. Rancho Dobe's Primo × Ch. Maedel v. Randahof ×. Bred by Mr and Mrs Brint Edwards, Dobe's Storm was a sensation in the ring and became the first Dobermann to win BIS at Westminster in both 1952 and 1953. He is one of only eight dogs to win BIS at Westminster more than once, and the only Doberman to have done so. Notably, his grandsire Ferry v. Rauhfelsen was the first Dobermann to win BIS at Westminster. Royal Doulton modelled their Dobermann figurine on him, and Rancho Dobe's Storm is so famous he even has his own Wikipedia page.

2 THE DOBERMANN IN GREAT BRITAIN AND IRELAND

Despite the breed being well established in the USA, only a handful of dogs were imported to the UK before World War II. One of the first Dobermanns in the UK was seen at Crufts Dog Show in 1928 at Crystal Palace, where it was then held. The dog was owned by a famous cookery writer, Mrs Elizabeth Mann, and for most, it was the first time a Dobermann had been seen. Her name was Ossi v. Stresow b.1925 (Cuno v. Stoizenberg × Flora v. Stresow), and she was flown in from Berlin in 1928 in whelp by (yet another) Harras v. Wendelstein, who was downline from Prinz v. Ilm-Athen. Ossi's litter produced six puppies born in late 1928, and records show that only one was subsequently bred from: a dog called Otto, who was later mated to an imported bitch Wally vd Margaretenau b.1928, whose great grandsire was Troll v. Blankenburg.

Names of Influence in the 1940s

Birling: George Lionel Hamilton-Renwick was born in 1917 at Birling Manor, Northumberland, and had a founding impact on the development of the Dobermann in the UK. He appeared in the Crufts Best in Show ring on no fewer than eleven occasions with three different breeds. He also judged many times at Crufts and abroad. Hamilton-Renwick was the first person to import Pharaoh Hounds to the UK but he was most famed for his Dobermanns, which were his real passion.

Renwick imported Birling Britta vd. Heerhof b.1944 from Holland, and Birling Bruno v. Ehrgarten b.1947 from Switzerland. These dogs were both descended from Troll vd. Engelsburg, and were later mated together in 1949. Their daughter Birling Rachel was BOB at Crufts in 1950 and 1951, and Birling Rogue became the first male Dobermann Champion in the UK.

Tavey: The Tavey name of the English kennels of Fred and Julia Curnow is synonymous with the history of the breed in the UK. The Curnows imported their first Dobermann, Roeanka vd Rhederveld of Tavey, and over the years have bred many champions. In 1943 they imported Pia vd. Dobberhof from Holland, where she was mated to Benno vd. Schwedenhecke before coming to the UK. Pia produced just two puppies born in quarantine: Bruno of Tavey and Don of Tavey, who later went to Durham police. Bruno later sired eight champions, among them the most famous Ch./Ob. Ch. Jupiter of Tavey CDex, who remains the only UK Dobermann to become a beauty champion and a working trial champion. His most famous daughter was Elegant of Tavey b.1950, who was the first UK Dobermann champion, having also won the first bitch challenge certificate (CC) on offer to the breed when Leo Wilson judged at Crufts in 1952. The dog CC on that inaugural occasion was awarded to Ingot of Tavey b.1951.

NAME VARIATIONS

In 1949 the Germans dropped the word 'Pinscher', as it was no longer felt that the word 'terrier' reflected the breed. The British have always used the double 'n' for 'Dobermann', but the Americans use 'Doberman Pinscher'.

THE DOBERMANN CLUB

In 1948 The Dobermann Pinscher Club (later The Dobermann Club) was formed by Sir Noel Curtis-Bennet as President, Mr Fred Curnow as Chairman, Mr Lionel Hamilton-Renwick as Vice Chairman, and Mrs Julia Curnow as Honorary Secretary and Treasurer. The Curnows provided facilities for committee meetings at their business offices in London, and rallies and shows at their home in West Sussex. In 1957 the club held its first championship show in London, where the DCC was awarded to Ch. Daybreak of Cartergate, and the BCC to Ch. Baba Black Pepper. There were eighty-nine entries in the obedience competitions, which were for all breeds.

Ch. Acclamation of Tavey, sire of thirty-two champions, and a cornerstone of the breed in the UK.

The Curnows had initially started with European Dobermanns, but after judging in the US they became enamoured with the American dogs, and in 1950 imported an American bitch called Rustic Adagio b.1949, granddaughter of Am. Ch. Dow's Illena v. Marienland, and Am. Ch. Gunther of Westphalia. Adagio was imported in whelp to the famous twice Westminster BIS winner Am. Ch. Rancho Dobe's Storm, and the Stormy A litter of three dogs – T. Stormy Abundance, T. Stormy Acacia, and T. Stormy Achievement – and one bitch, T. Stormy Adagio, were born in quarantine. Ch. Tavey's Stormy Achievement founded a line of BIS winners for the kennel in the 1960s.

Acclamation of Tavey b.1959 was line-bred on Rancho's Primo on both sides, and founded lines for Carickgreen, Triogen and Tumlow, amongst others. Acclamation sired an incredible thirty-two UK champions, a record unlikely ever to be beaten.

Juno of Cartergate b.1959, bred by Eva Would MBE, was of great value to the breed as she carried both the early Tavey imports from America and the Dutch/Swiss-based Birling lines. Juno was mated to Acclamation to produce the most important son Ch. Iceberg of Tavey b.1963, who had great success in the show ring, becoming Top Dog All Breeds in 1965 and runner-up in 1966 and 1967. In a two-year period between 1965 and 1967 he won six BIS at general championship shows, and with thirty-three CCs maintained his Breed Record Holder status for twenty years.

In addition to his show career, Iceberg sired many champions including Ch. Studbriar Chieftan b.1968 (× Eikon Jests Amazon); Ch. Yachtsman of Tavey and Ch. Yucca of Tavey b.1969 (× Nieta of Tavey); and siblings from repeat matings Ch. Tavey's Badge b.1970 and Ch. Tavey's Icypants b.1971.

Tumlow: Tavey Stormy Governess b.1958 was jointly owned by Julia Curnow and Elizabeth Hoxey of the Tumlow kennel, who had an arrangement that half of each litter would be registered to Tavey, and half to Tumlow. Governess was mated to Acclamation of Tavey and both the combination of dogs and the arrangement proved fruitful for both ladies. From the first litter in 1960 came Ch. Tavey's Stormy Nugget, winning ten CCs, and Ch. Tumlow Fantasy. A repeat mating in 1961 produced Ch. Tavey's Stormy Wonder, Ch. Tavey's Stormy Willow, Ch. Tavey's Stormy Wrath b.1961 with eighteen CCs, and Ch. Tumlow Impeccable with nine CCs and himself sire of eight champions.

In 1958 branches of The Dobermann Club were formally established in Nottingham (which in 1967 became the Midland Dobermann Club), and in Newcastle, later to become North of England Dobermann Club. In 1959 the Scottish Dobermann Club was established in its own right.

CHAMPIONSHIP SHOW
with
OPEN OBEDIENCE
(ALL BREEDS)

at the KINGS HALL and
WINTER GARDENS,
ILKLEY, Yorkshire

SATURDAY, 27th JULY, 1968.

Guarantors to the Kennel Club :
Mrs. J. IRVINE, Low Burnfoot, Featherstone, Haltwhistle, Northumberland.
Mrs. E. NICHOLSON, 246 Norfolk Road, Newcastle-upon-Tyne 6.
Mr. S. REGAN, 5 Police Houses, Harperley Hall, Crook, Co. Durham.
Mr. T. E. SESSFORD, 2 Westcott Walk, Newton Aycliffe, Co. Durham.
Mrs. P. THORNE DUNN, Holm Head, Greenhead, Carlisle, Cumberland.
Mr. D. WONTNER-SMITH, " Neves Hill." Ash Heads, Menston, Ilkley, Yorkshire.

Breed Judge :
HERR ERNST WILKING
(President of the German Dobermann Club)

Die Norden Dobermann Gewüzhaus vom England bittet eine Herzliche Einladung an Herr Ernst Wilking

North of England Dobermann Club.

Scottish Breeders

The **Auldrigg** kennel of Andy and Flora Auld based some of their breeding on Tavey and Tumlow. Ch. Auldrigg Cosair b.1958, owned by Willie Gallagher, was their first champion, winning five CCs. Their Ch. Auldrigg Pinza b.1970 won eleven CCs in one year, and sired two champions. They continued to breed champions into the early 1970s with Ch. Auldrigg Witchcraft b.1971. The Aulds imported Salvador v. Franckenhorst about whom we write later.

Other Scottish breeders such as Lachie and Joy Galbraith developed their lines and enjoyed success with their Ch. Rioghal Raquel b.1967.

Around 1960 a Dobermann bitch found stray in Scotland was taken in by a Mrs Brandon, and it was certified by two championship judges that she was a purebred Dobermann. She was later mated to Ch. Auldrigg Corsair and produced the 1964 Crufts BOB winner Ch. Ampherlaw Sir Galahad.

Clanguard based their breeding on Tumlow and Triogen lines, and produced many quality dogs. Ch. Clanguard Comanche b.1964 won nine CCs, and his full brother from a repeat mating, Ch. Clanguard Cadet b.1965, won twenty-four CCs, BOB Crufts 1969 from Alf Hogg, and BOB Crufts 1972 from Fred Curnow; he won many more BIS even well into his veteran years. Clanguard Cha Cha b.1964 was not made up, but was important in the development of the breed in Scotland.

Police/Service Dogs

Dogs have always been used to track criminals, but no formal system was ever established.

In 1946 the new Chief Constable of Surrey Police was Mr Joseph Simpson. He obtained permission from the Home Office and Police Authority to establish a dog section based on the continental method of training. He was supported in this by Harry Darbyshire, who joined Surrey Police in February 1948.

'Darby', as he became known, and later colleague Tom Roberts, visited Ulm in Germany to learn more about training and how to establish a good breeding programme. The traditional thirteen-week training course as practised at Mount Browne, where the dog section was based, was split into shorter sessions, with field experience in between. Surrey also followed the Germans by using their most popular breeds for working, which were Dobermanns and Alsatians. Equal numbers of GSD and Dobermann litters were bred at Mount Browne, and used by many forces throughout the country.

In 1948 a male called Ulf v. Margarethenof had been imported privately by a returning soldier,

Bob Ling and Mountbrowne Peter, one of the first Dobermanns at Mount Browne.

but on release from quarantine it was realized that he would be more ideally suited to an active working life. Ulf was offered to Mount Browne, where his training was taken up by Darby. Despite having bitten his handler on a few occasions, Ulf was particularly good at working around guns and was very quick to go in at the first shot. He later became a WT Champion. In 1948 two more Dobermanns were born and imported from Germany: a brown male Astor vd Morgensonne, and a black and rust female Donathe v. Begertal, who later gained Cdex, Udex and was the dam of two WT Champions. Both are recorded as having tracked and located many burglars and missing people. These two were later mated and produced six puppies, one of whom was WT Ch. Mountbrowne Karen.

Both Mr and Mrs Simpson were very keen that serving police dogs and handlers should continue their training, and encouraged forces and handlers to enter Working Trial Competitions, which many did with great success.

Until the dog section was established at Mount Browne, forces had relied on gifted dogs from the public, but Darby believed that dogs for police work should be bred for purpose. Mary Porterfield of Bowesmoor kennels supplied some Dobermanns to the police, and when Darby eventually retired, they became partners, breeding, training and supplying dogs to forces. Police dogs are not officially available to be used at stud on privately owned bitches, which left the best dogs of their time lost from future generations. Mountbrowne Joe CDex, UDex, TDex, PDex, and winner of one WT certificate, was an exception to this rule when he was given to The Dobermann Club for stud use by their members.

Dobermanns were used with great success by many other forces. Metpol Fritz with his handler PC Dines had 110 arrests to his credit, and won the annual 'Black Knight' trophy in 1959 ahead of all other breeds in the force. Durham Constabulary held annual competitions for 'Handler of the Year', and in 1960 nineteen dogs were entered, comprising eight Dobermanns and eleven GSDs. The Dobermanns took the first five places with just three-and-a-half marks between them. Nonetheless, in 1957 the Association of Chief Police Constables Standing Advisory Committee on police dogs stated 'The GSD is considered to be the most suitable breed for police work although there is no reason why other breeds should not be used.'

There may have been various reasons for this decision, not least that the GSD, with its naturally erect ears and impressively alert disposition, appears very intimidating to the public. Dobermanns are equally as quick to react to real threat, but as they often appear relaxed until movement or action prompts them into immediate response, this may seem less intimidating, particularly in crowd management, for example. Moreover the Dobermann's lack of undercoat leaves it shivering against the wet and cold whilst standing idle, and the comparatively 'over-thinking' Dobermann is not suitable for the novice or average police dog handler.

Fred Curnow and Jean Faulks' highly recommended book *The Dobermann* lists many stories of the courageous and exceptional traits of the Dobermann in service, so it is a pity the breed is now so rarely used. The only Dobermann known to work today in the UK is Diego's Bacarat, who is on active duty with Dumfries and Galloway Constabulary in Scotland.

Police dog handlers on parade in 1955.

Police dog handler and his cropped Dobermann.

THE NINETEEN-FIFTIES

In 1952 Kennel Club Challenge Certificates were awarded to the breed, which meant that Dobermanns could now become UK champions, and the breed boomed.

Names of Influence in the 1950s

Barrimilne: Margaret Bastable's Barrimilne kennel was renowned for breeding high quality European Dobermanns. Margaret was a talented dog handler who delighted in working her own dogs at trials. Her first Dobermann was Ch. Xel of Tavey b.1955, who had excellent German lines with many important dogs in her pedigree such as World Sgr Alfa V Hollingen, US/Can Sgr Ch. Troll von der Engelsburg SchHl, Int Ch, Sgrn Jessy von der Sonnenhoehe SchHlll.

The first of Margaret's many imports arrived in 1960 when she and her friend Peter Clark imported a bitch named Iris v. Wellborn in whelp to Urion v. Madurahof (litter sister to WW Lump v. Hagenstolz). Iris was registered jointly with Peter, and the litter of eight puppies were shared equally between them, half registered as Barrimilne, half as Carrickgreen.

In 1960 Margaret imported Gin v. Forell and took on his training to qualify him UD in a Championship working trial. With his excellent working skills Gin was used widely at stud by both private breeders and the Durham Police who needed tougher characters in their service dogs.

Over subsequent years Margaret imported eleven more dogs from Dutch/German bloodlines, including one of her most famous dogs

JEAN FAULKS

Jean Faulks remains one of the Dobermann world's most respected members, having reached the top in both working and showing. She discovered Dobermanns after a visit to Crufts in 1950, and became interested in working trials when she and husband Deryck visited the ASPADS (Associated Sheep, Police and Army Dog Society) Trial at Betchworth. They saw Harry Darbyshire qualify Ulf v. Margaretenhof PDex at that trial, later going on to achieve the WT Champion title.

Jean was so inspired by the dog, the work, and Harry himself, that guided by him she bought a twelve-month-old male called Viking Drum Major from Mrs Pamela Korda. Jean and her dog, whom she nick-named 'Pinscher', went on to work in both obedience and working trials where they won CDex, UDex, TDex and PDex. Until 1963 'Pinscher' was the only Dobermann, bred, trained and handled by a civilian to qualify in all four stakes of WT. Jean was very highly respected by all who knew her, and she and her dogs were called on more than one occasion by Grampian Police to help search for escaped prisoners from Peterhead prison. Jean and Pinscher would be escorted by guards while she tracked these men, just as the soldiers in war had done years before.

Jean later had a bitch called Lorelei of Tavey CDex, UDex, TDex b.1952 (Tasso vd Eversburg x Princess Anja v Scheepjeskerk), who demonstrated both her brains and beauty when at one championship breed show she won the CC in beauty and was placed in all the obedience classes. Jean trained, competed and judged in working trials for over forty years, and remarkably remains one of only two people approved by The Kennel Club to award championship certificates in show, obedience and working trials. In 1977 Jean judged the KC Working Trial Championships TD stake, in 1978 she judged the class C obedience class at the Scottish Kennel Club Championships, and the following year she judged both sexes in the show ring at Crufts.

Margaret Bastable enjoying a visit to South Africa.

Wilm v. Forell b.1965. Wilm sired just three champions, but his prepotency reached far beyond the first generation sired by him.

Licensed quarantine kennels were built at Barrimilne under the direction of Bob Ling, ex Chief Instructor at Surrey Constabulary Police Dog training Establishment, and this provided the many dogs that Margaret imported with personal attention.

Hazel Jones (Sigismunds) said 'in those days you could tell who was who. The Taveys were lighter in body, Triogens were between the two and a little longer, and Margaret Bastable's Barrimilnes were always ready for a bit of action!'

A later import to Barrimilne in 1972 was Greif v. Hagenstern, a dog Margaret had coveted since he was born. His parents were Bundesieger and Bundesiegerin winners opposite each other at

Wilm v. Forell.

DOG WORLD, MARCH 22, 1968

DOBERMANNS—continued

QUALITY
MUST IMPROVE BUT
COSTS
MUST DECLINE
Such advice is given to all of us by the Chancellor of the Exchequer and being good citizens we at Tavey have decided that in order to help breeders improve quality in their Dobermanns, costs of stud fees should be reduced. Accordingly, from now on, stud fees for the best dogs in Britain will be as follows:
VANESSA'S LITTLE DICTATOR OF TAVEY
25 guineas.
CH ICEBERG OF TAVEY
20 guineas.
CH ACCLAMATION OF TAVEY
15 guineas.
BAYARD OF TAVEY
10 guineas.
PUPPIES ARE USUALLY AVAILABLE
MRS J CURNOW
Colwood Court, Warninglid, Sussex.
Tel: Warninglid 233

Barrimilne Dobermanns
German Imported Dogs at Stud
The offspring of Show Champions with top working qualifications
BLACK OR BROWN PUPPIES
USUALLY FOR SALE
Inquiries:
MARGARET BASTABLE
Barrimilne Kennels
and International Quarantine
Great North Road, Baldock, Herts
Telephone: Stotfold 221

There was much competition between the two top breeders of their day, each with Dobermanns of quite different origins.

the German National All Breed Show in 1970. Following a visit to Germany in 1972, Margaret finally acquired him and brought him home to England where he sired seventeen litters, among them notable progeny particularly from Pompie and Metexa.

Some clever breeders did make use of Margaret's imports, and as we saw with Birling and Tavey, the combination of European and the finer American breeding often worked very well. An important bitch bred by Margaret was Barrimilne Helga b.1961. She was owned by Pat Quinn, who produced three champions from her when mated to Tavey and Tumlow dogs.

THE NINETEEN-SIXTIES

Names of Influence in the 1960s
Pompie: Hilary Partridge's Pompie kennel also used Barrimilne/Carickgreen dogs to great advantage. In 1959 Hilary bought a male and female

from Triogen at a cost of 21 guineas and 25 guineas respectively; the female Trisha became the foundation of the Pompie kennels. In 1961 Trisha was mated to Carrickgreen Cordon Bleu, producing just one puppy named Pompie Seaman, who was subsequently mated to a bitch called Jilharren Belling Belle of Pompie b.1963 (Tavey's and Triogen breeding). This produced Pompie Sea

BARRIMILNE PREFERRED TRAITS AND IDEALS

Margaret dedicated herself to studying the German breeding lines and spoke of how 'Dobermanns in the UK, especially those in the second and third generation of breeding after the introduction of the American bloodlines, were too light in bone and over-long in loin, pale in both eye colour and tan markings, and often insufficiently firm in character.'

She felt the essential features of any Dobermann that she imported or kept herself were 'shortness in loin, a level topline and good tailset (no falling croup), rich tan markings, a dark eye and a good head. They must also be firm in character but not vicious, honest but not mean, and while short-coupled and compact in body, must have elegance without exaggeration in either length of neck or bend of stifle.'

In an era when the Dobermann in the UK was dominated by the American style, Margaret's preference for the comparatively tough Dobermanns put her, as she herself said, 'in the wilderness for some time until the bigger breeders realized what the imports were giving to the breed then some turned up but a lot of them obtained the breed through the back door.' Notwithstanding, the lady had a quite extraordinary career in judging Dobermanns around the world and to this day remains the only judge from the UK to have judged at the IDC (the panel of which is notoriously impenetrable to even the most long-serving European breeders), at Strasbourg 1963.

Urchin, who established the strong bitch line for Pompie; downline from her came bitches such as P. Sea Dilettante, and from her came Pompie Sea Aphrodite b.1973.

Borains: In 1964 the Curnows imported Westwind Quintessence who had two litters, the first to Ch. Tavey's Stormy Achievement, which produced Tavey's Stormy Pride b.1964, owned by Mike Bradshaw in partnership with Jane Parkes, and the second to Vanessa's Little Dictator of Tavey. Little Dictator produced Ch. Royaltains Babette of Tavey b.1966, who won six CCs and was the foundation bitch of the Borains kennel of Pat Gledhill. Among the many winners for Borains were Ch. Borains Night Watchman b.1978, who won nine CCs and was BIS at Birmingham National 1981; and Ch. Borains Raging Calm b.1974, who won seventeen CCs and produced Ch. Borains Wild Alliance. Babette's litter sister Ch. Baroness of Tavey b.1966 went to Chater, where she produced Ch. Chater Man of The Moment.

Chater: Chater was the affix of Vicki Phillip, and her Chater Icy Storm was owned by Trevor and Noreen Simmons with the Javictreva affix. They bred Ch. Javictreva Brief Defiance of Chater b.1975, who was bought and shown by Vicki. One of his daughters, Ch. Maxtay Meritorious b.1980, won nine CCs, and another, named The Lotus Eater of Chater, was mated to Achenburg Andrew to produce Ch. Chater the Ferryman b.1983. He won four CCs, and sired the first

Borains Raging Calm, winner of seventeen CCs.

champion for Tony and Linda Fisher, Ch. Lintoya Secret Acclaim b.1988.

Chater Icy Storm also sired Thelma Toole's Ch. Chornytan Travelling Light b.1982, sire of siblings Ch. Dolbadarn Dirty Girty and Ch. Dolbadarn Nite Star b.1984.

Thelma's breeding had links back to Margaret Bastable's Gin von Forell, and the original Tavey lines. Thelma's Chornytan Midnite Mark b.1976 sired Ch. Chornytan Dinahawk b.1981 with five CCs, Ch., Ir. Ch. Dolbadarn Hawker Fury b.1983, and Ch. Fillidons Carltons Cuckoo from Chornytan b.1979.

Von Klebong: Jackie Perry of Von Klebong was born in India and lived in Malaysia and Thailand. Jackie had been breeding for some time before importing Ch. Carrickgreen Champignon from the UK in 1967, followed by two bitches from Tavey, and an Australian Ch. Delderland Black Regal, who became a multi BIS winner. Jackie produced eighteen champions around the world, including Ch. Von Klebong Solar Encore at Achenburg b.1978, owned by Margaret Woodward, who later won thirteen CCs with him; Can. Ch. Vonklebong Raja Muda (Ch. Swyndwr Storm Bearer × Johnsuree's Celestial Lady Imp Thailand); and Thai Ch. Vonklebong Kakak Di-Sting, who won Dog of The Year in Bangkok in 1997.

Phileens: Eileen and Phil Edwards of Phileens owned Ch. Yucca of Tavey b.1969, who was sired by Ch. Iceberg of Tavey. They made a joint trip to America with the Curnows, and jointly purchased three bitches from Jane Kay's Kay Hills kennels. One of those was Kay Hills Outrigger b.1970, who was imported in whelp to Am. Ch. Tarrados Corry and produced four puppies in quarantine in 1972. The litter was shared between the two couples, and the Curnows took home a brown male, Phileen's Duty Free of Tavey. He left a great legacy of top quality dogs.

In the late 1970s, the Curnows started to decrease the number of dogs at the kennels. Phileen's Duty Free and Tavey's Diploma went to live with Reg and Mary Barton, who subsequently purchased the Tavey prefix and continued to breed and show under it. This made the Tavey affix one of the most enduring UK show kennels, and very few UK bloodlines are without the name somewhere in their pedigree.

THE DOBERMANN CLUB WORKING TESTS

For some time the dominance of the American-style Dobermann had been of concern to some fanciers. Although they acknowledged the superb success of the beauty of the American imports and their descendants primarily through Tavey, they felt the breed was losing some of the character considered fundamental to the breed in their country of origin. This difference of opinion on the direction of the breed led to a great deal of division and friction within the fancy.

Responding to these concerns, The Dobermann Club set up a sub-committee working party in 1961, headed by Fred Curnow, and established The Dobermann Club working tests, adapted from the German Schutzhund tests. Notwithstanding that the American dogs were more closely related to the German lines in those days, it is of interest that the dogs who achieved their character diplomas originated equally from both the American and German bloodlines.

For many years there was a very active working dog membership, with working tests being run by The Dobermann Club, and most members did some level of working and/or obedience training with their dogs.

Roanoke: Daisy Richardson of the famous Roanoke kennels in Essex came into Dobermanns with Frenches Gaynos b.1953 and bred notable champions in the sixties. The first champion for the kennel was Ch. Cadereyta of Roanoke b.1964, soon followed by Ch. Triogen Tuppeny Feast b.1961, who won five CCs and founded a good line for Jean Scheja's Tinkazan dogs. A successful daughter of Cadereyta was Ch. Roanoke Bobadilla b.1968, who won eight CCs. Daisy's son Jimmy started showing in 1962; he was first awarded CCs at Southern Counties Championship show in 1972. He is Vice President of The Dobermann Club, and also the author of the well known book Dobermanns Today. Roanoke Dobermanns were later well known for breeding all four colours of Dobermanns: black/tan, brown/tan, blue and fawn.

Triogen: The Triogen name of Alf and Eleanor Hogg produced consistent quality dogs based on American and European breeding. They began breeding in 1956 with their foundation bitch Triogen Bandeau of Tavey b.1956, and between 1961 and 1970 Triogen produced no fewer than ten champions. Their Ch. Triogen Teenage Wonder b.1961 produced three champions: Ch. T. Tuppeny Feast and Ch. T. Tuppeny Treat b.1964, and Ch. T. Treble Chance; their litter sister Teenage Sensation produced sibling champions, Ch. Traffic Trouble and Ch. Traffic Cop b.1963.

Ch. Triogen Tornado b.1967 was tightly bred, being doubled up on Acclamation on Tavey on both sides, and on the Sensation and Wonder siblings on both sides. Tornado sired thirty litters and produced five champions: Ch. Chater Man of the Moment, Ch. Kenstaff Tornado of Achenburg, Ch. Ikos Valerians Valour, Ch. Zalpha's Harmony, and Ch. Royaltains Miss Haversham.

'Triogen' Inge aus Munchen had been imported from America originally by Alf and Eleanor Hogg at Triogen, and then on to Peter and Audrey Kelly (Rathkeel). One of Duty Free's brothers, Phileen's American Express, was mated to a brown bitch called Rathkeel Red Pepper b.1972. It took everyone by surprise when the litter produced puppies of all four colours: black/tan, brown/tan, blue and fawn.

The Triogen name was later transferred to John McManus, who continued the affix with his champion West Highland Whites, and Boston Terriers. Harry and Margaret Woodward (Achenburg) took on the Hogg's dog Ch. Triogen Tornado, who, having moved down from Scotland to the Midlands, was more widely used at stud.

Metexa: John and Irene McManus of Metexa are well known for their interest in European bloodlines, and have travelled extensively around the world judging the breed. Their foundation bitch was Triogen Tartan Hope b.1970, who was tightly line-bred: both Acclamation and Triogen Tullaherin were present four times in her four-generation pedigree. Tartan Hope was later mated to Grief v. Hagenstern, and the litter produced Metexa Midnight Surprise b.1973.

A great-grandson of M. Midnight Surprise was Ch. Metexa Movie Master b.1983, whose pedigree carried many of the best European dogs, including Gravin Weitske v. Neerlands Stam IDC winner 1979. He was also very tightly bred, carrying three full brothers from repeat matings in the third generation of his pedigree: Int., Multi Ch. Jurgen v. Hagenstern, Int., Multi Ch., DVSgr. Can. Ch. Rico v. Hagenstern, and DVSgr Greif v. Hagenstern, all by Int., Ger. Ch. Bonni v. Forrel × Int., Ger. Ch. Dona v. Eichenhain SchH1, Bdsgrn, DVSgrn.

Bonni was a litter brother of the important Bryan v. Forrel, who Han vd. Zwan references in his book *In The Beginning*. Carrying all this exceptional blood made Movie Master an excellent sire, and although his use was limited by his location in Scotland, he sired thirty-one litters, with his most famous son being a founder of Clive and Nancy Evans's Amazon lines.

THE NINETEEN-SEVENTIES

The 1970s were a rich time for the breed, with many talented breeders producing top quality dogs. Kennel Club Registrations were still increasing, and membership of The Dobermann Club reached around 600.

Breeders, particularly those who enjoyed the working aspects of the breed, were always interested in overseas dogs to complement the existing bloodlines, and many turned their attention to northern Europe where the quality of the Dutch dogs was attracting worldwide attention.

Names of Influence in the 1970s

Jimarty: Jim and Marty Burrell of the Jimarty kennel were great advocates of European breeding and imported many lines from overseas, such as v. Neerlands Stam, v. Franckenhorst, and v. Hagenstern to their kennels. The Burrells were committed to good health in the breed, having all their breeding dogs health tested, and were heavily involved with Dobermann Rescue. They were equally passionate about retaining the working ability of the Dobermann, organizing the Dobermann Club working tests.

There was great success for Jimarty's working dogs, the best of which was when John Fleet won the Kennel Club Working Trials with WT Ch. Jimarty's Citta b.1992. Born in the UK of Dutch parents, she was only the third Dobermann to gain her WTCh. since 1960. Her brother Jimarty's Fedor attained CDex, UDex, WDex, TDex, PD CoM.

Vyleigh: Heidi Vyse's first champion was Ch. Vyleigh's Valerian b.1972, and she bred many dogs of note. Vyleigh's Valerian sired Ch. Ikos Valerian's Valour b.1974 (× Ch. Triogen Tornado); siblings Ch. Chevington Royal Virginia and Ch. Chevington Royal Virtue of Mantoba b.1979 (× Ch. Chevington Royal Black Magic UDex); and Ch. Vyleigh's Zaxon b.1990 (Ch. Dimrost Freedom Fighter × Vyleighs Xanja).

Heidi imported Quinto van de Kunnemaborgh b.1984, and later bought Xantos vd Kunnemaborgh b.1985. Xantos was the sire of Schutz Lara Linda (× Lya-Linda v. Roveline), who was the dam of Heidi-Hi of Helmlake, and Quinto sired Linda Clayton's Ch. Essenbar The Challenger b.1986 (× Essenbar Athena).

David Crick's **Ch. Flexor Flugelman:** One of the UK's top winning dogs was David Crick's Ch. Flexor Flugelman b.1970 (Tumlow Green Highlander × Tumlow Radiance). Flexor Flugelman was a grandson of Ch. Acclamation of Tavey, who

appeared three times in Flugelman's five-generation pedigree. Flugelman won fifteen CCs, three BIS, won Reserve in Group in 1973, and won the Group at Crufts in 1975.

Ch. Flexor Adonis b.1979 was a double Flugelman grandson. He produced three champions: Ch. Tashatrend Son of Adonis, Ch. Margin's Flexibility, and most importantly, the bitch Ch., Ir. Ch. Pompie Sea Jade of Chancepixies.

Vom Franckenhorst: The Vom Franckenhorst kennel in Holland of Sonja von Franquemont and her husband David is revered as possibly the greatest Dobermann kennel in the world. Their breeding was famed for its correctness of type, being particularly coveted for their exquisite head quality. Sonja's very first litter in 1971 gave her World Winner Korung Alva v. Franckenhorst, and this early success was set to continue. Vom Franckenhorst breeding is found behind most quality pedigrees throughout the world.

Salvador v. Franckenhorst b.1978 was imported to Andy and Flora Auld in Scotland, but changed hands a couple of times as he was too much for most people to cope with. He had just thirteen litters in the UK before returning to Sonja in Holland, where he was used to great advantage. Ironically Salvador's bloodlines returned just two generations later in dogs imported to the UK from America. When mated to Vitesse v. Franckenhorst the litter produced the multi-winning EuroSgr, Int, Multi, Ned. Ch. Arrow v. Harro's Berg SCHh III, ZTP 1A b.1983. Although he was an excellent dog, he was so heavily used that breeders began advertising their dogs as 'Arrow free'. Notwithstanding, his many progeny included the eternally famous 'D' litter b.1984: Dea Dolores v. Franckenhorst, Dexter v. Franckenhorst, Dolly v. Franckenhorst (all out of Vivre Vivien v. Franckenhorst).

Pompie: In 1977 Hilary Partridge mated her Pompie Sea Aphrodite to Ch. Findjans Poseidon, which produced Ch. Pompie Alcyone. This initiated a hugely successful breeding enterprise, and the Pompie name is held in great respect worldwide. Pompie Alcyone was later mated to Gerry Young's Ch. Flexor Adonis, and the resulting litter contained a bitch who was bought by partners Dave Anderson and Jean Frost. Ch./Ir. Ch. Pompie Sea Jade of Chancepixies b.1983 held the Bitch Breed Record for eleven years. Hilary has always preferred strong European dogs for her breeding and despite public opinion used Salvador on Ch. Alcyone. Her instincts were right when she produced Ch. Pompie Dutch Leiveling b.1981, who won BOB at Crufts in 1984.

From the same litter P. Dutch Dewi went to Sonja von Franquemont in Holland, and P. Dutch Dictator went first to Holland, then Japan. When Mr Pezzano was judging in Japan he was so impressed with Dutch Dictator that he brought him back to stand at his world famous del Citone kennel in Italy, where he was widely used. The number of British Dobermanns being bought by European show/working breeders can be counted on one hand, so demonstrates the great respect in which the Pompie name is held worldwide.

Pompie the Blues Swinger of Chancepixies b.1994 (Pompie The Marksman of Vandenburg × Pompie Didja Ever, who were half brother and sister both sired by Ch. Dimrost Freedom Fighter) went to Dave Anderson's Chancepixies kennel, where she had just one litter to Ch. Marrijax Doobie Have, but it was a good one, as it produced champion siblings Ch. Chancepixies Monopolist, and Ch. Chancepixies Aura b.1988. Monopolist was BOB at Crufts in 2001, but was regrettably under-used, with only four litters and no champion progeny.

Pompie imported siblings from v. Neerlands Stam, and later another female Gravin D'Astrid v. NS, who won a CC in the UK.

Hilary has judged in many countries including Sweden, Australia, and Indonesia, and when judging the breed at Crufts in 1999, awarded the CC and RCC to sisters Ch. Sallate Striptease and Sallate Seduction respectively. Striptease went on to win the Group that year. Hilary later awarded Seduction the BCC at Welsh KC.

Findjans: Martin and Alma Page became involved with Dobermanns in the 1960s when Martin handled the first two Dobes to qualify in Club working tests, Pompie The Bosun b.1964, and his granddaughter P. Sunset Shell b.1967. Sunset Shell was by Easterns Own, who was by Vanessa's Little Dictator to Tavey × Pompie Sea Urchin, who went back to Carrickgreen, Triogen, Tumlow, Tavey, Prinses Anja vt Scheepjeskerk).

Alma mated Pompie Sunset Shell to a dog called Ch. Heidiland Trouble Spot who had already sired a champion – Ch. Royaltains Reluctant Hero b.1968. The litter produced a bitch called Findjans Fair Allyne, who in turn was bred to Ch. Tumlow Satan.

The combination of Pompie breeding with the early American import lines, gave Alma her first champion – Ch. Mitrasandra Gay Lady of Findjans b.1971. This founded one of the most important lines in UK Dobermanns, as Gay Lady was later bred to Phileen's Duty Free of Tavey to produce Ch. Findjans Poseidon b.1974, whose value to the breed is immeasurable.

Alma Page with Ch. Findjans Poseidon.

Ch. F. Poseidon sired many champion progeny, and left even more champion grandchildren for the breed, including such important dogs as:

Ch. F. Freya b.1977 (× Tanerdyce Michealia)
Ch. Pompie Alcyone b.1977 (× Pompie Sea Aphrodite)
Ch. F. Gelert b.1981 (× Pompie Dione of Findjans)
Ch. F. Bo Derek of Nyewood b.1982 (× Ch. Findjans Melee)

Siblings Ch. Perihelia's Resolution and Ch. Perihelia's Lili Marlene b.1981 (Ch. Perihelia's Madame Rochas)

Ch. F. Chaos b.1982 (x F. Atropos); Chaos was top Dobermann in 1984.

Ch. F. Chaos b.1982 was tightly bred on Ch. Mitrasandra Gay Lady of F., who was his grandmother on both sides. He was a prolific producer, siring an extraordinary eighty-seven litters, including many champions:

Ch. Crossridge Carbon Copy for Lynfryds b.1984 (x Dizown Copy Cat),

Ch. Dizown I Can Boogie Too with Holtzburg b.1984 (x I Can Boogie at Dizown)

Ch. Findjans Melee b.1985 (x Findjans Alita)

Ch. Borains Night Flyer b.1989 (x Borains Lorna Doone)

Ch. Ranlor Circuit Breaker, and his sister Ch. Ranlor Annie Laurie b.1993 (x Borains Freedom Lady)

Ch. Findjans Mêlée b.1985 (x Ch. Alita)

A later addition to Alma's kennel was Pompie Dione of F. (Borains Warning Shot × Pompie Idylla). Dione was a grand-daughter of Poseidon and Ch. Heidiland Trouble Spot with Greif v. Hagenstern in the pedigree, and was a fundamentally important addition to Findjans. Pompie Dione had five litters, and bred two champions from her first and second litter when mated to her grandsire Poseidon: Ch. F. Gelert b.1981, and Jackie Rutter's Ch. F. Boderick of Nyewood b.1982.

Pompie Dione did not produce any champions when mated to Chaos, but her daughter Boderick was later mated to him and produced two champions: Ch. Nyewoods Bo Street Runner at Tanbowtra b.1984, and full brother Ch. Nyewoods Excalibur b.1985. An important daughter of Dione was F. Le Crunch, who was the dam of Ch. Twinglo Le Juice at Bledig b.1984 (by Resolution), and grand-dam of Ch. Twinglo Love Apple.

P. Dione was also the grand-dam of Ch. F. Mêlée, grand-dam of Ch. Zordia's Magic Moments of Amazon and Ch. Zordia's Vigilante, and the foundation bitch of Woodbriar Twinglo Original Syn at Woodbriar.

This prepotent line underpins almost every infuential UK Dobermann in the country. Posei-

don's most important son was Ch. Perihelias Resolution: he sired fifty-eight litters, which included two of the most influential dogs of the nineties – breed record-holding dog Ch. Sallate Ferris (x Sigismunds Ice Cool Kate), and breed record stud dog Ch. Holtzburg Mayhem (x Dizown I Can Boogie Too With Holtzburg).

Ch. Perihelias Resolution was the sire of:

Ch. Jenicks Cruise Missile b.1984 (x Jenick's Missile Belle)

Ch. Twinglo Le Juice at Bledig b.1984 (x F. Le Crunch)

Ch. Sallate Frauline b.1985 (x Sigismunds Ice Cool Kate)

Ch. Sallate Impeccable and Ch. Sallate Islay b.1986 (Sallate Special Kay)

Olderhill: Sue Wilson's Olderhill breeding has its place firmly in the history books with her 1974 litter from Ch. Phileen's Duty Free of T. × Olderhill Dhobi, daughter of Iceberg. The litter contained a dog and three bitches, which would be a new foundation for the breed: Ch. O. Sheboygan, Ch. O. Seattle, and O. Sioux (two CCs, six RCCs). O. Salvador also did not gain her title, but proved to be of great value as the dam of three champions in one litter. Forty years later

Olderhill Sioux.

Ch. Olderhill Seattle.

Ch. Olderhill Sheboygan.

Sue remains the only person to have bred, owned and handled Dog CC and Bitch CC twice with a sibling.

Dizown: For any student of the Dobermann, the Dizown kennel needs no introduction, as Di Patience was one of the most talented breeders and exhibitors in the breed history. Di had kept Dobermanns since 1961, and she registered the Dizown prefix in 1974. She had an exceptional foundation bitch in O. Salvador, and when she mated her to Tavey's Satellite in 1975, she produced an extraordinary three champions in her first litter: Ch. D. The Hustler, Ch. D. Georgie Girl, and Ch. D. Bedazzled of Chaanrose. Bedazzled was Rosie Lane's foundation bitch.

This was a time when show entries were huge, competition was high in numbers and quality, and Dizown was the kennel to beat. Where some kennels often breed either a strong dog or strong bitch line, Di bred consistently excellent quality in both sexes. Dizown dogs were not just great winners but also great producers, and everyone coveted the Dizown lines.

Ch. D. The Hustler became the youngest male in the breed to become a champion, at just twenty months old. Although his champion progeny were not numerous, they were of great quality and provided a firm foundation for the future.

Ch. I Can Boogie at D. b.1976 was a Hustler daughter (× O. Sioux). She produced just one champion from her five litters, the bitch Ch. D. I Can Boogie Too with Holtzburg b.1984 (× Ch. F. Chaos). When D. I Can Boogie Too was mated to Ch. Perihelias Resolution in 1987, she produced one of the most important dogs in the UK: Ch. Holtzburg Mayhem.

The third Olderhill sister, O. Seattle, was mated to Ferrings Mike Victor, who was from two US imports: Gra-Lemor Demetrius vd. Victor × Amsels Andante of Marks Tey. This litter produced Ch. D. Razzamatazz b.1979, who sired over fifty litters. One of his best known champion progeny was Ch. Halsbands Helmsman b.1980 (× H. Manhattan).

Another son of Razzamatazz was D. All That Jazz b.1981. He wasn't made up, but sired many notable champions and producers themselves, such as Ch. Crossridge the Jazzman b.1983 (× Anna of Crossridge), and Ch. Jowendy's Into Jazz b.1984 (× Cracklin' Rosie of Jowendy).

Sibling Ch. D. Hello Darlin' from Estridge and Ch. D. Street Legal b.1986 (Marienburg's Firedanza v. Tavey × D. Daisy Brown) both produced well for other kennels.

Ch. D. Street Legal sired two champions in his second litter for Val Allen's Zordia's kennel, Ch. Z.

Vigilante and Ch. Z. Magic Moments at Amazon b.1988 (× Findjans Shelada of Zordia), and in the same year sired another pair of sibling champions: Ch. Jowendy's Infa Red for Maelstrom, who was the dam to an important bitch at Amazon, and Ch. Jowendy's Kia-Ora (× Ch. J. Into Jazz), the important foundation for Supeta. The following year Street Legal also sired Ch. Chaanrose Flashpoint b.1989 (× Chaanrose Sitting Pretty).

The Dizown bloodline was equally desired abroad, and in the late 1970s Dizown exported six Dobermanns to South Africa, which all became champions. Mr and Mrs Griffiths D. Dressed to Kill became the Southern African Supreme Dobermann 1977, with judges from Germany, UK, USA, Holland, Israel and Canada all greatly admiring this bitch. Remarkably during the year in which points were amassed and calculated towards this title, 'Scarlet' was flown to Germany to be mated, and back to have a litter.

Twenty years after Di's first litter she was still producing important champions, such as:

Ch. D. Dance with the Devil b.1992 (Ch. Lodgehouse Casablanca × D. Lucky Lady)
Ch. D. Tickled Pink b.1994 (Ch. Jowendy's Kilowatt × D. Playin' with Fire, litter sister to Ch. D. Dance with the Devil)
Ch. D. To Die For at Amazon b.1996 (Ch. Amazon Sound Machine × D. Playin' with Fire).

Di Patience stopped showing at the end of the 1990s, but her talent for producing excellent Dobermanns provided a solid foundation for virtually all UK breeders, who continue to revere the Dizown name.

Chaanrose: Di's very close friend and talented breeder Rosie Lane of the famous Chaanrose Dobermanns based her breeding on Dizown, her foundation bitch being Ch. Dizown Bedazzled of Chaanrose b.1975 (Tavey's Satellite × Olderhill Salvador). Bedazzled started a whole dynasty of top winning Dobermanns.

When Bedazzled was mated to Phileen's Duty Free of T. she produced the first Chaanrose champion, Ch. Chaanrose The Solitaire b.1979. Meanwhile Rosie had acquired Olderhill Salvador from

Rosie Lane and her foundation bitch Ch. Dizown Bedazzled of Chaanrose.

Di, and bred her to Heathermount Flitzenjager b.1976 (Ch. Flexor Flugelman × Heathermount Festive), producing the superb working bitch WT Ch. Chaanrose Night Queen b.1978.

C. Night Queen TDex, WDex, UDex, CDex b.1978 was owned and handled by John Fleet, qualified TDex an incredible twenty-four times, and won four Working Trial Challenge Certificates, including at the prestigious Kennel Club championships.

Ch. Chaanrose Elegantiae at Merryn b.1987 (Dizown The Heist × Chaanrose Lady Sun), top Dobermann bitch in 1991, produced two champion litter sisters to Ch. Jowendys Kilowatt, Ch. Stormy Romance with Chaanrose, CDex, and Ch. Wild Cherry at Chaanrose, bred in partnership with Jo Gibbs (Merryn) in 1992.

Ch. Stormy Romance with Chaanrose CDex and is thought to be only the second Dobermann bitch in the UK to have won BIS at a general championship show. Her award came from breed pioneer Lionel Hamilton-Renwick at Border Union in 1995, in which year she was also Top Dobermann. Stormy Romance is one of the very few Dobermanns with a working qualification as well as their show title. Handled by Rosie in the ring, she won four CCs, all with BOB, and was Top Dobermann in 1995. She was handled on the working field by her owner, Dawn Ferguson. Stormy Romance died a few months before her fourteenth birthday.

Her litter sister, Ch. C. Wild Cherry, was mated to Casablanca and produced the two top winning brothers: Derek Peters' Ch. Chaanrose Shock Tactic, who won seventeen CCs, Group 1, many Group placings and was Top Dobermann 1998; and Sue James' Ch. Chaanrose Don't Crowd Me at Jaegerson, who won thirteen CCs, also many Group placings, RBIS at WPBAW, was Top Dobermann in 1999, and Top Sire 2000.

Ch. C. Talking Point b.1998 (Dizown Prime Time × C. Don't Look Back from Regenka) was mated to Jowendy's Robin The Hood to produce Rosie's last Dobermann bitch, her Chaanrose Get-Oh-Fabulous CDex b.2004. The last Chaanrose champion was Tony and Elizabeth Lynch's Ch. C. Kiss Don't Tell b.2000 (Aritaur Midnight Rave × C. Let 'em Talk).

Chaanrose dogs gained great success in both show and work, and Rosie bred ten show champions from relatively few litters, with many working titles. The accomplishments of the Chaanrose bitches in working trials demonstrates that Dobermanns do not have to be either European-bred or over-driven to succeed at working.

Halsbands: The Halsbands kennel of Roger and June James also greatly benefited from Dizown breeding. Their Halsbands Manhatten b.1978 (Ch. D. The Hustler × Tarn of Halsband) was a great producer, with four champions from three litters:

Ch. H. Helmsman b.1980 (× Ch. D. Razzamatazz)
Ch. H. Redwing b.1982 (Rosecroft By The Way to Bilsam, Imp US), who amongst her many wins, won the RBCC at Crufts in 1985, and BOB at Crufts in 1986
Sibling brothers Ch. H. Wicked Wizard, and Ch. H. Bugenhagen b.1983 (× Wizz Bang of Vickisfree)

June handled many of the dogs that were bred at Halsbands, or that were by their dogs, one of which was Ch. Shirdawns April Rain b.1985 (Ch. H. Helmsman × Alphadobes Merry Contessa) who won the BCC at Crufts in 1989. Ch H. The Joker b.1992 (Bronco vd. Kunigundenhohe at Heimdall, imp. × H. The Sonnet), and a repeat mating in the same year of Ch. H. Canisp, were the last two champions born at the kennel.

Jowendy: Undoubtedly one of the most influential British kennels of modern times is Wendy Burge's Jowendy, whose breeding lies behind the majority of important British kennels. Wendy had her first Dobermann in 1966 and registered her kennel name when she started showing in 1977. One of her early bitches was a brown bitch called Quandri's Bitter Lemon (Hilmora The Corsair, son of Wilm v. Forell, × Wolfstone Harmony). Quandri's second litter was to O. Sheboygan, from which Wendy kept Jowendy's Bandido Migel. In 1980 Migel was used at stud to a bitch called Russtuns Miracle who had Tavey and Royaltain

Ch. Jowendy's Into Jazz.

41

lines, and in part payment for a stud fee Wendy had a bitch called Cracklin' Rosie of Jowendy from the litter.

All successful kennels need a great foundation bitch, and Cracklin' Rosie was one of the best. She proved her worth to the breed in her first litter when she was mated to D. All That Jazz and produced a champion daughter, Ch. Jowendy's Into Jazz b.1984. Like her dam, Into Jazz was also an outstanding brood bitch, giving four champions from three litters.

Amongst others, Into Jazz was tremendously important in the development of two of the top UK kennels today: Amazon and Supeta. In her first litter in 1988 she produced Ch. J. Infa Red for Maelstrom, who was the dam of Maelstrom Mor Than a Feeling at Amazon (who produced three champions in her first litter), and Ch. J. Kia-Ora (by Ch. D. Street Legal), who was the foundation bitch for Supeta. Her second litter was to Marienburg's Firedanza v Tavey (imp. US), and produced Ch. J. Tokyo Joe at Damarills.

In her third litter to Ch. Holtzburg Mayhem she produced Ch J. Kilowatt b.1990, who became one of the most significant UK stud dogs of all time. Ch J. Into Jazz was Top Brood Bitch in 1991 and 1992.

Wendy Burge with Ch. Jowendy's Kilowatt.

Ch. Jowendy's Kilowatt b.1990 sired eighty-three litters and ten champions:

Sibling sisters Ch. Stormy Romance with Chaanrose, and Ch. Wild Cherry at C. b.1992 (× Ch. Chaanrose Elegantiae at Merryn)
Ch. Holtzburg J'Adore du Boogie b.1992 (× Holtzburg Luvta Boogie)
Ch. Remesca Dream Lady b.1993 (× Ch. Remesca Firelight, a Mayhem daughter)
Ch. Dizown Tickled Pink b.1994 (× D. Playing with Fire)
Ch. Remesca Truly Madly Deeply b.1995 (× Remesca Firenza, sister of Firelight)
Ch. Nearctic Legal Protector b.1996 (× Zarleon Heaven Scent, a Mayhem daughter)
Ch./Ir. Ch. Supeta's Orangina (Ch. J. Kia-Ora) with seven CCs
Sibling brothers Ch. Michcar My Cousin Vinny, and Ch. Michcar Jumpin' Jack Flash b.1994 (× Lynfryds Chase The Ace)

Kilowatt's litter sister was J. Hooligan von Holtzburg, owned by Mayhem's owner Fiona Field; although she wasn't made up, was fundamental in the development of two kennels. For her first litter Fiona mated her to Sue and Spencer Houghton's Ch. Crislea on Target with Desuzer b.1993 (Ch. H. Mayhem × Better Be Good with Holtzburg); this produced Crislea Centrefold of Aritaur b.1996, who was the foundation for Martin and Jay Horgan's line.

Fiona later became ill, and Hooligan went to live with Toni and Ian Norman at Nearctic Dobermanns, where she was later mated to N. Big In Japan b.1994 (Kilowatt × Zarleon Heaven Scent, by Mayhem), producing Ch. N. Nearctic The Biscuit. He in turn was the sire of four champions: Ch N. High Treason of Shagraan b.1998 (× N. Hot Hatch), Ch. Amazon She's A Sinner for Tridon b.1999 (× Ch. A. Sinful Skinful), Ch. J. Dr Feelgood b.2000 (× J. Strikes Again), Ch. Woodbriar Serengetti Sky b.2001 (× Ch. A. Sealed With a Kiss at Woodbriar).

Jowendy's continued to be one of the very top breeders in the UK, and their J. Strikes Again b.1995 (Dobermoray April Fool × J. Wild Child) was a great asset for the kennel. Her second litter to Ch. Nearctic Nick The Biscuit produced Ch. J. Dr Feelgood for A. b.2000, and for her third litter she was bred to Victor van Roveline. Sue Mycroft had persuaded Wendy to consider the dog, and Wendy openly said she nearly got cold feet when he came up the garden path as, putting it mildly, Vito was not normally the style of dog Wendy would have chosen! However, the mating went ahead and Sue was proven right, as the litter produced some very special dogs. J. Enuf Said for Supeta became a great asset as a brood bitch for Sue and Pete Mycroft, Ch J. I'm So Excited at Zajonti won five CCs for Andy and Sharon Dzuba, and J. Robin The Hood, who was not shown, but stayed with Wendy and John, became a tremendously successful stud dog, siring many champions and a legacy of many more generations of champions.

Jowendy's Robin The Hood was Top Sire in 2003 and 2004, Top Stud Dog in 2004, 2006, 2008, 2009 and 2010. In 2008 and 2010 he was also Top Working Stud Dog.

Robin The Hood descended from a line of top winning and producing dogs. His sire Victor van Roveline was Top UK Sire 2001, Top Working Stud Dog 2002 and 2003, when he was also fifth All Breeds.

His grandsire Ch. Jowendy's Kilowatt was Top Stud Dog in 1996 and 1997, and runner-up Top Stud Dog All Breeds in 1996.

His great-grandsire was Ch. Holtzburg May-

hem, who was Top Stud Dog in the breed from 1991–95 and Top Stud Dog All Breeds in 1995.

Genetic excellence was not just in the male line, as Robin The Hood's daughter Ch. A. What's Up Pussycat JW was Top Dobermann Bitch in 2003 and 2004, and Top Dobermann Brood Bitch and Top Group Brood Bitch 2008.

J. Robin The Hood b.2001 (Victor v. Roveline, imp. Ned, × J. Strikes Again) sired fourteen champion progeny:

Triplets Ch. Amazon Under Fire at Liason, Ch. A. Cheek to Cheek at Lynfryds JW, and Ch. A. What's Up Pussycat b.2002 (× Ch A. Sinful Skinful)
Ch. Manzart Jalousie at Amical b.2002 (× M. Ever Smiling)
Ch. Supetas Top Tip for Mavson b.2003 (× Sallate Dixie)
Ch. Jaegerson Singing the Blues JW b.2003 (× Ch. J. Giggle n' Gossip)
Ch. Jojavik Dance Floor Diva b.2003, and SA Ch. J. You Dance I Dance
Ch. Freelance Temptation of Alcumlow b.2004 (× F. Galaxy)
Ch. Supeta's Wicked Wizard at Sonakint JW b.2005 (Ch. S. Witchy Woman)
Triplets Ch. Izralight New Year Dream, Ch. I. New Year Wishes, Ch. I. New Year Spirit b.2005 (I. Lady Madonna)
Ch. Jaegerson Imagination b.2005 (× Ch. Jaegerson Giggle n' Gossip)
Ch. Nearctic Jack Spicer b.2007 (Amazon All Out Of Love for Nearctic)

With this pedigree full of illustrious winning and producing dogs, it is not surprising that Robin The Hood was so influential for the breed.

Sallate: The world-famous Sallate kennel name was established in 1978 by Graham Hunt, whose mother supported and encouraged his early passion for Dobermanns. Graham bought Sigismunds Ice Cool Kate b.1980 (Ch. D. The Hustler × Sigismunds Bit o' Muslin) from Hazel Jones, and contested working trials with her.

With his first wife Maxine, Graham produced many of the best dogs in the UK, and theirs was the kennel to beat. Over the years Sallate bred fourteen UK champions and four Irish champions, and won 120 CCs. Kate was much more than just a good brood bitch: she had just two litters, but she was the dam or grand-dam of over ten ticket winners with more than forty CCs between them.

In her second litter she produced siblings who would establish the Sallate name as one of the greatest UK kennels of all breeds: Ch. Sallate Ferris and Ch. S. Frauline b.1985 (Ch. Perihelias Resolution × S. Ice Cool Kate). More is written on the famous Ferris later, but Frauline herself produced three litters, each containing a champion: Ch. S. Dignity, Ch. S. Qate, and Ch. S. Zoey at Manzart, who founded Mandy Everley's Manzart line.

Sigismunds Ice Cool Kate.

Amongst the very many Sallate champions are names such as:

Ch. S. Dignity b.1991 (Ch. S. Ferris × Ch. S. Frauline)
Ch. S. Gember b.1991 (Graaf Buco v. Neerlands Stam × S. Quina)
Ch. S. Hollywood b.1991 (Ch. H. Mayhem × S. Qala at Stroudley)
Ch. S. Liberty b.1992 (Ch. H. Mayhem × S. Standerbert Diploma)
Ch. S. Dexter b.1993 (Ch. S. Liberty × S. Finesse)
Siblings Ch. S. Schumacher and Ch. S. Striptease b.1997 (Graaf Xandy v. Neerlands Stam × S. Jenna)

Graham bred with equal consideration to character as conformation, and Sallate was a kennel of choice for the working competitor. In 1992 Yvonne Walker's S. Ming of Darcregan (Graaf Buco v. Neerlands Stam × S. Odette of Dundalk, out of a Ferris daughter), gained his CDex, and UDex titles. Yvonne later had Diego's Caught N The Act b.2014 (Ch., Ir. Ch. Bosskat Bonza × B. Designer) who also gained CDex, and UDex. Yvonne runs the very successful Darcregan Dog Training School near Edinburgh, where her intuitive and calm kind handling has established her as one of the leading trainers of Dobermanns in the UK.

In the 1990s Sallate complemented his existing lines with some fresh genes when he imported dogs from Holland. First was Graaf Buco v. Neerlands Stam b.1990 (Graaf Xuvier v. NS × Gravin Hera v. NS), who sired ten litters including Ch. Sallate Gember, and to Princess Paula V.'T Gronnigerland (imp.), produced WT Ch. Jimarty's Citta b.1992.

The following year he imported Nemesis Feo von Koepsel at Sallate b.1993 (Int., Multi Ch. Graaf Quirinus v. NS × the superb Kalina v. NS), and his son Graaf Xandy van NS b.1996 (× Gravin Beauty v. NS), who both feature prominently in the pedigrees of many of the successful dogs in the UK. 'Feo' sired twenty-one litters.

Dave and Barbara Mitchell (Bosskat) owned Sallate Jezebel b.1994 (Ch. Holtzburg Mayhem × Ch. S. Levi, who was the result of a father/daughter mating, Levi being a daughter of Mayhem). She was outcross mated to Feo and produced the Irish winning Bosskat siblings.

The Sallate name stayed at the top of the breed for many years, winning the annual Top Breeder title a record eight times, and giving great foundations for top kennels, including Diego's and Supeta's.

Krieger: Also in Scotland, one of the first Dobermanns at John McIlroy's Krieger kennel was Ibsen Jingo von Ferrolheim b.1977 (by Ger. Ch. Aldo v. Ferrolheim SchH II, Bdsr 76). He was originally imported by Stan MacDonald, who also imported Graaf Wodan v. Neerlands Stam. The first champion for the kennel was Ch. Krieger Rhythm 'n

Blues b.1996 (Idol v. Brandenburg at Brubacker × K. Luana). The following year Ch. Tavey's Uproar v. Davway was used on K. Pandora (Kinski Dirty Tricks × K. Luana), and produced sibling brothers Ch. K. Storm and Ch. K. Sure Shot b.1997. A sister from that litter, K. Satin, was mated to Drusus v. Adlercrest at Heimdall imp. US. Their daughter K. Xantia was mated to Ch. K. Sure Shot and produced sibling champions Ch. K. Endurance and Ch. K. Endless Love JW b.2003.

Ch. K. The Wizard of Oz JW b.2010 (Ch. Supeta's Wicked Wizard at Sonakint JW × K. Kinky Boots) sired Ch. Jojavik Molly Mobster b.2011 (× Ch Jojavik Gangsters Moll); he gained his third CC in 2013.

THE NINETEEN-EIGHTIES

From 1945 to the mid-1980s there were approximately 174 Kennel Club registered Dobermann imports to the UK: thirty-five American, forty-nine German and twenty-two Dutch. Annual KC registrations of Dobermanns peaked at nearly 10,000 puppies.

The breed had become extremely popular and fashionable through television programmes such as Magnum, which featured the immaculately well trained Dobermanns, Zeus and Apollo, who portrayed the glamour of the breed – but many owners were badly suited to Dobermann ownership and did not train their dogs to become the canine models of excellence as seen on the television. The backyard breeders who tried to 'cash in' provided no support when inevitably things went wrong, and breed rescue organizations overflowed, particularly with rejected dogs. Thankfully the breed never stayed high or reached the 'status breeds' list.

One benefit of the expansion in breeding was that it provided many new important dogs and talented breeders. Space limits mention of all the champions, but there are some particular dogs and kennels which have had a strong influence on the breed.

Names of Influence in the 1980s
A big-winning male in the 1980s was David and Edith Bamforth's Ch. Highroyd's Man of the Year,

b.1980 (Jacade Mercedes of Mantoba × Studbriar The Fortune Gal of Mantoba). He won twenty-five CCs including BOB at Crufts in 1985, where he is one of the rare few Dobermanns also to win the Working Group. Best Opposite Sex that year was the bitch Ch. Laurill's High Flyer, who was a daughter of another big ticket dog, Ch. Major Marauder b.1976 (Ch. Ainsdale Sea Marauder × Crudos Amoroso), owned by Tegwyn Jones, who forty years later remains one of the UK's top judges. Marauder also won twenty-five CCs, was BIS at the general championship show WELKS under Joe Braddon, and won the DCC at Crufts in 1981. He sired two champions: Ch. Laurills High Flyer b.1980 (× Royaltains High Hopes), and Ch. Vincedobes Eclipse b.1980 (× Vincedobes Aurora of Chancepixies).

Chancepixies: The Chancepixies affix was established by friends Dave Anderson and Jean Frost in 1980, when, having been around Dobermanns for a while, they became involved with showing and breeding. The first champion for the kennel was Ch. Vincedobe Eclipse of C. b.1980 (Ch. Major Marauder × C. Aurora, grand-daughter of Ch. Studbriar The Red). She produced only one litter, but her sister Eternity was bred to a Ch. F. Chaos son and produced another champion for the kennel, Ch. Chancepixies Friend or Foe b.1985.

Dave and Jean had been looking for a special Dobermann to further their joint interests in the

Ch. Pompie Sea Jade of Chancepixies, bitch breed record holder to 1998.

45

breed, and visited Hilary Partridge's Pompie kennels to view her litter by Gerry Young's Ch. Flexor Adonis × Ch. P. Alcyone. The litter contained a Ch./Ir. Ch. Pompie Sea Jade of Chancepixies b.1983, who would become the future breed record holder.

Sea Jade was awarded her first CC with BOB from judge John McManus at Darlington, in the Junior class. Her second CC came from her breeder (permitted in those days). Her crowning CC came in 1985, when she also became Top Dobermann. Having become Top Dobermann in Ireland, this was the first time that both UK and Irish titles had been achieved. In 1986 she won a further ten CCs, and was again Top Dobermann. She gained her twenty-fourth and final CC from Liz Cartledge in 1987, and held the Bitch Breed Record until handing it over to Ch. Dobermoray Whirl'n Dervish in 1998. Sea Jade was handled to all her wins by Dave. She died aged fourteen years and four months.

Dave Anderson also handled Ch. Sallate Ferris, so holds the unique honour of being the only person to have shown two UK Breed Record Holders in Dobermanns.

Dave later handled Vincent O'Brien's successful Irish male Ch./Ir. Ch. Vincenza Distant Thunder b.1995, and had continued success with his own breeding, titling the siblings Ch. C. Aura and Ch. C. Monopolist b.1998 (Ch. Marrijax Doobie Have × Pompie The Blues Swinger of C.). Later champions for the kennel were Ch. Gaindyke Keramia of C. b.2000 (Vito v. Roveline, who was by Randy van't Sabbatsveld) and Quelsey v. Roveline (× Gaindyke Molly Malone).

The most recent show champion for the kennel is Darren Joy's Ch. C/ Locomotive b.2007 (C. Auctioneer × Ch. C. Olive Oil), who sired the Crufts double winning siblings for Jojavik.

Dave later became involved in working dogs in the sport of Schutzhund (aka IPO/VPG), and has bred four of the first ten UK Dobermanns to have full working titles: C. Legend VPGIII, C. Angellica VPGI, C. Auctioneer VPGI, and C. Cherry Brandy VPGI; the latter two he also handled.

In recent years Dave and his wife Heidi opened a kennels and rescue centre near Dover, where they devote themselves to rescuing and rehoming Dobermanns and other dogs, and campaigning for improved policies for the breeding of dogs in the UK.

Crossridge: John Crossley and Margaret Detheridge bred their first Dobermann litter in 1983 using Dizown All That Jazz on their bitch Anna of Crossridge b.1979 (Drindod Sir Galahad, a Phileen's American Express son × Cassala Cassis with Tumlow parents). The litter produced Ch. Crossridge the Jazzman b.1983, owned and shown by Avril Stewart, making him the first champion for both Avril and Crossridge. Another successful champion from the kennel was Ch. Crossridge Carbon Copy for Lynfryds b.1984 (Ch. Findjans Chaos × Dizown Copy Cat), owned by Fred and Linda Wilkes.

Lynfryds: Fred and Linda Wilkes had been involved in Dobermanns for some time before they bought their Rathkeel bitch from Audrey and Peter Kelly. They then bought Ch. Crossridge Carbon Copy for Lynfryds, who was shown by Fred. He won four CCs, and sired twenty litters and three UK champions.

Ch. Sallate's Qate b.1988 (× Ch. S. Fraulein)
Ch. Bledig Bugatti b.1988 (× Ch. Twinglo Le Juice at Bledig)
Ch. Sallate Unison at Mattacane b.1989 (× Ch. S. Islay)

Ch. Crossridge Carbon Copy for Lynfryds.

From the success of his progeny, Carbon Copy won the Top Sire competition in 1989, and left many successful grand-progeny such as Ch. Kerajun Cousin Kate at Mytanamy b.1992 (Ch. Bledig Bugatti × Kerajun Head Over Heels). Carbon Copy also sired Am. Ch. Findjans Outrage b. (× Ch. F. Mêlée), who was the first ever uncropped Dobermann to become an American champion. Outrage sired over seven American champions, including three DPCA Top Twenty competitors, and one Canadian champion. He passed on his sound character aptitude by siring a SchHlll, and a Delta Society (service) dog.

In 1986 Linda heard of a litter from Olderhill Keyhole Kate, who was on joint breeding terms with Colin Macleod. Kate was from the last Olderhill litter, and Linda was understandably very keen to have a puppy from the line. The sire to the litter was a dog called Vidal's Boscowan, a son of Gloria Pascoe's Ch. Trevannick Master Mariner (Ch. Upfolds Admiral Blackfoot to a bitch of Tavey breeding) who won five CCs; the litter was split, with half being registered in Colin's prefix of Damocles, and the others as Olderhill. Ch. Penny Black of Olderhill at Lynfryds JW became the second champion for the kennel.

Carbon Copy and Penny Black were later mated and produced two notable bitches: L. Penny Royal of Marcavie, and L. Pennyfarthing. Neither was titled, but both made their mark on the breed through their grandchildren, with Penny Royal being the grandmother of the foundation bitch for the Jojavik kennel.

Fred and Linda Wilkes continued to produce top winning dogs for many years; their Ch. L. Domino b.2001 (Ch. Swyndwr Crimestopper × L. Smart Move) and Ch. Amazon Cheek to Cheek for L. JW b.2002 (Jowendy's Robin The Hood × Ch. A. Sinful Skinful) both won four CCs, as did Ch. Lynfryds Valentino JW b.2004 (Ch. Khaneve Gold'n Child to Amazon × Ch. L. Domino).

Valentino was mated to Cheek to Cheek and produced Ch. L. Raspberry Beret b.2006, who won five CCs. She was later mated to Ch. Amazon El Torro and produced the most recent champion for the kennel, Ch. Lynfryds Scaramouche b.2010.

Valentino also sired Ch. Amazon Kandy Kisses

b.2008 (× Ch. A. What's Up Pussycat), Ch. Jaegerson Man In The Mirror b.2009 (× Ch. J. Singing The Blues JW), and Ch., Lux. Ch. Jojavik Gangsters Moll JW b.2006 (× Ch. J. Dancefloor Diva JW).

Fred and Linda Wilkes continued to produce top winning dogs for many years.

Dolbadarn: In 1985 and 1986 Mick and June Higgins won the coveted Top Breeder title for their Dolbadarn kennel. Their breeding was based on Bremenville Miss Sonya, whose antecedants, among others, came from Heathermount, Jasmere and Flexor Flugelman. She had five litters and produced a champion in each of her first three litters:

Ch. D. Oriana b.1991 (× Merad Dark Tempest; also back to Flugelman)
Ch. D. Ace High b.1982 (× Davalog's Crusader, which tied in on Tumlow breeding)
Ch. D. Hawker Fury b.1983 (× Chornytan Midnite Mark)

Other champions bred by Dolbadarn were siblings Ch. D. Dirty Girty and D. Nite Star b.1984 (Ch./Ir. Ch. Chornytan Travelin' Light × D. Life of Avelion – daughter of Miss Sonya).

Dexter v. Franckenhorst.

Marienburgs: In 1984 Mary Rogers (Marienburgs) imported siblings Dolly and Dexter v. Franckenhorst (Arrow v. Harro's Berg × Vivre Vivien v. Franckenhorst) to America from Holland, and made great use of their depth of quality and substance to her generations of elegant breeding.

Dexter was later mated to her Marienburgs Hollyhawk to produce Am. Ch. M. Morocco, who was exported to Brazil. Am. Brazilian Ch. Morocco was then mated to Dolly to produce Marienburgs Dark Daimler, who was exported back to Holland to the joint ownership of Sonja v. Franquemont and Brigitte Schellekens (Ranisberk), where he was used widely at stud.

In 1985 Reg and Mary Barton at Tavey imported a male, Marienburgs' Firedanza v. T. (M. Don Diego × M Topaz Flame), and female Marienburgs Mitzi v. Dixifire (M. Morocco × Reisdorf Rage of Dixifire) from Mary Rodgers famous American kennel. Before leaving, Mitzi was mated to Dexter vom Franckenhorst and had the 'U' litter in quarantine. In the litter were Thelma Toole's Tavey's Uncle Sam for Chornytan, and Jenny Battershell's Ch. Tavey's Uproar v. Davway.

Uproar won four CCs, but should have been used far more than the thirty-two litters he sired considering the great value of his lineage. He sired three champions: Ch. Metexa Mastalinski (a granddaughter of Ch. M. Movie Master), and sibling brothers Ch. Krieger Storm and Ch. K. Sure Shot (× K. Pandora).

Ch. Dimrost Freedom Fighter b.1984 (Pompie Danger Man at Dimrost × Khasamari Sieglinde At D.) was a prolific sire of 257 puppies from thirty-one litters. Seven became UK champions, and two were BOB winners at Crufts. His champion progeny were:

Ch. Mansty's Prize Fighter b.1988 (× Othertons Liberated Lady Of M.)
Ch. Lodgehouse Casablanca b.1989 (× L. Camelia)
Ch. Borain's Carte-Blanche of Dobermoray b.1990 (× B. Sizzling Hot)
Ch. Pompie Ain't Miss Behaving b.1990 (× Gaby v. Okdorp of P., imp.)
Ch. Vyleigh's Zaxon b.1990 (× V. Xanja)
Ch. Gaindyke Fancy Free b.1991 (× Panha Riff At G.)

Ch. Halstatt Waldsteinia b.1991 (× Ritlo Royal Cressida)

Although not used widely at stud, Tim and Lita Lainchbury's Ch. Lodgehouse Casablanca produced four big-winning champions:

Sibling brothers Ch. Chaanrose Don't Crowd Me at Jaegerson, and Ch. Chaanrose Shock Tactic b. (× Ch. Wild Cherry at C.)
Ch. Dizown Dance with the Devil b.1992 (× D. Lucky Lady)
Ch. Marrijax Doobie Have b.1992 (× M. Mirrabelle)

From the success of his progeny Casablanca became Top Dobermann Sire in 1999 and Top Dobermann Stud Dog in 2000.

Ch. M. Doobie Have won eight CCs, six with BOB, and also sired four champions:

Siblings Ch. Chancepixies Monopolist, and Ch. Chancepixies Aura b.1988 (× Pompie The Blues Swinger of C.)
Ch. Jowendy's Let Loose at Mattacane b.1997 (× Jowendy's Wild Child)
Ch. Mattacane Green With Envy at Marrijax b.1997 (Ch. Holtzburg J'Adore du Boogie)

Remesca: Carol's first Dobermann was Achenburg Remy Martin b.1979, bred by Harry and Margaret Woodward (Achenburg).

In 1984 Carol had a bitch from the Torjet kennels of Ivan and Jean Wardropper called Firefly of Torjet (Chornytan Midnite Mark × Torjet Class Distinction), who was a granddaughter of Harry and Margaret's Ch. Von Klebong's Solar Encore at Achenburg. Firefly was later mated to Ch. Holtzburg Mayhem, to produce Carol's first champion Ch. R. Firelight b.1989, owned by Alison Moss. Firelight's litter sister Firenza was mated to Ch. J. Kilowatt to produce Ch. R. Truly Madly Deeply b.1995. Several champions have followed over the years.

Ch. R. Dream Lady b.1993 (Kilowatt × Firelight), owned by Nick and Kerry Pape, was bred to Mysel Rock on Tommy (Bronco vd K. at Heimdall imp. × Jowendy's Caught Red Handed at Mysel). The litter was split with the owners and Carol, half registered as Padharco, and half registered as Remesca, with Ch. Padharco Spirit of Evie b.1997 (Mysel Rock on Tommy × Ch. R. Dream Lady), shown by Carol and owned by the Papes.

Alison Moss later had Firelight's granddaughter R. Forget me Knot (Ch. Lodgehouse Casablanca × R. Dream of Darkness), who although was not made up, won the BCC at Crufts 2001. Ch. R. What Eva b.2009 (Ch. Supeta's Enuf's Enuf for Cooley × Remesca Majolica), Nicky Walton's Ch. R. Perfect Timing at Dabells JW b.2011 (Ch. Amazon El Torro JW × R. Magie Noire) followed, and the latest champion for the kennel was Zarina Brough's Ch. R. Rossini JW, ShCM (Ch. Aritaur Cardinal Red at Jodaseen × Ch. R. What Eva).

Holtzburg: Fiona Holt's (later Field) first Dobermann was a bitch from Hazel Jones called Sigismund's Fanlight Fanny (Ch. Dizown The Hustler × S. Bit O' Muslin), who was litter sister to Graham Hunt's Sigismund's Ice Cool Kate. A male from Olderhill followed, and then Fiona's first champion, a bitch called Ch. Dizown I Can Boogie Too with Holtzburg b.1984 (Ch. Findjans Chaos × Ch. I Can Boogie at D.). Fiona mated her with Ch. Perihelias Resolution, and one puppy stood out as something very special, a dog that would have enormous influence on the breed: Ch. Holtzburg Mayhem b.1987.

Ch. Holtzburg Mayhem with breeder Fiona Field. Mayhem was Top Dobermann Stud Dog from 1991–1995, and Top Stud Dog All Breeds in 1993.

Mayhem was handled by Fiona and won seven CCs, all with BOB. Where his half brother Ferris was the great showman, it was as a sire that Mayhem excelled. He was very tightly bred on both a great brood bitch Ch. Mitrasandra Gay Lady of Findjans, who appeared four times in four generations, and another great producer, Ch. Phileen's Duty Free of Tavey who appeared three times. This breeding on proven producing dogs and bitches made Mayhem a valuable stud dog. Mayhem sired seventy litters and produced fifteen champions:

Ch. Remesca's Firelight b.1989 (× Firefly of Torjet)
Ch. Sallate Zoey at Manzart b.1989 (× Ch. S. Fraulein, who was Ferris's sister)
Ch. Jowendy's Kilowatt b.1990 (× Ch. J. Into Jazz)
Siblings Ch. Albadobe Shalimar and Ch. A. Kouros b.1990 (× Kool and Kinky at Holtzburg and Sigismunds)
Ch. Crislea on Target with Desuzer b.1991 (× Better be Good with Holtzburg)
Ch. Sallate Carrie b.1991 (× S. Standerbert Diploma, a Ferris daughter)
Siblings Ch. Sallate Levi and Ch. S. Liberty b.1992 (× S. Standerbert Diploma)
Ch. Sallate Hollywood b.1991 (S. Qate at Stroudley)
Siblings Ch. S. Nostalga and Ch. S. Neptune b.1992 (× S. Unity)
Ch. Swyndwr Me and My Girl at Rocksea b.1993 (× Swyndwr Celebration)
Ch. Hikays Rumor Has It b.1994 (× Ch. H. Rock Folley)
Ch. Sallate Jigsaw b.1994 (× S. Levi, so a father–daughter mating)

Khaneve: This kennel is renowned for Ch. Sallate Ferris b.1985 (Ch. Perihelias Resolution × Sigismunds Ice Cool Kate), owned by Dave and Yvonne Bevans from Middlesex. Ferris won BPIS as a ten-month-old at an open show, followed a couple of weeks later with a BIS and BPIS. He took his first CC at just fourteen months old, shown by breeder Graham.

His second CC was from breed specialist Audrey Kelly, and his third and crowning CC came from Peter Kelly at National Working Breeds 1986,

Ch. Sallate Ferris, who won BOB at Crufts on four occasions and won the Group twice, with his breeder Graham Hunt.

Ch. Sallate Ferris winning the Working Group at Crufts in 1990 with Dave Anderson, under judge Leonard Pagliero.

where he also won BIS from Group Captain Sutton. Ferris became the youngest Dobermann champion in the UK to gain his title, at just fourteen months and fifteen days, and gained it most quickly, within fourteen days.

Graham won seven CCs with Ferris before handing him over to Dave Anderson (Chancepixies), who amassed thirty-one CCs, taking him to a Group win at Crufts in 1990. Ferris then took the title of Breed Record Holder from Ch. Iceberg of Tavey, who had held it for twenty years.

Derek King (Studbriar) subsequently won three CCs with Ferris, and also won the Group at Blackpool in 1991. In total, Ferris won BOB at Crufts an incredible four times, and won the Group there twice, once with Graham and the other with Dave. He was unbeaten in the breed at all his Crufts outings. Ferris held the Breed Record with forty-two CCs for twenty-eight years, until he was overtaken by Ch., Lux. Ch. Supeta's Ozzy Osbourne JW in 2011. He died in 1997 aged eleven years and ten months.

Ferris sired forty-two litters and six champion progeny:

Ch. Sallate Black Magic of Coltrac b.1990 (× Brookman Princess Stephanie), winner of twelve CCs, and BOB at Crufts 1994, beating her sire Ferris, who won the DCC. Incidentally Black Magic had a total hip score of fifty-six: obviously no hindrance in beating off the competition.
Siblings Ch. Tudor Tarrados and Ch. Charles Great Homestead b.1991 (× Lady Myfanwy Talbot), who won twenty CCs, and nine CCs respectively.
Ch. Khaneve Judgement Day b.1994 (× Dizown You Got it at K.), with five CCs and a CC at Crufts.
Ch. S. Dignity b.1991 (× Ch. S. Fraulein, litter sister to Ferris, therefore a brother/sister mating) with three CCs.
Ir. Ch. S. Legend b.1987 (× S. Extra Special).

Ch. Khaneve Judgement Day b.1994 was owned by Dave and Yvonne Bevans, who bred him from Ch. S. Ferris, out of their Dizown You Got it at Khaneve b.1989 (Marienburgs Firedanza v. Tavey, imp. US × Dizown Daisy Brown). He won five CCs and sired twenty-nine litters with two champions, both of whom had Mayhem and Ferris as grandparents in their quality pedigrees:

Ch. Jimbaros Steel Magnolia b.1998 (× Amazon Always An Angel for J.)
Ch. Estridge Sobriety of Doberlane b.1996 (× E. Move Over Darling).

Two other daughters who were valuable brood bitches were Marcavie Rythm 'n Dance from K. b.1999 (× M. Chorus Girl), who was the foundation bitch for the Jojavik kennel, and K. Dolly Daydream b.1997 (× Estridge Double Dare for Tirana), who was the dam of Ch. K. Gold 'n' Child for Amazon (by Ch. A. Oh What a Knight).

Studbriar: The Studbriar affix of Margaret and Derek King began with their foundation bitch Eikon Jests Amazon × Barrimilne The Minx. For her first litter she was mated to Ch. Tavey's Iceberg, from which came the first champion for the kennel Ch. Studbriar Chieftain b.1968. Later mated to Jatra's Commanche Princess of S. (a Duty Free daughter), Chieftain produced Ch. S. Dark 'n Sassy of Zarwyn b.1974, who won ten CCs for owner Mike Jones. A repeat mating produced Terry Lamb's Studbriar the Fortune Gal, dam of the top winning dog Ch. Highroyds Man of the Year b.1980.

Otherton: Lynn Rock had her first Dobermann in 1967, and shortly after established her Otherton affix with her then husband Paul Rock. Their first champion was Ch. Otherton's Statesman b.1980 (Ch. Merrist Reluctant Knight × Airborne of O.). In 1998 O. Touch of Genius was mated to Ch. Amazon Sound Machine, which produced sibling champions Mick and Eileen Matthews' Ch. O. Country Gent and O. Oasis. Ir. Ch. Otherton Mirage b.2001 (Ch. Cloudybay Dead Ringer for Amazon × Ch. Otherton's Oasis) was Lynn's last champion before she died.

Swyndwr: Hilton and Jean Quigley became involved in Dobermanns in the late 1970s, and their first involvement with the showing and breeding world was with Steveley's Black Jezebel, who was a Ch. Halsband's Helmsman daughter. She wasn't shown, but was a great asset to Swyndwr, with her three litters all to Ch. Crossridge The Jazzman. A succession of champions followed for the kennel, well into the twenty-first century.

Steveley's Black Jezebel's second litter produced the first champion for the kennel – Ch. Swyndwr Storm Bearer b.1989, who had various handlers. Avril Stewart showed him up to Limit Dog, then Hilton and Jean's son David handled him to his first ticket under Irene McManus. Jean then took him on herself and won seven CCs with him. John Hull stepped in for a few shows, then Pete Mycroft, and occasionally Sue, handled him to the rest of his total of fifteen CCs. Storm Bearer sired one UK champion, Ch. Manzart Black Humour at Sallate b.1995 (× Sallate Zoey at M.), and three overseas champions for Jackie Perry, but his value to the breed extended well past just the first generation as his descendants have themselves become successful champions and producers.

The third litter produced S. Celebration b.1990, who although she wasn't titled, produced Scott and Michelle Lyons Ch. S. Me and My Girl at Rocksea b.1993 (by Mayhem) in her first litter. Celebration's third litter to Reesharn's Hijacker produced Ch. S. Charlie's Angel b.1997. Charlie's Angel wasn't titled as she didn't like showing, but she secured her great value to the breed by being an outstanding dam, with five champions in four litters.

Charlie's Angel's first litter to Mansty Hooray Henry produced Ch. S. Crimestopper b.1999. Sue Day, who handled the Swyndwr dogs, had become a partner in the affix in 2001, and handled him to win all his twenty-seven CCs, apart from one occasion where a young Victoria Ingram stepped in to help out and won the CC with him at Richmond in 2004. Crimestopper was Top Dobermann in 2003 and sired two champions:

Ch. Lynfryds Domino b.2001 (× L. Smart Move)
Ch. Jojavik Wurlitzer b.2004 (× Marcavie Rhythm 'n Dance from Khaneve)

The Hooray Henry to Charlie's Angel litter was repeated, and produced Ch. Swyndwr Say The Word b.2001, and repeated again to produce the third champion from the combination, Richard Meredith's Ch. S. Hellfire of Tarchan b.2002. For her fourth litter, Charlie's Angel was bred (by frozen semen AI) to American Grand Ch. Cambria's Irish Rebellion b.2002 (Ch. C. Cavalleria × Ch. Orion's Rasberry Beret), who produced an extensive number of champion progeny in the US. This venture produced sibling champions Ch. S. Supatramp, who won fifteen CCs and was Joint Top Dobermann 2006, and Ch. S. Supacool. S. Charlie's Angel's progeny won a total of fifty-four CCs and won the Top Brood Bitch competition an amazing four times, including in 2004 when she was Top Brood All Breeds.

Helmlake: Karina Le Mare's famous Helmlake kennels were successful in various breeds, and her Dobermanns were handled for a long period by Barbara Harvey, managed by herself and her son Marc. Helmlake produced many champions, mainly based on European dogs.

Ch. Pampisford Promise of Glory of Helmlake b.1988 (Lexa Aldo × Ch P. Pepper) sired twenty-seven litters. His daughter Ch. Barrimilne Simply the Best for H. b.1993 was out of Thalia v. Franckenhorst at Barrimilne, imp. Ned, who carried Dexter v. Franckenhorst and Marienburgs lines. Ch. Cheapside Shoot to Fame at H. (Ch. Pampisford Promise of Glory of Helmlake × Baroness Of Cheapside) won eleven CCs and three BIS at breed championship shows. He was mated to his half sister (same sire) Vyleigh's Heidi Hi with H., producing Ch. H. Phantom b.1996, who won a CC at twelve months, twenty-three days, gaining his title at twenty-one months.

Gaindyke: Gaindyke was originally the affix of Lynn Glass, and later transferred into joint names with her husband John Hull. Lynn won her first CC with Boreamond Enforcement Agent b.1981 (Ch. Roanoke Swell Fella × Ch. R. Marigold at B.), and became interested in European breeding through John and Irene McManus.

One of Lynne's early bitches was Panha Riff at Gaindyke b.1985 (Ch. Metexa Movie Master × Bolac Britta, down from Quanto vom haus Schimmel), and she produced Lynne's first champion, Ch. Gaindyke Fancy Free b.1991 (by Ch. Dimrost Freedom Fighter). Fancy Free was later mated to Bronco Von Der Kunigundenhohe At Heimdall (imp.) and produced Ch. Lyntarski Ice Man for John Christie.

John Hull (Brubacker) had his first Dobermann Othertons Magic at Brubacker b.1986 (Ch. Vonmac Keegan × Red Skye at Otherton) with his first wife Andrea. At an obedience club run by Heidi Vyse, John became involved in showing, particularly admiring the European dogs, and imported Peggy van Roveline at Brubacker, imp. b.1991 (Int., Multi Ch. Graaf Quirinus v. Neerlands Stam DV Sgr'91, IDC Sgr'93, × Nathy v. R.) from Roland and Evelyn Beunekens famous Belgian kennel. She was followed shortly after by German Idol von Brandenburg at Brubacker b.1992 (Int., Multi, Ger. Ch. Eick v. Rappenau × BdSgrn'89 Athene v. Brandenburg), who sired Ch. K. Rythm'n Blues. John Hull also took on Xantos vd. Kunnemaborgh from Heidi Vyse to live with him.

In 1995 John and Lynn met at the World Dog Show in Brussels, where their love for Dobermanns and their enjoyment of European bloodlines gave them a shared mutual interest.

Victor van Roveline, or 'Vito' as he was known, became a most prolific and prepotent stud dog for them, siring fifty-six litters and twelve UK champions, and has had an enormous impact on the UK Dobermann through generations of champions and producers carrying his name. Victor became Top UK Sire 2001, Top Stud Dog 2002 in the breed, and topped the Working Group Stud Dog 2002, being third All Breeds. He repeated this success in 2003 when he was Top Stud Dog in the breed and Working Group, this time being fifth All Breeds.

His direct champion progeny are as follows:

Multi UK Ch. Gaindyke Flash Gordon b.1998 (× Schutz Mascha); he was the first UK dog of any breed to be shown in Holland under the Pet Passport Scheme, featuring on Dutch television and in the Dutch club magazine. He was the first UK-bred Dobermann to gain Dutch and Luxembourg titles

Ch. Knecht Merete b.1998 (× K. Margherita)
Multi Ch. Vonedstram The Vixen b.1999 (× Gaindyke Tamara at V.)
Siblings Ch. Supeta's Lyin Eyes for Sizlin, and Ch. S. Witchy Woman b.2000 (× Sallate Dixie)
Siblings Trystorme In Anticipation and Ch. T. Highlander b.2001 (× T. Indescretion)
Ch. Jowendy's I'm So Excited at Zajonti b.2001 (× J. Strikes Again)
Ch. Chancepixies Olive Oil b.2002 (× Ch. C. Aura)
Ch. Sallate Smugs Lady for Dejayotwo b.2003 (× Ch. S. Striptease)
Siblings Ch. Gaindyke Yuma v. Mansty, and AKC, UDC and Lux Ch. G. Yolo, re-import, one of the very few uncropped dogs to win in the USA, b.2003 (× Yeris Van De Wuytjeshoeve, imp. Bel) b.2003
Ch. Estridge Kanoute b.2003 (× E. Spice Gal JW)

He also sired the Top UK Sire 2003 Jowendys Robin The Hood.

The only litter sister to Ch. Gaindyke Flash Gordon was Gaindyke Molly Malone, who although she didn't gain her title, proved of great value as the dam of three important dogs:

Dave Anderson's Ch. Gaindyke Keramia of Chancepixies b.2000 (by Vito van Roveline, who was by IDC Sgr, Ch., Int., Randy Van't Sabbatsveld WW, EU × Multi Ch. Quelsey v. Roveline, who was litter sister to Quercia, Victor's dam.

Gill Cashman's Ch., Lux., Ned. Ch. Gaindyke Mirco at Lakehouse b.2002 (by Int., Multi Ch. Nitro del Rio Bianco Sgr AIAD 2001) was a winner at home where he won four CCs, BIS Birmingham Dobermann Club BOB Group 2 Bath Ch. Show, and abroad where he was Dutch Club Seiger 2005, Amsterdam winner 2004, Euro Sgr 2005, and Vice Euro Sgr 2003/2004.

Mirco's sister Ch. G. Martini b.2002, owned by John and Lynn, won top awards in many countries; she was the first UK bred dog to gain her BH, and the challenging French character test titles of TAN and TC. Her excellent litter in 2009 to It. Ch., IDC Sgr Ale Alamos del Citone produced Ch., Int. Ch. G. Eureka, Multi Ch. G. 'Ells Bells, and Indonesian Ch. G. El Alamain.

Vito and his daughter Supeta's Soul Sister for Gaindyke b.2001 (× Sallate Dixie) kindled John's working interest, which he continued after he and Lynn moved to France, where he trained G. Einstein b.2009 (Int., Multi Ch. F'Hiram Abif Royal Bell × G. Zulu) to his IPOIII.

The imports to Gaindyke, and their progeny, significantly changed the direction of the Dobermann in the UK, bringing their particular qualities of strong heads, more substantial bone and hard backs to the gene pool.

Knecht: Robert Downie and his partner Andy have bred Dobermanns for many years under the Knecht affix. Robert's first show Dobermann was Fra Hyzenflae of Knecht b.1983 (Kilmuir the Carpetbagger × Lucky Strike), who was not shown a lot but who introduced him to showing.

When he was looking to mate Hyzenflae he admired the Sallate breeding, and particularly those down from Ch. Perihelias Resolution, whom he mated to her. Their daughter Knecht Fra Ninotchka continued the line when mated to Kilmuir Caruso, and produced Knecht Margherita. Mated to Vito, their first champion, Ch. K. Merete b.1998, was born. Her grand-daughter, Knecht Magritte b.2009 (Aritaur Nominator × K. Maghera), was bred to Ch. Italo Elite House imp. Pol., to produce the kennel's most recent champion, Ch. Knecht Marek b.2012. Robert and Andy had meanwhile become partners with Lynn Glass on Ch., Int. Ch. Gaindyke Eureka imp. Fr. b.2009, who won seventeen CCs in the UK.

Supeta: Sue and Pete Mycroft came into Dobermann showing in the early 1980s, basing their Supeta kennel on Jowendy's bloodlines. Their first champion was a male called Ch. Jowendy's Kool Choice b.1986 (× Tamberg Ace High, who was a Resolution son out of Naughty but Nice for Jowendy's). Next came the bitch Ch. Jowendy's Kia Ora b.1988 (Ch. Dizown Street Legal × Ch. J. Into Jazz). The Supeta kennel has enjoyed an outstanding record of winning dogs and bitches from the 1980s right up to the present day.

Ch. Jowendy's Kia Ora was later mated to her half-brother, the top producing Ch. J. Kilowatt (Ch. Holtzburg Mayhem × Ch. J. Into Jazz), which produced Ch./Ir. Ch. Supeta's Orangina JW with eight CCs.

Orangina was that rare combination of being a winner and producer. In her first litter she was mated to Ch. Michcar Jumping Jack Flash b.1996 and produced Ch. Supeta's Caughtya' Dreamin', and her litter to Nemesis Feo produced Ch./Ir. Ch. Supeta's Positively Perfect for Cooley b.1998. He won six CCs, five BOB, and his Irish title for owner Sinead Taggart, and sired sibling champions: Ch. S. Enuf Alredi, who would be the dam of the future breed record holder, and Ch./Ir. Ch. S. Enuf's Enuf for Cooley b.2004 (× Jowendy's Enuf Said for S.), who won six CCs, three BOB and his Irish title.

In 1998 the Mycrofts imported a bitch called Sallate Dixie b.1998 (Nemesis Feo × Gravin Winey v. NS); she was mated to Vito and this litter produced Ch. S. Witchy Woman JW, who stayed at Supeta, and Jean Walker's Ch. S. Lyin' Eyes for Sizlin' JW b.2000, who although she did not gain any obedience titles, has the great honour of being one of the very few breed champions to have represented the breed by competing in obedience at Crufts every year from 2002 to 2009. She is believed to be the only Dobermann to have competed in obedience at Crufts over such a long period.

Sue and Pete then bought in a litter sister to Jowendy's Robin the Hood called Jowendy's Enuf Said for Supeta b.2001, who was mated to Ch./Ir. Ch. S. Positively Perfect for Cooley in 2004. A dog in the litter was Ch./Ir. Ch. Supeta's Enuf's Enuf for Cooley, who went to Sinead Taggart in Ireland, and his sister Ch. Supeta's Enuf Alredi JW was the dam of the future Breed Record Holder Ch., Lux. Ch. Supeta's Ozzy Osbourne.

Success continued at Supeta when they bought Ch./Ir. Ch. Talacre Vysan's Boy at Supeta JW b.2001 (Int., Multi Ch. Vysan van hof ter Eeckhout × Ch. S. Striptease), bred by Dave Gelderd and Lisa Sawyer, and owned by Pete and Dave. He had a tremendous show career, ending on twenty-six CCs, BOB Crufts 2004 and 2005, where he was third and second respectively in the group. He also became Top Dobermann in those years. Vysan's Boy won BIS at Three Counties Champion show in 2005, and later that year was RBIS at WPBAS.

His pedigree was excellent: his paternal grand-sire was the outstanding Dutch dog Int., Multi Ch. Jivago van het Wantij IPO3, ZTP V1A Angekort (Int., Multi Ch. Graaf Quirinus v. Neerlands Stam × Lara V H Wantij). His dam Vaya Vom Franckenhorst's ancestry included Dexter and Vivre Vivien v. Franckenhorst. Having just eleven litters was a great waste of Vysan's Boy undoubted qualities, and he did not sire any UK champions; however, he did leave champion siblings in Ireland: Ir. Ch. Supeta's Black Russian At Beechillawn CJW, and Ir. Ch. Supeta's Alcoholic Frolic For Cooley JW b.2005 (× Supeta's Sun Kissed).

Ch. S. Wicked Wizard of Sonakint JW b.2005 (J. Robin The Hood × Ch. S. Witchy Woman) won ten CCs, and even in his veteran years accumulated seventeen BVIS at breed club shows before he retired. Being only a singleton puppy the litter was repeated, and this time produced three puppies, of which Supeta's Witchqueen JW, ShCM b.2006 was one. Although Witchqueen was not made up, she was a super brood bitch, producing a champion in each of her three litters to Ozzy Osbourne. The first litter included Franck and Gay Pieters Ch. S. Grace Kelly to Ostertag b.2009, from her second litter came a big-winning dog Ch./Ir. Ch. S. Secret Wizard for Dronski JW, ShCM b.2010 for June and Andy Cairns who won nineteen CCs. From the third litter came Ch. S. Spells Trouble JW ShCM b.2013, who stayed very firmly at Supeta.

In 2007 Sue Mycroft used Ch. Korifey iz Zoosfery to Ch. S. Enuf Alredi, which produced the future UK breed record holder – Ch., Lux. Ch. Supeta's Ozzy Osbourne JW b.2007. It has been no surprise that Ozzy has had such an exceptional career, as the line is full of top dogs and proven producers. Owned by Tracey Bennett, Sarah Smith and his breeder and handler Sue, Ozzy won his first CC as a junior at fourteen months, and became a champion by sixteen months. In 2011 he took the title of UK breed record holder from Ch. Sallate Ferris who had held it for twenty-one years, at Paignton Champion Show under Jeff Horswell, aged just four and a half years old.

The old saying 'there are winners and there are producers' is certainly not true of Ozzy Osbourne, who in addition to his record-holding wins, sired 191 pups from twenty-seven litters, and eleven champions:

Sibling brothers Ch. A. El Torro and Ch. A. Eldorado at Whizzbean b.2008 (× Ch. A. She Will be Loved)
Ch. Jojavik Mafioso JW b.2008 (× J. Dirty Dancing)
Siblings Ch. T. Halestorm, Ch. T. Hrana, Ir. Ch. T. Fernando Torres b.2008 (× Ch., Ir. Ch. A. Hipnotique)
Ch. S. Grace Kelly of Ostertag b.2009 (× S. Witchqueen JW)
Ch. A. Russian Ice b.2009 (× Ch A. She Will be Loved)
Ch. Ashlain Makriammos b.2009 (× Ch. Trystorme in Association with A.)
Ch. J. The Heat Is On JW b.2010 (× Ch. J. Singing The Blues JW)
Ch., Ir. Ch. S. Secret Wizard at Dronski JW, ShCM b.2010
Ch. S. Spells Trouble JW b.2013 (× S. Witchqueen JW

Ozzy's record is truly outstanding. He won seventy-one CCs, forty-seven BOBs, twenty-five RCCs and an incredible fifteen Groups. He was BIS at WPBAW, and NWPBA in 2011, RBIS at LKA 2008, and Belfast 2011. He was Top Dobermann in 2010, 2011 (also Runner-up Top Dog All Breeds), 2012, and 2013. From his eleven champion progeny Ozzy was Top Sire All Breeds 2009, Top Working Stud Dog 2011, 2012 and 2013, and Top Dobermann Stud Dog 2014. In 2014 Ozzy won his seventy-first and final CC from the Veteran class at Richmond from judge Gary Daniel.

Amazon: In 1981 Clive and Nancy Evans had their first Dobermann and soon started showing. Clians Tanya was bred on American lines of the early Tavey imports. She was bred to Ch. Metexa Movie Master, which was essentially a complete outcross apart from a six-generation back connection to Acclamation. The combination gave the outstanding dog Ch. Amazon Brahms 'n Lizt JW b.1988, who brought big fame for the kennel. Amazon has continued to produce an outstanding succession of champions to the present day.

Ch. Amazon Brahms 'n Lizt, who won twenty-four CCs, BIS at all breeds at Bath Champion show in 1990, and was Top Dobermann 1990 and 1994.

THE KORUNG TEST

Korung is a test in Germany of character, performance and conformation to maintain breed standards. Dogs must be at least two years old with SchH1 or IPO1, AD (endurance) test, A-stamp or OFA of hips, and a show grading of at least good (SG). After the first breed survey the dog has two years to get deferred or to gain their second breed survey, which qualifies the dog for life, or start over. Angekort is the title awarded to dogs that have qualified Korung for life.

Ch. Zordia's Magic Moments at Amazon b.1988 (Ch. D. Street Legal × Findjans Shelada of Zordia) bred by Val Allen came next, followed by Ch. Vyleighs Zaxon b.1990 (Ch. Dimrost Freedom Fighter × V. Xanja).

Four years later the Evans brought Maelstrom Mor Than a Feeling at A. JW b.1992 (Ch. J. Kilowatt × Ch. J. Infa Red at Maelstrom) whose parents were half siblings. Being so tightly bred she was outbred to Brahms-n-Lizt, and the resulting all brown litter born in 1995 contained an Irish champion and three UK champions who, with the quality of their pedigree, were themselves excellent producers:

Ch. A. Iron Lion of Mirdale owned by Julie Kelly, who won seven CCs
Ch. A. Sinful Skinful won three CCs and was Top Dobermann Brood Bitch 2003
Ir. Ch. A. Justa Rumour
Ch. A. Sound Machine stayed whose progeny success earned him the titles Top Dobermann Sire 1997, and Top Dobermann Stud Dog 1998.

Sound Machine's direct champion progeny include:

Ch. Dizown To Die For at Amazon b.1996 (× D. Playing with Fire, who was a Casablanca daughter out of D. Lucky Lady).
Siblings Ch. A. Licensed to Thrill, and Ch. A. Ain't No Doubt b.1996 (× Keealto Bossy Boots, a Mayhem daughter)
Siblings Ch. A. Oh What a Knight and Ch. A. Sealed With A Kiss at Woodbriar b.1996 (× A. Almost An Angel)
Siblings Ch. O. Country Gent and Ch. O. Oasis

Amazon Almost An Angel b.1993 (Ch. Holtzburg Mayhem × Zordia's Magic Moments at A.) was Top Brood Bitch 2001, and also the dam of Ch. A. Dark Angel b.1998 (by Metexa Murphy's Surprise), who won four CCs for owner Caroline Friend-Rees. He descended from Mayhem, Dizown and Findjans on one side, and Dutch/Germanic on the other to Movie Master and Graaf Carlos vd Edele Stam.

Other champions in these years include Ir. Ch. A. Love Potion at Arbrodin b.1997 (Ch. J. Kilowatt × Tweedhall Cantata at A.) for Paul and Angela Andre, and Ch. A. She's A Sinner for Tridon JW b.1999 (Ch. N. Nick The Biscuit × Ch. A. Sinful Skinful).

Clive and Nancy then decided to introduce some fresh blood to their breeding, and imported from Holland Graaf Fela v. Oranje's Stam at A. and his sister Gravin Farrah v. Oranje's Stam at A. (Danyo vt Nordse Veld × Ziggy v. Franckenhorst), a daughter of Marienburg's Dark Daimler (imported to Belgium from America).

When Fela was bred to Jim McEwan's A. Careless Whisper b.1996 (Ch. A. Sound Machine × Keealto Bossy Boots) it produced Ch. Cloudybay Dead Ringer for A. JW b.1998, who won BOB Crufts 2002.

Ch A. Sinful Skinful had produced a champion from her second litter, Ch. Amazon She's a Sinner at Tridon JW b.1999 (by Ch. Nearctic Nick The Biscuit), but her success as a brood bitch was proven in her fourth and final litter by Jowendy's Robin The Hood in 2002 containing three champions: Ch. A. Under Fire at Liason, Ch. A. Cheek to Cheek for Lynfryds JW, and Ch. A. What's Up Pussycat, who stayed at Amazon, won eleven CCs, and became Top Dobermann Bitch 2003 and 2004, and Top Brood Bitch 2008.

In 2002 Dave and Yvonne Bevans used Ch. A. Oh What a Knight on their Khaneve Dolly Daydream and bred Ch. Khaneve Gold 'n' Child at A. JW, who went home with the Evans's to later win seven CCs, and became Top Sire 2005. Among his top winning progeny was Fred and Linda Wilkes Ch. Lynfryds Valentino JW b.2004, and another was Ch. Amazon Black Sabbath at Purroma b.2004 (× A. Infatuation at Purroma), who won twelve CCS and was BOB Crufts 2006. Black Sabbath was owned by Paul and Alison Richardson, and handled by Nancy to all his wins. When he was mated to A. Beautiful Stranger they produced Ch. A. She Will Be Loved JW, who became a champion aged fifteen months and one day.

More Amazon champions include:

Ch. A. She Will Be Loved JW b.2005 (Ch. A. Black Sabbath at Purroma × A. Beautiful Stranger JW)
Siblings Ch. A. Coldplay JW, SA Ch. A. Pussy

Galore of Nusu JW b.2005 (Ch. A. Black Sabbath at Purroma × Ch. A. What's Up Pussycat). Coldplay won BOB at Crufts in 2009
Siblings Ch. A. Talk of The Devil JW and Ch. A. The Devil Wears Prada b.2006 (Ch. Supeta's Enuf's Enuf for Cooley × Ch. A. What's Up Pussycat)
Ch. A. Kandy Kisses b.2008 (Ch. L. Valentino JW × Ch. A. What's Up Pussycat)
Siblings Ch. A. El Torro JW, and Ch. A. El Dorado at Whizzbean b.2008 (Ch., Lux. Ch. Supeta's Ozzy Osbourne × Ch. A. She Will Be Loved)
Ch. A. Russian Ice b.2009 (Ch., Lux. Ch. S. Ozzy Osbourne × Ch. A. She Will Be Loved)
Ch. A. Stormy Romance b.2009 (Ch. A. El Torro × Ch. A. Devil Wears Prada)
Ch. A. Russian Romance JW (AI) b.2010 (Int., Multi Ch. Grand Mollis Armani × Ch. A. She Will Be Loved JW
Ch. A. Cartier b.2011 (Ch. A. Russian Ice × Ch. A. Devil Wears Prada)
Ch. A. Davinci b.2012 (Ch. Lynfryds Scaramouche × Ch. A. Kandy Kisses)

A quality bitch line is the cornerstone of any kennel, and it is particularly noteworthy that three generations of Amazon brood bitches all won one of the most coveted of titles of Top Brood Bitch (based on progeny success). Although Maelstrom Mor Than a Feeling at A. was not made up, she became Top Brood Bitch three years in a row, in 1996, 1997 and 1998. Her daughter Ch. A. Sinful Skinful was Top Brood Bitch 2003, and her daughter Ch. A. What's Up Pussycat was Top Brood Bitch in 2008. Between 1990 and 2012 Amazon won the Top Breeder title no fewer than thirteen times, and have to date bred forty-two champions.

A great many more champions and important dogs contain Amazon bloodlines, such as Judith Balshaw's Ch. Janzins Jamelia JW ShCM b.2006 (Ch. A. Coldplay × Janzins Jade), bred by Peter and Janet Forshaw.

Woodbriar: The Woodbriar kennel belongs to Mike and Debbie Stansbury, and their daughter Tanya Pilgrim. The family's first Dobermann was Twinglo Original Syn at Woodbriar b.1985 (Ch. Perihelias Resolution × Findjans Le Crunch), and over the years they have produced several champions.

A top-winning bitch was Ch. Amazon Sealed with a Kiss at W. b.1996 (Ch. A. Sound Machine × A. Almost An Angel).

Later mated to Ch. N. Nick The Biscuit, this litter produced Ch. W. Serengetti Sky JW, ShCM b.2001. Her later litter, to Ch. Jowendy's Dr Feelgood at A., produced Ch. W. Shanghai Silk ShCM b.2003. In 2010 W. Silk was mated to Ch. Jojavik Mafioso JW, and this produced the most recent champion for the kennel, Ch. W. Luciano JW ShCM b.2010, who won Group 2 at Blackpool Champion show in 2015.

Hikays: The Hikays kennel of Keith and Irene Rushfirth bred sparingly, but with high quality. Their foundation bitch Neelans Cheringa at H. b.1985 was a Halsbands Halloween daughter. They bred a succession of champions up to the turn of the century.

Neelans Cheringa was mated to Jeniks Crakajack at H. (a son of Resolution) to produce Ch. H. Rock Folley b.1988. Mated to Ch. Holtzburg Mayhem, they produced Ch. H. Rumor Has It. In her first litter to Graaf Xandy v. Neerlands Stam (imp.) was Pam Newton's H. Rain Man, handled by Graham Hunt, who was unlucky not to gain his title. For her second litter in 1999 she was mated to H. Home Run (by Nemesis Feo), and this continued the unbroken champion bitch line with Pam Newton's Ch. H. In Yer Dreams b.1999, who was, as with all the Hikays bitches, shown by Irene to all her nine CCs. Her third litter was to Ch. Gaindyke Flash Gordon and produced another champion, Jo Dear's Ch. H. Rumors Have It b.2000 (× Ch. H. Rumor Has It), who was shown by Irene, and by Ian Norman.

Nemesis Feo to H. There's A Rumour produced their last Dobermann champion, Ch. H. She's Intoxicating at Marchtay b.1998, who won eight CCs and was Top Bitch 2000. Intoxicating was owned and handled by Linda Parkes, who also owned Ch. Sallate Hunter for Marchtay b.2000 (a double Feo grandson).

Keyala: Keyala Dobermanns was established in the UK in 1988 by Debbie Gamble, whose family bred and showed Pembroke Corgis. Debbie's first Dobermann and first champion was UK, Ir. Ch. Bilsam the Thriller JW b.1988 (Bilsam Sudden Impact × Bilsam Golden Girl), whose double grandsire was Am. Ch. Rosecroft By the Way to Bilsam imp. US, and whose ancestry included Kay Hill, and Highbriar breeding from the US. Debbie has continued to produce champions into the new millennium.

In 1989 Debbie bought a bitch named Andalucia's Song Bird at Keyala b.1989 (Vondobe Black Bird v. Andalucia imp. Aust × A. Eastern Star), who was shown for only a short time. She produced K. Ice Baby b.1992, who in turn produced Irish Ch. K. Kandy Kracker b.1994 (by B. The Thriller). Ice Baby won two CCs and thirty-seven Irish Green Stars, but just missed out on both titles. She was mated to Ch. J. Kilowatt and produced Irish Ch. K. Wot A Thriller b.1999.

In 2002 Debbie bought a brown, cropped male from Russia called Rensdorff Evsey at K. b.2002 (Int., Multi Ch. Tamerlan iz Slavnoi Stai × Russ Ch., IDC Sgr. Rensdorff Amaridge). Although the cropping ban had been introduced, it had not yet led to a show ban in many parts of Europe, so he could be shown in most countries, where he became int., multi champion.

When Debbie moved to France with her then partner Dean Spires in 2007, the Keyala affix could not be registered under the FCI so it was replaced with 'Wot A Thriller'.

Although he was under-used by UK breeders who were not yet used to driving overseas to use foreign dogs, Rensdorff Evsey sired three UK champions:

Siblings Ch. K. Wot A Dream, and Dave and Laura Wood's Ch. K. Dream Machine at Nytbonn VPG1 b.2004 (× K. Wot A Thriller), Crufts CC winner 2007
Ch., Ir., Multi Ch. Farentino Wot A Thriller at Ruholfia b.2010 (Int., Multi Ch. Pathos de Querce Nero × Ned, Lux Ch. K. Wot A Dream)

Tuwos: Billy Henderson in Northern Ireland owned his first Dobermann in 1977 and with his wife Michelle registered their affix in the early 1980s. Their first big winner was Ir. Ch. Schutz Ophilia b.1990 (Schutz Kazou at Franckenheim × S. Jup), and when she won the CC at Leeds Championship show she became the first Irish-bred Dobermann to win a CC on the mainland. The Tuwos kennel continued to breed champion dogs over the next twenty years.

In 2003, friends Hugh and Jewell Fleming used Tuwos Dark 'n Delinquent b.1996 (Pompie Dutch Dictator* × Ir. Ch. S. Ophilia) on their Vanlinberg Success at Franckenheim b.2001. Her pedigree went back to Victor v. Roveline and Schutz breeding, and the mating produced a bitch called Black Fuss Pot Belle, who was the dam of Ir. Ch. Tuwos Impeccable b.2010 (by Ch., Ir. Ch. Aritaur Tomahawk Marillium).

In 2005 Billy, Hugh and Jewell became partners in Ch., Ir. Ch. Aritaur Hipnotique b. 2004 (Int., Multi, Russ. Ch. Tamerlan iz Slavnoi Stai × Ned. Ch, A. Dominatrix EJSgrn. 2002), bred by Martin and Jay Horgan. Hipnotique lived with Hugh and Jewel, and handled by Billy, became the youngest Dobermann to gain both Irish and UK titles. Hipnotique won BOB at Crufts in 2008, Top Dobermann UK 2007, 2009, Top Dobermann Ireland 2005–2009, won RBIS at Driffield Ch. Show in 2007, and BIS at Belfast Ch. Show in 2009. Hipnotique eventually became the UK Bitch Breed Record Holder, taking over from Ch. Dobermoray Whirl 'n Dervish in 2009.

Billy and Michelle's son Josh Henderson won his first CC with Tuwos Emily b.2006 (Ir. Ch. Doberlane Strider Von Samenco × Black Fuss Pot Belle) in 2007, and after titling dogs for June and Andy Cairns at Dronski kennels in Scotland, he then moved to the Jojavik kennel in Essex.

In 2008 Hipnotique was mated to Ch./Lux. Ch. Supeta's Ozzy Osbourne JW, and this was the first time that two breed record holders were mated. The litter produced three big winners

---

*There were two dogs named Pompie Dutch Dictator, this being the second dog born in 1994 (Ch. Lodgehouse Casablanca × Gravin d'Astrid v. Neerlands Stam at P., imp.).

for the kennel: Ciaran and Ann-Marie Donnelly and Billy and Josh Henderson's Ch., Ir. Ch. Tuwos Hrana; Ch., Ir. Ch. T. Halestorm; and Ir. Ch. T. Fernando Torres b.2008, who later sired Ir. Ch. Roszar Falbrav via T. IKC b.2010 (× Ir. Ch. T. Ellie).

Dogs of Influence

The history of Irish dogs and their owners would be another chapter in itself, but many notable kennels have enjoyed success with their dogs at both the Irish and UK shows.

Metexa Movie Master was grandsire through the maternal line to Bill and Karen Castle's Ir. Ch. Amazon Dare to Dance at Chenick b.1991 (Ch. Swyndwr Storm Bearer × A. Slightly Sozzled, who was a Brahms-n-Lizt sister), and his paternal grand-sire was Ch. Crossridge The Jazzman.

A Crossridge decendant and big winner in the mid-1990s, gaining both titles, was Vincent O'Brien's UK and Irish champion, Ch. Vincenza Distant Thunder b.1995 (Ir. Ch. Assisi State of the Art × V. Distant Surprise). His ancestry also included Dizown, Royaltains, Marienburgs and Borains, but despite this he was very unfortunately unused by the UK breeders.

Donal and Beverly Gormley's Ch./Ir. Ch. Bosskat Bonza was one of the very few dual-titled dogs, and Trevor and Elaine Smyth owned his successful sister Ir. Ch. Bosskat Bagatelle b.1998 (Ch. Nemesis Feo v. Koepsel at Sallate × S. Jezebel).

Irish Breeders of Influence

Irish breeders generally prefer European breeding, and continue to import dogs. The gene pool is varied in both Southern and Northern Ireland, and some of these quality dogs are occasionally seen at UK shows.

Breeder Stephen Richardson (Spitori) has owned and handled many dogs to their Irish championship titles, including Anne Moore's Ir. Ch. Spesmagna In Search of a Hero.

Dione Fitzsimons has bred numerous Fitzkin champions, including Ir. Ch. Fitzkin Eternal Elegance, with a rich pedigree back to Chancepixies, Royal Bell, Norden Stamm and del Citone. Eternal Elegance was Ireland's Top Dobermann Bitch in 2013 and Reserve Top Dobermann in 2012.

Sam Walsh had bred many top winners at her Samenco kennels, including her Ir. Ch. Doberlane Strider von Samenco (Ch., Ned. Ch. Ace van hof ter Eeckhout at Siboveld × Ch. Estridge Sobriety of Doberlane); sibling champions Ir. Ch. Samenco Hitman, and Ken and Margaret Foley's Ir. Ch. S. Mr Perfect Jaysbury (Int., Multi Ch. Vysan van hof ter Eeckhout × Ir. Ch. Doberlane Glory Seka at Samenco JW).

Seamus and Moira Gettings also made up their Ir. Ch. Supeta's Black Russian at Beechilawn (Ch. Talacre Vysan's Boy at Supeta's × Supeta's Sun Kissed JW).

More recently Triona Ni-She's Ruholfia kennel in Southern Ireland has had great success with her dogs. Two of the first imports to the kennels were Ch., Ir., Multi Ch. Farentino Wot A Thriller at Ruholfia b.2010 (Int., Multi Ch. Pathos de Querce Nero × Ned., Lux. Ch. Keyalas Wot A Dream) and his sister Fiastra Wot A Thriller. With Dean Spires, they added further imports and used top European dogs to gain success showing on mainland Europe. At the IDC 2016 their Ruholfia Giorgia (Lucinio del Diamante Nero, ZTP V1A X × Ch. Ruholfia Bardot, ZTP V1A) won a coveted first in Baby Black Female.

> ### THE DOCKING BAN
>
> Docking in England was banned in 2007, and as docking was banned much later in Ireland (2013 in Northern Ireland, and 2014 in Southern Ireland), exhibitors have not entered many UK shows with their docked dogs in recent years, except at Breed Club Shows where there is no entrance fee so docked dogs may be shown.

THE NINETEEN-NINETIES

Heimdall: In 1990 David Stafford and Wendy Crick imported Bronco von der Kunigundenhohe at Heimdall (Ch. Baron Bryan v. Harro's Berg SchHlll, ZTP V1A × Ch. Alexa v. Frankenland SchHl, Angek 1A, ZTP V1A).

Bronco von der Kunigundenhohe.

Bronco sired twenty-seven litters, which included siblings Ch. Halsband Canisp and Ch. H. The Joker b.1992 (× H. The Sonnet), and Ch. Lyntarski Ice Man b.1994 (× Gaindyke Fancy Free). Bronco is the grandsire of Ch. Dobermoray Whirl 'n Dervish.

In 1999 David and Wendy imported a dog from the US Adlercrest kennels of Philip and Linda Calamia, who had flown their bitch Athena v. Karat (Int. VDH Ch. Shogun v. Roveline IPO1 × Lambada v. Brandenburg SchH3) to Italy to mate her to the prolific sire, Gino Gomez del Citone.

Very tight incest matings are uncommon, but Pierluigi Pezzano (del Citone) felt he knew his lines well enough to try it. Gino Gomez was born in 1997 from the brother/sister mating of Astor del Citone × Arielle d'Amour del Citone. Gino became World Champion, IDC Sieger, SchHlll, AD, ZTP V1A, and Angekort 1A, and became a significant producer with winning progeny around the world.

From the Adlercrest litter, Drusus v. Adlercrest al Heimdall b.1999 was imported to the UK. He did not sire any champions directly, but through his daughter Krieger Xantia came sibling champions Ch. K. Endurance and Ch. K. Endless Love JW b.2003 (by Ch. K. Sure Shot).

Dobermoray: Another kennel that also used very tight in-breeding to seal their type was Alison

Dougherty's Dobermoray kennel. In 1993 Alison used Bronco on her Ch. Borains Carte-Blanche of Dobermoray b.1989 (Ch. Dimrost Freedom Fighter × Borains Sizzling Hot). The litter produced a male called D. April Fool, born on 1 April 1993. In a practice now banned under KC rules, Alison bred April Fool back to his mother Carte-Blanche, and in a quirk of fate their litter was born exactly two years later, on 1 April 1995. Like Pezzano, Alison also knew her lines intimately, and through this incest mating, produced the future breed record-holding bitch Ch. Dobermoray Whirl 'n Dervish.

Ch. Dobermoray Whirl 'n Dervish, bitch breed record holder: bred by Alison Dougherty, owned by Tony and Carol Avard, and shown by Alison's daughter Tracey Dougherty to all her wins.

Whirl 'n Dervish's first ticket was LKA 1996 under Margaret Everton aged twenty months, and she gained her title a few months later from Nancy Evans at Three Counties in 1997. 1998 was a great year for her: she started the year by winning the Bitch CC at Crufts from Audrey Weston (although BOB at Crufts always eluded her), was BIS at both WPBAW and Southern Counties, was Top UK Dobermann, and also in this year became the new bitch breed record holder with twenty-five CCs, which she won at SW Dobermann Club 1998 from Gloria Pascoe. She swept the board in an amazing career with BIS awards, and dominated the ring for many years. In total, Ch. Dobermoray Whirl 'n Dervish won twenty-seven CCs with twenty BOB, and held the record for eleven years until 2009, when she was overtaken by Ch., Ir. Ch. Aritaur Hipnotique.

Manzart: Mandy Everley had been raised in a dog breeding and showing family before she became interested in Dobermanns. Ch. Sallate Zoey at Manzart b.1989 (Ch. Holtzburg Mayhem × Ch. Sallate Frauline) was the first champion for Manzart. She was later mated to Ch. Swyndwr Storm Bearer to produce Ch. M. Black Humour at Sallate b.1995.

Ch. Manzart Black Humour at Sallate, who won eight CCs, two Groups, RBIS at Southern Counties in 2000, and was Top Dobermann 2000.

Black Humour was not used as widely as he should have been, and only sired four litters, but left some quality champions. Other champions at the kennel were:

Ch. Manzart C'est La Vie b.1996 (Dobermorays April Fool × M. Alexis)
Ch. Jaegerson Giggle 'n' Gossip JW b.1999 (× Merryn's Double Take for Jaegerson)
Ch. M. Jalousie at Amical b.2002 (Jowendy's Robin The Hood × M. Ever Smiling)
Ch. M. Naughty Nora b.2007 (Ch. Amazon Black Sabbath at Purroma × M. Knock 'Em Dead

Jaegerson: Merryn's Double Take at Jaegerson b.1994 was the foundation bitch of Sue James' Jaegerson kennel. She was from a repeat mating of Ch. Stormy Romance with Chaanrose (Ch. J. Kilowatt × Ch. Chaanrose Elegantiae at Merryn), bred this time under Jo Gibb's Merryn affix. The foundation male for the kennel was Ch. Chaanrose Don't Crowd Me at Jaegerson b.1995 (Ch. Lodgehouse Casablanca × Ch. Wild Cherry at C.). He became Top Dobermann in 1999 and Top Sire in 2000.

Ch. Chaanrose Don't Crowd Me at Jaegerson. Handled by Sue James to all his wins, he gained thirteen CCs, a Group 2 and a Group 4.

In the following years the Jaegerson kennel produced a succession of top quality Dobermanns.

Merryn's Double Take at Jaegerson was later mated to Ch. Manzart Black Humour at S. to produce Ch. Jaegerson Giggle 'n' Gossip b.1999, who was valuable in both the ring and the litter box by producing a champion in each of her three litters. In her first litter she produced Ch. J. Singing The Blues JW b.2003 (by Jowendy's Robin The Hood). A repeat mating in 2005 produced Ch. J. Imagination, and her third litter produced Ch. J. Hot Gossip b.2006 (by Ch. Trystorme Highlander JW). This strong producing bitch line was continued when Ch. J. Singing The Blues produced Ch.

Jaegerson Man In The Mirror b.2009 by Ch. Lynfryds Valentino JW, co-owned with Steve and Jo Goscomb, and another champion Ch. Jaegerson The Heat Is On b.2010 by Ch., Lux. Ch. Supeta's Ozzy Osbourne.

Vonedstram: Steve and Avril Waldie had Dobermanns before they started showing seriously with their Gaindyke Tamarra at Vonedstram b.1993 (Metexa Maritsa Magnum × Gaindyke Prairie Rose, who was litter sister to Ch. G. Fancy Free). They mated Tamarra to Victor van Roveline and had their first champion, the bitch UK, Lux., Dutch Ch. Vonedstram the Vixen b.1999.

UK, Lux., Dutch Vonedstram The Vixen won eighteen CCs, BIS Scottish Club show, BIS at the Dutch Club show in 2002, and was the first UK-bred Dobermann to win at the IDC when she won the champion class in Paris 2001. Owned, bred and handled by Steve Waldie.

The Vixen was one of the first UK-bred Dobermanns shown in Europe under the Pet Passport scheme, which had been changed to allow dogs to move from Europe to the UK without quarantine. Although she was docked, she had natural ears, but despite this, she won against many impressive cropped bitches in Europe, and her elegance, compactness and overall harmony appealed to a wide range of judges at home and abroad.

The Vixen had one litter, which produced a champion for Derek Elmslie, Ch. Vonedstram Vir-

tuoso b.2003 (by Int., Multi Ch. AIAD Sg. Gemini Ginga House, a son of Gino Gomez), who won BOB at Crufts in 2007 from Rosie Lane. The most recent champion for the kennel, Ch. Coltregan Prada at Vonedstram b.2009, is a Vixen granddaughter (by V. The Viking) and descends on her maternal line from the combination of Nitro × G. Molly Malone.

Trystorme: The Trystorme Dobermanns of Mick and Irene Pagan in Scotland began with two litter brothers sired by Kinraith Blackchat, whose paternal grandsire was Auldrigg Pinza × a bitch of Metexa and Kilmuir breeding. Success came with sibling champions born in 2001 from Victor van Roveline and their Trystorme Indescretion (Ch. Lodgehouse Casablanca × Chancepixies Lady Luck at T.).

Ch. Trystorme Highlander JW won his first CC as a puppy at only his fifth championship show, and Ch. Trystorme In Anticipation JW won her first CC at Crufts 2002 as a junior from judge Wendy Crick (Highlander also won his junior class that day). Highlander proved himself as a sire with two champion daughters: Lainchbury's Ch. Trystorme In Association with Ashlain JW, and Ch. Jaegerson Hot Gossip.

Diego: Twiggy The Tearaway Flame b.1982 (Ch. Swanwite Flame Successor × Kingsmeadow Crystal Gayle) was the first Dobermann owned by Tracey Feeney; with her second Dobermann, Austanns Brown Lady at Diego b.1983 (Greenholmn Sea Quest × Kazan Brown Princess), Tracey started showing. This began a long career of breeding and producing champion Dobermans.

Tracey first bred Austanns Brown Lady at Diego to a Canadian imported dog Freespirits Elian Robin At Koriston. Her second litter was to Ch. Jenicks Cruise Missile b.1984 (Perihelias Resolution × Jenick's Missile Belle) gave John Harkness his first Dobermann, Diego's Double Trouble.

Sallate Jenna b.1994 (litter sister of S. Jezebel) was owned by Tracey, and co-bred with her and Graham under the Sallate affix to Graaf Xandy v. NS. The litter was superb, containing Ch. S. Striptease, Ch. S. Schumacher and S. Seduction b.1997. At Crufts in 1999, Striptease and Seduction did the double by winning both the CC and the RCC from Hilary Partridge, with Striptease going on to win BOB and the Working Group. Hilary later awarded Ian Broughton's Seduction the CC at the Welsh Kennel Club. It was a matter of general regret that Seduction never gained her crown, ending on two CCs and three RCCs, as she was more than worthy of being titled. S. Jenna became Top Brood Bitch in 2000.

At the IDC in Belgium in 1998, a then eighteen-month-old bitch Come As You Are Alabama (Baron Nike × Galaxi Gwendy) entered the ring, and the spectators literally packed around it to see her. The IDC crowd is made up of strongly dedicated Dobermann enthusiasts who are always keen to demonstrate their pleasure when good dogs win, and equally to voice their protest at poor judging. When Alabama was initially placed second in the final four bitches, the thousand-strong spectator crowd erupted with unanimous boos of derision for the judging. The judges re-conferred, and then, acknowledging the views of the crowd, reversed their decision, awarding her first place! The crowd was ecstatic. CAYA Alabama became probably the youngest IDC Siegerin in history. She later won the World Championship (Italy) title.

Hilary was determined to have a puppy from her, and when Alabama was mated to It. Ch. Ilane Darafal, Hilary imported CAYA Gwen At Pompie, imp. Yug. b.2001.

Gwen was later mated to Ch. Gaindyke Mirco at Lakehouse, and although no champions were produced from the litter, when Tracy Feeney took a daughter Pompie Wham Bam with Diego and mated her with Ch. Amazon El Torro, it produced Ch. Diego Temptation for Stormhold in partnership with Matt and Elaine Sommerville.

Tracey then bought Pompie Wham Bam at Diego b.2003 (Ch. Gaindyke Mirco at Lakehouse CAYA Gwen At Pompie, imp. Yug.) from Hilary. When she was mated to Ch. Amazon El Torro they produced Ch. Diego Temptation for Stormhold b.2009, owned by Matt and Elaine Sommerville.

In 2010 Tracy Feeney imported Ch. Italo Elite House from Poland (Int., Multi Ch. Zordan Zewi del Citone IDC Sgr, World Sieger, AIAD Sgr 2008, whose sire was Gino Gomez – × Ciara Elite House,

who herself has equally impressive parentage, being by Int., Multi Ch. Pimms No. 1 iz Doma Domeni × Yalla iz Slavnoi Stai). Ch. Italo Elite House has to date won sixteen CCs, a Group 4 at WKC 2013, a Group 1 at Bournemouth 2013, BIS at Bath 2014, and BIS Border Union. He has also become a very popular stud dog, and his early champion progeny so far include:

Ch. Knecht Marek b.2012 (× Knecht Magritte)
Sibling brothers Tony and Linda Fisher's Ch. J. Elite Mafia b.2013 and May Michael's Ch. J. Swedish House Mafia (× Ch. J. Bella Mafia)
Ch. Cockneyoka High Society of Diego b.2011 (× Diego's Addiction with Cockneyoka)

Diego has also been influential in helping other breeders develop, and Ch. Cockneyoka Hi Society from Diego, owned by Tracey Feeney and Wendy McColl, was the first champion bred at Steve and Debra Roberston's Essex kennels. Hi Society descends on the maternal line from Diego's Maranello b.1999 (Graaf Xandy v. NS, imp. × S. Jenna).

Korifey: Lynne Jones has been involved in showing Dobermanns since 1991 with her Crossridge Night Star (a granddaughter on the paternal line of Dizown All That Jazz, and on the maternal line from Ch. Crossridge The Carbon Copy at Lynfryds). Success followed with her bitch Amazon It Started With A Kiss b.1996 daughter of Ch. A. Sound Machine, and then with Moordale Ever So Supeta's b. 1998, whose pedigree included Jowendy's, Supeta's and Dizown lines.

Lynne then decided to import a Dobermann, and having seen Ch. Nestor iz Zoosfery (sired by Nivago) at the IDC Bratislava 2000, she knew that he was the type of dog she was looking for. Evgeny Rosenberg (Zoosfery) told her he had a planned litter by Nestor's half brother (both by Int., Russ. Ch. Sant Kreal Nivago), and offered Lynne a male puppy from the litter.

Ch. Korifey iz Zoosfery b.2001 (SK Nivago × Russ Ch. Gretchen iz Z.) became a UK champion, winning three CCs each with BOB, and in 2006 won the prestigious Dobermann Classic competition against sixty-four other top-winning Dobermanns from judge Alma Page (Findjans).

Korifey began his stud career on his first birthday and became very popular, siring twenty-three litters. He sired just one champion, but it was a very worthy one, being the future UK breed record holder Ch. Supeta's Ozzy Osbourne. Korifey's champion grandchildren are:

Ch. Leibwache Al Capone b.2006 (Int., Multi Ch. Aritaur Histabraq SchH3 × Leibwache Wild 'n Wicked, daughter of Korifey)

Ch. Cockneyoka Hi Society From Diego b.2011 (Ch. Italo Elite House, imp. Pol × Diego's Addiction with Cockneyoka, daughter of Korifey)

Ch. Jasprico Jazz Master Flash b.2012 (son of Korifey, Trystorme Zhivago × Ch. Trystorme Boogie Woogie at Jasprico)

Lynne has handled many dogs to win CCs, and in addition to her own dogs she titled Ch. Aritaur Helina b.2004 (Int., Multi, Russ. Ch. Tamerlan iz Slavnoi Stai × Ned Ch A. Dominatrix), and Paul and Alison Richardson's Ch. Jasprico Jazz Master Flash b.2012 (Trystorme Zhivago JW × Ch. T. Boogie Woogie To J.).

In 2009, Lynne bought Ch. Amazon Russian Ice b.2009 (× Ch. Amazon She Will be Loved), and a year later, bought his half-sister Ch. Amazon Russian Romance JW b.2010), who had been conceived by AI to the Russian dog Int, Multi Ch Grand Mollis Armani (descended on the maternal line from Nestor iz Zoosfery, whom Lynne first saw at IDC).

In 2013 Lynne used frozen semen from Am, Can Ch Dabney's Phenomenon to her UK, Lux Ch Amazon Russian Romance. The litter has been very successful. Lynne's daughter Sam Jones has also become a talented handler, and made up a daughter from the litter Ch K. Black Diamond JW ShCM in 2016. Karen Moore and Stephen McPhee's Ch K. Onyx handled by Lynne, won the prestigious Dobermann Classic competition 2016 and gained his title at Blackpool in 2016 , and to date has won 9 CCs.

Aritaur: Jay and Martin Horgan's foundation bitch was Crislea Centrefold of Aritaur b.1996 (Ch. Holtzburg Mayhem x Holtzburg Dior from Crislea), bred by Spencer and Sue Houghton. Centrefold's first litter to Khaneve Rage n Honour produced five stud book number winners, and

her second litter to John and Marcia Rinaldi's Ch. Miendy's Soba Up JW b. (Manzart Black Secret × Jowendy's Casta Spell at Miendy's) b.1997 produced the first two champions for the kennel: Ch. A. Surprisingly Soba, and Ch. A. A Little More Soba b.2000.

Having become interested in European lines and with C. Centrefold being so tightly bred (Mayhem featured three times in three generations of her pedigree), an outcross mating was chosen to a dog in Belgium, Ger. VDH Ch. Ramonburg's Valdo b.1997 (Marienburg's Dark Daimler imp. US to Bel × Qalina van de Donken, a daughter of Int., Multi Ch. Graaf Quirinus v. Neerlands Stam). Valdo's paternal line was Marienburgs, which already combined the Dutch breeding of Dexter v. Franckenhorst with Mary's American bloodlines. The litter included Ned., Lux. Ch. A. Dominatrix b.2001 and Ned., Lux. Ch. A. Dolce Vita.

Dominatrix won the Europa Jugend Sgrn 2002 from Pezzano (del Citone), gained her Dutch title in just four visits, and was a finalist at IDC 2004 (the only uncropped bitch). Her first and most famous 'H' litter to Int., Multi, Russ. Ch. Tamerlan iz Slavnoi Stai (Int., Multi, It. Ch. Ugor di Villa Conte × Russ. Ch. Indira vd Rauberhohle) in 2004 produced the following champions:

Ch., Ir. Ch. A. Hipnotique, owned by Hugh and Jewell Fleming and Billy Henderson, became the youngest champion to gain both UK and Irish titles, was BIS at Belfast Ch. show 2009, and became the UK bitch breed record holder with twenty-eight CCs

Ch., Irish, Lux. Ch. A. Heracles owned by Colin and Karen Wakefield

Int., Lux. Ch. A. Histabraq SchH3

Ch. A. Helina, owned by Lynne and Les Tilley, and handled by Lynne Jones

Histabraq SchH3 was worked by Martin, and remains the highest scoring dog in UK breed history at all three levels. He was also one of only three UK dogs to achieve the ZTP V1A grading at the ZTP (fit for breeding test) assessment from H. Wiblishauser in 2010, the others being Inguna Grase's Amber Sea Adele Great LV Jnr Ch., BH

(Pluto de Grande Vinko × Imidz Galaxy Great), and Chris and Tracy McMullen's A. Vincent Vega EJgSr'09, b.2008 (A. Nominator BH × A. Hastra Kastra).

Due to the success of the litter, Tamerlan became Top Dobermann Stud Dog 2007, and Dominatrix was Top Dobermann Brood Bitch, and Top Group Brood Bitch 2007.

Histabraq sired two champion sons, Ch. Leibwache Al Capone b.2006 (× L. Wild 'n Wicked, a Korifey daughter), owned by Richard Milne and Andrea Williams, also owners of Ch. Leibwache Sunset Stripper (A. Nominator BH × Khaneve Chicargo Flirt to L.). Both were bred by Dianne Burree, and both were shown by Mel Merchant. Histabraq also sired Ch. A. Cardinal Red at Jodaseen b.2010 (× L. Honey Hustler to A.), who with owner Joanne Sanderson won nine CCs including the CC at Crufts in 2014. Another son, Sue Thorn's Bel., Ned. Ch. Grafmax Louis Armstrong b.2009 (× Cosajora Nina Simone, a Jowendy's Robin The Hood daughter) won the CC at Crufts in 2013.

The second litter from Dominatrix was to Int., Multi Ch. F'Hiram Abif Royal Bell IPO1 b.2003 (Int., Multi Ch. Eko Royal Bell – vom Franckenhorst blood × Eboni v. Residenschloss, a Gino Gomez daughter) produced Tony Sheldon's Aritaur Notorious SchH3, the second highest scorer for a UK Dobermann behind his half brother Histabraq.

Marion and Bill Mulholland's male from Dominatrix's last litter was Ch., Ir. Ch. A. Tomahawk Marillium b.2007 (Int., Multi Ch. Tom-Dober Hagi IDC Veteran Sgr 2013 × Ned. Ch. Aritaur Dominatrix.

Names of Influence

Notable individual dogs in the first decade of the new millennium were Jivago Van Het Wantij, Ace van hof ter Eeckhout, and Ch. Siboveld's Helluvan Angel. Jivago was owned by Jaap van Gelder in Holland, and was a big, bold dog. At the Bundesieger show in Dortmund 2000 it was a great sight to see four of his top winning sons, Multi Ch. Vysan vh ter Eeckhout, Multi Ch. Wanja Wandor v. Stevinhage WW, Ch. Vero vh Wantij WW, and Ch. Falk v. Markischen Land, showing next to each other on the end of long leads with

Matt Holmes with his Ch. Ned. Ch. Ace van hof ter Eeckhout IPO1, ZTP 1A, BOB Crufts 2003, bred by Marc Michels, and Ch. Siboveld's Helluvan Angel, who won the BCC at Crufts 2003.

the crowd cheering for these stallion males. 2000 being a special year, the Bundesieger was held on two days with full titles on each day, and the winner on both days was Wanja Wandor. Jivago sired many significant winners, especially the Russian dogs such as Pimms No. 1 iz Doma Domeni and Nestor iz Zoosfery (half brother to Korifey), and was also used by the Russian kennels Sant Kreal.

In Belgium, Vysan vht Eeckhout had been mated to a daughter of Gamon di Campovalano and had produced a bitch called XLvalentyn van de Doberhoeve. She was named XL as she was a substantial but very elegant bitch with great charisma, and whose protection work was tougher than most males. XL was mated to Gino Gomez del Citone, and produced a son, Ch., Ned. Ch. Ace van hof ter Eeckhout IPO1, ZTP 1A b.2001, who was imported to the UK by Matt Holmes after spending six months in Holland under the original Pet Passport scheme. Ace gained his UK and Dutch title, and won three CCs in the UK.

Ace also sired Irish Ch. Doberlane Strider von Samenco b.2003 (× Ch. Estridge Sobriety of D.); Ch. Siboveld's Sauron at Rocksands b.2003 (× Mysel Lady in Red at S.); and Ch. Helmlake by Design for Tuwin b.2004 (× H. Performing Magic).

Matt's bitch Mysel Lady in Red at S. b.1998 (Ch. J. Kilowatt × Mysel Money Penny) was later taken to Belgium to mate to Vysan. The mating produced Ch. Siboveld's Helluvan Angel b.2001, who won seven CCs. Unfortunately she had just one litter, but none were bred from, so her undisputed qualities for the future were not passed on. In 2003 Matt achieved what few have even dreamed of when he won the double at Crufts with Ace winning the DCC and BOB, and Angel winning the BCC.

Resident at the same home in Holland for six months' 'Pet Passport' (quarantine) before import, was Lynne Jones' Korifey iz Zoosfery. The timing of their import was coincidental, as was the fact that they were both grandchildren of Jivago van het Wantij.

Jojavik: The Jojavik kennel of mother and daughter team Jackie and Victoria Ingram began their notable kennel with a bitch called Marcavie Rhythm 'n' Dance from K. b.1999 (Ch. K. Judgement Day × Marcavie Chorus Girl). They bred her to Jowendy's Robin The Hood (tied into Findjans Chaos), and the first Jojavik champions were born.

The first Jojavik champions were Ch. J. Dancefloor Diva JW, and SA Ch. J. You Dance I Dance JW b.2003. Another sister, J. Save The Last Dance, did not gain her title but was valuable to the breed through her progeny.

In 2005 Jackie and Victoria began their long friendship with Alma Page, whose Findjans bloodlines were behind their breeding, and with her guidance the kennel flourished. The first champion for the kennel was in 2006 with Ch. J. Dancefloor Diva JW (Marcavie Rythm n Dance from Khaneve x Jowendy Robin the Hood). Many more champions and titles have been won since:

Ch. J. Wurlitzer JW b.2004 (Ch. Swyndwr Crimestopper × M. Rhythm 'n' Dance from K)

Ch. J. The Gigolo JW b.2005 (SA Ch. J. Ministry of Sound × J. Dirty Dancing, who are half siblings, sharing the same dam Marcavie Rhythm 'n' Dance from Khaneve

Ch., Lux. Ch. J. Gangsters Moll JW b.2006 (Ch. Lynfryds Valentino JW × Ch. J. Dancefloor Diva JW)

Ch. J. Mafioso JW b.2008 (Ch., Lux. Ch. Supeta's Ozzy Osbourne JW × J. Dirty Dancing)

Ch. J. Bella Mafia JW b.2009 (Ch. J. Mafioso JW × Ch. J. Dancefloor Diva JW)

Ch. Tronjheim Belladonna from Jojavik JW, ShCM b.2010 (Ch. J. Mafioso JW × J. Save The Last Dance), bred by Alistair and Lynne Holmes

Ch. J. Molly Mobster JW ShCM b.2011 (Ch. Krieger's The Wizard of Oz JW X Ch., Lux. Ch. J. Gangsters Moll JW), five CCs and BCC Crufts 2014

Siblings Ch. J. Elite Mafia b.2013 and Ch. J. Swedish House Mafia (Ch. Italo Elite House imp. Pol. × Ch. J. Bella Mafia)

Ch. J. Constanzia JW, ShCM b.2013 (Ch. J. Mafioso × J. Jezebel)

Siblings Ch., Ir. Ch. Jojavik Poison Ivy JW, ShCM, CW16, and Ch,, Ir, Ch, Jojavik Midnight Express JW, ShCM b.2013 (Chancepixies Locomotive x Ch, Tronjheim Belladonna from Jojavik JW, swept the board since they won their first CCs aged thirteen and fourteen months respectively. Just another month later, Poison Ivy became the joint youngest Dobermann Champion aged fourteen months. She was Top Dobermann Bitch 2014, and Top Dobermann 2015, won the Bitch CC at Crufts in 2016, and in July 2017 she became the new UK Bitch Breed Record Holder taking over from Ch., Ir. Ch. Aritaur Hipnotique. At the time of writing she has thirty CCs, and in July 2017 Poison Ivy won BIS at NWPBA.

Her brother Midnight Express now has twenty-nine CCs, and won BOB at Crufts 2016 from

Judge Sue Brassington, making this the first time since 1958 that siblings have won the double at Crufts. Midnight Express has now won two BIS at all breed championship shows; Three Counties 2016 and Windsor 2016 and was Top Dobermann UK 2016, a year in which Jojavik achieved the outstanding accolade of becoming Top Breeders of All Breeds in the UK.

Dronski: The first Dobermann for June and Andy Cairns was Aritaur Vodkatini at Dronski b.2008, who gained her stud book number and had two litters, but was not made up. The couple then bought Ch, Ir Ch Supeta's Secret Wizard JW, ShCM who was the first champion for the kennel.

He was first handled by Josh Henderson, who won thirteen CCs with him, and was then shown by his breeders from Crufts 2014, where he won the CC and BOB. Ch., Ir. Ch. S. Secret Wizard for Dronski JW, ShCM won nineteen CCs with twelve BOBs. He won the Group on two occasions, with many other Group placings, BOB Crufts 2014, and in the same year won the prestigious Dobermann Classic 2014. He was Runner-up Top Dobermann 2012 and 2013, beaten by his sire.

The couple also imported a bitch from Ireland, Ch. Tuwos Jackie O' at Dronski JW, ShCM b.2011

Ch., Ir. Ch. Supeta's Secret Wizard for Dronski JW, ShCM.

(Aritaur Navarro via Tuwos × T. Erica), who gained her title in May 2015.

FOREIGN INFLUENCE ON UK DOBERMANNS

There have been many European kennels in modern years that have contributed to, and continue to contribute to, the development of the breed in the UK.

Holland: Dutch kennels have probably had the greatest effect on the UK Dobermann, and the van Neerlands Stam kennel of Mrs Knijff-Dermout (latterly taken over by Han vd Zwan, author of the book *In The Beginning*) has provided many important dogs to the UK over an extended period.

Graaf Quirinus v. NS b.1987 is heavily behind the imports to Sallate, being on the paternal line down to Ch. S. Schumacher, Ch. S. Striptease and S. Seduction. He is also behind Victor van Roveline through both Kastra and Jenna v. Roveline, Supeta Aritaur, Siboveld and others.

Franckenhorst lines have had enormous influence on the UK Dobermann, from Jimarty to Pompie through Salvador, Metexa, Barrimilne, Chornytan and Krieger through Firedanza v. Tavey, to Amazon through Ziggy, to Supeta through Nemesis Feo v. Koepsel at Sallate, whose paternal line returned to Dea Dolores v Franckhorst, to Chancepixies through Graaf Odin v. Neerlands Stam and Schutz Jari, subsequently to Trystorme, and to Aritaur through Ramonburg's Valdo from Marienburg's Morocco from Dexter v. Franckhorst, and influenced much American breeding through him.

Jens and Alison Kollenberg v. Norden Stamm lineage lay behind Heidi Vyse's Quinto van de Kunnemaborgh b.1984, who was the sire of Linda Clayton's Ch. Essenbar The Challenger, and later from the same kennel Xantos vd Kunnemaborgh.

In the same period of 1984, Int., Multi Ch., Multi Sgrn, Alida v. Flandrischen Löwen, owned by Ray Carlisle in the USA, who became SchH3 by thirty months, was the dam of two famous sisters. Int. Ch., Multi Sgrn WW Kalina v. Norden Stamm was mated to Quirinus to produce Graham Hunt's import Feo. Feo was a major influence at Supeta, and used by Hikays, Bosskat, Jeujann, Jimarty, Knecht and Marchtay amongst others. Kastra v. Norden Stamm SchH 3, Angekorung, was the dam of Int., It. Ch., AIAD Sgr Prinz v. Norden Stamm. He sired siblings Astor del Citone IPO1 and Multi Sgrn, Arielle d'Amour del Citone, parents of Multi Sgr, WW Gino Gomez del Citone. Litter brother Multi Ch., Multi Sgr Alfa Adelante was the sire of Victor van Roveline.

Graaf Fela v. Oranje's Stam at Amazon, imported by Clive and Nancy Evans, and sister Gravin Farrah descend on the paternal line from Salvador v. Franckenhorst in the fourth generation, and on the maternal line back from Dexter v. Franckenhorst through Marienburg's Dark Daimler.

Int., Multi Ch. Jivago van het Wantij ADPr, IPO3, ZTP V1A, Angekort V1A, Int., Multi Ch. Vysan van hof ter Eeckhout Angekort 1A sired Ch./Ir. Ch. Talacre Vysan's Boy at Supeta JW and Ch. Siboveld's Helluvan Angel. Jivago was the grandsire to Korifey iz Zoosfery who was very widely used throughout the UK.

Belgium: The Belgian van Roveline kennel of Roland and Evelyn Beunekens has had a long period of influence over the UK breed for many years. Lya Linda v. Roveline imp. b.1987 (Baron Bryan v. Harros Berg × Hera v. Roveline) was mated to Graaf Odin v. Neerlands Stam at Chancepixies, from whom Dave Anderson and Jean Frost took a dog and a bitch back, then to Schutz Kaiser Bill to produce Schutz Mascha, the dam of Ch., Lux., Ned. Ch. Gaindyke Flash Gordon, and to Xantos vd. Kunnemaborgh to produce Schutz Lara Linda, who was the dam of Vyleigh's Heidi-Hi of Helmlake. Victor van Roveline was extensively used by Jowendy, Supeta, Trystorme and Vonedstram, and through Ozzy Osbourne to Amazon, Manzart and Tuwos and most other prominent UK kennels.

America: America has always had an influence on UK breeding from the very start, and Fred and Julia Curnow's Tavey kennel imported many American dogs, which were used by just about all UK breeders. In later years Reg and Mary Barton continued the tradition, importing dogs from Mary Rodgers, such as Marienburg's Firedanza v Tavey.

Am., Braz. Ch. Marienburg's Morocco was the paternal grandsire of Twinglo Love Apple at Elsco through her sire Tavey's I Yodel at Wolfstein, and through his son Marienburg's Dark Daimler who was also the grandsire to the Aritaur litter of Dominatrix and Dolce Vita.

Jean Quigley's Swyndwr kennel used Am. Ch. Cambria's Irish Rebellion (grandson of Am. Ch. Cambria's Cactus Cash) by AI on Swyndwr Charlie's Angel to produce siblings Ch. Swyndwr Supatramp and Ch. Swyndwr Supacool.

Simon Molloy and Emma Edwards' US import Tevro D'Vines Last Heir to Wintablizard is a Cactus Cash grandson through the paternal line of Ch. Foxfire All That Jazz. He is the sire of the Multi BISS, BIS Protocol's Veni Vedi Vici, Westminster Winner in 2012 and 2013, who is a double granddaughter on the maternal line of Cactus Cash.

Mike Bradshaw's Perfex Vengeance at Zeitgeist (US imp.) is descended from Cactus Cash on both sides of his pedigree, and has so far sired two CC-winning progeny in the UK: Karen King's male Ch. Nerak American Dream, and his sister Ch. Nerak Twist Of Fate, who remarkably both gained their championship titles at different shows but on the same weekend in 2016.

Italy: Italian lines have featured in UK dogs in recent years, particularly through del Citone and Multi Ch., Multi Sgr Nitro del Rio Bianco.

Gino Gomez del Citone continues to influence UK breeding. He sired Multi Ch. Gemini Ginga House, who was bred to UK, Lux., Dutch Ch. Vonedstram The Vixen to produce Derek Elmslie's Crufts BOB winning Ch. Vonedstram Virtuoso. Both Aritaur and Krieger used Gino's son Drusus vom Adlercrest at Heimdall (although a US import, his line was all European), and Gino also sired Ch., Ned. Ch. Ace v. hof ter Eeckhout. A recent dog to come to the UK with Gino bloodlines is Tracey Feeney's BIS-winning Ch. Italo Elite House from Poland, through his sire Zordan Zewi del Citone.

Gino's grandson Multi Ch., AIAD Sgr Ale Alamos del Citone is the sire of Ch., Int. Ch. Gain-

DOCKING AND REGISTRATIONS

On 6 April 2007, the UK docking ban came into force. This had a significant effect on KC registrations, which dropped by around 1,000, as many breeders feared they would be unable to sell their undocked Dobermanns, or because they themselves did not want dogs with tails. Registrations did slowly recover once breeders realized there was still a demand for Dobermanns with tails, but registration numbers have never fully recovered. Later the same year the UK was hit by a national outbreak of foot and mouth disease, which stopped all UK dog shows. There have been many reasons for the decline in show number entries, which have affected breeds across the board. Fuel prices, and the general cost of keeping any dog, quite apart from the larger breeds, are expensive. Entries at UK Championship shows once averaged 250 Dobermanns, but that has now dropped to around half that number.

Dobermann registrations peaked at 13,000 in the 1980s, and the impact on rescue organizations was immense. In 2012 Dobermann registrations were just 1,346; although it seems a lot, with less than 1 per cent of dogs going in the show ring, this means that just thirteen new dogs are now going into showing each year.

dyke Eureka, and Ryan Lack's Indonesian import, Ch. Garuda von Dockerman, handled by him and Naomi Cowley. Garuda is a great grandson of Int., Multi Ch., IDC Sgr Fedor del Nasi on the maternal line.

Nitro del Rio Bianco was Best Producer at the IDC 2003, and when mated to Gaindyke Molly Malone, produced the UK 'M' litter of champions, Mirco, Martini and Mercedez in Norway. Sire to Ch. Chancepixies Locomotive, who produced two champions for Jojavik, is Chancepixies Auctioneer, who was by Nitro × Ch. Gaindyke Keramia of Chancepixies BH, whose paternal grand-dam was Quelsey v. Roveline, litter sister to Quercia, Victor van Roveline's dam.

Int., Multi Ch. F'Hiram Abif Royal Bell ZTP V1A, IPO1 was used by Aritaur, Gaindyke, Supeta and Wot A Thriller; he is a grandson of Nitro through his sire, Int., Multi Ch., Multi JgSgr Eko Royal Bell from the famous Croatian Royal Bell kennel.

Russia: Russian kennels such as Sant Kreal and Smart Wood Hills are attracting much interest from UK and Irish breeders, and exhibitors who have either imported or used dogs from the region.

Int., Multi Ch. Ugor di Villa Conte SchH1 was the sire of the Russian dog Int., Multi Ch. Tamerlan iz Slavnoi Stai IPO1, who had a major influ-

ence at both Keyala through Int., Multi Ch. Rensdorff Evesy at Keyala, sire of Ch. Keyala's Dream Machine at Nytbonn VPG1, and through the Aritaur litter of Int., Lux. Ch. A. Histabraq SchH3, ZTP V1A, Ch. A. Helina, Ch., Ir., Lux. Ch. A. Heracles at Brintala, and Ch., Ir. Ch. Hipnotique.

Supeta's Ozzy Osbourne, whose maternal line goes back through Ch., Ir. Ch. Supeta's Enuf's Enuf at Cooley and his sire Nemesis Feo v. Koepsel at Sallate, to Quirinus v. Neerlands Stam and Kalina v. Norden Stamm. Ozzy's sire was Lynne Jones' Russian import male Ch. Korifey iz Zoosfery, whose great great grandsire was Ch. Quirinus v. Neerlands Stam.

Int., Multi Russ. Ch., IDC Sgr, WW Grand Mollis Armani, was used via AI by Amazon in 2010 to produce Lynne and Sam Jones' Ch., Lux. Ch. Amazon Russian Romance JW. She was later mated to the American Multi BIS, BISS Ch. Dabney's Phenomenon, and produced siblings Ch. Korifey Black Diamond and Ch. K. Onyx. Cambria's Cactus Cash is in the fourth generation on the paternal line of D. Phenomenon, and Gino Gomez is paternal great grandsire to Armani.

Russian and Italian influence is prominent in Kevin and Angela Goodwin's Ch. Satinea Alonzo JW b.2013, who is sired by Malibray Lagavulin (son of Sant Kreal Obelix in Ireland), out of Gianna de la Maison de Keyala pour Satinea imp. Fr.

She is a daughter of Int., Multi, AIAD Ch. Nibbio del Diamante Nero, who is a son of Int., Multi, AIAD Ch. Urbano del Diamante Nero. His double great grandsire is Graaf Quirinus v. Neerlands Stam.

The Goodwin's Sant Kreal Certero of Satinea (Imp. Rus.) (Int., Ch. Tahi Reme Gerett x Rus. Ch. Sergius Aleksandrija Fabula is also attracting interest from UK breeders.

Another Russian import is Sant Kreal Focus on Supeta with Korifey, jointly owned by Sue Mycroft and Lynne Jones. He won the Junior Ch. title at Luxembourg in 2016 and is worked in IPO (Schutzhund) by Pete Mycroft.

DOBERMANNS AT CRUFTS

No Dobermann has ever won BIS at Crufts, but three Dobermanns have done so at the American equivalent Westminster: Ch. Ferry v. Rauhfelsen in 1939, Ch. Rancho Dobe's Storm in 1952 and 1953, and Royal Tudor's Wild as the Wind CD in 1989.

A review of the Crufts 2014 Dobermann entry reveals that 93 per cent of Dobermanns have European dogs in the first three generations. The remaining 7 per cent comprise those with European dogs further back in their pedigree or whose antecedants are American bred.

Crufts BOB Winners Since 1950

The BOB winner is listed first, followed by the Best Opposite Sex (BOS).

1950 Birling Rachel (B), BOS Birling Rebel (D) (no CCs) (siblings)
1951 Birling Rachel (B), BOS Ch. Wolfox's Birling Rogue (D) (no CCs)
1952 Ch. Elegant of Tavey (B), BOS Ingot of Tavey (D)
1953 Ch./Ob. Ch. Jupiter of Tavey (D), BOS Ch. Francesca of Fulton (B)
1955 Ch. Precept of Tavey (D), BOS Ch. Juno of Tavey (B)
1956 Ch. Ace of Tavey (D), BOS Ch. Reichert Judy (B)
1957 Ch. Challenger of Sonhende (D), BOS Ch. Baba Black Pepper (B)

1958 Ch. Tavey's Stormy Abundance (D), BOS Ch. Tavey's Stormy Adagio (B) (siblings)
1959 Ch. Tavey's Stormy Abundance (D) (Group 2), Ch. Baba Black Pepper (B)
1960 Ch. Tavey's Stormy Achievement (D), BOS Tumlow Storm Away (B)
1961 Ch. Tumlow Storm Caesar (D), BOS Ch. Tavey Stormy Daughter (B)
1962 Ch. Tumlow Fantasy (B), BOS Ch. Tavey's Stormy Nugget (D)
1963 Ch. Edencourts Avenger (D), BOS Ch. Tumlow Fantasy (B)
1964 Ch. Ampherlaw Sir Galahad (D), BOS Ch. Kerstins Pride of Oakfair (B)
1965 Ch. Iceberg of Tavey (Grp 2) (D), BOS Ch. Tavey's Stormy Wrath (B)
1966 Ch. Iceberg of Tavey (Grp 2) (D), BOS Ch. Gurnard Gemma (B)
1967 Ch. Iceberg of Tavey (Grp 2) (D), BOS Ch. Rajada Juliet (B)
1968 Ch. Delmordene Buccaneer (D), BOS Ch. Rajada Juliet (B)
1969 Ch. Clanguard Cadet (D), BOS Ch. Dizzy Debutante (B)
1970 Ch. Kingroy Carla Kay (B), BOS Heidiland Trouble Spot (D)
1971 Ch. Tumlow Satan (D), BOS Ch. Tumlow Bonanza (B)
1972 Ch. Clanguard Cadet (D), BOS Bulpine's Carissma (B)
1973 Ch. Flexor Flugelman (Group 2) (D), BOS Sophie Copperbronze (B)
1974 Ch. Tumlow Satan (D), BOS Ch. Vyleigh's Valerian (B)
1975 Ch. Flexor Flugelman (Group 1) (D), BOS Ch. Abbeyville's Shooting Star (B)
1976 Ch. Kenstaff Tornado of Achenburg (D), BOS Ch. Kaiserberg Helen (B)
1977 Ch. Borains' Raging Calm (B), BOS Ch. Studbriar The Red (D)
1978 Ch. Merrist Reluctant Knight (D), BOS Studbriar Dark 'n' Sassy of Zarwyn (B)
1979 Ch. Borain's Raging Calm (B), BOS Ch. Davalog's Crusader (D)
1980 Ch. Sandean Aquarius (D), BOS Ch. Findjans Freya (B)
1981 Ch. Zalpha's Midland Miss (B), BOS Ch. Major Marauder (D)

1982 Ch. Zalpha's Midland Miss (B), BOS Ch. Vonklebong's Solar Encore at Achenburg (D)

1983 Carhis Blues Singer (D), BOS Ch. Magana's Dark Damask (B)

1984 Ch. Pompie Dutch Lieveling (B), BOS Ch. Torjet's Colonial Boy (D)

1985 Ch. Highroyds Man of the Year (D) (Grp 1), BOS Ch. Laurill's High Flyer (B)

1986 Ch. Halsbands Redwing (B), BOS Ch. Findjans Chaos (D)

1987 Ch. Sallate Ferris (D) (Group 1), BOS Ch. Halsband's Redwing (B)

1988 Ch. Sallate Ferris (D), BOS Ch. Chevington Royal Kashmere (B)

1989 Ch. Essenbar The Challenger (D), BOS Ch. Shirdawn April Rain (B)

1990 Ch. Sallate Ferris (D) (Group 1), BOS Ch. Elroban Scheherazade (B)

1991 Ch. Sallate's Ferris (D), BOS Ch. Borain's Carte Blanche of Dobermoray (B)

1992 Ch. Autolander General (D), BOS Ch. Albadobe Shalimar (B)

1993 Ch. Autolander General (D), BOS Ch. Twinglo Love Apple at Elsco (B)

1994 Ch. Sallate Black Magic of Coltrac (B), BOS Ch. Jowendy's Kilowatt (D)

1995 Ch. Charles Great Homestead (D), BOS Ch. Sallate Black Magic of Coltrac (B)

1996 Ch. Kamroyal Krystal (B), BOS Ch. Khaneve Judgement Day (D)

1997 Ch. Amazon Sound Machine (D), BOS Halsband's Pillow Talk (B)

1998 Ch. Amazon Sound Machine (D) (Group 2), BOS Ch. Dobermoray Whirl'n Dervish (B)

1999 Ch. Sallate Striptease (B) (Group 1), BOS Ch. Chaanrose Don't Crowd Me at Jaegerson (D)

2000 Ch. Sallate Striptease (B) (Group 4), BOS Ch. Ikons Charmer (D)

2001 Ch. Chancepixies Monopolist (D), BOS Remesca Forget-Me-Knot (B)

2002 Ch. Cloudybay Dead Ringer for Amazon (D), BOS Ch Trystorme In Anticipation (B)

2003 Ch., Ned. Ch. Ace Van Hof Ter Eeckhout at Siboveld, imp. (D), BOS Ch. Siboveld's Helluvan Angel (B)

2004 Ch. Talacre Vysans Boy at Supeta (D) (Grp 3), BOS Ebrill Chocolate Orange at Tackstone (B)

2005 Ch. Talacre Vysans Boy at Supeta (D) (Grp 2), BOS Ch. Siboveld's Helluvan Angel (B)

2006 Ch. Amazon Black Sabbath at Purroma (D), BOS Ch. Krieger Endless Love JW (B)

2007 Ch. Vonedstram Virtuoso (B), BOS Siboveld's Sauron of Rocksands (D)

2008 Ch./Ir. Ch. Aritaur Hipnotique (B), BOS BOS Ch. Keyala's Dream Machine at Nytbonn (D)

2009 Ch. Amazon Coldplay (D), BOS Ch., Lux. Ch. Jojavik Gangsters Moll JW (B)

2010 Ch./Ir. Ch. Vanhallen Black Velvet with Darkiss (B), BOS Ch./Lux. Ch. Supeta's Ozzy Osbourne JW (D)

2011 Ch./Lux. Ch. Supetas Ozzy Osbourne JW (D), BOS Ch. Jojavik Bella Mafia (B)

2012 Ch. Liason Latanya (B), BOS Ch./Lux. Ch. Supetas Ozzy Osbourne JW (D)

2013 Bel./Ned. Ch. Grafmax Louis Armstrong (D), BOS Ch. Liason Latanya (B)

2014 Ch./Ir. Ch. Supeta's Secret Wizard at Dronski JW, ShCM (D), BOS Ch. Jojavik Molly Mobster (B)

2015 Ch. Supeta's Spells Trouble JW (B), BOS Ch. Aritaur Cardinal Red at Jodaseen (D)

2016 Ch. Jojavik Midnight Express JW, ShCM, BOS Ch. Jojavik Poison Ivy JW, ShCM (siblings)

2017 Ch./Ir. Ch Jojavik Midnight Express JW, ShCM, BOS Ch Stormhold Enigma from Diego JW.

It has obviously not been possible to list every UK champion, or human or canine contributor to the breed, and any important omission is unintentional.

3 CHARACTER AND TEMPERAMENT

The fearsome reputation of the Dobermann has been reinforced for many years by films portraying a vicious, sharp and aggressive 'devil dog'. The black coat, muscular and agile body, and dark eyes all add to the infamy of the breed – which of course is exactly what Louis Dobermann intended when he created it.

The UK breed standard for character requires the Dobermann to be 'intelligent and firm of character, loyal and obedient'. The temperament is described as 'bold and alert. Shyness or viciousness very highly undesirable'. These descriptions are similar to other breed standards in Europe (FCI) and America (AKC/UKC).

The Dobermann is the only breed in the world to have been specifically created to guard man and his family. He retains this mindset to this day, and finds separation from his human pack tremendously depressing. The breed is poorly suited to living outside, even in a heated kennel. Their coats are not double layered, and they feel the cold considerably.

The Dobermann is often considered to be an aggressive breed, but the core motivation of the breed is not aggression, it is defence, which we want in our care for our families.

New owners to the breed are often amazed by the polar reactions to the breed from the public, with people crossing the road to avoid them, and others asking 'why would you risk your children being around a Dobermann?' The best response is that there is no better guardian for them: a companion and protector rolled into one great dog is an asset to any owner and family. Others are genuinely delighted to see the Dobermann, knowing them for their affectionate and reliable character, especially around children.

Graaf Buco v. Neerlands Stam, imported by Graham Hunt of Sallate, in 1990.

Baby and his guardian Dobermann.

These days the Dobermann is very different to the notably sharp breed of old. With selection for more passive traits in breeding, they are now known more for their general sociability. They were traditionally wary around strangers, but that is also now less often the case, and Dobermanns are known for their habit of leaning against friendly people when they want a bit of fuss and affection. Despite this, most Dobermanns still retain an acute sense of potential danger, and many owners have been shocked (albeit pleasantly) when their usually placid dog has defended them from threat, saying they 'didn't realize he had it in him'.

UNDERSTANDING BEHAVIOUR

Behaviours are formed from character, which is an inherited trait, while temperament can be considered an acquired trait. All Dobermanns share the same breed traits of loyalty and depend-ability, but they can be as behaviourally distinct as any two humans. When selling a puppy, good breeders will try to match the characters of the potential owner and the dog from the outset. Even the most easy-going pup can become 'dominant' when owned by a weak person, but will behave quite differently with another, perhaps stronger-willed owner.

Dogs inherit character traits naturally, but certain behaviours result from the way a dog is raised: thus chewing furniture, pulling on the lead, jumping up and tearing clothes, howling from being left alone, knocking people over, and ferociously guarding the boundary fence, are not inherited traits, but behaviours that are solely due to the owner not having trained their dog properly, and allowing aberrant behaviours to develop. When a child behaves badly we blame the parents, and it is no different with a dog. However, having said this, we can't blame incompetent owners for everything, and some dogs have a genetic predisposition to aggression or fear.

Understanding the Dog's Mind

To change a dog's behaviour we need to understand how his mind works. In simple terms we refer to the 'forebrain', which controls rational thought functions, and 'hindbrain' which is responsible for instinctive reactions. The forebrain (cerebrum/cerebral cortex) forms the main part of the brain and receives and analyses sensory information such as is provided by the voice, touch, hearing, smell, taste and pain. This

The Dobermann enjoys close contact with people. One of the nicknames for the breed is the 'Velcro dog'.

is where thought processes occur. The hindbrain controls hard-wired instincts such as fear, aggression, sex drive and food drive. The dog in hindbrain state is adrenalized and can't think clearly, so his mind needs to be changed if we want him to follow our instructions.

Motivating Drives

Drives are our motivations for eating, hunting, sleeping, mating, fighting or fleeing, and they shape our motivation – they drive us – to behave in a particular way. Most of us understand 'fight or flight', which come under the defence banner – if you feel defensive you will either fight or run – but there are other fundamental basic drives. Most of us train our dogs instinctively without knowing the technical sequencing of drives, but learning how drives work together and how to shape them is a fascinating and useful skill.

Pack drive: This drive dictates how much (or how little) a dog needs to be with his (human) family or pack. Pack is probably the most important drive for a dog to be in. It generally reflects a calm state of mind, typical of a relaxed, secure dog.

The pack drive of the Dobermann is very high, and they are never happier than in the company of children. Russ Ch Zenith of Fame de Grande Vinko IPO1 with his family and friends in Russia. DINA DAMOTSEVA

The bitch protecting the children is acting in two drives: in defence and in pack drive.

Prey drive: This drive motivates the dog to chase and hunt fast-moving objects. Some dogs are highly motivated by a falling leaf, while others barely raise a glance when a rabbit runs under their nose. Rather than suppress a high prey drive, harness it by playing with a ball on a rope, tug games and retrieve.

Defence (fight/flight) drive: In defence drive a dog will fight for its own safety, or for resources (food, mates or territory). The dog in defence drive feels afraid or threatened, and will either attack or run. Fear aggression is one of the most difficult behaviours to overcome. It is an instinc-

tive defence reaction, and like many fears, is not always rational.

Behaviours may seem to appear unexpectedly, but there is always an underlying reason. Humans miss the very subtle signs exchanged between dogs: the hostile glance, or the nudge or shove which gauges how far they can push each other before one or other reacts more strongly.

Drives are equally important in everyday life. Anxious and defensive dogs can be taught to focus on prey (controlled toy) and pack drive to overcome their stress. This is really useful for dogs that chase other dogs, horses and livestock, and for defensive/aggressive dogs that need to stay close, but also need to go off lead for proper exercise.

The Importance of Companionship

A common question asked by prospective owners is 'how much exercise does a Dobermann need', and 'how long can they be left for'? The breeder may rightly wonder if those people are trying to fit a dog into their busy lives, and may respond by asking 'how much time do you want to give the dog?' The intelligence of this breed attracts many people, but they neglect this integral part of Dobermann ownership. When asked what they plan to do with their dog, most prospective owners respond that they will 'take the puppy to training classes' and then…. silence, because they have thought no further ahead than that.

Imagine the child who was taken to nursery school a couple of times, but who was then kept at home alone, with nothing to do, no games, no television or computers, and just a walk around the same park each day. With nothing to fill his empty days, the dog turns to destruction to relieve his boredom. He often reacts dispro-

Clay, Gwen and Kodi have learned to control their natural prey drive through training.

portionally to visitors or people walking past the garden, and may race around barking constantly. On walks he has so much pent-up frustration that he lunges and barks at everything, so the owner gives up walking him. Despite his siblings being model citizens, the owner blames the breeder for breeding an aggressive dog. The dog is re-homed and loses his family.

Coping with Dog Aggression

Unlike hounds, gundogs and herding breeds, which have been bred for generations to work together, the Dobermann was bred to be a personal protector, and not to be part of a multi-dog pack. Also be aware that despite all the best socialization, direction and training from the owner, Dobermanns are not generally male-male compatible. Some may co-habit up until they are fifteen months or so, but usually they then want their own space. Breeders will rarely, if ever, home two dogs of the same sex together, because if they fight, they will have to be kept separated both in the home and on exercise for life, or re-homed. It is rarely worth the risk or the heartache.

Male dominance/aggression doesn't mean that a dog is bad or nasty. Males of most species jostle for prime position, and it is only our human social inhibition that stops fights breaking out every Saturday night! Fighting is normal behaviour for the dog that feels his resources are at risk. Remember the origins and purpose of the Dobermann: this is not a pack breed in the way that hounds are.

Research (Hart and Eckstein, 1997) has shown that castration does not affect territorial aggression, so it is pointless in these dogs.

Frieda loves her couch, but leads a very active life, running regularly with her owner, and training in the sport of IPO (Schutzhund).
RUTH ROBINSON

Dog aggression can arise from many reasons: stress, excitement, frustration, high fight drive, resource guarding, weakness, illness, fear. Dobermanns rarely start fights, but they won't tolerate being pushed by another male. Bitches can also be difficult with other dogs, but much less so. Opposite sexes rarely fight.

Avoiding and Breaking Up Fights

Dog fights come down to dominance and submission: one has to yield, it is just a matter of when. Happily, although they may posture around each other, dogs usually work things out themselves

Fortunately these two males are just play-fighting. They have been friends since puppyhood, but this is very unusual with males.

This play has not yet tipped over to fight, but it takes just one small step for full-scale war to break out, so it is generally sensible not to allow this type of play.

before a fight develops, so generally the safest bet is to leave them to back down in their own time (even if this does take nerves of steel). Problems occur if neither dog gives or recognizes submissive signals, and fights on regardless.

Controlling a dog by physical dominance is like keeping a lid on a powder keg, because that adrenalin has to go somewhere. Dogs that are held back or yanked by the neck in a heated situation may well turn and bite their owner, because they are not being rational and react to what they think is another dog attacking them.

Stand-up boxing may seem fun, but it can be a

fight-inducing 'game' that rapidly tips over into a squabble, especially if the dogs are the same sex. Games exist to enable dogs to assess the strength of their opponent in a real fight. If it looks as if a game is getting rough and out of hand, call the dogs away to calm things down; at least one of them will be relieved to have the game ended.

When two dogs stand over each other, stiff as a board and about to go into a fight, owners must never try and pull the dogs away, as a fight will be inevitable, just as it would be if they were to rush in screaming and shouting. Although it is our nature to try to prevent our dogs from being hurt, if you try to separate fighting dogs you will be bitten even by your own dog, as they are blinded by the survival drive into fighting for their lives. (Note that if people are injured from breaking up a dog fight, the police and judiciary rarely view that as an attack on a human.) Similarly, screaming at them drains physical energy that is needed to separate them. Two equally matched dogs will not kill each other immediately, so you have time to think tactically about your options.

Dogs quickly lock on to each other, and begin twisting and shaking their heads in a kill motion (this is why puppies and dogs should never be shaken by the scruff, because in dog language the only time a shake is used is in a kill manoeuvre). Once locked on, it becomes very difficult to get them apart. The problem with equally matched dogs is when you get them apart they will charge back in for a better bite. If they are not equally matched, focus on the aggressor, because if you can get them released, the victim is likely to run and not continue the fight.

If you are at home and can drag the dogs to either side of a door, you may be able to ram the door on their heads to force them to release; if you are in the garden, leash one dog to a tree or solid gate to stop it going back in, once released. Trying to pull apart two locked-on dogs will just cause them to inflict deeper flesh wounds on each other.

If this is a first fight you may sometimes be able to make them stand back from each other if you sound a loud air horn or spray hairspray in their face. Water makes everything slippery and you won't be able to get a good hold to force them apart, but it does make their fight more difficult, so weakens them more quickly.

If there is any tension between dogs you have at home, separate them before visitors arrive to avoid flash points, particularly round gates or doorways. Excited barking prompts dogs to turn on each other in frustration, and a vicious fight can develop in seconds. Forcing a dog to be in a roomful of other dogs, or to walk past them, will not make him less aggressive unless he has had a course of professional rehabilitation.

Naturally the dog that is attacked or bullied by other dogs, especially as a puppy, will mistrust other dogs. This is why every inter-dog experience as a puppy is critical, and will dictate whether in later life a dog is stable in company, or whether it is immediately aggressive. No matter how domesticated and well socialized the dog, we cannot apply social human niceties to dogs.

MANAGING BEHAVIOURS

When a dog behaves aggressively he is operating in hindbrain defence (fight or flight) and can't think clearly. If the owner tries to dominate the

A dog 'checking in' with her owner for guidance and direction: the pack drive overcoming the prey or defence drive.

dog into submission by checking and yanking him, this will push him further into defence. The clever owner can direct a dog out of instinctive/reactive hindbrain response, into a calm, thinking forebrain state. Hindbrain response can never be removed entirely – it is a body part just like a limb – but filling the mind with thoughtful processes effectively re-maps the brain and provides an alternative path to the usual default response.

The horse trainer Clinton Anderson says, 'A well-trained horse has a big thinking area and a small reacting space. With training, the react-ing part gets smaller and smaller, but you will never get rid of it completely … you must always be aware of its existence.' It is the same with dogs.

Stress and its Impact

Aggression is the result of a stressed mind, result-ing in a dog that can't concentrate; therefore rec-ognizing the signs of a stress in a dog, and learn-ing how to direct the dog out of a stressed state, will help in managing aggression.

Stress produces adrenalin for an explosive reaction of fight or flight hormone. If adrenalin is not used it literally gets stuck in the muscles. This is why dogs that have been standing for a judge to assess them, or who get in conflict ten-sion with other dogs, literally shake themselves down as they move away in order to release ten-sion, to clear stress build-up, and to loosen tight muscles and joints that have been in preparation for action.

The stressed dog keeps his muscles rigid perma-nently, which inhibits calm brain function. Just as we hold our breath in a stressful situation, so does the dog, and he may pant to re-oxygenate, or yawn to take in deep breaths after even mildly stressful events. Stretching is a tension reliever to allow muscles and nerves to relax, and to boost circulation to the body and brain.

Eye staring is a sign of confidence, assertive-ness and alpha status, and in stare-downs, each dog holds an unblinking stare to his opponent until one of them yields and looks away. During a stare the lower ranking dog will lower his head and repeatedly blink to signal that he is yielding, thereby acknowledging the superior status of the other dog. When the stare or threat is over, the dog relaxes his eyes and blinks to re-lubricate them. During stalk and chase, the eyes remain fixed on the prey subject; blinking will also be part of the eye relaxation.

The Palliative Effect of Touch

Touch is a vital aspect of human-to-human and human-to-animal social behaviour, helping us bond with, and care for each other. If we are feel-ing anxious our friends will often touch our arm, or give us a man-to-man pat on the back. Touch can release calming hormones of dopamine and serotonin in the brain, and transfers nerve sensa-tion to the area touched, rather than focusing on the cause of the arousal.

Dogs are very sensitive to even the slightest touch from the pressure of a collar, or a gentle touch from a kind hand. Using touch to lower the defence or prey drive and take the dog into the more desirable state of pack drive, is a non-confrontational way to introduce calmness. How-ever, never touch a dog when it is in full defence or aggressive mode, because that may result in it spinning round to snap at what it believes to be another dog coming in to bite. If your dog is reactive, visit a trainer who specializes in han-dling reactive dogs, so they can teach you how to manage the behaviour, and show you how to take the dog into another drive.

The Palliative Effect of Flank/Blanket Sucking

Flank or blanket sucking is a comfort habit and is normal in the Dobermann, and is not detrimental to the dog in any way. Some veterinary articles allege that it is a medical condition that Dober-manns 'suffer from', and incredibly recommend that in 'severe' cases drugs are prescribed to pre-vent the habit. Any Dobermann owner whose dog indulges in this habit will tell you that this is complete nonsense, in the same way that no one would consider medicating children who suck their thumb for relaxation. Some Dobermanns suck a blanket, while some suck their flank, loin or leg, in the same way that an infant puppy suck-les, with the paws kneading the blanket or cush-ion and the eyes usually either closed or 'glazed over' in contentment.

Flank or blanket sucking is normal in the Dobermann, and is not detrimental to the dog in any way.

THE DOBERMANN CHARACTER

The Dobermann character is the same the world over in terms of loyalty and protective instinct for their families, but differs markedly in the levels of drive and behaviour. As dogs are no longer used to guard us in our daily business or to work alongside us on farms, few owners train their dogs for work. Breeders realize that whilst they may be able to handle an active dog, not all their buyers can, or want to, and although owners claim they will do a lot of training with their Dobermann, in reality very few manage more than just the basics; breeders therefore select for a much more passive character to suit their buyers.

The working Dobermann has never featured strongly in either the UK or the USA, but in mainland Europe there is a sports dog club virtually on every corner. This is partly due to the fact that although working breeds can win some country championship titles in Europe, they cannot win the important Sieger (breed championship) titles without a working qualification.

One of the biggest misconceptions about working dogs is that they need to be aggressive to work. But aggression is the result of a stressed mind, resulting in a dog who can't concentrate, and no respected working handler wants a dog who perceives a threat in every situation, or who is so defensive around other dogs that he can't

Int., Lux. Ch. Aritaur Histabraq SchHlll, ZTP V1A. Protection on the field and at home.

A Dobermann is bred for a strong stable character who is as comfortable with the family as he is on the working field.

concentrate on his work. Bite work is part of a working dog's training, but teaching a weak or nervous dog to bite is a terrible liability, and no registered working club would ever allow an owner to do just bite work with their dog without requiring evidence that it is sound in character.

The 'architect' of the breed, Phillip Gruenig, makes the following observations regarding the Dobermann's character and position as a worker in his published masterpiece *The History of the Dobermann Pinscher*:

> His position in the country, where he fits himself into the family as its guard and protector, is our best assurance against his body and mind degenerating into the over-delicate form of the greyhound and its stupidity. The breed must assert its position as a worker and a guardian, by which I do not propose to endorse the transition from one extreme to the other. The organized training of the breed for sharpness and viciousness is just as senseless and obnoxious as the acceptance of the greyhound type.

Most owners think they know how their dogs would act if faced with real threat, but may be surprised at the outcome, whichever it is. This was why working tests were created, to enable breeders to expose the real merits and faults of a dog's character when under pressure.

Ideally a Dobermann is bred with a strong, stable character to ensure he is as comfortable with

Dobermanns are very respectful around children, and are smart enough to lower their strength around the young and very old. DINA DAMOTSEVA

the family as he is on the working field, and this can now be tested in a test called the ZTP. This is a 'Fit for Breeding Test' established by German Shepherd breeders in Germany to assess a dog's suitability for breeding. In addition to examining conformation and the physical attributes of the dog, it also tests his basic skills and character. As regards Dobermanns, outside Germany and de Verein (the German Dobermann Club), there are only three judges who are permitted to test Dobermanns for ZTP in other countries. The UK Dobermann Association (UKDA), based in Kent and headed by Dave and Heidi Anderson, is now the only UK breed club to run character tests in the form of the ZTP. The UKDA held the first ever ZTP test in 2010, and the second in 2016.

Some UK Dobermann owners believe that the character of European dogs is too high in drive, but interestingly a review of the Crufts catalogue in 2014 revealed that 93 per cent of UK Dobermanns have European ancestry in their first three generations, as a result of imports to the UK or from bitches bred to overseas sires. The remaining 7 per cent have European breeding further back in their pedigree, or who are down line from American dogs.

Although European dogs are bred for a generally higher work ethic that reflects a need for training, it is not possible to categorize all Euro-bred dogs as having the same character, any more than it is with English or American bred dogs. It can only be a generalization of character type.

Whether you prefer the working dog from Europe, the more passive American form, or the mix of the two in the UK and northern Europe, never choose a dog from nervous bloodlines.

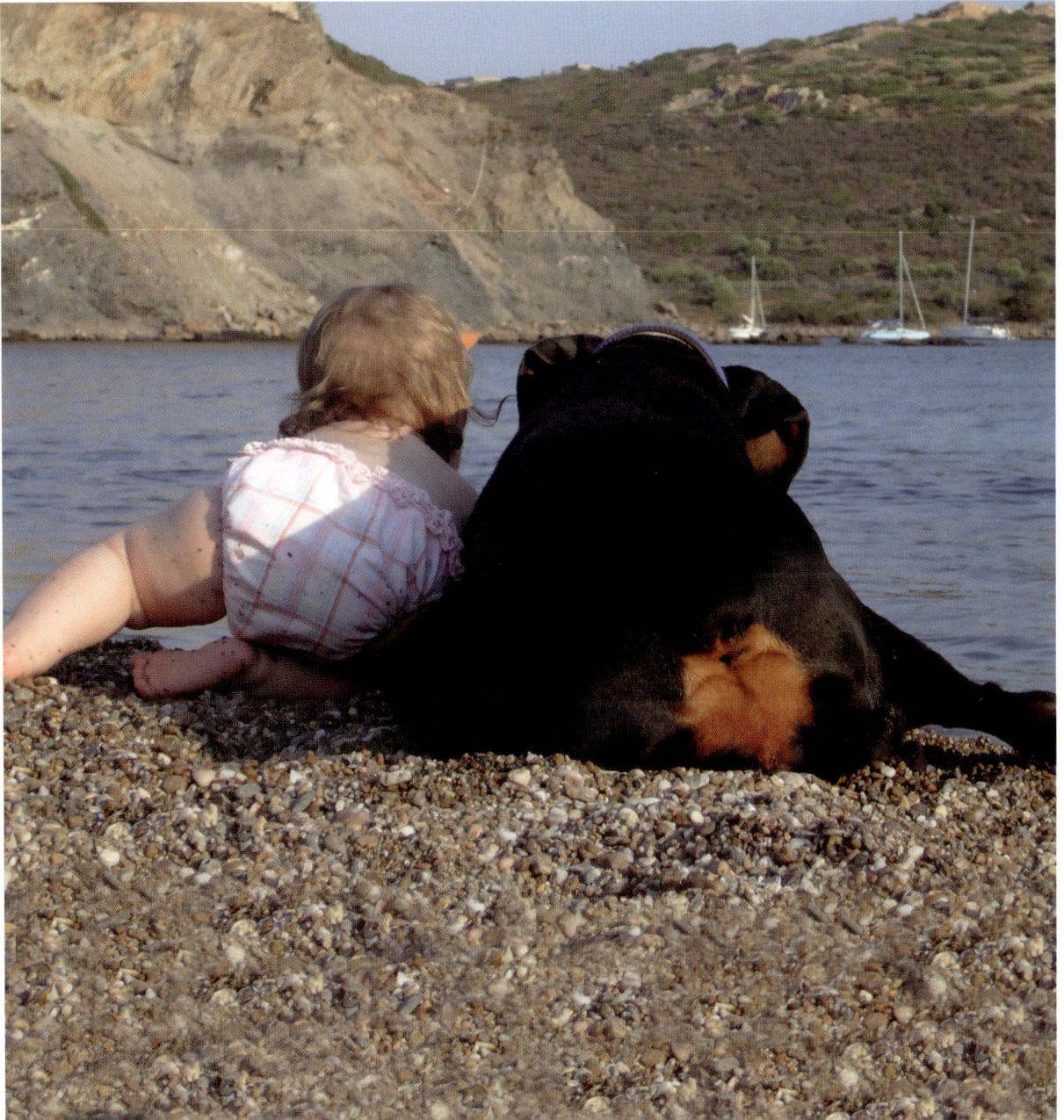

The best guardian for a baby: 'Maya' with Aliki. ELENI KLAVDIANOU

That way you can enjoy a dog that embraces family life without losing the natural protective instinct for which he was originally bred.

It is contended by some that Dobermanns are dangerous, but is this really true? In the UK there is no licensing requirement for any breed, and although the media over-excitedly reports any dog bite-related injury, successive governments have not extended specific breed legislation beyond the four breeds that are currently banned in the UK: the American Pit Bull Terrier, the Tosa-Inu, the Dogo Argentino and the Fila Braziliero – these may not be bred, owned, imported or sold. Unlike the media, most authorities (except Northern Ireland) sensibly focus any legislation on 'deed, not breed'.

Small breeds are much more likely to bite than large breeds, although large dogs can obviously inflict considerable damage if they do bite. The ten breeds in the UK most commonly known for bite injuries are the Dachshund, the Chihuahua, the Jack Russell, the Australian cattle dog, the Cocker Spaniel, the Beagle, the Border Collie, the Pit Bull Terrier, the Great Dane and the English Springer Spaniel (*see* Further Information).

Mike Mullan is a Dobermann (and Rottweiler) breeder, owner and judge; he is also a renowned dog behaviour specialist for all breeds. He is regularly called upon in court cases as an expert witness in dog bite incidents in all breeds. During the past thirty years he has represented dog owners in over 350 UK court cases, and in that time has not had one Dobermann owner to represent in any biting incident. Interestingly the Dobermann is not used as a status dog by criminals, who find them far too soft compared to some other breeds.

4 CHOOSING A BREEDER AND BUYING A DOBERMANN

With its impressive athletic physique and its high intelligence, the Dobermann is one of the most alluring breeds, while the short, easy-to-maintain coat is an added bonus for an owner. Breed guides boast an impressive and enticing list of attributes and features for the family seeking a loyal and energetic companion.

Nevertheless, although the Dobermann can be the best companion and partner, if the potential owner chooses the breed on looks alone without considering their own capabilities and character, this will often result in disappointment for both dog and owner. Despite convincing themselves that this is the breed for them, some people are simply not suitable for the breed, and vice versa.

Dobermann character varies widely in different bloodlines. Some breeders want to maintain the original purpose of the breed and select stronger working lines, while others prefer less demanding dogs who are content with no more than a daily amble round the block. Rather than just choosing the breed from books and breed booths, the potential owner would be advised to go to some dog shows to meet the breed and talk to the breeders and owners, or ideally visit a breeder and ask to go out for a walk with them and their dogs to really get a feel for the Dobermann. Visiting the breeder prior to buying a puppy will also help identify whether the type of Dobermann they breed will fit with their lifestyle and requirements.

Shiny puppy. JANE RYMAN

CHOOSING A GOOD BREEDER

In 2005 The Kennel Club introduced the Accredited Breeder Scheme; later this became the Assured Breeder Scheme (ABS), when it gained UKAS accreditation. This requires that certain recommended health tests are undertaken on stud dogs and bitches, and that all premises are visited and approved by the KC (*see* Chapter 13 for further details). Some high quality breeders choose not to be ABS members as they feel their standards already exceed those required by the KC.

There are many different standards of breeder, from puppy farmers, dog dealing and back yard breeders, to commercial kennels, individual bitch owners and show and/or work breeders.

Puppy farmers: Usually keep their over-bred brood bitches outside or in kennels where there is poor human interaction. There will be no pedigree, health testing or worming for either dam or pups, and the puppies will not be KC registered. Dam and pups are fed low quality food, and puppies are taken from the mother at a young age so that she can be bred again soon after. Puppies are sold to dealers, who may falsely affirm to the buyer that the puppies have come from a good breeder, or that they have rescued them. They may offer to drive to the buyer's

Shiny, happy puppies with a confident, relaxed and friendly dam are the first things to look for when choosing a puppy.

premises with the puppies in the back of their van (as they are 'just passing'), or they will deliver at a motorway services. Buyers are often shocked when they see the condition of the puppies, but often they will already have paid a deposit or in full.

Dog dealing: Puppy dealing is big business. Dealers have connections with breeders in Ireland and now Europe to import and re-sell cropped and docked puppies. However, breeders of quality dogs will never sell to someone they have not met. Papers for puppies bought from a dealer are often false, if indeed they ever arrive at all. Puppies come from both puppy farms and individual breeders, who may sell whole litters to the dealers.

Back-yard breeders: Are usually connected with dealers to whom they sell their pups, or they sell through general websites and local papers. They will never travel for a good stud dog, and will often use the local stud dog, who himself has no health testing. Health testing is never undertaken, and puppies are rarely KC registered.

Commercial kennels: Are licensed, and breed regularly. On the down side, handling and interaction will be limited, as time is money. There may be some health testing. Food quality will be acceptable, and bitches and pups are usually wormed.

Individual bitch owners: May not show or work their dogs themselves, but often decide to have a litter for various reasons. The good individual breeder will health test their bitch and travel for the best dog because they want to breed quality puppies. Puppies will be raised in the home with care. Most will KC register their puppies (some are ABS members, see above), and their care of bitch and puppies is usually excellent in all respects.

Show and/or work breeders: May own many bitches, or just one. They may also have agreements with owners of bitches they have bred, to breed on terms under the original breeders affix.

They have the latest health information from breed clubs and colleagues. Some will choose to be ABS members, others purposely do not wish to join the scheme as they feel they already exceed the ABS requirements.

There are now far fewer quality breeders than there used to be, and prospective buyers must be prepared to travel to find the right breeder and puppy. The Kennel Club holds a list of breeders with puppies for sale.

It is worth bearing in mind that although flashy websites give the impression of top quality dogs and premises, the reality of a breeder's set-up can only be revealed by a visit. And although you may see adverts in the local paper, good breeders in fact rarely advertise in the papers.

VISITING THE BREEDER

When you approach a breeder you like the look of, offer them a brief introduction about yourself, your experience with dogs, your lifestyle, any particular activities you want to do with the dog, and any sensible questions about their health and character. The breeder can then be assured that you are genuine about the breed, and will be happy to invite you to visit to meet their dogs.

All good breeders will also want you to visit them before buying a puppy so they can assess you as much as you are assessing them and their dogs. They will ask personal questions about your work/home life balance, and your experience with dogs in general, to ensure they would be sending one of their dogs to a good home. Quality breeders take great pride in what they do, and if a breeder doesn't ask you any questions you can assume they haven't bred conscientiously, don't care if the puppy goes to live in a high-rise flat and will be left alone all day, and will certainly have no interest in supporting you when things go wrong.

Breeders who allow strangers to view puppies before they are three weeks old are disregarding the bitch's need for privacy – but puppies who don't see visitors until they are six weeks old will be nervous of people they don't know. And

Most breeders use a drop-down bed to sleep on next to the whelping box. Dobermann bitches are usually very 'needy' when they have pups, and will move to be next to their owner even when suckling their pups.

*Gentle early handling
from the breeder is
essential.*

Gentle early handling from the breeder is essential.

when you visit, watch how the breeder handles their dogs and puppies: if they are careless and handle the pups roughly, avoid buying one as it will be nervous of human contact for life.

All these things should ring alarm bells for you, because a puppy will never overcome these early negative experiences despite the kindest socialization – that blank slate is already marked, and you will have a difficult dog for life.

You should expect the one-off breeder to raise a litter of pups with as much success as any top quality breeder. The dam should be in good condition and not worn down from breeding, and the puppies should be raised in a healthy, spacious, stimulating environment. Quite soon a dam will need a break from being with her puppies, otherwise they will mob her continually for food, and the conscientious breeder will provide a sofa or raised bench for her, so she can get away from them but still be close. No bitch should be shut in with her puppies continually.

Check references, health testing and KC registration before you visit. If you know the registered name of the parents, you can find out if they are KC registered and check their health test results by looking on the Kennel Club's website: www.thekennelclub.org.uk. You must have the exact spelling of the dog's name to find the dog or bitch. This avoids the heart-breaking situation of going to see a litter of pups and being so horrified at the conditions that you let your heart rule your head, and buy a puppy 'just to get it out of there', ending up with a sickly, ill-tempered, under-socialized dog that you are stuck with for life.

Never be embarrassed to ask to see KC registration and health testing papers. A good breeder will be pleased that you asked because it shows you are serious. You should expect to see health tests for the sire and dam for at least vWD (von Willebrands disease, see Chapter 8) and hip dysplasia. Some breeders also test for eye health,

Once her pups are over three or four weeks old, the dam is no longer as protective as she was and wants to leave the box more. In her absence she is happy for family members to entertain her puppies. It is vital during this important formative time that only gentle handling is allowed.

Eating outside for the first time on a sunny day.

notably PHPV (*see* Chapter 8), although this is not a condition that presents any major problem in the breed.

Few top quality breeders use their own stud dog unless it is the ideal combination, so don't expect to see the stud dog at their home. It may be possible to see the sire of a litter at local shows or trials.

Be aware that most quality litters are already pre-booked by the time they are born, so unless there has been a cancellation or perhaps a larger-than-expected litter, you may be unlucky and not make the list. Never give or send a deposit to anyone for puppies not yet born.

You may feel you can ask a breeder to recommend another breeder: their response may be influenced by whether they are friendly competitors or deadly rivals, but most will refer you to other good breeders with available puppies.

CHOOSING THE RIGHT DOG

Choosing the right dog for you will be the next task, and you should consider how your lifestyle and capabilities will match the character and capabilities of the puppy. Don't expect breeders to let you choose from the entire litter, as they will already have selected puppies for work or show homes, and they don't even choose their own puppies until they are seven weeks old.

Dogs are born with the basic character they

93

inherit from their parents, but their temperament will depend on their upbringing. If you meet the parents you will have a good idea of the character of the puppy; the way you treat it after that point, and how you raise it, will dictate how it behaves in later life. And be aware that even the most laid-back puppy from two easy-going parents can become a hooligan without a good upbringing. Furthermore, if a new owner doesn't follow through with their promised intentions and the advice given, the breeder cannot be held to blame for the wayward dog.

If you don't have much dog experience, you may struggle with a male Dobermann as your first dog. A sexually mature male (usually seven months plus) can become territorially and sexually dominant with other males, and if he is feeling full of testosterone in the local park, that is a lot of dog to have on the end of the lead. There are, of course, exceptions to the rule, and many males are quite happy around others, but that usually depends on the socialization they have had. Bitches are not as sexually territorial, but can be the stronger guarders.

Keeping a litter of puppies entertained isn't easy, but an inventive breeder can make the most of the space they do have by being creative with tunnels and things to climb on to keep puppies amused.

Puppies enjoying a walk and play in the garden.

The breeder producing Dobermanns for work or competition will monitor and character test the individual puppy, to identify which puppies have an aptitude and drive for work. They must then be sure to place them with a suitable owner, because no active working dog should have to end up where his wonderful mentality and spirit of character is wasted; it would be truly unfair to put that sort of dog in a dull environment.

If as a new owner you want to show your dog, obviously choose a breeder whose dogs have already had success in the ring, and visit shows to see dogs and meet breeders. Puppies are not selected for show purposes until they are around seven weeks, so if you are serious you must be prepared to wait. There is more information on the selection of puppies for exhibition in Chapter 11, Showing.

COLLECTING YOUR PUPPY

When the new owner collects their puppy from a breeder it will be accompanied by a puppy pack and documents, and these will vary between breeders. Some provide just a basic one-page feeding guide and the KC registration document, while others send off the puppy with a full folder of information on everything from feed-

These puppies are being highly entertained by the adult entire male in the home.

RESCUE AND RE-HOMED DOGS

Many lovely dogs turn up in rescue centres through no fault of their own. Specialist breed rescue organizations assess dogs that come into their care, and although the process may take a little while due to completing application and adoption forms, they are always careful to achieve a good match between new owner and dog.

Dobermanns are often found advertised on general sales websites or in the local papers. Buyers may be lucky to find a good one, but not all owners are honest about their reasons for re-homing their dog. Good breeders always take back dogs they have bred for re-homing.

For registered breed rescue organizations, see Further Information.

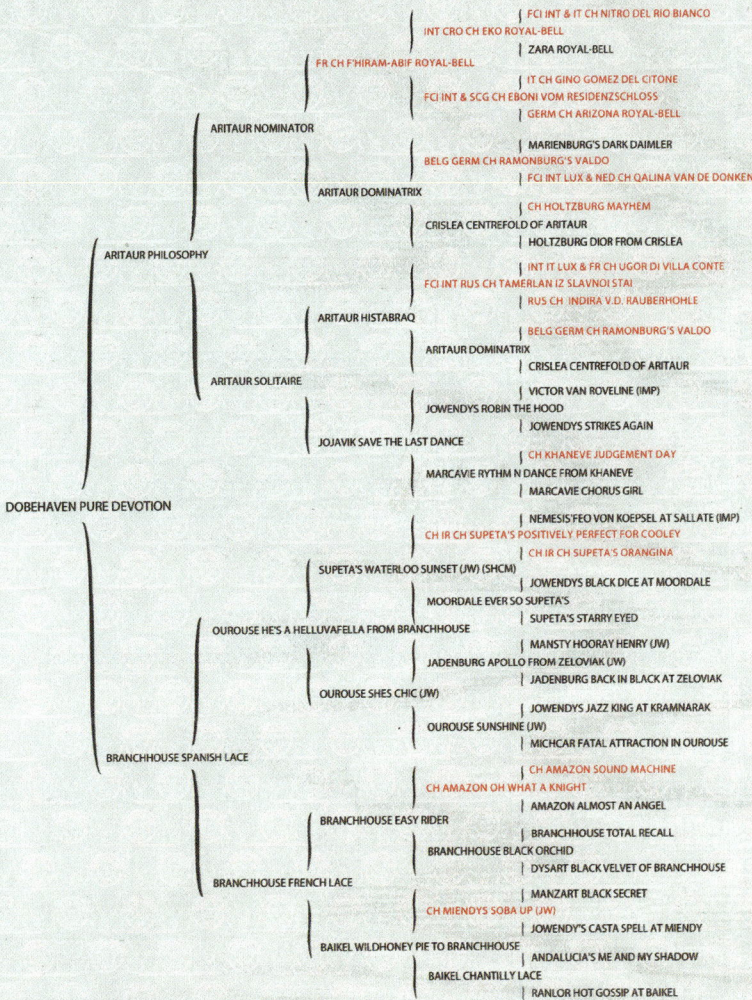

FIVE GENERATION ENHANCED PEDIGREE

DOBEHAVEN PURE DEVOTION

				FCI INT & IT CH NITRO DEL RIO BIANCO
			INT CRO CH EKO ROYAL-BELL	
		FR CH F'HIRAM-ABIF ROYAL-BELL		ZARA ROYAL-BELL
				IT CH GINO GOMEZ DEL CITONE
			FCI INT & SCG CH EBONI VOM RESIDENZSCHLOSS	
	ARITAUR NOMINATOR			GERM CH ARIZONA ROYAL-BELL
				MARIENBURG'S DARK DAIMLER
			BELG GERM CH RAMONBURG'S VALDO	
	ARITAUR DOMINATRIX			FCI INT LUX & NED CH QALINA VAN DE DONKEN
			CH HOLTZBURG MAYHEM	
		CRISLEA CENTREFOLD OF ARITAUR		
ARITAUR PHILOSOPHY			HOLTZBURG DIOR FROM CRISLEA	
				INT IT LUX & FR CH UGOR DI VILLA CONTE
			FCI INT RUS CH TAMERLAN IZ SLAVNOI STAI	
	ARITAUR HISTABRAQ			RUS CH INDIRA V.D. RAUBERHOHLE
			BELG GERM CH RAMONBURG'S VALDO	
	ARITAUR SOLITAIRE	ARITAUR DOMINATRIX		CRISLEA CENTREFOLD OF ARITAUR
				VICTOR VAN ROVELINE (IMP)
		JOWENDYS ROBIN THE HOOD		
	JOJAVIK SAVE THE LAST DANCE			JOWENDYS STRIKES AGAIN
			CH KHANEVE JUDGEMENT DAY	
		MARCAVIE RYTHM N DANCE FROM KHANEVE		
DOBEHAVEN PURE DEVOTION			MARCAVIE CHORUS GIRL	
				NEMESIS'FEO VON KOEPSEL AT SALLATE (IMP)
		CH IR CH SUPETA'S POSITIVELY PERFECT FOR COOLEY		CH IR CH SUPETA'S ORANGINA
	SUPETA'S WATERLOO SUNSET (JW) (SHCM)			JOWENDYS BLACK DICE AT MOORDALE
		MOORDALE EVER SO SUPETA'S		
OUROUSE HE'S A HELLUVAFELLA FROM BRANCHHOUSE			SUPETA'S STARRY EYED	
			MANSTY HOORAY HENRY (JW)	
		JADENBURG APOLLO FROM ZELOVIAK (JW)		
	OUROUSE SHES CHIC (JW)			JADENBURG BACK IN BLACK AT ZELOVIAK
			JOWENDYS JAZZ KING AT KRAMNARAK	
		OUROUSE SUNSHINE (JW)		
			MICHCAR FATAL ATTRACTION IN OUROUSE	
				CH AMAZON SOUND MACHINE
		CH AMAZON OH WHAT A KNIGHT		AMAZON ALMOST AN ANGEL
BRANCHHOUSE SPANISH LACE	BRANCHHOUSE EASY RIDER			BRANCHHOUSE TOTAL RECALL
		BRANCHHOUSE BLACK ORCHID		
	BRANCHHOUSE FRENCH LACE			DYSART BLACK VELVET OF BRANCHHOUSE
			MANZART BLACK SECRET	
		CH MIENDYS SOBA UP (JW)		
			JOWENDY'S CASTA SPELL AT MIENDY	
		BAIKEL WILDHONEY PIE TO BRANCHHOUSE		
			ANDALUCIA'S ME AND MY SHADOW	
		BAIKEL CHANTILLY LACE		
			RANLOR HOT GOSSIP AT BAIKEL	

Kennel Club Registration Number

Miss K Bullock

Breed
Dobermann
Colour
Black With Red Rust (tan)
Sex
Bitch
Date of Birth
7th April 2014
Breeder
Mrs J & Mr D Ryman
Owned by
Miss K Bullock

000052

I certify this pedigree has been compiled from official records. This is not an export document.

Signed by

C Kisko

Caroline Kisko
Secretary
Issue Date: 18th June 2014

THE KENNEL CLUB
Certificate

KC/REG/107A/02/14

Although the KC version is very smart, the breeder pedigree form may be more detailed as the KC does not include all overseas championship titles (for UK or overseas dogs).

OWNER REGISTRATION CERTIFICATE

THE KENNEL CLUB
Making a difference for dogs

CURRENT REGISTERED OWNER:

Miss K Bullock

...e, West Derby, Liverpool, ...

REGISTERED NAME:	DOBEHAVEN PURE DEVOTION (AR2)
PREVIOUSLY REGISTERED AS:	
TITLES:	
BREED:	Dobermann
DATE OF BIRTH:	07/04/2014
COLOUR:	Black With Red Rust (tan)
SEX:	Bitch
IMPORTED FROM:	
BREEDER:	Mrs J & Mr D Ryman
	Transferred on 02/06/2014 from Mrs J & Mr D Ryman

REGISTRATION NUMBER:	
STUD BOOK NUMBER:	
DNA PROFILE:	
MICROCHIP NUMBER:	977200008.
TATTOO NUMBER:	
ENDORSEMENTS:	R - Progeny Not Eligible For Registration
	X - Not Eligible For Issue of Export Pedigree
HEALTH SCREENING	
KC/BVA SCHEMES:	
DNA TESTS:	vWD Hereditarily Clear

SIRE:		**DAM:**	
REGISTERED NAME:	ARITAUR PHILOSOPHY (AK1)	REGISTERED NAME:	BRANCHHOUSE SPANISH LACE (AL3)
TITLES:		TITLES:	
REGISTRATION NUMBER:	A 0307 2	REGISTRATION NUMBER:	AL 67 05
STUD BOOK NUMBER:	22 CV	STUD BOOK NUMBER:	
HEALTH SCREENING		**HEALTH SCREENING**	
KC/BVA SCHEMES:	Hip: (13/05/2011) - 5/5	KC/BVA SCHEMES:	Hip: (09/08/2013) - 4/4, Eye: (13/06/2013) - UNAFFECTED by PHPV
DNA TESTS:	vWD Hereditarily Clear	DNA TESTS:	(08/07/2013) - vWD Clear

THE KENNEL CLUB LIMITED, REGISTERED IN ENGLAND AND WALES, REGISTERED NUMBER: 8217778, REGISTERED OFFICE: 1-5 CLARGES STREET, PICCADILLY, LONDON W1J 8AB

KC/104A/11/13

A Kennel Club registration document. The back of the KC registration form details how to transfer the registration into your own name.

ing to exercise requirements and training, a full pedigree (usually done by the breeder, but sometimes purchased from the KC), and four or five weeks free insurance. Food is usually supplied to avoid the puppy suffering a tummy upset from a sudden change of food, and first vaccinations are sometimes done, but not always. A comfort blanket is often included. From April 2016 it has been a legal requirement that all puppies are micro-chipped before leaving the breeder.

The KC requires the KC registration form and pedigree to be given to the new owner at the time of sale. If the breeder has registered their puppies by two or three weeks of age, the KC registration documents will usually be back in

time to accompany the puppies when they leave for their new homes. If there has been a delay for some reason, the breeder may send these on to you later. You can ring the Kennel Club to check if there is a litter registration pending. If the breeder tells you the KC papers will follow but you don't ever receive them, there is nothing the KC can do for you: it is not their responsibility to chase up a breeder on your behalf.

IMPORTING A DOBERMANN

Importing a Dobermann has become easier and more commonplace since the relaxation of quarantine with the Pet Passport scheme in 2000, and subsequently the UK docking ban of 2007. Prospective owners who have researched thoroughly and have gone to visit the breeder and the parent dogs will be able to see a litter of quality puppies raised in good conditions – but just as in the UK, many people buy directly over the internet, often to their downfall. Many of these kennels will sell to anyone for the asking with no questions asked: just wire the money, and 'shipping' will be arranged for an extra cost. If a breeder is prepared to sell their puppies to someone who can't be bothered to travel to see the parents, and doesn't ask any questions of the buyer, then they won't be taking much pride in their puppies.

As championship titles cannot be gained in most countries without the dog also having earned a working title, most European dogs have an aptitude for work. In view of this, you may well end up with more dog on your hands than you can manage, particularly if you do not plan to give your dogs an interesting life with plenty of mental activity. The websites and list of wins are often impressive (note that it is far easier to gain a European or US championship title than in the UK), and obviously thoroughly check out the parents and the health results.

Ear cropping is now banned in all parts of Europe except Hungary, and many have banned tail docking, so if you are importing a cropped and docked (c/d) Dobermann, it will usually have been bred in Hungary. Some of the Eastern European kennels are amongst the best breeders in the world, but there are a great number of backyard breeders who cash in on the demand for c/d dogs.

For any good breeder, anywhere in the world, you should expect to have to work hard for a good puppy, and must earn the respect and trust of the breeder if you wish to have one. There will always be a waiting list for a quality litter.

5 BRINGING YOUR NEW PUPPY HOME AND THE FIRST YEAR

The first year of puppy ownership is obviously fundamental to forming his behaviour and turning him into a dog to be proud of. It is about education and socialization, not exercise, and will be a busy one, in which you will be providing him with all the skills and experiences he needs. If you know you have a busy year coming up and will have to fit in puppy education between other commitments, postpone buying a puppy until you do have time for him, or you won't have the beautifully behaved dog you hoped for.

The TV celebrity dog trainers, online training videos and various books seemingly make it much easier to having a perfect dog. However, although you can gain some great ideas on training your dog from books, they are each just the author's personal opinion, and none will teach you the actual 'hands on' of dog ownership. Furthermore the Dobermann is a particularly intuitive breed, quickly sensing strength or weakness in a person. If the clever puppy realizes you need a book to tell you what to do, how can he respect

From five weeks of age, the good breeder's home provides physical space for puppies to run around freely with plenty of entertainment.

you? For the owner of a passive breed that may not be such an issue, but for a bold breed it is a big problem.

Prepare for ownership by spending time with a breeder and their dogs. Join them for walks, or offer to help out at the local rescue kennels in return for them teaching you how to work around dogs. Visit a training class and ask if they can help teach you some basics before you get your own dog. A good breeder should provide support for you if you encounter any problems. If they can't help you directly, maybe due to distance, they will have a network of contacts you can call on for help if needed.

Don't set yourself or the puppy unreasonable expectations. Just like having a newborn baby, a demanding puppy can be a shock to the system, and with problems such as lead pulling, nipping, chewing, jumping up and house-training accidents to deal with, the whole experience can turn into a bit of a nightmare, even though it won't last forever. However, it is no coincidence that the most common time for young Dobermanns (usually males) to be given up for re-homing is at around ten to eighteen months, when they are at their most difficult.

On the plus side, there is the fun of teaching puppy the exciting things in life, watching him play with other pups, his first trip to the school to collect the children, and learning his first few commands. Don't be afraid to persevere, put the work in, and eventually you will have the excellent dog you can be proud of by your side.

STAGES OF DEVELOPMENT

Understanding a puppy's stages of development in the first months of his first year will prepare you for some of his perhaps more perplexing behaviours.

The Imprinting Period

The first four months (sixteen weeks) of a puppy's life are known as the 'imprinting period', and puppies absorb more during this time than they can learn in a lifetime. The puppy that encounters bad experiences in the imprinting stage carries fears for life. Therefore never let him meet antisocial, bullying or snappy dogs, or he will always fear other dogs. Make all experiences – car journeys, outings to town, interactions with other animals and people – very easy going.

The first few weeks of the puppy's life are known as the 'first socialization period'; during this time, gentle care from his dam and breeder shape his future behaviour. The second socialization period begins from seven weeks. Although puppies usually leave the breeder from eight weeks of age, confident young males that are already guarding and squabbling may benefit from going to their new homes a few days earlier.

Socialization is not just about meeting other dogs, and a puppy is not 'socialized' just because he plays with the other dogs at home or goes training once a week. He needs to accept new situations in various environments with confidence. Dogs who spend their lives out and about with their owners, whether on the farm, the office, or as a travelling companion, never need to see a dog 'behaviourist' because they are too busy to become neurotic. Waiting until after the puppy is twelve weeks old, or until he has had all his puppy vaccinations, is far too late to take advantage of the socialization window. You may not have exposed him to any risk of infection, but an under-socialized dog is a burden for life.

Avoid the local park where unvaccinated dogs toilet, but carry the puppy to visit schools at leaving time, sit on the bench in town, visit the local stables so he can get used to horses in the yard, watch sheep and cows in the field, and find a dog-friendly pub (take a comfy rug so puppy learns to lie down quietly next to you). A papoose or baby carrier is perfect for carrying him around in.

At 7 weeks: Start imprinting 'basic training' – sit, down, stand, lie down, roll over, crawl, back up, wait and so on. We start these routines with our puppies at seven weeks and repeat them twice daily as the puppy is highly receptive to new skills at this age, and muscle memory of positions will always be remembered, especially if reinforced with clicker training and treats. Maintain the

Quality puppies ready for their new homes.

recall programming (*see* Chapter 5, on working and training) at each mealtime.

At 8–9 weeks: Let him get used to the home and garden for the first few days after you have brought him home. Let him meet the family and the neighbour's cat and other pets, and other calm visitors. He could be taken on short car journeys, though keep him on your lap for the moment.

At 10–12 weeks: Puppy can now travel in his own crate; use plenty of bedding so he doesn't roll

around and feel sick. Visit the vet for some treats from the staff so he learns it is a good place. Get him used to being examined – teeth, ears, feet and so on – both at the vet and by you. Visit friends with kind dogs and children; maybe leave puppy there for a few hours of playtime. Owners sometimes ask if it is safe to take the puppy to someone else's home, but why shouldn't it be? He could have gone to live at their home rather than yours.

At 12–14 weeks: With his vaccination course complete, puppy can now walk safely on the ground, though areas at high risk of possible infection should still be avoided. Ask the vet if there have been any recent outbreaks of parvo virus or kennel cough in the area. Invite nice dogs and children to your home for a puppy party. Drop down to three meals daily, and take his lunch out with you to feed him when you visit friends or go to the pub. (Note that he should not be exercised after meals.)

15 weeks onwards: Puppy can start to cope with noisier places such as the local market and the town centre. Carry him often to save his joints. Continue inviting visitors and their nice dogs to your home. Sit near livestock in the fields watching them grazing, or even better, find a local farmer who will let you visit his farm with the puppy. Visit the local stables to watch horses in the yard and being ridden round the school. Start training the basics (sit, stay, down) in different environments under light distraction (*see* Chapter 5, Working and Training). Use your imagination for training games.

The Post Imprinting Period

5 months plus: If you plan to put your puppy in boarding kennels at any time, put him there for half a day or overnight so he gets used to the sights and sounds. Once he is six months old move on to feeding twice daily, as this may make him keener to work for food rewards between meals. Increase his training repertoire, and maintain recall programming.

Off-lead socialization and natural interaction with other dogs is essential to a happy puppyhood. In group play like this, it is important to remind the pushy puppy to calm down a bit, and ensure that the shy puppy isn't overwhelmed. Call all the puppies back in occasionally to their owners for a treat, and so they can sit, wait and re-release.

Owner Nicky introducing Aggro to a steady donkey. Let your puppy meet steady animals before progressing to flight animals such as sheep.

Always keep training fun: teach puppy the rules and boundaries, and that good things happen when they are respected. There is no place for harsh or corrective handling, especially with a puppy who is still learning. Dogs who are well occupied have nothing to rebel against – bear in mind the old adage 'the Devil makes work for idle minds'.

6 months to a year: This is a difficult time for dogs (and their owners): puppy is now an adolescent and can be as trying as a hormonal teenager. The male's testosterone levels are surging, and he is starting to cut the apron strings to test what he might get away with. A raised eyebrow with an 'I don't think so!' expression usually corrects minor transgressions, but be quick to correct him if he really over-pushes things – and be sure to praise him when he stops. He may start chewing on household objects again, pulling on the lead when he has always walked perfectly to heel, and he may become a bit of a thug with other dogs in the park.

This also often coincides with a stage when owners feel they no longer need to go to training class. However, if you are not teaching him anything new or taking him to fresh environments, he will be deeply frustrated and desperate for activity.

Teething: External signs of teething are 'flying ears' and flat feet (*see* Chapter 9, General Health

Puppies have to chew on something. Old shoes (minus laces) will hopefully keep him away from your new ones. If he chews your best shoes, reprimand yourself for leaving them lying around!

and Welfare). Puppies are fractious and destructive when they are teething heavily. Give him something he is allowed to chew on: a cold carrot will ease sore gums, and lamb ribs or a 'recreational' knucklebone will keep him occupied for ages. Play a thinking training game, or give him a soothing massage to calm him down.

Fear Phases

Neophobia is the fear of new things, and fear phases are a normal stage in the puppy's development in learning how to avoid dangerous situations. Terrors can appear out of the blue, and the puppy that has calmly walked past a rattling gate for weeks can suddenly jump when it bangs one day. Other puppies may go through longer phases where everything is a perceived threat. They can be humble, extra snappy, won't leave their owner's side, and are scared of pretty much everything except in their own safe little world.

Frightening or painful experiences have a more lasting impact if they occur during fear phases, so don't push your puppy to experience new things at these times.

The first fear phase starts from around five weeks, peaking between eight and eleven weeks. The second phase usually occurs from five to six months onwards to a year, and perhaps another at around fourteen months. These phases are not specific to points of time.

Distance is the dog's friend: he can stand back from a situation so as to assess it more calmly, and can weigh up his response to something potentially frightening without feeling the need to run. Don't mollycoddle him, but take extra care not to put him in stressful situations. Never let anyone tell you that it's only natural for their big dog to push your puppy around: he will feel he can never trust you if you allow him to be bullied. Shield him from the over-enthusiastic stranger who rushes at him shrieking, or who plays rough

This puppy is watching the donkey in the yard from a safe distance. Townie pups can benefit from a trip to the countryside, and the country pup should see crowds and traffic.

IN SUMMARY

- Whether or not the danger is real, give him distance until he can better cope with it
- Don't overwhelm him with other dogs or loud noises. He is too young to face all the 'threats' at once
- Take a shy puppy out to a quiet pleasant place so he can learn things in his own time
- Avoid eye contact when he is fearful or hiding behind your legs as it reinforces the fear. Gently ask him for a 'check in' eye contact when he is over his fear, and he can have a treat for calmness
- Fill his mind with positive thoughts, and never leave him to face a potentially frightening or over-bearing situation alone

with him: ask them to back off and wait for the puppy to approach them, but never force or coax the puppy to them. Let him work things out himself, and don't feel you have to be polite; your puppy is more important than worrying about offending people.

If the puppy is nervous and starts to run away from or back off something, kneel down next to him with a steady hand on his side and wait for him to relax. *Don't* make eye contact or talk to him to reassure him – just like a child hiding behind mummy's skirts, baby talk reinforces fear. Once he realizes that nothing awful is going to happen, he may start being curious of the thing that frightened him. Tell him he's a good pup, and carry on with your walk.

BRINGING YOUR PUPPY HOME

Crates and their Use

Crates and cages can be very useful when used correctly, such as for overnight sleeping and for security if you are out, but shutting your puppy or dog in one when you are at home can cause him to feel great frustration. Imagine being caged yourself when you are wide awake.

Don't use a crate to try and calm a puppy down: caging a puppy that is having a mad five minutes is going to have the opposite effect, as he will view it as a trap and will hate it for ever. When a puppy gets frantic in his cage, the old school of thought is to leave him to it to exhaust himself – but just as we wouldn't leave a tiny baby to work itself into a frenzy, the puppy should be released long before he even starts to panic. He should see the crate as a place of comfort rather than a trap.

If you use a cage to stop a puppy jumping up at visitors, he will never learn any self-control or manners.

Puppy must be able to turn round in the crate that he is to sleep in, but don't buy one so big that he can avoid his bedding to wee or poo if he needs to go in the night. Dobermann puppies are usually very clean and will not want to soil their bedding unless they are really desperate, so will learn to 'hold on'.

On the first night in his new home a puppy is often exhausted from a long day travelling and all the new experiences, so this is a good time to get him used to the crate for bedtime. A crate used for puppy to sleep in is ideal for overnight house training, as it can be put next to your bed for the first week or two, then moved downstairs once puppy is settled in his new home. Dobes like to snuggle into bedding rather than just lie on top of it, so make it really comfortable with a thick piece of vetbed on the base, a snug single duvet and a soft blanket. Last thing at night when he is already sleepy and has had a wee, carry him upstairs – don't let puppies walk up and down stairs as their joints are not yet fully formed – and place him gently in it.

Some feel that the puppy must get used to being downstairs on his own, and that if he starts sleeping in the bedroom it will be difficult to move him later. Strangely we don't hear the same about a new baby sleeping in the parents' bedroom. Move him downstairs after a week or two, by which time he will at least have settled down and will be feeling more secure in his new home.

If you crate him when you go out, give him a recreational bone to keep him occupied.

A standard 'medium' dog crate is 29.5in long by 18in wide and 20.5in high. It will be a bit big for him to start with, but should last him until he is four or five months old. After that you don't need a crate – and if you do, something is going wrong.

Toys

Toys don't have to be expensive, and sometimes a regular supply of big cardboard boxes filled with empty plastic bottles and balls, or others made into a mini assault course of tunnels and caves, are the best fun. Huge soft teddy bears (charity shops are full of them) are always welcome. Anything that makes a noise is particularly fun for puppies, and empty plastic bottles make great rattles – though watch that he doesn't destroy them and eat bits of plastic.

There are very few really indestructible toys for Dobes, and even the hardest rubber toys on the market have been found in bits in a dog's stomach. A juicy raw bone fresh from the butchers is a natural treat which satisfies the primal need for the dog to chew and exercise the jaw.

Don't buy toys made of latex – very flimsy rubber – as they will be eaten in minutes. If you give rope toys, remove them when the bits of rope start to fray as they compact into a ball of material in the gut, or come off as long strands which can cause blockages. Felt-covered tennis balls are fine, but remove them when they start to be destroyed. We use the tough rubber 'pimple'-covered balls on ropes, and big socks knotted inside other socks as they are a lot cheaper than shop-bought tug toys. Beware of anything that frays.

Puppies can't differentiate between the toy you bought them from the store and the shoe you left on the floor, so unless you catch them with it in their mouth, you have only yourself to blame for not having put your precious things out of reach, however infuriating it is. If the puppy starts chewing on furniture, don't leave him unsupervised in that room, and keep him occupied with mind games. And if he has made a mess out of something unimportant, ignore it, as it really isn't worth making a fuss about in the greater scheme of things.

EARLY TRAINING

House Training

Dobermanns are generally clean dogs and usually try to go outside if possible, but just like a baby, they will sometimes forget to hold themselves. As soon as you arrive home, put your new puppy outside so he understands where to wee and poo. He has never had to hold his bladder before now, so even if the door is open, take him out every hour to remind him to wee. Set an alarm if necessary. After a while with no accidents, gradually lengthen the duration between trips outside.

As soon as pup comes home with a full bladder from a long journey, take him straight out to do his business where you want him to go, and praise him with a particular command word such as 'do your business' or 'be quick'. Use the command word every time he pees, and he will soon realize what is wanted of him. Wait until he is

actually peeing, and repeat the phrase continually.

If he keeps peeing inside, restrict access to the place where he has previously weed, and clean it thoroughly, using antibacterial spray to leave no residual smell, which attracts him back to the place.

Overnight house training is easy with puppy in a crate by your bedside, as you can quickly get him out and downstairs, pop him out to do his business, and then straight back to bed. If you house train him in this way it usually takes just a couple of nights for him to go straight through till morning. If he is downstairs or shut away in a separate room you won't hear him so quickly, and by the time you reach him he will be either frantic to get out of his crate, or has already messed.

Dobermanns hate the rain, and if you put the pup outside on his own when it is raining he will not do anything, but will just cry to come back in. Go outside with him somewhere under cover, such as a garage or shed, but if it is really lashing down, put a towel down at the back door for him to go on.

Don't make a big issue of a small accident. Dogs forget what they did just a moment before, so pointing to the offending area after the event and telling him off will mean nothing to him, except he will worry that you are cross for some reason. He will then try to offer you an appeasement gesture, such as looking humble, in the hope that you will calm down. No, he doesn't know why you are angry, and he is not 'ashamed of himself': he needed a wee, and just like a baby, he hasn't quite learned to hold it yet. You weren't looking, so reprimand yourself, clean up and do better next time!

One of the wickedest things that an owner can do to a puppy that has pooed in the house is to rub his nose in his mess as punishment. It is difficult to imagine that anyone would think this would be at all educational, or that it is ever a decent way to treat a dog.

During teething and the second fear phase, puppies often forget their house training. Be careful how you behave at this stage, as brandishing a newspaper and chasing him out of the room would really frighten a puppy in fear phase.

As before, there is no point in reprimanding him unless you see him do it. Go back to basics as above. (The exception is with young males cocking their leg in the home, *see below*.)

Teaching Self-Control

A puppy with self-control means that you don't have to force him to sit, or hold him to stay, or haul back on his lead, because he respects what you want of him. The puppy that has self-control will sit patiently to have his collar and lead put on and off, so there is no need to reach out and grab him.

Self-control must be learned both indoors and out – for instance, he must learn not to charge through doors like a hooligan. Use your calm friends as training stooges: give them some treats and ask them to get him to sit before they reward him; or teach him to give his paw to people when he meets them, which is always a winner. This doesn't just teach him to sit, it also teaches him that if he is calm around humans he gets a reward.

Youngsters can become very disrespectful, deliberately barging past anyone in their way. A 40kg dog running at a child or old person at full speed can knock them off their feet, so you must teach puppy that the house is not a racetrack, and to be respectful of others, for example by teaching him to walk steadily through doorways (for a treat). Use a quick finger snap to teach him to pause just long enough for you to go through first, then invite him to follow you; this is better than going for a long controlled stop.

A puppy learning self-control from her grandmother. Older bitches love to nurture and discipline young puppies, and are the very best teacher for a pup.

Similarly a dog that jumps up on his owner has no respect for humans because his owner did not train him to show respect – so he will jump on strangers in the park. Jumping up is attention seeking from a dog that hasn't been taught that sitting gets him a better reward. As with any undesired behaviour, the owner can either ignore it and reward the positive, or work through it (*see* Chapter 5 for various training methods).

And if he barks constantly, teach him to bark on command. In both of these situations the pup must learn self-control.

'Time out' is often used by parents whose children have been bad, when they are made to sit on the proverbial naughty step until they have learned their lesson. The equivalent for a dog is to be ostracized from pack membership until he behaves properly. He should lie relaxed, because if you keep him on tenterhooks for the release, he will burst off from his sit point. Don't use a crate or close the door on him, as forced separation teaches nothing.

The 'invisible line' is a good way to teach the puppy to stay away from areas where you don't want him, such as the cooking area or dining table. You draw an invisible line that he must not cross, and each time he approaches it, click your fingers at him and flick your hand to make him step back. At first he will, of course, walk through it, but he will soon learn not to cross it and to lie behind it (a mat or bed there provides a good marker point). You must remember to give him calm praise when he does it right.

The invisible line is also used for sitting back from the door when the bell rings, for not jumping out of the car when the boot opens, and for not going past the garden gate.

Positive Training

As your puppy's teacher, teach him positively by not saying 'no' all the time. Dogs are constantly told not to do this and not to do that, but are rarely told 'yes, clever dog, good job'. You will be amazed at the difference it makes for a dog that is so used to hearing what a bad, naughty dog he is, suddenly to hear 'Yes, what a good boy!' and see you smiling. Plan interesting things to teach him, then you won't need to keep reprimanding him because he's bored. Don't play hard games, but teach 'thinking' and activity games; these range from simply throwing toys for him to retrieve, to hiding food or toys for him to find, to get his nose working.

Nipping and Biting

Puppies learn 'bite tolerance' – that biting hurts – from their siblings and dam, and they instinctively know which dogs and humans not to mess with. Owners who complain that puppy keeps biting them or the children, and who display wounded arms, can only blame themselves for allowing it. When they are told to reprimand the dog, they meekly reply 'but I don't want to hurt him'. Allowing your puppy to bite you means that he will grow up disrespecting humans. Stop it now, and if it hurts him when he bites you, he will learn not to do it.

If you snatch your hand away with a loud yelp, the puppy will realize he has the power to make you move and cry, and will do it again. Keep your hand still at your side and hiss under your breath 'don't you even think about it!' When he looks up to see how serious you really are and releases, acknowledge he stopped, and praise him. Divert him on to some training, a toy or chew.

IN SUMMARY

- Ask him to 'check in' with you by giving you eye contact, and give him a small smile of approval before going through doors or sitting for a reward
- Aim to get the dog achieving something, however small, which allows you to praise him
- Don't wait for the puppy to be bored before giving him attention. Take time out to initiate play

IN SUMMARY

- It is not advisable to let a puppy chew on your fingers, so don't leave your finger idly in his mouth as a teething tool. He won't understand why it was all right at nine weeks but not at nine months
- Very few puppies are born 'dominant' or 'stubborn'. Cheeky or bored puppies try it on to get a reaction
- Stop misbehaviours before they become established. Divert the puppy's attention to training so you can reward him for good behaviour

If he doesn't stop, keep your hand there but make him remove his mouth from your hand by making it really uncomfortable for him, by squeezing his tongue or lips. If this sounds terrible, understand that if you don't stop this behaviour in its tracks, he will become bolder and he will hurt someone properly in future because you let him get away with biting.

The correction level depends on the age of the puppy and how hard he bites. But no matter how much it hurts you, if he nips never smack or even tap either a puppy or a dog across the face or nose, because you will make him head shy. And there is a very big difference between giving a quick physical correction, as any other animal parent does to a naughty youngster, and resorting to physical violence out of temper.

Not all mouth contact is intended badly, and some dogs like to hold their human's hand or arm in their mouth affectionately to lead them somewhere. One of our bitches loved to do this, and she was the least dominant dog imaginable. She had a very soft mouth and always carried things around, but she never nipped.

EARLY SOCIALIZATION

Introducing Other Pets

Other pets should be introduced to the puppy soon after his arrival, and he must learn right from the first moment that he is not allowed to approach them, but must wait for them to approach him. Sit on the sofa or floor with puppy on your lap, and place the cat or other pet alongside. The cat can approach the dog, but not the

other way. If you do this on the first evening when the puppy is still new to the house, the pup will be quieter as he is still taking in his surroundings. He is allowed to look on curiously and sniff, but may *not* stare. A click of the fingers with a gentle 'no' should get the message through. However, it is equally important that the cat respects the dog. Do not allow the cat to smack the puppy if the pup has done nothing wrong.

Never allow the new puppy to chase the cat, in the belief that this will 'get it out of his system'. All it will do is terrify the cat and teach it to run from the dog every time they see each other, and you will never stop the dog from chasing it. It is a truly unkind thing to do to a cat.

Play-fighting

Dobermanns are always quite noisy when they play, with loud, blood-curdling snarling and snapping mouths. However, watch to see that both dogs are playing, and that it isn't becoming one-sided: if they are tense and are putting their head over each other's back, or standing on their hind legs boxing, then one is trying to dominate the other, and play-fight is becoming fight.

Puppies must be allowed to play naturally together, but be sure that your puppy rolling on his back and chasing his playmate with teeth snapping isn't actually feeling overpowered and is trying to back the other dog off. Intervene to curtail heavy play before your puppy feels bullied, or vice versa, giving both a chance to back down without losing face. Otherwise the puppy will feel either victimized or victorious, neither of which is a positive state.

There is nothing funny or clever about encouraging your puppy or dog to chase cats and other animals when you are out. Owners who do that will regret it when their dog chases a cat on to the road and is run over.
ALEX LOCKE

Playfighting or bullying?

This x-ray image of a two-week-old puppy clearly shows how much further the bones have to grow to join up with each other. Even three-month-old puppies should have only small amounts of steady exercise for no more than fifteen minutes twice daily.

PUPPY EXERCISE AND MENTAL STIMULATION

Up to ten weeks of age, puppies get quite enough exercise running around the house and garden. It is heartbreaking to see tiny puppies being walked far more than their little legs can take, but they keep going despite them hurting because they don't want to be left behind. No one would ever walk a human infant for miles. Although puppy may seem keen, he should be occupied with more socialization and teaching games than exercise to tire him out. His physical exercise routine might be as follows:

At twelve weeks: 5–10 minutes slow road walking with 5 minutes in the park, plus plenty of socialization.

Up to sixteen weeks: A maximum of 20 minutes' walk daily on the lead, with 5–10 minutes free running.

From six months onwards: Gradually increase road walking to 45 minutes or so a day, and then up to an hour and a half at a year old.

At around five to six months: Minimize free running as puppies are teething heavily.

(*See* Chapter 10, General Health and Welfare Part 2.)

At eight months: The adolescent dog needs physical and mental freedom, so start increasing the difficulty of the brain-training games. (*See* Chapter 5, Training, for ideas.)

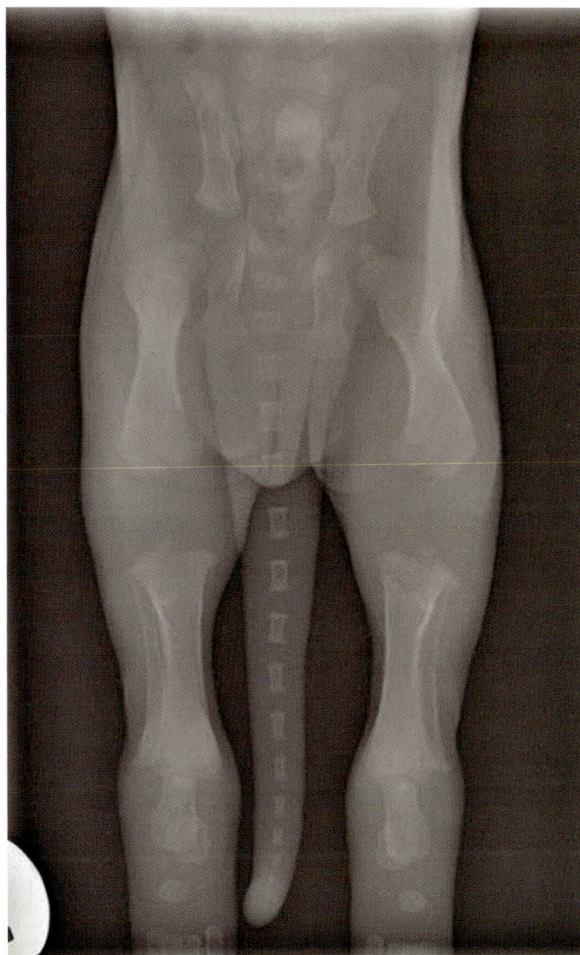

Note that exercise will not satisfy the energetic dog: it will make him worse. (See Chapter 7, Conditioning and Exercise.)

Jumping is the main cause of spiral fractures in puppies, and too much walking and bouncing before their bones are fully formed – at around eighteen months – can damage unformed joints. Stair gates are essential, and if your puppy likes to come up on the sofa with you, lift him on and off, and put a duvet on the floor in front of the sofa so he doesn't crash land. Once puppy is eight or nine months old he can do a lot more.

If you want to do a long walk with your puppy, put him in a baby sling or carry him most of the way.

A six-month-old puppy being brave.

Off-Lead Freedom

The freedom to run around off the lead is essential for the puppy as early as possible, or he will feel captive and will be desperate to break free from you. From your first trip out, let him off the lead in a safe place. At this age puppies know they are too young to look after themselves and will always follow their leader, so you can take advantage of this from the outset.

If you are nervous about losing your dog, go out with a friend and an older, well trained dog that is reliable on recall, and which will teach the young pup how to behave. We let our eight-week-olds toddle around outside under the supervision of the adults, and this results in them not feeling the urge to escape as they don't get frustrated, and don't see the door/gate as somewhere to bolt through. Even if they wanted to run away, they are too small to outrun their humans.

By using the recall programming (*see* Chapter 5, Training) he has his embedded response to return in an emergency. Let your puppy grow a little bit without you. It is all about choices, and he will choose to return to you rather than being made to. Just as with children, you have to loosen the apron strings.

Lead Training

From eight or nine weeks of age, clip a very light (cat weight) collar and lead on the puppy and let him walk around the house and garden for a little while to get used to the feeling of it. If you go out in the garden with his lead on, he won't understand how he can't go to the places he normally goes to, and that's when you get lead resistance. If you know of a clean area not used by other dogs take him out for a little lead training.

Ask him to come with you by your voice. Don't allow him to pull to go forwards, because he soon learns that if he heaves hard enough it will get him where he wants to go. When he pulls, stop and attract his attention by a little treat or a gentle stroke and ask him to come back again.

When you are out with your young male, don't let him pee up every post. He doesn't need to pee – watch the trickle coming out and you can see he doesn't have a full bladder. This is territory marking, and by pulling you to the place where he wants to pee, he expects you to follow him. Instead, take him to a particular tree or area of your choosing, and ask him to 'do your business' or whatever phrase you use. Dog must follow human, not the other way around.

It's not what you use, but how you use it. Dogs can lean and pull against a harness just as much as a solid collar. Use them as a safety line, never to pull him around.

MANAGING EARLY BEHAVIOURS

Puppy Separation Anxiety

In the early days, and even later, a puppy or young dog may suffer separation anxiety, and this can develop into a real problem: his mental state may approach near hysteria, manifested in non-stop howling, pee and poo everywhere, the destruction of furniture, and trying to escape from his crate. It is awful for the dog, his owner and the neighbours.

However, a puppy on his own will naturally cry and whine when he is left, even when you just walk out of the room for a couple of minutes, and this doesn't mean that he is suffering from separation anxiety. A wild-born wolf puppy would feel very vulnerable when separated from the pack, and if he is not near his den when he is alone, will cry for rescue and safety. This evolutionary safety response is no different in domesticated dogs or most other young creatures.

Dogs are pack animals, and few more so than the Dobermann, whose main purpose in life is to bond with and protect his owner and family. It therefore makes absolutely no sense to break this bond the moment the puppy comes home by leaving him on his own to miserably sob himself to sleep for a few nights. Just as a baby wants to be close to his parent, the puppy has only ever known the comfort of his mother and siblings, and being separated from them is hugely unsettling for him and a great deal for him to cope with anyway, without being put into forced isolation. The distress felt by a domestic puppy is no different to that of a wild dog puppy which fears he has been separated from safety and is isolated and alone.

Moreover, as the first fear phase begins at around eight to eleven weeks, putting a puppy through the terrors of abandonment at this age is contrary to everything we know about puppy development. The wicked person who thought up the theory that puppies have to endure such an awful introduction to their new home at this most vulnerable age is probably responsible for having caused separation anxiety for generations of dogs and their families.

Like any young creature, puppies become independent over time. The human infant starts to toddle off to explore, and young kittens go exploring, but they do this from a secure foundation when they feel ready, without being rushed by enforced separation, and certainly not when they are tiny babies. There is no benefit in rushing this initial stage, and with the right introduction to your home you can avoid the situation developing into a full-blown issue. Most separation problems come about because puppy panics without his parent. He will initially follow you like a shadow, because you are his parent and he is out of his comfort zone. Don't feel you have to push this point: after a couple of days he will have started to settle in and will feel less panicky about you being out of his sight.

Nevertheless, even though you may think it is very sweet to let him follow you everywhere, for his own benefit it is important that you teach him to be alone for just a little while, knowing you will return. Later on you may have to leave him for some reason, and he must learn not to panic.

As he settles into the house and gets used to you walking around, leave the room, shut the door for literally two seconds, not giving him the time to build up any panic, then walk back in and straight past him. If you return to a screaming puppy and make a fuss of him, he will know next time to scream to get you to return, so when you do go back in the room, just go past him without giving him any attention. Turn on the TV or make a cup of tea, and only when he is calm and settled give him some gentle praise. After some time of this, you can leave the house in the same way:

shut the door and then open it again, all without fuss. Save a fresh bone for when you leave the room because he will be concentrating on that so much he won't notice you've gone before you're back.

It is good practice to teach the puppy 'sit stay' whilst you do this: walk initially a step away from him, and eventually go out of the room and around the corner whilst still calling sit stay. Give him a small food reward on your return. This teaches both obedience and self-control through play, so he thinks it's all a good game. Use different rooms for the exercise, including the room he is to be left in. Once he is relaxed about you being out of the room and knows you will always come back, shut the room or crate door, count to five, and return. The greeting on return should be a simple 'well done' and a smile, not over-enthusiastic cheering.

If you are going to use a crate, gradually build up the closed door/crate time: leave puppy for five minutes one day, leading up slowly to one hour a day, then up to two to three hours if necessary. That is the maximum time a puppy should be left alone anyway, due to his feeding requirements. After their morning meal, puppies usually play for a shorter time than in the afternoon, so if you have to make a choice of when during the day to leave him, make it the morning.

It is not a good idea to take two weeks off work to settle puppy in, then suddenly return to work: this would be really unsettling for a puppy who has been used to constant company. Puppies don't really need you at home when they are tiny, as they sleep a lot, but from five months onwards they are more in need of company and mental stimulation. No dog should be left alone all day.

When you plan to go out and leave the puppy, ignore him for some time prior to leaving. Dogs who have had attention such as playing or cuddling with their owner directly before being left, often find the separation a bigger issue than if they have been left alone in the house before the owner ups and leaves.

Resolving separation issues takes a long time, but take it slowly, and be careful not to push the time you spend out of sight too quickly or the dog will come to seek you out, and then you will have to start this process all over again.

The Male Puppy

The owner of a male puppy must be aware of the youngster producing testosterone, and must realize that play isn't always innocent, but a way of assessing the strength of an opponent. What seems to be play-fighting can tip into a serious fight in a fraction of a second, so never allow stand-up boxing. A first squabble usually ends quickly, but won't be forgotten.

Whilst it is quite possible for well socialized males to be happy in the company of other males, it is not that common in the Dobermann. Males rarely fight with bitches, but if they fight with other males it is never a quick spat – it's generally a very nasty fight with the intention to wound or kill. Furthermore, if you failed to defend your puppy when he couldn't protect himself against a bigger, aggressive dog, don't be surprised if he becomes dog aggressive or fearful as an adult: you weren't there for him when he needed you, so he doesn't need you in the future.

Keep in your mind that a Dobermann is your guard, and as he grows older, other dogs coming into your vicinity may be seen as a threat. Learn to read both your dog and the other dog, and if it feels as if things are getting out of hand, both owners should walk away in the opposite direction.

No matter how much you tell some owners not to play rough with their puppy, it seems they can't help themselves, and play tough power games with the puppy who jumps on them and rags their clothes (interestingly women rarely, if ever, play such games). Advising people not to do this isn't about being a spoil-sport, and no one would dream of not playing with a dog, but think about what you are teaching him: when he is fully grown with big teeth he won't understand why he can't tear at your clothes and jump all over you and other people. It stops being as funny when a big Dobe is roughhousing the human. Playing a gentle tug of war is fine as long as it's not done aggressively (watch baby teeth), but avoid physical plays of strength. Dogs that jump on people in the home are always the ones

This dog sits calmly assessing his environment. A penetrating stare from the dark eyes of the Dobermann is usually a sufficient deterrent for most criminals.

that jump on people in the park. If the dog is disrespectful to his owners, he will be disrespectful to all humans.

Occasionally young males will cock their legs in the home or, even worse, on someone's leg! This is because he is trying to make his mark on both his territory and on the human, and it is behaviour that needs to be stopped very quickly. As with all behaviours, pointing to the offending mark and shouting will only result in confusion for the dog, which really has no idea why you are so angry. However, if you do catch him in the act, a loud shout, a smack on the backside and chasing him out of the room gets the point across. *Note that this is absolutely not to be done with a young puppy, where shouting would be terrifying* – but the 'teenage' male needs to know he just got unlucky!

Guarding

Guarding can start to occur at any age, but the confident puppy may first bark on alert from hearing something by the time he is around five to six months old. At first it may be amusing to see your puppy barking for the first time, but he should not be allowed to become an 'over-guarder' – the dog who barks insanely at the windows of their car or home at anyone walking past. Such behaviour is neurotic, because the dog is not differentiating between a real or a perceived threat. An owner might like to have a vicious-looking Dobermann barking like crazy, but most criminals know that these dogs would probably immediately back off and run if they were approached. The criminal is much more wary of the dog that sits quietly, carefully watching their every move: they know that these dogs are the thinkers who consider and assess a real threat, and who will usually follow through with any action if needed.

When the puppy charges up and down the fence line, it may impress the owner, but hearing the dog endlessly barking all day at people innocently walking by will eventually become very tiresome for all within earshot. Rather than just standing watching him bark – which conveys permission to carry on – or trying to suppress his barking – don't buy a guarding breed and expect it not to guard – stand with him by the gate and show him that you have things under control. Think ahead to what you are planning to teach him, and guide him to react to threats rationally and sensibly. Teach him to bark on command (*see* the training advice in Chapter 5).

Finding a Good Club

A training club is not about socialization – you should have been doing that already – but it should help you learn how to train your puppy under distraction. Extraordinarily some owners say that they didn't start any training with their puppy because 'the local training classes were fully booked and they were waiting for a space'! Imagine a parent not teaching anything to their child before pre-school and then expecting it to suddenly become 'socialized and trained', as if by magic!

Good clubs are run by generous people who really care about dogs, and who offer a stimulating range of entertaining training in a fun environment. Other, not so good clubs are run by perhaps more old-fashioned people who belittle owners and bore dogs with unimaginative routine exercises. Young, mentally active dogs rapidly tire of the routines and the oppressive atmosphere, and will start to play up from boredom and frustration – so if you don't enjoy the atmosphere and your dog is starting to play up, leave quickly and socialize with good, calm dogs on a one-to-one basis.

Never be afraid or embarrassed to walk straight out of a class if the club trainer does something that is obviously unpleasant to your dog, or if you are not enjoying the classes. Trainers who use squirty water bottles on dogs who are barking disruptively, rather than providing those dogs with interesting training routines, should be avoided. Bad behaviour tells us the dog is not benefiting from the situation. Don't punish him for being bored.

There are often loud and naughty dogs at training classes, and of course those dogs do need to be trained somewhere, but this is such a critical period for your puppy that it is not up to you to help with someone else's under-socialized, badly mannered dog. Leave as quickly as you can.

Classes usually last an hour, which is far too long for puppies. Dogs learn in short bursts of module training, and intelligent breeds can often become bored and fractious. It's like taking a five-year-old to the museum for hours; interesting at first, then dull enough to make them throw themselves on the floor in a tantrum. Let the trainer know beforehand that you would like to keep sessions short, and train what you have learned at home. That way if you feel your puppy starting to get bored, you can excuse yourself from the class before he gets bored and naughty.

Good clubs will invite you to watch and check them out first. Never feel awkward about querying the advice given. Good trainers will be glad to advise. Good classes will limit the number of puppies they take, so book a place when you get your puppy.

Some vets offer puppy parties held at the surgery, which are usually well managed. They may try to persuade you to sign up to sales schemes about health plans, early neutering, flea treatments, worming every month, and annual vaccinations whilst you're there, but even if you choose not to take these up, it's worth going as a new experience for your puppy.

The Kennel Club provides a list of accredited trainers in your area. Also, look for a BIPDT (British Institute of Professional Dog Trainers) trainer. Take up references from local friends with dogs. People are usually quick to tell of bad experiences with clubs.

Take out insurance for at least the first year of your puppy's life. Puppies will eat things they shouldn't, and regularly injure themselves. Minor disasters such as a broken toenail can be fixed at home quite easily, but big bills are never far away when keeping dogs.

6 WORKING AND TRAINING THE DOBERMANN

For the forward-thinking owner and trainer, the Dobermann's mental acuity is a wonderful gift, and their ability to master various skills enables them to succeed at virtually any sport or hobby. For the more laid-back owner, on the other hand, the Dobermann's mind is a constant source of

Dobermann guarding in 'bark and hold' in IPO/ Schutzhund protection work. Int., Multi Ch. Tahi-Reme Max IPO3, AIAD Ch. 2014.

exhaustion, and such owners never realize how much so until puppy is home and they start finding out what they have taken on.

Novice dog owners should generally avoid taking on a strong working dog as their first choice of breed, as confidence in management and training only comes through experience. However determined they are to 'make it work', and however dedicated to the task, without basic skills the dog will very quickly lose respect for them.

Involving your children with the training increases their bond with the young dog, and creates a natural authority from the child to the dog. The dog soon realizes that for even the most basic sit on command, the child has the capability to provide good things. Later in this chapter are suggestions for various games that you or your children can teach to dogs.

UNDERSTANDING TERMINOLOGY

Dominance

This is a word barely used in this book for a very good reason, and that is because the theory that all dogs try to be dominant over humans has been responsible for a great deal of misery for both dogs and their owners since it became popularized. The same school of thought advised leaving baby puppies all on their own crying pitifully on their first night away from home, in the contention that they must 'learn their place early on'.

Dogs naturally want to please us, and good trainers and handlers do not want submissive dogs. The best relationships occur where the dog and his owner and family are in harmony, not when he feels oppressed. Dominating a dog makes everyone miserable, but you can still be

The perfect combination of Dobermanns and children.

the boss without having a humble dog. Instead of constantly reprimanding the dog for being a nuisance, find something he is good at, and watch him come alive when he is told he is a good boy.

When a strong-minded dog ignores a weak owner, it is labelled as dominant and punished for its behaviour – but very few dogs are born 'dominant': they are made so by a weak owner.

With so many different advice books and 'experts' available, owners become very confused about training. They are told to be 'the pack leader', but don't know what that actually means. When the dog disobeys or ignores them, they try to remember how to be assertive, but the dog will see through their indecision.

If you have to work hard to get your dog's attention, you are not in control, he is – but if a dog gets a bit hot-headed or ignores a command, it doesn't mean he is dominant. We don't call an unruly child 'dominant', we say he is over-excited or needs manners (because his parents didn't teach him properly). Go back to basics, and praise the dog for remembering good manners.

'Pack Leader'

'Pack leader' simply means being a parent who spends time teaching their children or dog good manners, and rights and wrongs, whilst instilling mutual respect and trust. Such parents don't behave aggressively, or dominate their children/

Yvonne Walker's 'Marley', Diego's Caught 'n' the Act, CDex, UDex.

dog, or show weakness: being bolshy and aggressive are not good leadership qualities in humans or dogs. Real 'Alphas' are the cool, calm people in life whom others naturally follow; they rarely need to resort to physical oppression, and would certainly not need to 'pin down' a dog to discipline it.

Self-Control

Control is not about dominance, it is about the dog using self-control through your direction. The well-trained dog runs to the door when the doorbell rings, and then sits and waits just back from the door a little whilst it is answered, because that is what he has been taught to do. He does not have to be held back by the collar to stop him from barging past, because his owner has taught him the self-control to greet visitors politely.

Praise and reward the dog when he is calm, and not when he is jumping hysterically, barking constantly, spinning around, doing anything else disruptive to gain your attention. Block this behaviour with a gentle touch on his side, a 'watch me' eye contact with a smile, a whispered 'shhh, watch and wait'. The act of putting on his collar and clipping the lead on and off should never be a struggle: a quiet 'sit and wait' whilst you fix it on is calmer for owner and dog.

Even in the busiest of households when everyone is rushing to go to school, take one calm moment to check in with each other. If you start running around trying to grab the dog to physically restrain him from racing out of the front door, you only add to the madness. Take a treat out of your pocket and quietly ask the dog to come and sit next to you. With self-control he won't be fighting any restraint. Think about the youngster as a hyperactive child. After they have burned off energy, ask them to stop, sit, and take a deep breath, and then give them something valuable as a reward. Bring the mind back to calm.

UNDERSTANDING BODY LANGUAGE

Eighty per cent of communication in humans is non-verbal, so only 20 per cent of what we say

The self-controlled wait is one of the most useful exercises you can teach for everyday life. Use 'wait' for meals, treats, toys, not barging through doorways, and walking nicely to heel.

IN SUMMARY

- Reward positive, calm behaviour. Don't reward a dog that is jumping, growling, lunging, barking, shaking or urinating
- Don't give something for nothing. Sooner or later the dog will want something from you: get him to work for you, don't work for him

is spoken. We are poor at recognizing signals even in other humans, so it isn't surprising that we miss the gestures that are so fundamental in dog behaviour: lowering the head as a calming signal often used when meeting other dogs or to calm angry humans, a flicker of the eyes to show pleasure or anger, the twitch of a cheek betraying a tense jaw.

Dogs are masters at reading both body language and micro-facial expressions, watching for subtleties they can pick up on to help them assess their owner's moods.

Appeasement gestures are the signals given by the dog to the human when the dog sees that the human is angry. The more frustrated the human becomes trying to train his apparently stupid dog, the more the dog tries to calm the human – thus he may lick his lips to signal supplicant behaviour, turn his head away yawning, or go into avoidance by sniffing the ground. It is terribly sad to see people misunderstand these signals, believing the dog is being disrespectful or stubborn. The dog tries his best, but the owner completely fails to 'see' what the dog is trying to 'say', and then even punishes the dog.

Turid Rugaas is one of the world's foremost lecturers in animal behaviour, and specializes in educating dog trainers and owners about the hidden meaning behind a wide range of canine postures, facial expressions and movements. He makes the following point:

> Dad calls Prince, and has learned in class that he should sound strict and dominant so that Prince will know who is in charge. Prince finds Dad's voice to be aggressive, and being a dog he instantly give Dad a calming signal in order to make him stop being aggressive. Prince will perhaps lick his own nose, yawn, turn away – which will result in Dad becoming angry for real, because Dad perceives Prince as being pig-headed, stubborn and disobedient. Prince is punished for using his calming signals to calm Dad. This is a typical example of something that happens on an everyday basis with many dog owners. If we ignore what dogs are trying to tell us, we can never have a complete relationship with them in training.

Recall, for example, is probably the most important behaviour, but owners destroy the natural inclination of a dog to return by giving mixed signals. Calling the dog, the owner leans forwards with arms outstretched, which in fact puts him in defence and repels him. The owner then calls in varying tones: pleading, frustration and anger, and even occasionally lunges forwards to try and catch the dog. The totally confused dog now runs around just out of reach from the furious owner, who thinks the dog is mocking him.

In contrast a welcoming body position slightly side on, with a kind and happy facial expression, encourages the dog to approach.

A quick 'check-in' of eye contact between you provides a strong connection. Rather than just wearing out his name to get his attention, make a small sound such as with a whistle, or hum, or make a tutting noise, and ask for a quick glance. When he looks at you, smile with your eyes, and reward him with verbal praise or with a click and treat reward. Don't get down to his level to try to force eye contact or hold his gaze, as that is

An inviting posture without leaning forwards increases pack drive and reduces defence.

This is the keen and adoring expression you want looking up at you. ANNIINA LANTTA

threatening. A dynamic game obviously requires a more upbeat attitude, but you will achieve more with a whisper of praise and a kind smile to encourage the dog to listen to your every word.

If we want the dog to be close by our side, or to retrieve and present an object to us, don't lean over him invading his space, as this will make him feel defensive. Encourage close pack drive by leaning slightly back and softening your face.

Dogs meeting assess each other from a distance, and then either avoid or approach each other. Forcing them to walk towards each other is confrontational: their heads are raised because their owners hold the lead tightly, so they each appear aggressive to the other. If neither owner wants to let the dogs play off lead, move on quickly. Static introductions increase tension, so when introducing dogs to each other, keep walking forwards together to build pack drive. Avoid owners who rush to put their dogs on the lead as soon as they see another dog. For whatever reason, they have probably not allowed their dogs to socialize properly and the dogs will be uneasy.

TRAINING BASICS

Despite their tough exterior Dobermanns are a very sensitive breed, and being hard on them in training makes even a strong dog nervous. No creature can concentrate when stressed, so never train in a bad mood as a dog will pick up on it. Keep training light-hearted and happy.

A calm moment between Dean Banks and his dog on the working field. Although this dog is a high-energy working dog, he is calmly in 'pack drive', and able to receive clear instructions.

Dobermanns get bored with repetitive exercises at any age, so keep sessions small and sweet at just a few minutes. Watch for him starting to switch off from training, and finish quickly with an easy and fun exercise on a positive note before having a play break, a game of tug or ball. Return later with a fresh mind.

Although dogs need to train and socialize in a different environment, don't set him up to fail by pushing training too long, too far, or too soon. If he breaks the command, go back to basics and make your training solid elsewhere before trying this environment again.

Each day differs in the ability of the young dog to concentrate. Their hormones are raging, they will still be teething up to fourteen or fifteen months old (they will be pushing molars), and their legs are growing and will sometimes ache (from panosteitis, or growing pains). So if everything goes wrong, leave it and come back later or on another day, or it will be worse than not doing any training at all. Technical and position training needs calmness to enable the dog to absorb the information.

Motivations and Rewards

Rewards can be toys, food, or emotional (verbal/touch) praise. Food is ideal for technical or position training, and Dobermanns are generally easy to train as they are usually very food motivated. Toys will motivate high prey-driven dogs. It is also important to use appropriate treats – for example, training under distraction requires treats of a higher value than just plain kibble.

There is a strange theory that once dogs have learned a particular skill they should no longer have food rewards, or treats – but who would be motivated to work without being paid? However, moving to intermittent rewards *once a behaviour is established* can actually strengthen a behaviour. This is because if the dog isn't always sure he's going to receive something, his desire to get it increases. When omitting regular rewards, replace the missing reward with verbal emotional praise.

Remember, too, that dogs don't offer food to each other: they have to get it when they can, and they are more excited by scraps of food dropped on the floor than with food being pushed in their face. Thus a dog offered a treat by the owner keen for him to take it, may turn his head away and ignore it, but the same treat given by someone who motivates the dog's seeking behaviour by whispering 'wait for it', changing the treat from one hand to another, or hiding it behind their back, will be devoured.

Some foods are of such high value, such as liver, chicken or fish bits, that the dog is over-stimulated and can't think straight. A mid-value treat such as Edam or ready-cooked cocktail sausage cut into small squares is ideal. Keep treats small so the dog is focusing on your cues, rather than chewing a large piece of treat.

Be imaginative and use main meals as a send-away target, or lay a track with his breakfast. Always think of the end goal, which is being interactive with your dog to keep his focus on you. Avoid the situation where the dog comes in, grabs the food treat, and races off again. Bring him in with a 'whoop, whoop', or a joyful return hug or pat, but then make him sit for a treat. Doing a few paces of active heelwork and down-stays before releasing him makes him realize that returning is rewarding.

A great game is 'throw rotation', where the handler throws out a food treat for the dog, which runs out to get it, and runs back to the owner for another go. Do some quick-fire routine exercises – sit/down/stand/wait – between throws, rather than just delivering food treats.

Clicker Training
Clicker, or marker training is operant condition-

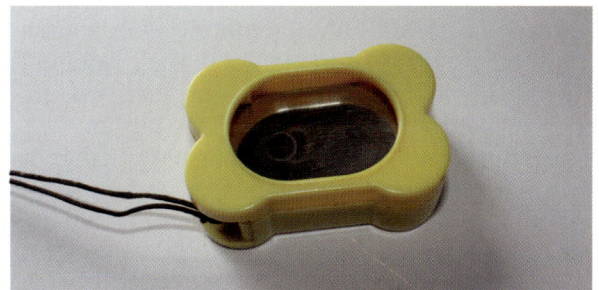

A palm-size plastic clicker with a metal piece that clicks when pressed.

125

ing where a neutral sound is made when the dog completes a task to indicate that a reward will follow. The world's top canine competitors now train with clickers, and even sceptics have been converted to the method. The noise can be made with a physical clicker instrument, or a tongue/cheek click, or a snap of the fingers. A word such as a 'yes' could be used, though ideally it should be a unique sound not heard by the dog in other circumstances.

Training starts by clicking and rewarding the dog when he does something that you want, such as performing sit, down, lift a foot, touch a target. The timing of the click followed by the reward is crucial, and must be at the very moment the desired behaviour is offered. It must not be used to get a behaviour, but to reward it.

Start all training at home, then once the dog is solid with his skills, take him out to train under light distraction, progressing to training at the park, the market place and so on.

Timing and Anticipation

Timing and anticipation is fundamental in training; therefore if you have asked the dog to sit and he does so but gets up immediately, you must correct it next time before he gets up. Don't let him get up and wander around before replacing him. If his attention wanders, correct his gaze as soon as he looks away from you, and make sure he has eye contact with you. Early corrections are much more effective than letting a behaviour become established.

Training and Trainers to Avoid

For many years dog trainers used hard methods to teach dogs, routinely dominating and demeaning them physically and mentally. They would hit them, yank their collars, and string them up until they choked and gave in, suppressing any free spirit. Such methods achieve passive obedience, but teach nothing constructive, inhibiting learning and demeaning the dog, which meekly and abjectly obeys his owner to avoid punishment. It is an appalling way to train.

Then there are weak owners, always self-doubting and relying on others for guidance: the dog may love them, but there is nothing to respect.

IN SUMMARY

- Timing is paramount in any training. Give that click or reward just a moment too late and the dog won't link his action with the reward
- Remember that young dogs are teething throughout the first year, and expecting to teach a retrieve, hold and present when he is going through a particularly chewy phase may not be the best time for him to learn
- For baby training during teething, hide an ice cold carrot or chilled raw meaty bone in the garden and send him out to 'find it'
- Whenever training any skill or game, always be clear when the task or game is over; use hands up/all gone, to show you have no objects or treats and say a clear 'game over'

And there are owners who become increasingly frustrated when they can't convey their request to a dog, and are then determined that it is the dog being stupid, stubborn or dominant, rather than their failure to train properly. These people should not own any dog, especially one as intelligent as the Dobermann.

Nonetheless a high-drive bull-headed dog that ignores his owner is a potential danger, and he must learn that there are unpleasant consequences for bad behaviour. But if such a dog is reprimanded fairly and proportionately, he will respect the trainer and will learn from the reprimand.

POSITION TRAINING

The Sit

With your dog next to you, ask him for eye contact. He will naturally look up and his back end will automatically go down, and at the very moment he sits, you say 'Sit', and click and reward. If he is distracted, take a treat in your hand and pass it over the back of his head to make him sit. Only treat when his bum is on the floor, so keep giving him treats as he is sitting. Don't overdo the

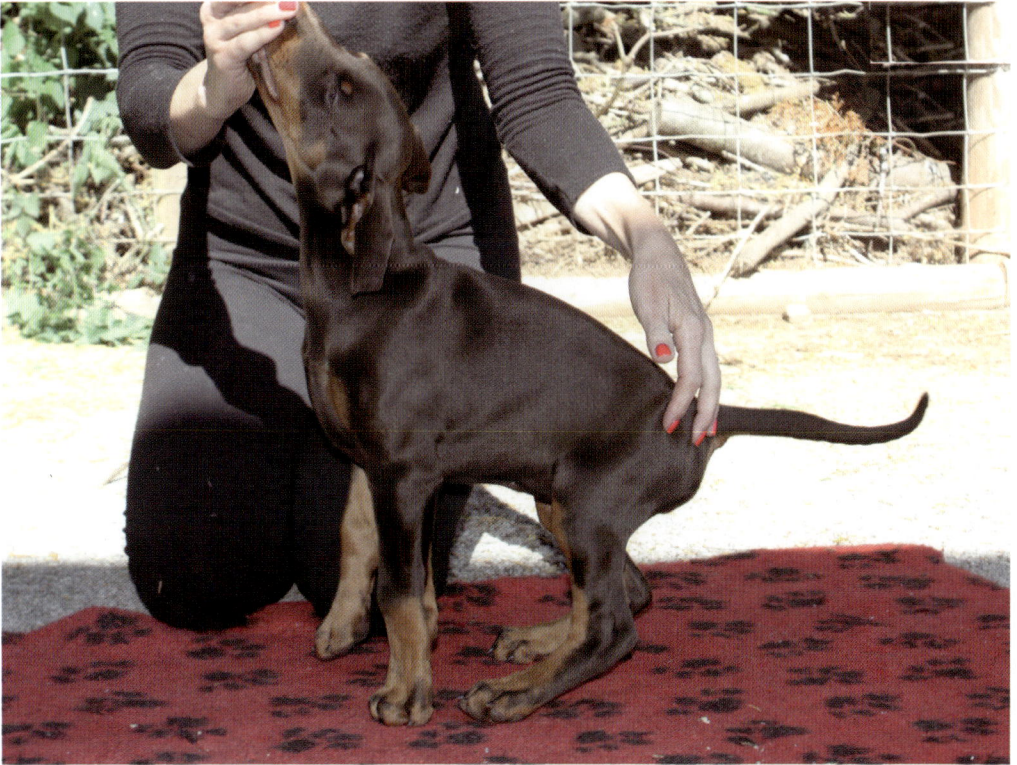

A very gentle touch on the puppy's back end will help him remember the move. The touch is a tuck under, not a push down, which will damage your puppy's bones and ligaments when he braces his legs against the push.

length of time you keep him in sit, but slowly build up the duration of the sit.

After a month of sit with rewards, progress to intermittent rewards by occasionally replacing treats with praise. Make his default position at your side looking up at you, rather than in front, which has no practical use in daily life.

The Lie Down

The lie down can make a dog feel defensive, especially if you lean over him. Teach the down from sit, as the dog is halfway there. With food in your fist get him to follow your hand with his nose down towards his feet and along the floor, just enough for him to lie down. The moment his elbows touch the ground, click and reward. Drop food every few moments between his front legs whilst softly repeating the 'down' command. Start with a ten-second down before release, and increase the duration of the down gradually. If he breaks the position, gently repeat, treat, then release on your command. Always return to basics.

The Down and Stay

Ask the dog to lie down and stay on a mat at the side of the room. Stay close to him at first so that you can return promptly if he breaks the stay – which he will do repeatedly until he understands the exercise. Start with a one-minute down, and gradually increase its duration over the next few weeks to half an hour or more. It will help if he lies down with one hip on its side rather than sphinx-like. The dog in a long down and stay should be relaxed, and not be staying alert waiting for a release, but both exercises are valuable for self-control. Release him calmly so he is in a relaxed state of mind.

Lying Flat

Teaching the dog to lie flat on his side is useful for grooming, examination, and even for veterinary care such as x-rays without sedation in an emergency. This must be done slowly and steadily as dogs can panic and become defensive when being rolled over. From the lying down position, and using high value food, tuck his opposite hind

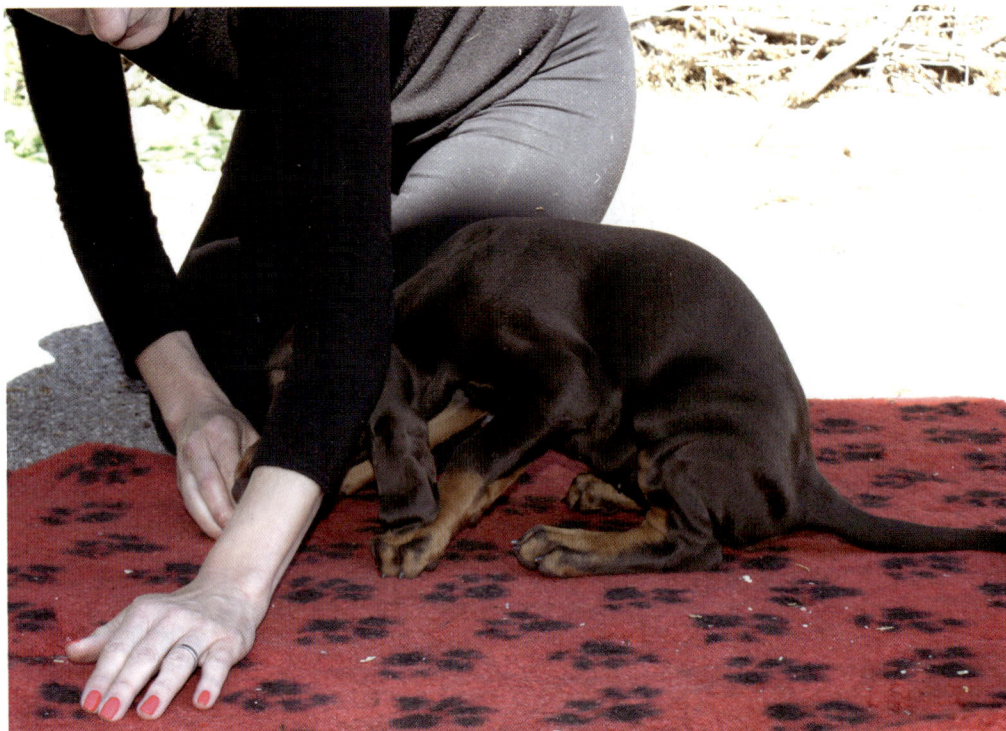

Make a barrier of your arm for him to crawl under to get the food. The moment he lies down, click, treat and stroke him, repeating the 'down' command.

Do not hold or pin him down. This must be a voluntary exercise. If he struggles, let him up and find a different game to teach until trying again later.

TRAINING TERMINOLOGY

The following are some of the technical terms you may come across when training your dog:

Chaining: Combining multiple behaviours into a continuous sequence linked with cues, maintained by a reward at the end of the chain. For example, the sequence of stand, sit, down, sit, stand would initially be taught in separate modules with a marker reward treat at each successful action. These are eventually chained together, with one reward given at the end of the sequence.

Classical conditioning: Places a neutral signal before an initially involuntary (auto) reflex to mark the response until the behaviour becomes a conscious response.

Clicker: A small plastic and metal mechanical noisemaker. The sound of the clicker is quick, unique and consistent. The tongue/cheek can also be used to make the sound.

Clicker training: Precedes and indicates a reward. Uses positive reinforcement (see below) in combination with an action marker.

Compulsion training: The dog is compelled to carry out a behaviour and physically corrected for non-compliance.

Luring: Using a treat to guide the dog towards a desired position.

Operant conditioning: Uses both rewards and punishments (consequences) after behaviours. Rewarding a desired behaviour causes the dog to do it more often. Punishing an undesirable behaviour causes the dog to do it less often. Behaviours without any consequences (negative or positive) lead to behaviours occurring less frequently. First described by B. F. Skinner.

Proofing: Teaches the dog to carry out required behaviours under distraction – he works/performs reliably despite other things going on.

Reinforcement: There are four types of reinforcement: positive, negative, punishment and extinction:

Positive reinforcement: A pleasant experience of treat, toy or emotional reward when the dog carries out an instruction well. Praise increases the chances of the good behaviour.

Negative reinforcement: Removing unpleasant pressure, giving relief for a correct behaviour response. Lions in a circus are trained with whips and without reward. When they complete the command the whips and pressure from the handler are decreased. They move unwillingly, displaying highly defensive and suppressed body language, so it is no surprise when their bottled-up stress sometimes causes them to turn on their trainers, with dreadful results.

Punishment: Adds something unpleasant (aversive) to decrease a behaviour – for example, a dog is asked to sit and does not obey the command. He is pulled up by the collar and his back end is pushed down, and when he sits, the aversive pressure is removed, which reinforces the correct response. Negative reinforcement can also mean withholding punishment to get the dog to perform correctly, such as 'Do it and I won't smack you'.

Extinction: All undesirable behaviours are ignored – if the dog doesn't sit correctly or returns with an incorrect item, the trainer ignores it; the dog is only rewarded for good work.

Reward-based training: The dog is given a reward for carrying out a required behaviour.

Shaping: Encouraging the dog to follow instructions by rewarding behaviours which come progressively closer to the end goal.

A perfect example of putting these technical terms into everyday practice is the most important thing to teach from day one: the recall (*see* Technical Training).

Learning positioning for heelwork with muscle memory.

leg to you under his back end, so he is lying on his hip rather than in the sphinx position.

When he is relaxed in that position and focused on the food, slowly and gently tuck his opposite elbow under him to prevent him bracing himself, and slowly roll him on to his side. Continually feed the high value food, repeating 'flat' and stroking him.

Later, link together individual skills for a sequence such as stand, sit, down, roll over, sit, left paw, right paw, spin and so on.

Once he has learned his positions you can switch to toys for a faster and more driven response.

TECHNICAL TRAINING

Lead Training
Puppies learn to pull on the lead from their first walk, when the owners enjoy seeing their puppy confidently race ahead on the end of a long lead.

From the first walk, teach the pup that pulling does not get him ahead. Shorten your lead, keep him on your left side, and give regular treats by your side until he learns the self-control to walk on a loose lead at heel. Say 'Heel' when he is walking nicely at your side so he learns what it means.

Owners often try various collars, half-checks, harnesses, head-collars and choke chains to control their dog, but it is not what you use (except a full choke chain, which is dangerous in novice hands), but how you use it that is important.

Head-collars are useful for a dog not already taught to heel, but if he walks up ahead and is pulled back, his neck twists, and if this happens repeatedly it will cause aggravation, muscle tension, nerve damage and even cervical spondylitis (inflammation of the vertebrae). Head-collars must not ride up into his eyes, so try different ones for size at the pet shop or training class. Use them as a training aid, and phase them out once the dog has learned to walk to heel.

Don't wrap the lead round and round your hand in preparation for a battle with him! Big heavy chains and massive collars for a strong dog just give him more to lean on.

Small 'reminder' checks with an immediate release of tension mean you don't have to haul back a 50k dog on a solid collar, which is not good for human or owner. Remember to keep treating.

A half-check collar and leather lead.

Chain leads are unpleasant to hold even with a double-handed death grip around the lead, and thick nylon leads have sharp edges that can cut the hands. Leather leads provide grip if needed, but are also light enough to give soft contact with the collar. Use a lead that is approximately ⅝in wide for a male and ¾in wide for a female.

The Recall

When you call your dog, he consciously decides whether to return or not. If he ignores you, you might try a squeaky happy call, a serious commanding tone, a jolly 'tra la la' call, then frustration and panic lead to furious yelling, and desperate pleading. The dog hears all these emotions, and realizing how livid you are at him, can't be blamed for staying out of reach to avoid retribution. Finally cornering him, our emotions can be overwhelming, but we must curb our temper, say well done for coming (even if you had to catch him on a fly-past!), clip his lead on and go home, because if you punish him you won't even catch him next time. However, using classical conditioning you can instil in your dog a really reliable and immediate recall using a particular sound and/or visual cue.

To instil this reaction in your dog, proceed as follows. First you must consider his brain as being separated into forebrain (conscious thought) and hindbrain (instinctive reaction). Any new action or skill takes twenty-eight days to embed in the muscles and neurological system. Next, choose an exciting sound that carries a long way. It needs to be a unique sound, not his name or a sound you normally use, nor one he has already learned to ignore. You can whistle, but in the field, if you are running after your dog who is heading for trouble, you physically can't whistle as your throat constricts with panic – so use an actual whistle or a siren-type 'whoop, whoop!'.

Use his regular meals for the conditioning process: each time you put his meal down, every day for twenty-eight days, make your sound – the whoop or whistle. Don't use it where there are distractions until twenty-eight days of consistent programming have passed, because if he ignores it, you will have to start over with a new sound. Be patient and don't over-use it.

In a couple of weeks you can start to use the sound when calling the dog in from the garden or from another room, as that's a fairly failsafe recall (in that there are few other distractions).

Once you have a solid response in home and garden, you can try it out at the park. Always accompany the sound with something wonderful at the end of it: it doesn't have to be food, but you must make a great fuss of your dog when he returns.

Remember your body language, and never lean towards the dog (which puts him in defence/makes him back off). Most importantly, always welcome him in with plenty of joy. Don't nag him to keep with you, but just let him continue

---

IN SUMMARY

- Get firm foundations in place before moving on too fast. Don't set your dog up to fail by overloading him with information. His learning will only be as good as your teaching
- Dobermanns switch off at slow routine work or robotic training, so limit each game/task to no more than three times per session. If your dog succeeds after the second try, finish on a win for the day
- Keep toy or food rewards proportional. If he is so hyped up by the reward that he can't concentrate, drop to a lower value reward
- Stay slow to teach foundations. Learning two objects a month is far better than trying to teach him multiple objects too early
- If he fails a task, it means your training wasn't good enough, so go back to basics to re-train the foundations

to keep tabs on where you are, rather than you doing all the work and being his echo-locator.

Although a big Dobe charging back to you joyfully can be intimidating, don't stop him approaching or shout 'Stop!', as this is confusing and puts him in defence drive just as you called him into pack. Let your puppy come racing into you on recall – you can calm that down later – because now is the time to get into his mind that coming back to you is wonderful! To stop him crashing straight into you, use a toy – a ball on a rope, for example – in your outstretched arm away from your body, or direct him to one side of you with a big sweep of your arms.

Freedom is essential for dogs, but being charged by a big dog is terrifying. Who can blame owners of children or small dogs for picking them up in case they are attacked or squashed? Owners who have taught their dogs a polite, self-controlled approach rarely get into squabbles with other owners in the park.

USING TOYS FOR TRAINING

Using toys for training enables you to build the dog's prey drive in a dynamic and interactive game. A ball on a rope is invaluable for recall: as he sets off to chase something, you can whizz it round and call 'Hey, look what I've got!' Dogs love to pick things up and carry them around, and they quickly learn that the toy becomes a whole lot more fun when the owner is involved in a game of tug or throw and bring back. This is the start of 'drive training' for working dogs.

Most dogs have a natural desire to catch and hold moving objects. With a young dog that comes a little late to toy training we need to activate his instinctive 'seeking behaviour' by teasingly putting a small soft toy or ball on a rope on the ground and encouraging him to catch and grab it whilst you pull it.

Ignore the old myth that the dog must never win, because if he realizes he will never get it, he gives up wanting it. If he is possessive over an object he will work harder to get it, but we also want him to realize that the game is even better when his best friend is also playing, so we build the prey and pack drives simultaneously.

When he takes the toy or ball, play a gentle game of tug, being careful not to lean over him with your body straight on to him because he will interpret this as confrontational and aggressive: keep him in pack and prey drive, not defence.

When trying to get a dog 'on to' a toy, think of the toy in dog terms as a prey object, for instance a mouse or rabbit. Therefore don't just dangle the toy in his face: make it move like a small animal by flicking it around and behind your legs, or swapping it between hands behind your back, to activate his seeking/hunting drive. (Keep your legs still or you will become the focus and the dog will think you're inviting him to join in a game of jumping all over each other instead!)

A 'flirt pole' with a toy on the end is a great game to build prey drive focus.

This owner's posture – leaning over and face on to the dog – would be interpreted by the dog as aggressive and confrontational, and will push him into defence (fight) mode, which is not what we require at this stage when building drive work.

Remove confrontation from the game by turning side on, and when the dog has a calm, solid, steady grip without growling, the owner will release the ball to him.

Don't yank it (and especially not in a baby mouth – mind the teeth), just give a gentle heave.

Note: if the dog growls, the game has become too aggressive and he has switched into fight drive (defence). Let go of the toy and walk away. He will know that it is not a win, as he will have read your displeasure. When you develop your skills and learn more about drives, you can manipulate him out of defence (fight) drive, and into pack/ prey drive.

Once he has won the toy, he will proudly prance around with it for a while. Tease him a little that you are trying to catch it; this will increase his possession, but the eventual aim is that he brings it back to you for another game.

If he won't return (we want him to be possessive, so don't squash that), take out the second ball or toy on a rope that you have had tucked in your pocket, and make out that this one is even better than the one he has. Pretend to have your own game with that ball, or ideally get someone else to join you for a game of throw and catch. It won't be long before your dog realizes your game is better than his on his own, and that the toy only becomes 'alive' and of interest when you are involved.

When asking him to release the toy, slack the tension on the rope so there is nothing for him to pull against – but don't expect a young dog

When asking him to release the toy, slack the tension on the rope so there is nothing for him to pull against.

Taking a few moments to mentally rest and come into 'pack' drive during the game.

to release the ball like this. The dog that gives it up easily doesn't want it enough to work for it. Release teaching comes later.

As the dog grows bigger, a tennis-size ball on a rope is ideal for these games; it can be moved quickly, flicked along the ground to simulate prey, used as a light game of tug, thrown easily for retrieve, and whisked up quickly to the shoulder for a few paces of heelwork.

You can also start to use his increased prey drive to ask for a sit, down, stand/whatever behaviour you want, in really quick succession. To build prey drive, put the ball up to your shoulder and ask for a sit, and the very second that he sits and makes a moment of eye contact, drop the ball to him or throw it. Later, put the ball up to your shoulder and take him straight into a few paces of heelwork.

Using prey drive to teach dynamic heelwork is

the foundation of working in most disciplines. Initially the dog will be very bouncy, jumping up and even grabbing your clothes, but work through this by walking forwards – and don't talk to him or stop whilst he is jumping – and if you can get just four or five paces of focused heelwork from it, quickly drop or throw the toy as his reward. Don't push it too far: ten paces of good heelwork is worth more than fifty with the dog losing interest at the end. And don't play the heelwork game any longer than for five minutes to prevent boredom.

Your dog is now working in combined drives of prey and pack. Because he wants to play an interactive game with you, he maintains his focus on you and the toy, rather than on other dogs or livestock in the field, and has a great recall. Prey and pack drive training is meant to be dynamic: the aim is to keep his eyes on you in keen antici-

Although he will keep jumping up at you for the ball, keep walking forwards – push through the jumping – and get just a few paces of heel before releasing the toy. Remember this exercise is about harnessing prey drive, not technical precision.

Encouraging prey drive and courage by jumping up for a toy.

pation, and not just plodding along at your side. Keep your expression enthusiastic; technical positioning comes later.

Always remember to give him the ball, or click and reward him at the very moment he does what you have asked him to do. Training with toys really stimulates the dog, and you have to react quickly to keep one step ahead of drive work games. Mind your fingers! Always leave him wanting more, and never leave the special toy or ball lying around on the floor: if you leave him with it, it loses its magic powers!

If you want to progress to full working IPO, you need to teach your dog to track (many tracking books are available); he must also be impeccably obedient, have fearless courage, and have absolute control in all aspects for protection.

BRAIN GAMES AND TRAINING

Brain games are essential for the clever Dobermann, and can be played with the family both indoors and out to keep everyone occupied and to help build relationships. The skills your dog can learn might include fetching the remote control or your slippers, bringing specific toys from the box, and returning them after play. He could deliver things from one person to another (a great party piece), or take the post nicely from the postman.

These skills make him feel a really useful member of the family, and are a perfect way for children to be involved in training. One child could teach him to commando crawl along the floor, another to 'sit up and beg', another to 'play

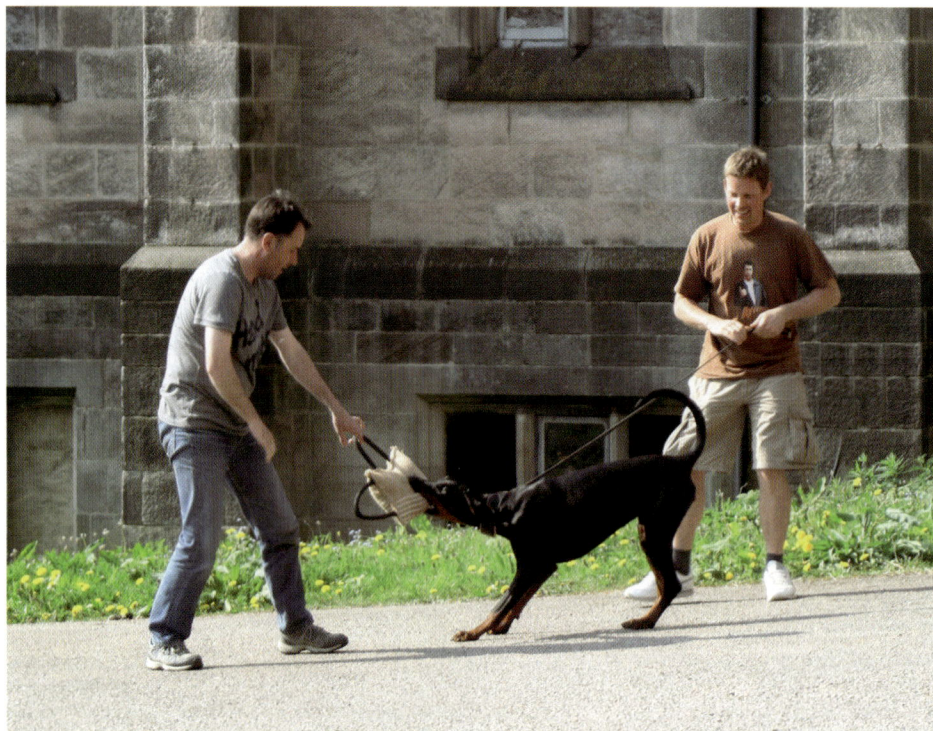

Early bite training on a hessian handbag for future protection work in IPO. This will later progress to a full sleeve, which the helper wears.

dead'. These skills can be chained together and put in a training demonstration to show what they have all learned. Dogs naturally respect the humans who teach and reward them, whatever their age, size or gender, so this form of training has the double bonus of keeping dogs and children occupied whilst building mutual respect in the process.

Article ID

Article ID is great game, and it can be developed into a way of training where the dog is of invaluable assistance to the disabled.

Having taught him to retrieve, now start to introduce different objects. As you give him a new toy, announce its name, such as slipper/phone/red teddy/blue box. It will take a few weeks for him to learn the individual objects. Once you think he can differentiate between them, take two of the objects, place them slightly apart, and then send him out for one of them. If he collects the wrong one, don't receive the proffered toy,

IN SUMMARY

- Building prey and pack drive is totally opposite in its approach to the old method of 'the dog must never win'. For the toy to be of any value to him, he must know he can win it occasionally or he will give up. Let him win the prize, but don't leave him with it
- Neither dogs nor humans can think or concentrate when they are angry or defensive. We want calm minds able to think clearly, so learning to calm your dog is more important than whipping up the game into a frenzy
- Increase the speed of his responses by increasing his desire for the object, thereby instilling a higher drive

but repeat your request that he collects the toy you first asked for. With these basic skills your dog can be trained to accomplish the following tasks:

- Pick up dropped objects
- Help you carry your bags in from the car
- Find your lost keys or phone
- Bring a phone to you when it rings
- Fetch shoes and slippers
- Bring a cushion or blanket
- Alert you to an alarm
- Put away his toys

These games can also be played outdoors; for example, you could place his breakfast behind a tree, and teach him to find it by following your track to it. Such games are perfect for children to play with the dog, as both have to complete a task to achieve the goal.

Directional Commands

Directional commands are used to advantage not only in agility training, but also around the house. For example you can simply ask the dog to go in and out of rooms without having to grab hold of his collar and push or pull him to where you want him to be.

Using a small fluffy toy or a favourite toy that he is keen to hold, start by building self-control into your normal 'throw and fetch' exercise: tell him to sit stay, then walk away – reminding him to stay – and place the toy on the floor. Return to his side, point to the toy and say 'find it!'

Directing the dog for the send-away.

Once he understands the sit/stay and what send-away means, you can start to link the skills that he has learned, such as 'send away' and 'lie down on the mat'. You can place a pot there with a treat inside it, which he has as a reward for lying down at that particular point.

Initially he will be working visually (just seeing the object), but as he gets the hang of it you can vary the placement of the article, and progress to placing it out of sight – just around the cor-

Young handler with his Dobermann training for calm food control.

ner of the sofa, or into the hall where you might place it to the right, then the next day place it to the left, or on the bottom stair, into each of the bedrooms, into a cupboard (with the door slightly ajar), under the dining table, outside the back door.

Once you and your dog have accomplished these skills, you can try some targeting, aka touch training.

Touch Training

A dog can be taught to turn lights on or off, or to close doors, by training him to target particular areas with his nose or paw. A good way to teach a dog to target things is by using sticky notes. Initially put the sticky note on your palm and hold it out for the dog to sniff: the moment he touches it, click and reward. Play this game a couple of times a day until he gets the hang of it. You can then put the sticky note on the door, or on the light switch, and so on. If you have taught him to give a paw, put a sticky note on your hand so he learns to target with his paw.

If you want him to learn to close a cupboard door, obviously it must be light enough for him to push closed. Using the sticky note on the door, start to introduce another cue as he touches the door: point to it and say 'close it', or 'push it'. Each time he touches it, click and reward, and this will continue over various sessions/days/weeks whilst you gradually increase how hard he has to push before he gets a reward; quite soon he'll be shutting the door in one touch.

Eventually the sticky notes can be faded out, as the cue from you to any object is to point to it and ask him to 'push it'.

Sending the dog in to search for human casualties. ERDÖPBERKI RAMONA RASHI

Erdöpberki Ramona Rashi (Pride of Russia Amadey × CsiniBaba Charlotte): Rashi is a live human search dog trained by her owner Betty Orbán in Hungary; she began searching at five months of age. During training one day she was searching for a helper, but before she found him she noticed a homeless person lying in some wasteland, and indicated by barking that she had indeed found a live person.

Assistance dogs for deaf people are trained to get their owner's attention by touch, not sounds, and use either a nose or paw nudge to alert the owner to the source of the sound, such as the doorbell, phone or cooker timer. Dobermanns are used a great deal in service in the USA, but because organizations in the UK don't like to use guarding breeds, their abilities remain sadly unused over here.

Teaching your dog to use his brain and exploiting his desire to please you keeps him occupied and makes him feel valued. Being mentally satisfied he won't pester you for attention whilst you are resting. He may not be able to fetch you an ice-cold beer or a glass of wine whilst you're lying on the sofa, but he can at least pass you the television remote control to save your weary legs.

PREVENTATIVE TRAINING

Stealing and Swapping

If anything is going to make the dog hang on to the dead bird he has found, it is when you run towards him shouting 'drop it!' because in his eyes this increases its value. Instead, teach him to bring it to you, and offer him an exchange. Remembering not to dominate with your body language, hold him gently under his chin and say 'show me'. Swap is easily taught from the game of catch and return with a toy, where he realizes that the game works better if he gives up the ball to his owner and shares the fun, rather than just running around with it on his own.

As an example, one of our terriers is a terrible thief, and often steals food from the worktop; she then takes her prize to her lair in the box under the table. If I am quick enough to realize she has stolen it, I kneel beside her, hold her under-jaw gently for a release, and quietly ask for a handover. I then thank her for giving it up and give her a piece of the (now ruined) quality cheese.

Much as I want to scold her for stealing, this would make her extra defensive and she wouldn't give up anything in the future. Many owners disapprove of this approach, thinking it rewards theft, but dogs understand being rewarded for immediate behaviour, which is doing what we ask. Unless you have actually seen your dog in the act of thieving, there is no point at all in punishing him – smack yourself for leaving stuff within reach!

Turn undesirable behaviour into a training opportunity by giving the dog a verbal or visual cue when he behaves in a way that you endorse.

Bark and Stop Barking on Command

Teaching a dog to bark and to stop barking is achieved through visual and verbal cues. When he barks, give this behaviour a name, such as 'talk' or 'speak', thus linking his action with a verbal cue word. At first he will look at you curiously, and the moment he stops, give him the visual 'stop signal' of the flat hand and the verbal cue of 'enough' or 'shh'. As soon as he barks again, put away the visual hand cue and ask for 'talk' again. It will take at least twenty-eight days (muscle memory) for him to learn this, so wait for him to bark at something, rather than keep saying it to get the behaviour.

Although you need some excitement in your expression, train the 'speak' using a whisper, because if there is an intruder outside, or if you are followed in a dark alley, you want them to think that your dog is barking of his own accord, not because you are commanding your dog to bark.

Preventing Chasing

Dogs, and particularly those with a high prey drive, will go through a behaviour sequence in hunting of eye, stalk, chase, grab-bite, kill-bite, dissect and consume: this is called the predatory sequence.

If your dog knows that chasing your house cat is off limits but does it anyway, he must be punished immediately for lack of self-control. If you catch him in the act, give him a hard smack across the backside and tell him it is not to happen again under any circumstances: he will slink away with his tail down, but this punishment is fair and proportionate as he acted deliberately.

This will offend some trainers who prefer (as we all do) the idea of only training positively, but dogs in high prey drive will kill, so if a once-off hard physical correction saves the cat's life, it's a small price to pay. It's the same with livestock: if you let him chase stock animals such as sheep or alpacas he could potentially kill them – but he could also be shot by the farmer, or run over if he chases them across a road. If the dog lowers his head and goes into 'eye, stalk, stare' the owner must recognize this as the predatory sequence and give him a quick, hard check to jerk him out of his prey drive. If you didn't notice, it is useless to reprimand him later.

Make him 'stock-proof' from puppyhood, so he is reliable with other pets and stock animals: take him out to the countryside and sit at farm gates to watch stock moving around, and instil into him that chasing must never happen. Don't let him chase birds in the park, which could develop into a compulsive obsession; this behaviour might be amusing initially, but when he chases a bird across the road, being run over isn't funny.

Preventing Jumping Up

Puppies will jump up at their dam, which in the wild would encourage her to regurgitate her prey when she returned from a hunting trip. In domesticity they jump up at people for attention. If you push the puppy down, make eye contact and say 'no, don't, no, off', the puppy is in fact getting the attention (any sort) he is asking for. Instead, stand still and don't make any eye contact with him – but the moment he stops jumping, smile, praise and treat reward him. Turning your back when he jumps up rarely works because he just jumps at that instead. Pre-empt bad behaviour by playing a game with him before he seeks attention, and remind him what a good boy he is. From day one reward him verbally and with treats for staying down.

Despite advice never to play rough games with puppies, men and boys in the home often ignore this, resulting in dogs that have no respect for humans, and who think it is quite all right to jump on everyone. Play clever thinking games, not powerhouse battles.

Stopping Disruptive Behaviour

Owners often complain that 'my dog won't stop barking/chasing/jumping' whilst simply watching the dog continue to pursue the behaviour they complain of! These undesired behaviours develop into behaviour patterns (muscle memory), so if you don't want your dog doing something, stop him immediately before the behaviour becomes established. Distract him with a treat, a sound, or a new movement, thereby re-wiring his brain and introducing a positive behaviour.

Putting a 'naughty' dog outside, or caging him, teaches nothing at all. Dogs don't reflect on previous actions, and caging teaches no self-control: it just makes him wild with frustration, and is a ridiculous attempt to control him.

DISCIPLINE IN TRAINING

In these modern times when physical corrections are frowned upon, is there ever an appropriate time to physically correct a dog? The word 'discipline' has become synonymous with the image of a mean-minded dog trainer beating his dogs, and in truth, there is no more miserable sight than that of a subdued dog sitting humbly next to his master living in fear of moving for doing something wrong, with the light gone from his eyes. That is not a well-trained dog: it is one living in constant fear of punishment from a bullying owner.

The discipline that we refer to is the one that all creatures need, of structure and self-control.

Humans need self-discipline to get up in the morning for work, wolves need discipline to co-ordinate a hunt together, ants need discipline to function as a community. Good discipline means that in a pack situation, everyone knows their role in life and works together – if one member of the family (pack) runs riot, then chaos is the result.

Out-of-control dogs were not born that way, and the sooner that owners take personal responsibility for having failed in their training, the sooner they will recover the situation. Insufficient training, poor manners, and a lack of socialization and mental stimulation collectively results in bad behaviour. How can you punish a dog for jumping all over people, mouthing arms or running off in the park if you haven't taught him how to behave? It is like punishing a child whose parents never spent time teaching it. These animals run wild because they have learned they don't need to follow any rules because their owners have never taught them anything better, or applied any consequences for ignoring them.

Any large, out-of-control dog is potentially dangerous, especially if he jumps on people or start fights with other dogs. If your dog is trained and ignores a command, he is either wilfully disobedient or he isn't trained properly (it is usually the latter). A bold and headstrong young Dobe must realize that humans are the boss, and if your dog deliberately disobeys an important command he must receive correction to realize that there are consequences if he ignores you.

In any training there is no 'one size fits all'. Be steady with a soft or nervous dog, and firmer with the alpha male – but understand that the alpha male is just doing what is natural. Acceptable punishment differs between people, as it does between dogs. It has to be appropriate to the crime (and the individual); it must be immediate and timely; the dog needs to understand why; and it should never be done in anger.

If you catch him thieving something, a loud shout and 'drop it' should suffice. If you don't catch him in the act, you can only smack yourself for so stupidly leaving whatever it is in reach. Don't believe it when people say that the dog knows what he has done: 'just look at his guilty expression' they say. But this is a ridiculous idea, and what the dog is actually trying to convey is, 'I don't know why you're angry, but I'm going to look humble to try and appease you'. Punishing a dog after the act is useless and just frightens the dog, who has long forgotten what he has done (even a minute ago): the owner who does this is both mean and short-sighted for punishing their dog, which has no idea why you are angry.

If a dog barges through a doorway knocking a child over, is this bad behaviour? Even if he didn't intend to knock the child over, it is still behaviour that needs correcting, and it is your responsibility to teach him to walk calmly through doorways in the first place.

Even the best-trained puppies and adult dogs get things wrong from time to time. Sometimes they simply forget, and at other times they may just refuse to do something. Refusing to comply isn't necessarily some kind of dominance rebellion; there may be a very good reason the dog doesn't want to sit down, such as teething making him feel fractious, backache, a bad knee or sore hip in an older dog, or even a bad smell where you are asking him to lie down.

Try again in a different place, at another time, or in a different tone, and finish on a quick win. Don't get into a power struggle, but think how you can motivate the dog to get him to do something for you; this is not about rewarding him for disobeying you, it is quite the opposite. You have the control because you have what he wants, and he has to do what you ask to get the reward. Of course it is bribery to begin with, but it is actually far better because first, the dog did the task, and second, you get the chance to tell him he was good.

ACTIVITIES AND TRAINING

Imagination (and motivation) is needed to move on from sits, stays and ball throwing, and the Dobermann is such a multi-purpose breed that it can excel in pretty much anything. There is a variety of activities – or 'disciplines', as they are referred to – in which they can participate, and these vary in levels of difficulty and competition. The Kennel Club's Good Citizen schemes begin with the Foundation Puppy Course, and progress from bronze, through silver to gold, where dogs undertake various obedience and general good manners tests. These tests provide a good foun-

Three impressive Dobermanns owned by Simone van de Haar. Much time and work is taken to achieving such well-trained dogs. SIMONE VAN DE HAAR *www.dobermannpedigrees.nl*

Rosie Lane's Chaanrose Get Oh Fabulous CDEx over the long jump.

dation for any future training, whether competitive or otherwise.

Working tests were originally designed to assess a working dog's desire to work, its trainability, its stamina and endurance, agility, courage, intelligence and loyalty, its temperament, and how stable its nerves are. The UK culture of working dogs differs vastly from that in Europe, where there are dog sport training clubs in almost every town. Although some breed clubs hold obedience competitions they are not well supported. There are now just a few owners dedicated to competing in sport with their Dobermanns.

Obedience competition classes: These are graded according to the dog's standard of experience and ability, and range from Pre-Beginner, Beginner, Novice and Championship, where successful competitors can qualify to compete at Crufts. The tasks include heelwork with complexity and length dependent on the class being judged, recall, retrieve, send-away, stays where the length is dependent on the grade of class. In more advanced classes there are Scent Discrimination, and Distance Control tests. The sport is held under KC rules.

Working trials (WT): These tests are broken down into three main sections: tracking, agility and control. The increasingly demanding grades are known as stakes. These progress from Companion Dog (CD), Open Utility Dog (UD), through Championship Utility Dog (UD), Open and Championship Working Dog (WD), to Open and Championship Patrol Dog (PD) and at the very top Working Trials Tracking Dog (TD). The sport is held under KC rules.

IPO (Internationale Prüfungs-Ordnung)/**Schutzhund:** These tests also include three elements, tracking, obedience and protection, but the dog must show excellence in each discipline simultaneously.

WORKING TRIAL CHAMPIONS

WT Ch Ulf Von Margarenthof (first UK Dobermann WT Champion)	Sgt Harry Darbyshire	1946
WT Ch Mountbrowne Karen	PC Bob Ling	1950
WT Ch Joseph of Aycliffe	Sgt W. Corrigan	1952
WT Ch Mountbrowne Julie	Sgt T. Tessford	1955
WT Ch Chaanrose Night Queen	John Fleet	1978
WT Ch Linrio Domingo (won the KC WT Championships, the top trialling award)	J. Middleweek	1979
WT Ch Jimarty's Citta	John Fleet	1996

WINNERS OF ONE WT CERTIFICATE

Mountbrowne Jenny	Sgt G. Jones	1952
Mountbrowne Joe	Mrs Porterfield	1953
Vyking Drum Major	Jean Faulkes	1953
Anna of Aycliffe	PC Hutchinson	1955
Arno of Aycliffe	Sgt H. Garth	1955
Mountbrowne Olaf	Sgt Taylor	1956
Mountbrowne Amber	PC T. Yeouart/later Sgt J. Hyslop	1956
Hawk of Trevellis	H. Appleby	1962

OBEDIENCE

Ob. Ch. Lady Gessler of Bryan (won the obedience championship at Crufts)
Ob. Ch., Ch. Jupiter of Tavey.

SCHUTZHUND/IPO

Askya from the Dobergang	George Robinson	IPO3 2009
Int., Lux. Ch. Aritaur Histabraq	Martin Horgan	IPO3 2009
Aritaur Notorious	Tony Sheldon	IPO3 2012
Chancepixies Legend	Des Connolly	IPO3 2007
Dark Hill Belona	Gabriela Szabo	IPO3 2008
Darkiss Maximus Decimus at Kinmonth	Derek Elmslie	IPO3 2015
Edmondo vom Bayerischen	George Robinson	IPO3 2007
Jobergs Ducati	Gary Booth	IPO3
Mianna Cracklin Rose At Luftez	Amelia Murray	IPO3 2017
Oberstein Arabs Fantasy	Andrew Ball	IPO3 2010
Vyleighs Heartbeat	Carl Gucker	IPO3 2000
Revolution von Warringhof (Imp Deu)	Julie West	IPO3 2017
Chancepixies Angelica	David Anderson	IPO2 2009
David von Hunnoterra	James Weller	IPO2 2013
Devil Dragon vom Jahrestal	Michael McCann	IPO2 2014
Florentina Texas Dawn for Oberstein	Dave Humphries	IPO2 2004

Chancepixies Auctioneer	David Anderson	IPO1 2006
Chancepixies Cherry Brandy	David Anderson	IPO1 2007
Ch Keyala's Dream Machine at Nytbonn	David Wood	IPO1 2006
Mikjulora's Crysla	Julie West	IPO1 2014

In 2010 the first ZTP (Zuchttauglichkeitsprüfung), 'Fit for Breeding Test' was held at Chancepixies kennels in Dover. Herr Wiblishauser, who was President of de Verein (German Dobermann Club), judged the event.

Dogs are graded into V (excellent), SG (very good). Three Dobermanns at this ZTP gained Excellent gradings:

Amber Sea Adele Great	(B) V1A PASS
Int, Lux Ch Aritaur Histabraq	(D) V1A PASS
Aritaur Vincent Vega Eur JgSgr	(D) V1A PASS
Axel von Schattenjagger	(D) SG1A PASS
Chancepixies Femme Fatale	(B) SG1B PASS
Chancepixies Juggernaut	(D) SG1A PASS
Oberstein Arabs Fantasy	(B) SG1B PASS

In addition to their Schutzhund successes, Int., Lux. Ch. Aritaur Histabraq SchH3 and Ch. Keyala's Dream Machine at Nytbonn IPO1 remain to date the only two Dobermanns to have won CCs at UK shows, with Dream Machine having won the CC at Crufts in 2008 under Lynne Rock (Othertons).

LEFT: *Rosie Lane's Stormy Romance with Chaanrose CDex, on the scale in Working Trials.*

RIGHT: *Julie West with her Revolution von Warringhof IP03.*

Qualifications to enter Working Trials Stakes

Instructions:

1. Find the Stake you want to enter down the left hand side.
2. Then look across the row to see which qualifications are required, and which qualifications debar you from entering this Stake

☒ = You cannot enter the Stake on this row if you already hold this qualification

✓ = You need this qualification to enter the Stake on this row. Except where shown for WD Champ, you need all the ticked qualifications

✓✓ = You need to have gained this qualification on at least two occasions

START HERE Stake you want to enter ↓	Qualifications your dog must (or must not) hold														
	CD			**UD**			**WD**			**TD**			**PD**		
	Open: Cert Merit	Champ: Qual	Champ: Ex	Open: Cert Merit	Champ: Qual	Champ: Ex	Open: Cert Merit	Champ: Qual	Champ: Ex	Open: Cert Merit	Champ: Qual	Champ: Ex	Open: Cert Merit	Champ: Qual	Champ: Ex
Intro Stake			☒			☒									
CD Open							☒	☒	☒	☒	☒	☒	☒	☒	☒
CD Champ									☒						
UD Open							☒			☒			☒		
UD Champ				✓					☒						
WD Open				✓						☒			☒		
WD Champ			✓			✓	✓ -of-		✓			☒			☒
TD Open							✓				☒				
TD Champ									✓✓	✓✓					
PD Open							✓								☒
PD Champ									✓✓				✓✓		

NOTES:
- You cannot enter a UD Championship Stake and a WD Championship Stake at the same Trial
- You cannot enter a WD Championship Stake and a TD or PD Championship Stake at the same Trial
- You can enter an eligible dog in both the Introductory Stake and the CD Open/CD Championship Stake at the same Trial

Open: Cert Merit - a Certificate of Merit is gained at an Open Trial where the dog has gained at least 70% of the marks for each group of tests and has gained 80% or more of the total overall marks

Champ: Qual - A dog qualifies at a Championship trial where it has gained at least 70% of the marks for each group of tests but has not gained 80% or more of the total overall marks

Champ: Ex - a Championship 'Excellent' is gained at a Championship Trial where the dog has qualified by gaining at least 70% of the marks for each group of tests **and** has gained 80% or more of the total overall marks

EXAMPLE: To be eligible for WD Stake at a Championship Trial, the dog must have qualified Excellent in a CD Stake at a Championship Trial, **and** qualified Excellent in a UD Stake at a Championship Trial, **and** have either gained a Certificate of Merit in a WD Stake at an Open Trial or have qualified Excellent in a WD Stake at a Championship Trial. However it ceases to be eligible once it has qualified Excellent in a TD Stake or a PD Stake at a Championship Trial.

Qualifications for entry to Working Trials Stakes. THE KENNEL CLUB LTD

Int., Lux. Ch. Aritaur Histabraq SchH3. 'Bracco' was clicker trained by Martin in all elements of Schutzhund tracking, obedience and protection, and remains the highest-scoring UK Dobermann in history.

To work in IPO, dogs must pass the BH, literally translated as companion dog test. This ensures the dog is of suitable character to progress into full training.

Working Trials and Schutzhund/IPO are extremely demanding tests for any dog, and very few Dobermanns in the UK have gained the highest grades of Working Trials Champion, Schutzhund /IPO, and Obedience Champions respectively.

For the roll of honour, *see* sidebar.

Agility: A dynamic sport that tests the dog's fitness and the handler's ability to train and direct the dog over jumps and through obstacles. The course is timed, and the fastest clear round is the winner. Although dogs cannot compete in agility until they are eighteen months old, they can start basic training at home, in the woods, and at local agility clubs. Dogs can progress through the grades of their agility

A hold and bark in the hide: Matt Holmes with his Ch., Ned. Ch. Ace van hof ter Eeckhout at Siboveld, IPO1, ZTP 1A.

Retrieve over a jump: Aritaur Notorious SchH3.

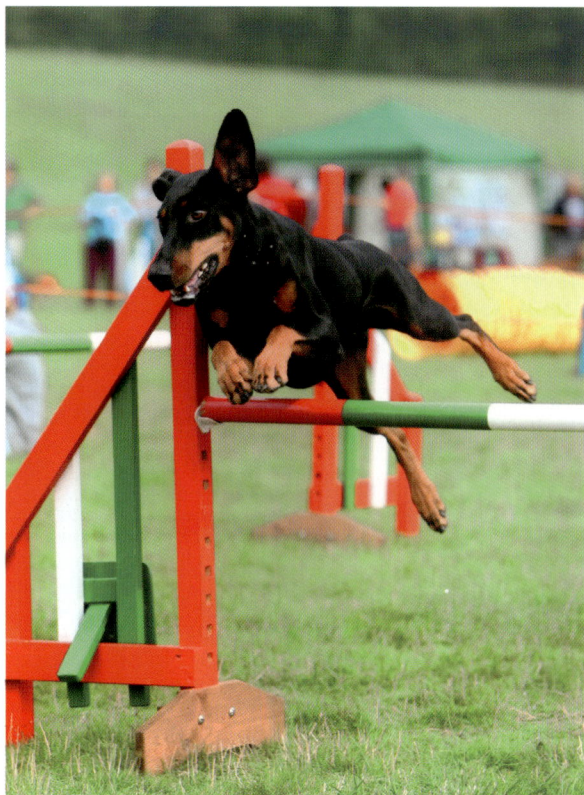

Nicky Warren's Aritaur Cavallo Vira. Grade 4 Agility, Bronze and Silver Agility Warrants. DE PHOTOS

Sam Jones with her bitch Ch. Korifey Black Diamond.

career from the lowest Grade 1 to the highest Grade 7. The sport is held under KC rules.

Endurance tests: Held under GSDL/BAGSD regulations over a distance of 20km (approximately twelve miles). The dog must run on the lead on the left side of the handler, who is riding a bike. It is not a race, and should be completed at a speed of 12–15km an hour with timed rest periods.

Cani-X: Cross-country running with the dog over a timed course. Competitors usually wear a waist belt attachment so they can run free with a harness for the dog, which runs in front. A 5km CaniX should take around 30 to 40 minutes. There are even night runs, which are held over a shortened course with glow sticks marking the route. The sport is organized by CaniX.

Rally-O': Short for 'Rally Obedience', which is a relatively new sport to the UK having been established in the USA some years ago, and is now held under KC rules. The sport involves the handler and dog working through a ground level course to demonstrate the dog's understanding of basic commands such as sit, stay, down, and come and heel position.

Heelwork to Music: (Dancing with Dogs), managed by the Kennel Club, with classes and competitions for beginners up to advanced level. Handlers devise their own routines set to music of up to 4 minutes, which they perform with their dog. It is divided into two categories – Heelwork to Music (HTM) and Freestyle, and most events hold classes in both categories.

7 CONDITIONING AND EXERCISE

One of the first questions often asked by prospective Dobermann owners is 'How much exercise does the breed need?' There is no prescriptive amount: it depends how fit you want both you and your dog to be. The exercise requirements of the Dobermann are no different to that of any large athletic breed, and the freedom to run is the cornerstone of good health and well-being in any dog. However, mental exercise is equally as important as physical exercise for the Dobermann, and if you want a well balanced dog that is easy to live with, you must include interactive exercises.

Most dogs are given a run-around in the park for an hour or so, maybe with a little ball throwing if they're lucky. Weekends may provide more variation, with a trip to a different park, but the type of exercise will be the same: more free running. The dog eventually becomes hyper fit and his energy demands continue to increase, with the result that he is not a pleasant dog to live with. Despite having been out sometimes for hours, he is pumped up and unable to relax. He paces up and down, whines, demands constant attention and continually wants to be let out to run around the garden, only to come in and repeat his nervous behaviour. It is simply caused by the owner spending more time on the dog's physical energy demands, and not enough on their mental demands.

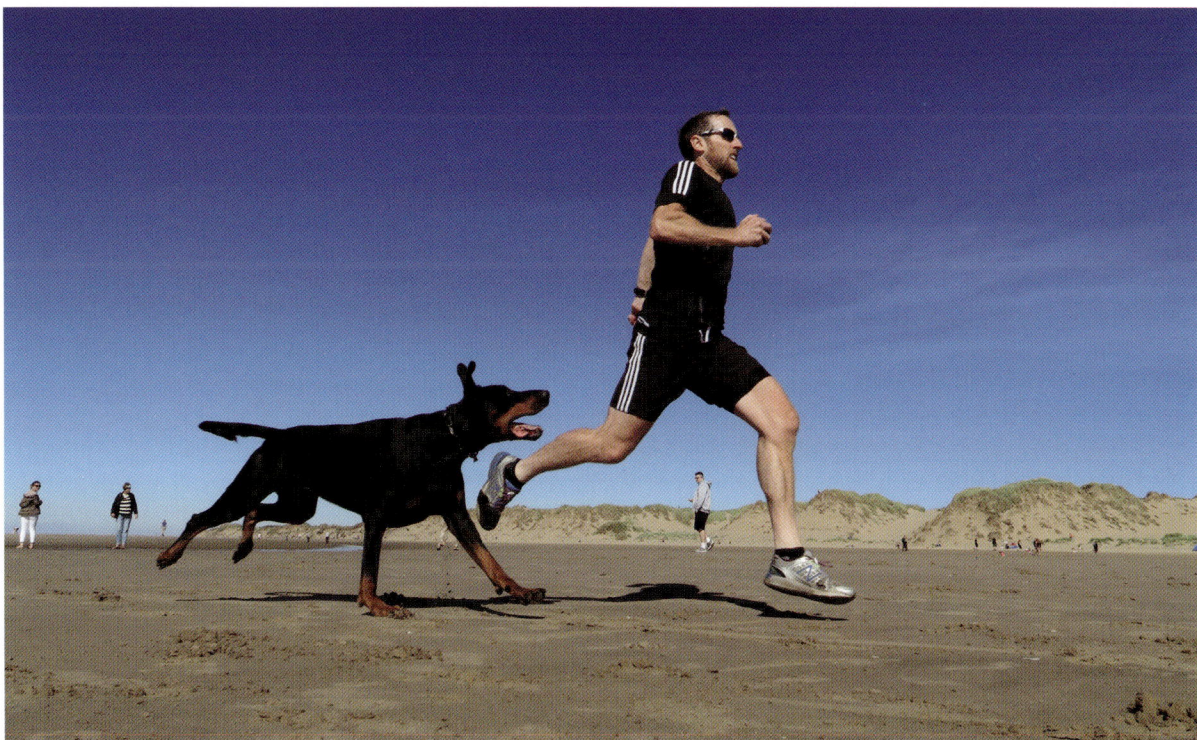

Keeping each other healthy and fit: long-distance runners Simon Liptrott and Hachi.

Wild dogs and wolves do not spend energy running wildly in every direction just for the sake of it. They maintain fitness by roaming over large areas of territory in a steady trot, which keeps their muscles in tip-top condition, waiting for the spurt of energy needed to catch their prey, for which they can attain speeds as high as 40mph.

The US Fish and Wildlife Service reports that wolves can regularly travel up to 30 miles a day, and dispersing wolves have travelled as far as 600 miles from their original location. Although evolutionary domesticity has made the companion dog of today far removed from their lupine forebears, they retain the instinctive urge to roam. Whilst few of us can achieve that level of endurance with our dogs, we can replicate these behaviour patterns in a scaled-down version by providing mostly road walking or trotting instead of free running.

UNDERSTANDING BREED TYPE AND FUNCTION

Understanding breed type and function is important in assessing the exercise requirements of any breed. 'Fit for function, fit for life' is a phrase coined by the Kennel Club some years ago, to convey that every dog bred should be capable of leading a fit, full and happy life. Of more relevance is the fact that a dog should be capable of carrying out the function *for which it is bred*. We don't expect a chihuahua to do personal protection work (although they are very sure they can), and mastiffs lack the quick turning ability of a terrier to catch rodents. Although Dobermanns are generally no longer required to be the tough deterrent they were in the last century, they should still have the mental acuity and peak physical fitness to do their job if necessary. The Dobermann is a multi-purpose breed, so it is fulfilling for them to be exercised both mentally and physically in accordance with their breed function.

Categories of Gait
There are basic categories of gait (movement styles) into which different breeds fit for their particular purpose. Common to all breeds is the

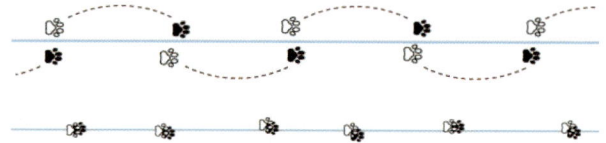

'Pacing' or waddling is when the two legs on one side move together and the two legs on the other side move together, producing a swinging action. Although it looks relaxed it isn't economic because the bodyweight and muscle is distributed unevenly. In comparison, look how efficient the trot is, where the legs move in diagonal pairs, as each side of the body works equally as hard.

walk, pace and trot. The canter and gallop are more suited to breeds such as the sight-hounds, who need to have quick bursts of speed to catch distance-running prey, whereas terriers characteristically use hair-trigger turns to catch their small, fast-moving quarry.

The trot is the preferred gait for the Dobermann, who carries his lean body squarely over long, strong legs with medium angulation in his front and back legs for a balanced, even stride. He moves forwards in a two-time gait with his feet touching the ground in diagonal pairs. During a normal trot there is a brief moment of suspension during weight transference from one pair of legs to the other; in a faster trot the stride and suspension period is longer, when it is referred to as a flying trot. When trotting naturally he moves with his head held low in front of him, with efficient movement and balance.

The average speed of the Dobermann at a steady trot is around 6–7mph. His feet are tightly bunched, like a cat, to absorb impact from the walking and trotting that Herr Dobermann required of him in his work.

The show dog with his head held artificially high is very flashy and impressive, but although the long neck muscles can sustain the position for some time, it is an inefficient style of movement.

The canter is a smooth, three-beat stride of low-impact gait giving a ground-covering stride without expending an excessive amount of energy.

Hugo and Zede trotting in relaxed extension, with good front reach and rear rotary action.
PETER WILLIAMS

The canter is an economical, ground-covering stride that the dog can sustain for long periods.
PETER WILLIAMS

Archie and Jedi showing a double suspension gallop. PETER WILLIAMS

The gallop is a four-beat gait with a brief moment of suspension. It is only used for rapid spurts of high energy, and is not an endurance pace. Breeds with a very flexible spine and high tucks-up are designed to achieve a double suspension gallop, which literally means that the dog is suspended in the air in mid-stride in two phases. In the first phase the powerful hindquarters thrust off and overtake the front legs, which are by now under the body, so the legs are tucked up and almost folded inwards on themselves before the second phase, in which the dog lands and pushes off again from the ground in full extended suspension.

Limited records show that some Molosser-type dogs – a category of solidly built, large breeds – were used in the development of the Dobermann. These breeds are 'front loaded', in that their centre of gravity is over their front end, with about 60 per cent of their bodyweight distributed over the front legs and 40 per cent at the rear. Sight-hounds such as the greyhound, on the other hand, have stronger hindquarters, which enables them to achieve the double suspension gallop needed for great speed. The Dobermann combines the strength of the Molosser with the speed of the greyhound.

The Dobermann's body is compact and muscular with tremendous energy capacity, the chest and ribcage provide large heart and lung capacity for endurance, stamina and rapid exertions, and the long bones with wide joint angles allow a long stride: put together, these features make the Dobermann a highly efficient canine athlete.

Conformation and its Effect on Function

Correct conformation is vital for general health, and not just the show ring. It enables muscles to operate efficiently, providing maximum power and essential shock absorption. It is also essential that the body parts are in balance, because if one element is out of line, another will be subjected to added stress. Faults in conformation, such as front loading and cow hocks, will therefore compromise a dog's general health and ability.

Front-Loaded Breeds

In a front-loaded breed the development of the muscles of the hindquarters is neglected, leading to weakness in the dog's rear end. If a dog pulls on the lead during walking he will develop an over-heavy front. The rump (the equivalent of our buttocks), which should be firm, rounded and well muscled, is narrow and soft toned, the adductor (inner thigh) muscles do not develop equally to the stronger outer thigh muscles, and the biceps (hamstrings) become weak through lack of work, all of which leaves the knee and hock joint unsupported.

Cow Hocks

The phrase 'cow hocked' means that the dog's hocks (the equivalent to the human ankle) are bent towards each other. Cow hocks are usually a conformational problem resulting from the dog having a long second thigh (femur) so that the weight is not carried to best advantage with his legs under his body, and this puts pressure on the stifle (knee) and hocks.

However, cow hocks are also often caused by a puppy being exercised incorrectly. Young dogs that launch off on their back legs, or which pull against the lead, put great pressure on their hocks before the muscles on the inside of the thigh (the 'second thigh' in dogs) are strong enough to counteract the pressure of the stronger outer muscles. This pushes the knees and hocks inwards so they are angled towards each other. As the puppy matures, because the hocks are now bent towards each other, even steady road-walking exercise, which should be corrective, will not develop muscle correctly, as the joint is not held in the right place.

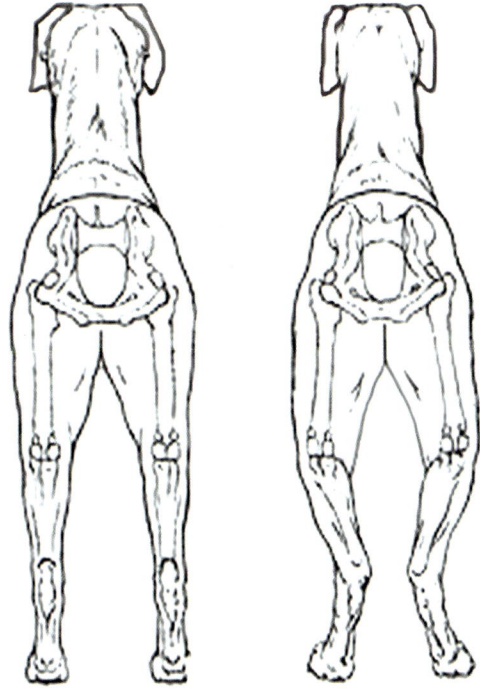

Viewed from behind: on the left are normal straight legs, and on the right are cow-hocked rear legs.

The situation is made worse by more free running, as the dog, which now has very little hindquarter strength, literally hauls himself along using his front end, with his hindquarters acting only as a stabilizer. Movement becomes inefficient, and the strain on other areas of the affected joint, which now does not function smoothly, usually results in arthritis.

COMPLETE BODY CONDITIONING

Complete body conditioning is important whether you are conditioning your dog for showing, agility, working or general fitness. Regular road-walking develops even tone around the body, avoiding strain on individual joints, muscles and tendons.

This mature male has fully developed muscles around his joints. He is not going to collapse inwards on the hocks due to any muscle weakness when pulling forward like this. Int., Multi Ch. Tahi Reme Max, AIAD Champion, ZTP V1B, IPO3.

Promoting Evenly Distributed Muscle Development

Many different exercises help promote evenly distributed muscle development in the body, combining balance front and back, and hindquarter proprioception (awareness of self). These exercises might include the following:

- Walking backwards
- Sit, to stand, to down, to sit etc
- Balance beam – on the floor at first
- Crawling
- Sit-ups
- Rocking a ball, with the front paws on the ball whilst moving it around
- Jumping over small objects
- Game of tug – gently, not a fight
- Balance boards

These exercises should be introduced slowly, and it is important not to overdo them: the benefits will be in small, steady movements. Top agility trainers do a lot of this sort of training with their dogs, as it helps the dog to be aware of his body movements.

Agility training: An excellent all-round occupation for the dog, as all the different tasks under direction from his owner keep his mind occupied, besides helping to promote his all-round physical development by increasing suppleness, exercising all the muscle groups, and improving co-ordination. Agility training also builds the dog's confidence, and benefits the owner-dog relationship as you are working together.

Obedience work: The routine exercises in obedience work are perfect for conditioning. The small, light movements of precision work may not look like much, but they add up to a great deal. Small, isometric movements work specific muscles rather than groups (compound) of mus-

---

IN SUMMARY

- Mix up the exercise routines and provide a variety of thinking games and functions such as tracking and obedience exercises during the walk
- Don't create a hyper dog that can't focus on anything but needing more exercise
- If you have even just half an hour spare, use it for training rather than just running

cles. The brain is focusing on the obedience tasks, while the body is incidentally targeting each muscle to fatigue. Obedience workouts offer low-grade impact on the body, making them ideal for general fitness and injury recovery. Ideally they leave the dog physically and mentally tired but satisfied.

Cycling and/or jogging: With your dog running alongside, this provides a good aerobic work-out for physically mature dogs of over fifteen to eighteen months. Muscles are evenly developed around the body, and, most importantly, it satisfies the innate and primitive canine urge to roam and trot with the pack, providing far deeper fulfilment than galloping at full speed around the park.

Swimming: A perfect exercise for dogs, as it allows muscles to move freely and increases

Despite having had his foreleg amputated because of cancer, Jed kept fit and healthy through exercise.
PETER WILLIAMS

cardiovascular endurance without stressing the skeletal system. If you go to a hydrotherapy pool make sure the hydrotherapist keeps the dog level in the water, and that the dog isn't 'doggy paddling' with his front end raised higher: if he is, it will over-develop the thoracic part of the trapezius muscle, which will lead to a bulging muscle over the shoulder. This is undesirable, particularly in show dogs, as the big muscle mass spoils the clean shoulder line; it is especially prominent on the move.

Water treadmills: These treadmills are now routinely used to keep competition dogs in peak shape, and are ideal for injured and elderly dogs. Their use can improve mobility and also the speed of recovery from injuries by strengthening muscles with minimal impact, and by increasing cardiovascular fitness. It is very useful for increased hind proprioception (awareness), and is particularly important in the Dobermann, who uses his front rather than his hindquarters for propulsion.

Use a member of a regulatory body such as the National Association of Registered Canine Hydrotherapists or the Canine Hydrotherapy Association.

Steady Exercise
First of all, steady exercise helps reduce the psychological effects of stress by producing the calming hormones of brain dopamine, serotonin and noradrenalin. The particular exercise of trotting alongside his human owner when they are either jogging or cycling, provides the dog (and the human) with more than simply a good form of exercise: it also allows the prefrontal (thinking) brain to switch off and relax, whilst the locomotive system continues to function automatically and rhythmically. This combination of factors releases 'feel good' endorphin hormones through the limbic system and the hippocampus, the two parts of the brain controlling motivation and mood, both of which are stimulated by exercise.

However, *even* though you may be happy to pedal along at full pelt, be careful that you are not pushing your dog to the point of exhaustion and beyond. To be most effective remember the relaxed loping of the wolf, which does not trot flat out, pounding the ground. This is not meant to be a race or an exercise in endurance, but the pack instinct is so high in a dog that he will continue to do his best to keep up with his owner, despite fatigue. So take it slowly and steadily, stopping occasionally for a rest and to check his feet.

Furthermore, we can't always avoid tarmac roads and lanes, and the hard surface can cause abrasions on the pads; also, if the dog is pounding along heavily at too fast a trot, his joints and bones will suffer from compression injuries. Glance down to check on his gait and stride, which should be balanced; take frequent breaks, and build up slowly to a full level of fitness.

See Chapter 5, Working and Training, for more details of the AD (Ausdauerprufung) Endurance test and Cani-X, which are both tests of fitness, and sports that an owner and his dog can undertake together.

MANAGING EXERCISE AND ITS EFFECTS
Warming Up and Cooling Down
Whether you are planning on doing any type of endurance training, or if you are just going in the fields to give your dog a long run, ideally you should prepare him before he starts any strenuous exercise. Cold muscles, ligaments and tendons are prone to injury if they are not stretched and warmed up before being put under pressure, so if you let the dog out of the car at the field, try to get him to do some warm-up stretches in the car park before you set off.

Dogs can be taught to stretch just as they can be taught to sit. Encourage stretching by massaging along the spine and down the legs: asking for a spin turn to the left and a spin turn to the right will loosen the body. Ideally walk to the field for ten minutes or so before letting him run free, as that will loosen up any tight muscles.

Cooling down is equally as important as warming up, and just as the dog should not go from crate to field, neither should he go directly from field to crate without settling his heart rate down and letting his muscles relax, in the same way as when warming up.

Lactic Acidosis

This is an unusual painful condition that can occur in healthy human and canine athletes after exercise. During normal exercise the liver and kidneys maintain the balance of lactic acid produced by the muscles for energy, and remove it from the body. When the body is tired and working anaerobically (without oxygen), lactic acid is not adequately cleared from the blood and accumulates in the muscles, causing lactic acidosis. Common symptoms include excessive panting, sickness and abdominal cramps. Persistent lactic acid in the body can affect cardiac and other organ function.

Progress Gradually

If you are planning to start running or cycling with your adult dog, ease him into the new exercise routine slowly as you would for yourself, by including just a minute or two of a steady trot in your normal walk. Gradually progress to more small runs a few times a week, rather than one long run a week, which puts both you and the dog under duress, and which will be less beneficial in the long term. Little and often is the key to building fitness. If you and your dog are overweight, you will both struggle with the extra stress on bones and joints, so work into running slowly and avoid strenuous endurance or speed work until you are both at peak fitness.

Walk Purposefully

Like all dogs, Dobermanns prefer an active and purposeful walking pace rather than a meandering wander, so if you can't manage a run or a cycle ride, provide a satisfying route march to get the dog into a good stride and workout. The discipline of structured exercise can be very satisfying, and if the dog spends the whole walk sniffing the floor, he is not making the most of the walk – there is plenty of time for sniffing when he is off lead in the woods on a recreational walk.

Similarly, with both males and females, don't let them stop and pee every few minutes. Males in particular like to mark every lamp-post, but you are playing a poor leader if you follow your dog to each pee stop he fancies. There is plenty of time for both scent stops and pee stops on a recreational walk; try and get into a good rhythmic stride on your walk or run, and let the brain switch off whilst the body moves forwards.

INJURIES

Identifying Injuries

Ligaments and tendons are very similar to each other in their functions: tendons attach muscle to bone, and ligaments attach bone to bone. This can make identifying injuries quite difficult as the symptoms of injury are similar. Both are made of collagen fibres for elasticity, but they are created differently for each function. The fibres in tendons run parallel to each other to allow for more stretch in the muscles, while in ligaments the fibres are formed in a cross-hatch pattern to help keep the joints stable.

The relative rigidity of ligaments can cause them to tear or rupture when they are under strain or subjected to sudden force, and cruciate ligament injuries are common in both human sportsmen and women, and in some dogs. Both humans and dogs are susceptible to cruciate injuries, particularly when turning fast at high speed, where strain equivalent to G force is exerted on joints and ligaments.

Tendons can become partially torn but will heal, but a total rupture can cause complete loss of movement.

These types of injury may result in the dog pulling up suddenly, usually with a yelp, and limping, so if you suspect this has happened, you should see the vet to ascertain if any treatment is needed, or just rest. Do not continue with exercise if ligament or tendon damage is suspected, as more damage can occur.

For this very good reason puppies should have only limited exposure to hard or long durations of exercise, otherwise their joints will suffer, and their tendons and ligaments are not strong enough to support excessive stress. Even games on flat ground, such as chasing a frisbee, can put extreme force on the soft tissues on the outside of the carpal joints when the dog stops and turns.

Assessing for Injuries

Whether you are conditioning your dog for performance work or the show ring, or just going for a hike through the local woods, it is useful to have a professional assess your dog at least once or twice a year to prevent small problems developing into more serious conditions.

Dog competition is contended very seriously nowadays, and the owners of dogs competing in top-flight agility, working trials, Schutzhund and so on will have their canine athletes assessed regularly by professionals to ensure the dog isn't carrying even a small injury which could be impacting on its performance. Even minor injuries can affect the way a joint works, as the dog will develop alternative movement styles to avoid stressing the injured part further. Compensatory issues can then occur as the body isolates areas of pain to reduce stress to the affected area, and as a result stresses are added to other areas, changing how the dog walks, runs and jumps.

The observant owner who notices that something is not quite right can glean much more information than just the fact that the dog is lame. For example, is he weight bearing evenly, or leaning slightly one way? Is he resting one leg by dropping down from the hip (as a human would stand relaxed with one hip dropped), or is one foot being raised slightly off the floor and then put back down again? Are his muscles the same size on each side, or do some bulge more, or are some flatter than others? A healthy solid spine has strong lumbar muscles on each side, and by feeling or looking at those, the owner may see if some of the spinal segments stick up further than others, or if the muscles are shrunken or enlarged on one side or the other – this could indicate a long-standing lower back problem, possibly from pain and/or nerve compression.

Raised hair is a very useful indicator of a potential problem as tense muscles and nerves create a dimpled effect over the area of tension, causing the hair around it to stand on end. Excessive licking is also symptomatic of injury. Other signs of underlying tension may be:

- stiffness after exercise – even if it wears off
- restlessness
- a change of shape
- tightening of the collar without any weight gain
- loss of hindquarter muscle
- a dry nose
- unusual performance
- concentration errors
- lack of enthusiasm for an exercise the dog has previously loved

(See Chapter 9, General Health and Welfare, for more information on injuries.)

Treatment Options

If a dog is injured there are a various treatment options available apart from veterinary care, ranging from chiropractors, remedial sports masseurs, and hydrotherapy/water treadmill gait analysis; these will also ensure the dog stays in peak performance condition.

Hydrotherapy centres: Can now be found in most big towns, and usually include both a warm pool, and more commonly these days a water treadmill where gait can be analysed. Hydrotherapy works all the muscles in balance without the stress of impact. A good canine hydrotherapist will hold dogs steady and horizontal in the pool to work muscles evenly. In some older pools the water is cold, which is not as beneficial for muscles that have not already been warmed up, as working 'cold' and unloosened muscles defeats the purpose of any exercise.

Chiropractic treatment and physiotherapy massage: Invaluable for any dog, and particularly those which regularly take part in sports such as agility and IPO (Schutzhund). Chiropractic treatment may also be useful in preventing lick sores, as dogs often chew areas of discomfort on the body. Puckered areas or raised hair often indicate underlying damage and strain, which can be relieved by a combination of approaches.

Galen myotherapy: A long-established method of assessing and treating dogs with postural and loading issues, and which suffer muscle pain caused by repetitive strain or injury, or compensatory problems from such conditions as arthritis or joint disease. Before treatment the dog is assessed to identify any behavioural traits specific to the muscular pain and dysfunction, along with observation of posture and loading, gait analysis and hands-on palpation of the whole dog to identify muscle dysfunction that may be causing the lameness or lack of mobility. Once the source of the problem is identified, the hands-on treatment relieves the inhibited muscle congestion to help restore posture, ease pain and facilitate eased joint function. (Reference Galen Myotherapy, West Sussex, England, 01403 740189.)

Thermal radiographic imaging: This very clever system uses a thermal sensitive camera to take a graphical image of the infrared radiation (heat) being emitted by the body called a thermogram. Hot areas show up on a camera monitor as red, and cool areas appear blue.

Physiotherapists: Vets are the general practitioners of the animal world, but unless they specialize in a particular area they can't reasonably be expected to spot every out-of-place hair. There are now many good canine physiotherapists in most regions. Anyone working with animals in these professions must be registered with their relevant regulatory body.

8 NUTRITION AND FEEDING

All disease begins in the gut.

Hippocrates

In 1913, fifty-seven leading researchers and doctors of the Royal Society of Medicine met in London to discuss alimentary toxaemia. Their 382-page report was entitled 'Death Begins in the Colon', and it stated that 'almost every known chronic disease is directly or indirectly due to the influence of more than 30 bacterial poisons that are absorbed from the intestines which accumulate because of poor eliminations from the colon.' Despite incredible technological advances this statement holds true today.

Puppies doing what comes naturally.

HISTORY OF NUTRITION

Wolves and dogs shared their last common ancestor around 32,000 years ago, and the process of domestication of the dog gradually occurred between then and 18,000 years ago. The divergence of wolves and dogs is so recent in evolutionary terms that many of the genes have not yet separated into distinct lineages.

Canids have always been opportunist eaters, originally scavenging from the waste of human settlements. The early diet of these scavenger dogs consisted of the scrap remains of the meat the hunters brought home, and the discards of the gathered vegetable and other carbohydrates. The canine diet remained unchanged for many thousands of years, with food supplies being so precious that little more than scraps were left spare for dogs. But as man began using dogs as an aid to hunt or in defence of his property, their value increased, and with it the food they were given.

2,000 years ago the first farming books were written by the Roman Marcus Terentius, who wrote:

> The food of dogs is more like that of man than that of sheep: they eat scraps of meat and bones, not grass and leaves. They are also fed on bone soup and broken bones from sheep as well for these make their teeth stronger and their mouths of wider stretch, because their jaws are spread with greater force, and the savour of the marrow makes them more keen.

As the growing middle classes in the eighteenth and early nineteenth centuries kept more dogs as household pets, entrepreneurs started selling meat to them. At the other end of the social scale the big sport of dog fighting required prize animals to be at peak fitness, and an interest in nutrition became more important to owners. In 1833 *The Complete Farrier* advised:

> The dog is neither wholly carnivorous nor wholly herbivorous, but of a mixed kind, and can receive nourishment from either flesh or vegetables. A mixture of both is therefore his proper food, but of the former he requires a greater portion, and this portion should be always determined by his bodily exertions.

PROCESSED FOODS VERSUS RAW (BARF) FOOD

In 1860 the first basic dog biscuits of flour, water and salt were made by James Spratt, who later added vegetables and beef blood to his mix. Then in around 1918 canned dog meat (the meat being mostly horse) started development, and by the mid-1930s 50,000 horses were being slaughtered annually just for dog food. By 1941 tinned dog food held a 90 per cent share of the market. But by the time the USA entered World War II both tinned meat and meat were rationed, and the nation returned to dry food for their dogs.

In the 1960s the Pet Food Institute was established to lobby for the pet food industry, which was spending $50 million a year on advertising. Their aim was to persuade owners to feed their dogs only packaged or canned dog food, and they did this by funding 'scientific research' to prove the benefits of 'complete' dog food; they even produced a radio advert warning of the 'dangers' of feeding table scraps to dogs, claiming that the only responsible way to feed dogs was with processed 'complete' food.

But in 1993 the Australian nutritionist, agricultural scientist and vet Ian Billinghurst published a book called *Give Your Dog a Bone*. This caught the imagination of many thousands of dog owners around the world, and gave the generations who had grown up knowing only processed food for their dogs, the first glimpse of what 'real food' was. This natural feeding method was given the acronym BARF – 'Biologically Appropriate Raw Food', and/or 'Bones and Raw Food'.

Many dog owners now questioned whether the rise in allergies, dietary complaints and other

Raw carrots have little nutritional value as dogs can only digest plant proteins which have been crushed (by a prey animal or machine) or cooked to make the proteins accessible. Dogs still enjoy chewing them, and cold or semi-frozen they are soothing for a puppy's gums when it is teething.

illnesses could be attributed to the modern processed food they had been feeding for years. In 2014 a TV programme called 'The Truth about Your Dog's Food' claimed that the pet food industry was profit-motivated, and that poor quality and harmful ingredients were included in the food produced by the corporate brands. It also alleged complicity between veterinary schools, the veterinary profession as a whole, and corporate pet food producers.

Although veterinary teaching colleges now include reference to raw feeding in their syllabus, it is in order to debunk it; they provide scant evidence to support it. In fact vet schools are actively sponsored by pet food companies, who 'contribute by providing additional lectures and branded text books' (source: Pet Food Manufacturers Association – PFMA). They also state that 'this will enable students to be familiar with the products available on the market so they can discuss nutrition with pet owners to help them make an informed choice'. But in the words of Shirley Chisholm: 'When morality is up against profit, it is seldom that profit loses.'

'Complete' food, or kibble as it is known, comes in pre-prepared formulas to suit the age, weight and breed of the dog.

An ideal 'complete' raw meal for a dog, known as 'prey model raw' (PMR), is something like a whole rabbit. This contains all the elements the dog needs for a perfect balance of vitamins, minerals and nutrients, proteins, fats and bone matter, in one sitting. The dog will firstly eat the rich organs of the liver, kidneys and heart, then the muscles and remaining soft tissue, then the nutritional (edible) bones, and lastly the skin and hair (jacket) that will wrap around any potentially damaging bone fragments in the dog's gut.

Wolves and wild dogs naturally balance their diet over time, eating various grasses, herbs, seeds and berries, and wild bird eggs, between kills.

COMPLETE FOODS VERSUS BARF FOOD

Both complete and BARF methods of feeding have advantages and disadvantages. As not all complete foods and not all raw feeding methods are equal, the following is a generalization based on the 'traditional' complete food (excepting grain-free foods).

Advantages of Complete
Convenient
Clean, with lower hygiene risk
Volumes and ingredients pre-prepared
Age-specific diets pre-prepared

Advantages of BARF
Biologically appropriate
Reduced risk of bloat
Improved absorption/small stools
Harder body tone and condition
Clean teeth and gum margins
Normal anal gland function
Full knowledge of contents
Cheaper (versus quality complete)

Disadvantages of Complete
Risk of bloat
Increased allergy risk (moulds)
Large stools
Majority grain/starches rendering of meat
Unknown sources (cheap foods)
Preservatives and colours (some)
Plaque accumulation on teeth
Expensive (for quality food)

Disadvantages of BARF
Risk of incorrect diet
Hygiene risk from handling raw meat
Inconvenient
Storage – freezer space and storing Processing/ defrosted meat in the fridge

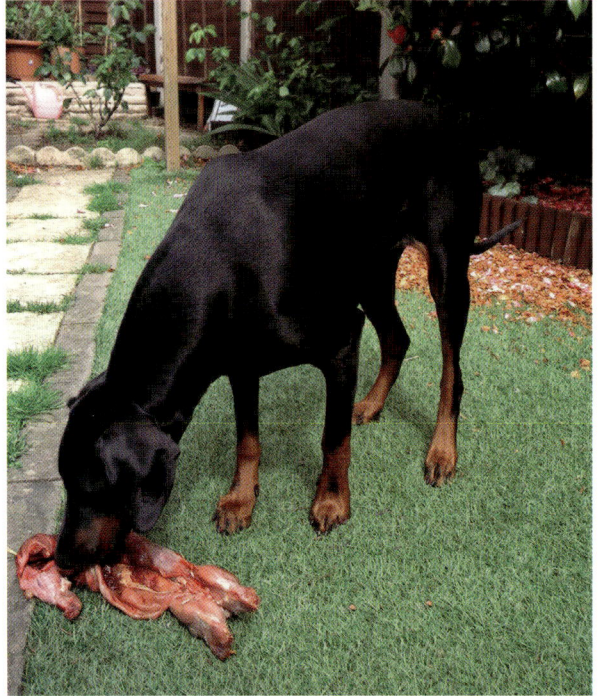

Leica eating a whole rabbit. This one has been skinned, but dogs can eat the whole animal; jacket (skin and fur), nails, and head. KATIE BULLOCK

There is just 0.2 per cent difference in the DNA of the grey wolf and the domestic dog, and canids will eat whichever prey is dominant in the region. Analysis of 2,063 wolf scats collected over thirteen years in Scandinavia found that moose comprised 68.9 per cent of their diet, whilst a four-year study on 1,682 wolf scats in Mexico showed that elk comprised 72.8 per cent of the diet, and that 25 per cent consisted of various smaller prey species. A smaller study in the Himalayas showed a 91.4 per cent prey diet.

Thus clearly the natural diet preference for the wolf/dog is proteins over carbohydrates in an approximate ratio exceeding 90:10.

Commercial dog foods on average comprise 70–90 per cent carbohydrates (consisting of grains, vegetables, rice, and potato or vegetable based foods) and 10–30 per cent protein: in other words, a complete reversal of the natural canid diet. Notably the Pet Food Manufacturers Association (PFMA) states that 'dogs have no absolute dietary requirement for carbohydrates'. In fact the carb/non-carb argument has raged for years, and even the BARF community disagrees on the amount of carbs a dog benefits from, if any.

Having watched their owner picking blackberries, these dogs quickly learned how to pick their own food. Whether through colour or odour, they always find the ripe berries and ignore the rest.

COMPLETE/ KIBBLE FOODS

Complete/ kibble foods consist of a set of ingredients that are mixed together, cooked at a very high temperature (200°C), and then extruded into shaped pellets and coated with oils and fats. These foods are easy to store and serve, and if it is a quality product, most dogs do well on it. Over half the pet owners in the UK feed their dogs on kibble. There are around fifty UK manufacturers who are members of the PFMA, and 90 per cent of brands in the UK come from just four corporate multi-national companies; smaller independent labels make up 10 per cent of the market.

Pet food manufacture is governed by the Department of Food and Rural Affairs (DEFRA) under the EU Animal By-Products Regulations.

CONSTITUENTS AND MANUFACTURE OF KIBBLE FOODS

Kibble meats are acquired from rendering plants, which collect products from slaughterhouses. Most source from excellent plants, but others do not, and these can legally include animals classified as '4D': 'Dead, Dying, Diseased or Disabled (downed)'. If the animal is condemned as 'not fit for human consumption' it must be 'denatured' to differentiate it, either with a dye or charcoal. Note that pet food labelling using charcoal may identify it as containing denatured meat.

DEFRA licenses manufacturers to use any processed or factory-rejected pet food from animal by-products: hides, skins, hair, horns, feet, pig bristle, feather or blood, placenta, wool, raw milk, hatchery waste, eggs, eggshells, day-old (live ground) chicks, and fish and its by-products, such as degreased bones and seafood shell waste.

The combined products are rendered, separating fat from the bone and protein, converting tissue into protein meal, and bone into bone meal. It is all edible, with varying nutritional values, and is classified as follows:

Meat and bone meal: This is the dry matter from all animal tissues, which is cooked down like a large stew, heated at very high temperatures to evaporate the water, and baked. It is typically around 50 per cent protein, 35 per cent ash, 10 per cent fat, and 5 per cent moisture.

Animal fat: The greasy debris that remains after rendering and extracting. It is listed as inedible for humans. Fats are necessary for dogs as they are one of their primary energy sources, so listed ingredients such as poultry fat, beef fat, salmon oil and chicken fat are acceptable fats.

Animal digest: The liquid resulting from the chemical or enzymatic washing of clean and undecomposed animal tissue. This heat-treated broth is usually sprayed on to the kibble to make it smell and taste more appealing to the pets that eat it. The source must have been produced from tissues belonging to the listed animal species, but could include 4D-sourced meat.

Notably the UK PFMA states that 'digests ("flavouring innards") can be imported from *non-EU countries*, for the manufacture of pet foods'.

READING LABELS AND CHECKING INGREDIENTS

On bags and packaging the largest ingredients of any food must legally be listed first. Foods should ideally have an animal protein listed in its first three ingredients, with no more than two grain sources in the first five ingredients. A misleading practice is to itemize the ingredients separately to make it look as if there is more protein includ-

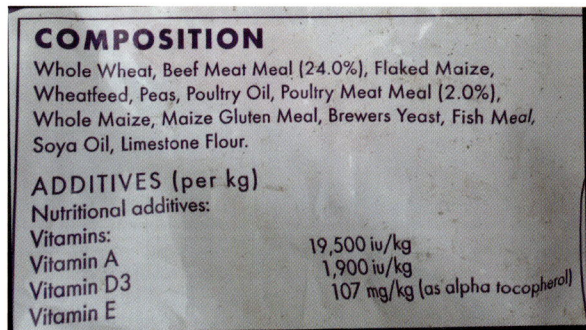

COMPOSITION

Whole Wheat, Beef Meat Meal (24.0%), Flaked Maize, Wheatfeed, Peas, Poultry Oil, Poultry Meat Meal (2.0%), Whole Maize, Maize Gluten Meal, Brewers Yeast, Fish Meal, Soya Oil, Limestone Flour.

ADDITIVES (per kg)

Nutritional additives:

Vitamins:

Vitamin A	19,500 iu/kg
Vitamin D3	1,900 iu/kg
Vitamin E	107 mg/kg (as alpha tocopherol)

A food composed of mostly grains.

Some manufacturers now list 'total meat content', rather than itemizing the ingredients, which is much clearer.

GB/IRL/RSA/AUS - Complete feed for dogs
For adult medium breed dogs (from 11 to 25 kg)
From 12 months to 7 years old

COMPOSITION: dehydrated poultry protein, maize flour, maize, wheat flour, animal fats, dehydrated pork protein, wheat, hydrolysed animal proteins, beet pulp, fish oil, soya oil, yeasts, minerals, hydrolysed yeast (source of manno-oligo-saccharides). ADDITIVES (per kg): Nutritional additives: Vitamin A: 12000 IU, Vitamin D3: 800 IU, E1 (Iron): 46 mg, E2 (Iodine): 4.6 mg, E4 (Copper): 9 mg, E5 (Manganese): 60 mg, E6 (Zinc): 181 mg, E8 (Selenium): 0.12 mg - Preservatives - Antioxidants. ANALYTICAL CONSTITUENTS: Protein: 25% - Fat content: 14% - Crude ash: 5.9% - Crude fibres: 1.2% - Per kg: Manno-oligo-saccharides: 0.5 g - Omega 3 fatty acids: 6 g including EPA/DHA: 3.1 g. FEEDING INSTRUCTIONS: see chart. Batch number, factory registration number and best before date: see information on packaging. To be stored in a cool, dry place. For RSA: Guaranteed analysis g/kg: Crude protein (min) 230 - Moisture (max) 110 - Crude fat (min) 120 - Crude fibre (max) 22 - Crude ash (max) 65. Product registration number: - Act 36/1947.

ed – for instance 'fresh chicken, chicken fat, chicken digest'.

'Chicken' is the wet weight of the animal. As water makes up around 65 per cent of the weight of fresh chicken or lamb, once the water is removed the actual amount of meat is far less, so on labelling this would move chicken down the list and other ingredients would move to the top. To make 1kg of dried chicken meat requires 2.8kg of fresh chicken. Choose *dry* weight of meat meal (only around 5 per cent water), rather than just 'meat'.

Comparing ratios between canned and dry food is only possible once the moisture content has been removed; it leaves the true nutrient value of a food expressed as 'dry matter basis'.

The True Value of Kibble Food Ingredients
The ingredients of a kibble/complete food as presented on the bag don't always tell the full story regarding their nutritional worth. Below are some common examples.

'**Natural**': This description isn't always what it may seem, as by law manufacturers can claim the product is 'natural' if *just 10 per cent* of the product comes from natural food sources.

'**Derivatives of animal origin**': Legally this allows manufacturers to avoid specifying the origin of the protein source. Low quality pet food companies use the cheapest protein available at the time of processing their foods. This could include euthanased and dead pet or farm animals, and restaurant and slaughterhouse waste such as feathers, fur, beaks and claws. If a label doesn't state which 'meat' or 'animal', the protein source will be varied and of low quality.

'**Derivatives of vegetable origin**': Legally this allows manufacturers to avoid specifying the ori-

What is the first ingredient in your pet food?

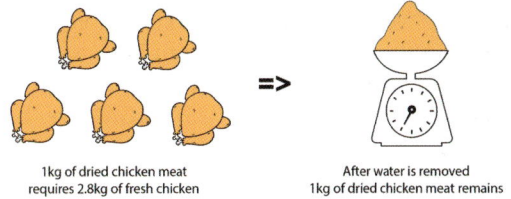

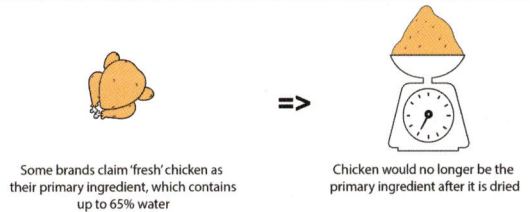

1kg of dried chicken meat requires 2.8kg of fresh chicken

=>

After water is removed 1kg of dried chicken meat remains

Some brands claim 'fresh' chicken as their primary ingredient, which contains up to 65% water

=>

Chicken would no longer be the primary ingredient after it is dried

If dried meat is used as the primary ingredient

=>

Dry chicken meat remains the primary ingredient in the finished product

By using dried meats as a primary ingredient there is 4 times more real meat protein in every bag

Scales of food. GEORGE MEADEN

PETS IN PET FOOD?

When the drug Pentobarbital, which is used to put animals to sleep, was found in some kibble, it seemed that euthanased pets were being included in pet food. However, a 2002 US FDA study found no dog or cat DNA in samples that had tested positive for Pentobarbital. It was proposed that any Pentobarbital residues that had survived the cooking and rendering processes, entered the pet food chain from euthanased farm animals and horses. No manufacturer who values their brand would knowingly include meat from dead pets in their food.

gin of the vegetable matter. They can change the formula to any vegetable of low nutritional value according to availability and price.

Soya/soy: Part of the legume family (peas, beans), and used to increase protein (it is cheaper than meat protein) and bulk. But soy is difficult to digest, and dogs produce a lot of gas on it; it is also a leading cause of food-related allergies in dogs. Soy will be listed as vegetable broth, textured vegetable protein (TVP), textured soy flour (TSF), tofu, vegetable protein, guar gum etc. Around 90 per cent of the soya produced in the USA is GM. Soy bean acids bind to dietary minerals such as iron, zinc and manganese, and block their absorption.

- A 2004 reproduction and growth study at the University of Pennsylvania of twenty-four random commercial dog foods revealed that 'all the foods containing Soy had concentrations of phyto-oestrogens in large enough quantities to have a biological effect on the animal.'
- One of the canine world's leading health experts Dr Jean Dodds states 'Soy interferes with the thyroid gland's ability to make T4 (thyroxine) and (T3) tri-iodothyronine, hormones necessary for normal thyroid function. In dogs, the result is hypothyroidism.'

Wheat: Harder to digest than rice, and because many dogs appear to be intolerant to wheat gluten, many pet foods are now wheat gluten free.

Corn: A cheap cereal crop which provides bare nutritional value to a dog. Unless correctly pro-

cessed, it is largely indigestible and has a poor amino acid profile. Barley is a starchy carbohydrate with medium energy value.

Dried whey: A by-product of the cheese industry, which is low in protein and has around 75 per cent carbohydrates.

Vegetables and cereal-based food: Grains, vegetables and fillers such as beet pulp and corn may satisfy the dog with a full stomach but leaves him craving nutrition because carbohydrates are not digested as efficiently as fats and proteins. Cereal-based food is of low nutritional benefit and financially wasteful, with nearly as much coming out as going in.

> Colonic bacteria ferment unabsorbed carbohydrates into CO_2, methane, H_2, and short-chain fatty acids (butyrate, propionate, acetate, and lactate) which can cause abdominal gases with distension and bloating.
> *'Malabsorption Syndromes', The Merck Veterinary Manual of Diagnosis and Therapy.*

Rice: For dog food rice is mostly 'feed grade', made up of the pieces left over when rice is processed for human consumption. Sick dogs benefit from eating fresh rice (mixed with lightly cooked chicken, fish stock or soup), as the rice acts like a sponge to absorb bacteria. This ability to absorb bacteria also means that once rice is cooked, it must be fed promptly, as rice is one of the fastest breeding grounds for bacteria.

'**Various sugars**': These are difficult to avoid as they may be added as a flavour enhancer, but they may also be natural sugars from carbohydrates, or even the browning from cooked meats. Sugar contributes to dental disease and diabetes. Note that sugar contents can reach 25 per cent in some foods.

PRESERVATIVES (ANTI-OXIDANTS) IN PROCESSED FOODS

Preservatives (anti-oxidants) in processed foods can be synthetic or natural. 'E' indicates EU-approved preservatives, and are usually labelled as EEC- or EU-permitted anti-oxidants and preservatives. The most common preservatives used in pet food are BHA (E320), BHT (E321) and Ethoxyquin (E324).

Ethoxyquin: Developed as a rubber stabilizer, and an insecticide. In studies on pregnant animals it has been found to cause gross birth deformities. In 2012 the FDA issued an industry reminder stating 'if Ethoxyquin is added to an animal feed, either directly or indirectly (as the component of an ingredient), this information must appear on the label.'

Butylated Hydroxytoluene (BHT) and Butylated Hydroxyanisole (BHA): Used to stop fat becoming rancid. The US DHHS classify them as 'reasonably anticipated to be a human carcinogen'. BHA is banned in infant foods throughout the EU, and in Japan. BHA/BHT is used in 9 per cent of kibble.

Propylene glycol: A preservative often used in semi-moist kibble to maintain water content and texture. It is an ingredient in anti-freeze (along with ethylene glycol) and can be fatal to dogs and cats which are attracted to licking the sweet tasting solution.

Propyl Gallate (E310): An anti-oxidant banned from children's foods in the US because it is thought to cause blood disorders.

Synthetic anti-oxidants: Often added pre-mixed, enabling some manufacturers to misleadingly claim 'No added colourants or synthetic preservatives', on the basis that if they didn't put the preservative in there themselves, they don't have to list it amongst their product ingredients.

Sodium nitrate: A mineral salt powder found in processed meat to prevent it turning grey. It is a flavour enhancer and preservative, and increases the weight of the meat. Salt causes water retention, which raises blood pressure and places strain on the heart and other organs. Studies on pregnant mammals showed that 'high levels of nitrite result in foetal loss, lower litter numbers and neonatal mortality.' (Ref. Fan A.M., Willhite C.C., Book S.A. *Regul Toxicol Pharmacol*, 1987.

Colours: Added to make pet food attractive to the owner. Red No. 2 and Violet No. 1 dyes were banned from human foods in the 1970s as they were linked to cancer, birth defects and skin lesions. In 2008 the UK FSA banned six food colours that were found to increase hyperactivity in children. This ban was later replicated in the EU, but is not yet implemented in the USA. There are no legal limits on the use of colours in dog food.

More on Preservatives
- If a food is synthetically preserved, Burns Pet Foods® calculate that the average 25lb dog will consume 6–9lb of chemical preservatives a year. With the bodyweight for the Dobermann being double that, the average Dobermann therefore consumes around 18lb of toxins annually
- Wet (canned or pouch) food contains fewer synthetic preservatives because ingredients are sealed and prevented from oxidizing and degrading. Some smaller producers steam-cook foods to maintain natural vitamin and mineral values
- Choose foods that are preserved naturally. Buy smaller bags as the shelf life is shorter

CONTAMINATION IN COMPLETE FEEDS

Grain infestation of mould, weevils and mites and their droppings is a big problem in the storage and feeding of any complete food. A dog suffering allergies is not usually intolerant to the grain, but to the poisonous fungal spores and storage mites in many foods. Poor harvesting and storage conditions of grains can lead to toxic mould growth, which is then spread by mites and insects carrying contamination.

Aflatoxin (one of the Mycotoxin group) is a by-product of a mould that thrives in dry conditions. Aflatoxin B1 is the most deadly as it accumulates in the liver where even trace amounts can cause cancers and liver failure. Although cooking can kill the mould and mites, the toxins are stable and resilient to very high temperatures, and retain their toxicity even when baked into the finished product. There is no cure for, or safe level of, mycotoxins.

Research published in 2006 in the *Journal of Agricultural and Food Chemistry* confirmed that 'mycotoxins are present in pet foods around the world, and contamination in pet foods can lead to chronic effects on the health of pets.' Manufacturers now regularly test each batch of grain for mycotoxin presence prior to use.

In 2005 and 2007 the US Food and Drug Administration (FDA) received reports of around 8,500 pet dog and cat deaths that were found to be the result of eating contaminated feeds, and this resulted in major pet food recalls. Most originated from one single company that supplied 100 brands of cat and dog food, including those from major pet food corporations. This linked the shared feed origins of top quality 'trusted' brands with those at the bottom of the market. This and the Melamine recall (used as a fertilizer, banned in US food but imported in wheat gluten from China) was a catalyst for many to change to home-prepared diets for their pets.

Kibble foods may last well beyond their sell-by date due to the preservatives, but should be kept in a sealed food bin to prevent potentially lethal degradation by insects, rodents and mould.

SPECIALIST KIBBLES

Grain-free kibble: In 2003 the first grain-free complete food, with 80 per cent dried meat and 20 per cent fruits and vegetables (later 70/30), was introduced to the UK, and many others have since followed. These foods are closer to the biological balance of the natural canid's food than standard complete food. Importantly, they do not swell in the stomach.

Organic kibble: Of the same composition and cooked at the same high temperature as normal kibble, but the ingredient quality is superior, and manufacturers don't go to the expense of using organic ingredients only to ruin the product with colours and preservatives.

Cold pressing: This process preserves dried food by processing and pressing the mixture at a low temperature of 40–75°C (as compared to the normal 200°C), thereby retaining essential nutrients. Importantly for the Dobermann, which is prone to bloat, the kibble does not swell as much as normal kibble, and breaks down in the body within twenty minutes.

CHOOSING A GOOD COMPLETE FOOD

Apart from grain-free foods, the £40 bag of food and the £10 bag of food both contain around 50–60 per cent carbohydrates, but they will differ in the quality of their ingredients; note that some costly foods can also contain many additives and preservatives. The most expensive food is not necessarily the best, but the cheapest will definitely not be.

Various breed, age and exercise appropriate foods are available, such as fish-based, which is ideal for overweight dogs, lamb-based for underweight dogs, and grain-free and specific formulas for dogs with skin or stomach disorders. 'Large breed' food is formulated for slow-growing breeds such as Great Danes and Mastiffs, with low levels of protein to maintain a steady growth rate. Some manufacturers class Dobermanns as a 'large breed', but these formulas provide insufficient protein for the Dobermann, which needs a higher volume to maintain weight. Food travels quickly through the body because he is too full to properly digest his food, and a large quantity of waste is produced.

A food can never be better than the ingredients used to create it. Buying British food with good online reviews, backed up by the expertise of a sensible, independent pet food shop adviser, may lead you to one of the smaller labels whose product ingredients are carefully sourced and manufactured.

VITAMINS, EFAS, MINERALS AND SUPPLEMENTS

Vitamins

Vitamins support cell repair, circulatory activities and collagen production. Multi-vitamins were originally made from dried and compressed natural vegetable and fruit concentrates. Today, 95 per cent of supplements are synthetic because when any food is cooked it loses some of its nutrients, so manufacturers replace these essential ingredients with a standard pre-measured mix of synthetic vitamins and minerals.

Omega Essential Fatty Acis (EFAs)

Omega 3 and omega 6 are essential for good health. Populations that eat mostly omega-3 foods live longer, healthier lives than those whose diet is low in them.

Omega 3s (ALA, EPA, DHA) are best sourced from diets rich in fresh fish, and are beneficial for breeding dogs and puppies. ALA reduces arthritis and inflammatory skin conditions. DHA from sources of fish oil can improve trainability in puppies (source: Kelley *et al,* 2004). Omega 3s may benefit good cardiac function and prevent arrhythmias. Sources of omega 6 are poultry, eggs, nuts, cereals and vegetable oils.

Deficiencies of EFAs can cause growth and reproduction problems, hair and weight loss, also thickened skin (hyperkeratosis), eczema and susceptibility to infections.

Some kibble manufacturers include omega 3 supplements to counter the excessive omega 6 levels in kibble.

Minerals

Minerals comprise around 4 per cent of the body, and are obtained through foods and water. Deficiencies can lead to minor ailments such as muscle cramps and fatigue, or major conditions such as osteoporosis (brittle bone disease). Some are

Raw mackerel or sardines are an ideal oily fish for Frieda's meal.

multi-functional and intrinsically linked, such as calcium (Ca), magnesium (Mg) and phosphorus (Ph).

Mineral deficiencies take a long time to become noticeable and to correct, whereas vitamin deficiencies operate on a short time-scale and are quickly corrected.

Supplements

Supplements are obtained naturally from food, fresh meat, fresh fish, fresh vegetables and fruit. As much harm can be done with an excess as with a deficiency, so don't 'chuck a bit in and hope for the best'.

Natural supplements: There are many on the market; two well established old remedies are Keeper's Mix from Dorwest Herbs®, which comes in powder form, and Hokamix from Kroeske BV® in powder or tablet form. These contain 100 per cent natural different herbs, which, with their vitamins and minerals, have a positive influence on the joints, providing good metabolism/digestion and restoring food deficiencies. Be careful with any supplement that contains kelp (iodine) if your dog has a thyroid problem, as it may interfere with thyroid production.

Chondroitin, glucosamine and MSM: For joint health; they are sometimes included in higher quality kibble foods. Check the levels to assess whether it is worth adding any more. The quality may be better in a product you buy and add in yourself.

Apple cider vinegar (unfiltered): An internal and external cleanser valuable for nail and skin infections, sores, warts and yeast infections. It also inhibits the growth of pathogens such E. coli. The father of modern medicine, Hippocrates, used it for wound cleaning over two thousand years ago. It is particularly useful for yeast infections.

Blackstrap molasses: A rich source of iron and B vitamins.

Nutritional yeasts: Brewer's yeast is an inactivated by-product of beer production derived from hops; pure nutritional yeast is derived from sugar cane or beet molasses and grown specifically for food consumption. Both are very rich in B vitamins and minerals.

Raw eggs: Full of protein and easy to digest. Eggshells are a good source of calcium (free-range hens peck in the soil for silicates that help in the formation of egg shells) and are enjoyed by puppies as a first easily crunched and digestible step towards bones.

*Visiting a dog we had bred, called Vince, I remarked how really well he looked. His amused owner said he was 'on the raw egg diet', explaining that Vince had learned to recognize the sound the hens made when they were laying in the barns around the farm, and had been seen taking eggs still warm from their nests. He was thieving seven or eight eggs a day until he was discovered, but he did look amazingly well on it!

Probiotics: These are beneficial bacteria, such as Lactobacillus Acidophilus, that colonize the bowel and displace unfavourable bacteria. They are very useful after taking antibiotics that destroy both good and bad bacteria. Tripe is full of natural probiotics (see below).

Coconut oil: Very popular as a food and skin supplement taken internally to promote joint, skin and dietary health; it can also be applied topically to improve itchy and flaky skin conditions. It is anti-fungal and anti-viral, and has no reported side effects.

Grass: Grass-eating enables dogs to be sick, which is a natural and beneficial action. Dogs

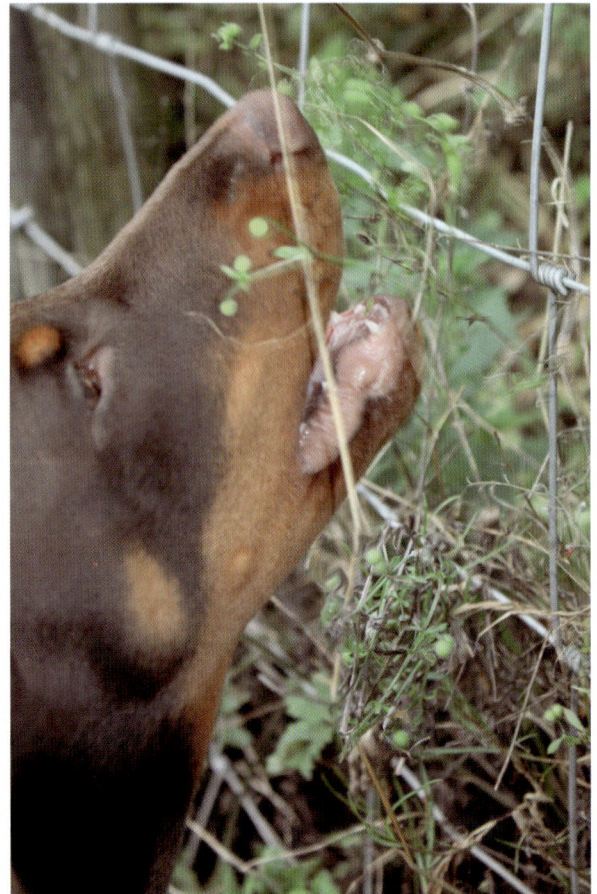

Clivers is a diuretic with mild astringent properties, which helps to keep the kidneys and bladder clear of toxins.

obviously suffering from a stomach upset, indicated either because they are tucked up in the belly or because they have diarrhoea (*see* a vet if either of these indicators continues for longer than a day), will often head directly for the rough grasses that grow at the sides of hedgerows or posts and eat them to aid vomiting. Objects that are hard to digest, or even foreign objects, may be found vomited up with coarse grass wrapped around them. Allow your dog to eat as much grass and seeds as he wants.

Dogs often enjoy eating sticky weed (clivers or goosegrass). The seventeenth-century herbalist Culpeper believed it to be 'excellent for cleansing the blood, strengthening the liver, and overall to get the body in good health ready for the change in season'.

TAKE NOTE

Whilst this section outlines the potential benefits of nutritional supplements and ingredients, it is against the law for anyone other than a qualified veterinary surgeon to make medical claims. None of the advice contained in this section is intended to be a substitute for veterinary intervention.

NATURAL RAW FEEDING (BARF)

Natural raw feeding (BARF) follows the wild canid flesh-based diet rather than a diet of cooked proteins and carbohydrates. Although dogs can digest carbohydrates, they cannot do so anywhere near as efficiently as they digest proteins and fats. These can be found in the following foods:

DANGEROUS AND TOXIC FOODS FOR DOGS

Although many things are poisonous to dogs if taken in sufficient quantity, particular foods, even in small doses, can be highly toxic. Chocolate is one of the best known toxins because it is high in theobromine, with dark chocolate being very high in theobromine. The lethal dose of both caffeine and theobromine is around 100–200mg/kg, although it is variable to the individual, and toxicity and death may occur at much lower dosages. Even 1oz of milk chocolate per 1lb of bodyweight is a potentially lethal dose in dogs. This means that a Dobermann weighing 35kg (77lb) would need to digest around 2.2kg (5lb) of milk chocolate for death to be likely.

Grapes and raisins are themselves not toxic, but the mycotoxin moulds, which are in some batches, are highly toxic. Nuts, particularly macadamia, have also been linked with some poisoning cases. Green tomatoes contain tomatine, which is harmful to dogs, although as the tomato turns a ripe red the tomatine disappears and it is then safe and enjoyable for dogs to eat.

Discarded kebab sticks are very tempting to dogs, which can eat them whole. Sweetcorn cobs are particularly lethal because they cannot be digested by the dog, and once eaten the barbs prevent them being vomited back up.

If the dog has projectile diarrhoea or is being sick/constantly retching he may have either swallowed a foreign object or developed an infection, so see a vet promptly to determine whether either is the case. Anti-emetic injections (anti-sickness) are not always sensible unless the stomach is in spasm and retching on empty, because if something needs to come out it will be stopped from doing so. If the dog is hunched up it is often an indication of a blockage, and it is not uncommon for dogs to continue to poo apparently normally despite having foreign objects lodged in the stomach.

Proteins: Meat, eggs, fish.
Fats: Animal fat, animal and plant oils, dairy products, nuts, oily fish.
Carbohydrates: Vegetables, fruit, seeds, grasses, rice.

Raw feeding uses the two basic ingredients of meat and bone, and usually a small amount of carbohydrates.

The basic BARF diet may be a protein-to-carbohydrate ratio of anything from 70:30 to 90:10. BARF diets do not feed specific portions, but ideally the dog will acquire the nutrition he needs over a succession of days or even weeks, in a system where he takes what he can find and what his body tells him he requires. On this premise his diet will achieve 'balance over time'. It is incorrect and dangerous to just feed meat without the other components of a raw diet.

Feed the bagged meat meal in the morning: this is ready prepared, minced meat available in different formulas – lamb and tripe, chicken and tripe, oily fish – with/without tripe, with beef, or minced meat with vegetables. Feed whichever mix you prefer – lamb/tripe/beef/chicken – and a carcass or lamb ribs at night so he is not exercised during the day with a stomach full of pre-digested bones.

BARF requires little more preparation than it does to put down a scoop of pellets, because all you need do is take the meat out of its bag and put it in a bowl.

Many established companies across the UK deliver by courier. Meats are individually bagged, and once defrosted are ready to feed. You will need to take the evening meal of carcass/bones out of the freezer and defrost it overnight ready to feed the next day.

Use a separate freezer for the dog meat, as the smell of tripe in particular will taint your human food.

When feeding BARF, don't expect all poos to be the same, because you are not feeding the same at every meal. After a large meal of bone the dog will deposit mostly white, chalky, crumbly faeces the next day, while after a rich organ meal he will have dark, tarry poos.

WHICH MEATS TO FEED?

Meats in a BARF diet include chicken, beef, lamb, heart, organ meats and tripe. The diet will also feature bones.

Chicken is high in protein, and low in fat; it is ideal for dogs in high energy work. Beef is high in protein, with medium fat levels, while lamb is high in protein and in fat. Fats are one of the dog's primary energy sources, and are particularly beneficial for young growing Dobermann puppies who need substance and energy without high proteins. (*See* growing pains 'Panosteitis' below, and in Chapter 10, General Health and Welfare.)

Heart Meat

Heart meat is high in protein and in fat. It is also high in B vitamins, and has some vitamin A, and some EFAs. Dark meat indicates hard-working muscles, and the heart as the hardest-working muscle in the body contains the highest amounts of the essential amino acid taurine, which is beneficial for eye and heart function, and reproduction. Large animals (such as cattle and horses) have low taurine levels, while small animals, fish, birds and rodents have higher taurine levels.

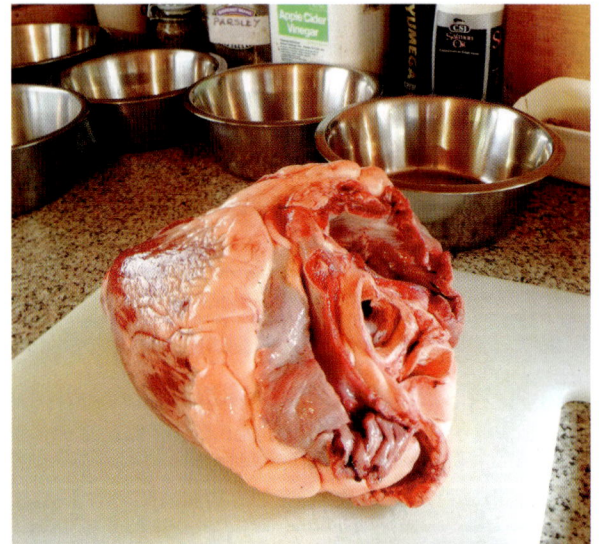

A whole cow heart. Feed in big slices to encourage chewing. Avoid feeding large chunks of meat that can be swallowed in one gulp.

Organ Meats

The liver and kidneys are high in protein, with medium fat; they contain nearly every essential nutrient the dog requires. Raw liver is one of the most concentrated sources of vitamin A. It aids digestion, is a great source of iron and folic acid, and is an anti-oxidant. It also has high levels of B, D, E and K vitamins. It is full of minerals – zinc, manganese, iron and selenium – and is rich in omega 3s and 6s. Feed little and often.

Limit organ meat to around 5 per cent of the dog's diet.

Tripe

Tripe is the lining of the stomach, and is low in protein, and high in fats. It is a valuable and nutritious food for dogs, full of omega 3s and 6s, natural probiotics, enzymes and phytonutrients. Paunch tripe is the first large stomach division, honeycomb is the second division. Raw – green aka 'dirty' – tripe is rich in the valuable probiotic Lactobacillus Acidophilus, a digestive enzyme. Cooking destroys digestive enzymes, so feed tripe raw for maximum benefit.

Digestive enzymes break down food and extract the maximum nutritional benefit from food. They purify and cleanse the blood to remove toxins, parasites and fungus, improve metabolism, hormonal function and boost the immune system. Processed food contains few enzymes.

Bones

Bones are either nutritional or recreational. Nutritional bones are soft and fully edible, such as chicken pieces, lamb ribs, rabbit, turkey necks and pigs' trotters. Mineral levels balance those of the dog's own bones.

Owners preferring not to feed carcass could feed minced chicken with ground bone to provide essential bone matter, but a lot more meat is fed that way (carcasses are mostly stripped), and the protein is very high. Also the teeth are not cleaned by chewing.

Recreational bones are thick, weight-support bones, or marrow/knuckle bones; they are of low nutritional value. Restrict the dog to an hour's chewing at a time, or the heavy bone settles like cement in the stomach. Provide softer

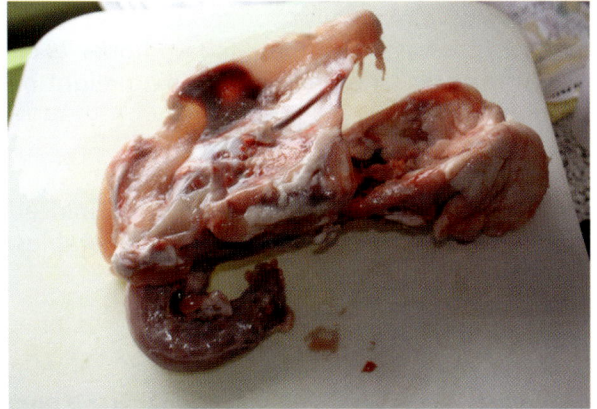

Chicken carcass. This large size would be a normal whole meal for an active male.

bone such as lamb or beef ribs for young dogs with soft teeth. Once the marrow is gone, you can stuff the bone with peanut butter, or smear the inside with yoghurt or cottage cheese. Don't leave bones lying in the garden for rodents and slugs to eat.

Roast bones from pet food shops have no nutritional value, and as they are cooked and brittle they are potentially lethal. They are sprayed with preservative, and are often stuffed with preservative and colourants.

Although anti-raw vets may warn of the dangers of raw bones, they remove many more cooked or nylon bone pieces, hide chews, plastic and rope toys, underwear and leather pieces from dogs' stomachs.

HOW MUCH TO FEED?

Initially feeding BARF you will be measuring and weighing foods, but you soon learn what works for your dog. Research by the author of 107 raw-fed UK Dobermanns found that their daily food intake is around 2.8 per cent of their bodyweight.

1lb = 454g, and the average chicken carcass weighs 500g.
For a male weighing 42kg, that would be 1.1kg (2.42lb) of food.
For a female weighing 33kg, that would be 0.8kg (1.7lb) of food.

An example of a daily food guide for a Dobermann which has around one to two hours' exercise of road walking and field running might be as follows:

MALE: 40–45kg (90–100lb):
Breakfast: 680g (1.5lb) lamb and tripe minced mix, a handful of biscuit or ground vegetables, and a raw egg.
Evening: Large chicken carcass.

FEMALE: 30–35kg (70–80lb):
Breakfast: 454g (1lb) lamb and tripe minced mix, handful of plain wheatmeal biscuit or ground vegetables, and a raw egg.
Evening: Medium chicken carcass.

Provide occasional variety for supper by changing a chicken carcass for a pig's trotter, a rack of beef or lamb, a salmon head or five or six mackerel.

The liver and kidneys of carnivores are comparatively larger than other species, enabling them to cope with the nitrogen burden produced from digesting flesh, but your dog should have regular rest days free from a protein-rich diet. Full starve/fast days are natural for wild dogs and have positive health benefits, reducing biomarkers linked to ageing, diabetes, cancer and heart disease, boosting the immune system, and reducing body fat. Old stockmen used to give a fast day once a week to all their dogs.

Provide occasional variety for supper.

FEEDING PUPPIES

With their small stomachs, puppies need meals little and often. However you space it out, their schedule should be as follows:

From 8–12 weeks   Four meals per day
From 3–6 months   Three meals per day
6 months + onwards   Two meals per day

Raw-fed puppies eat the same food as adults. At eight weeks feed around 115g (¼lb) of meat with a handful of carbohydrates per meal, and maybe a raw egg a day. By nine weeks feed around 150g (1/3lb) per meal, plus the extras. Rather than go suddenly from a large night-time meal to none at all, reduce its size gradually whilst increasing the size of the other meals, and finally give a small snack in place of the meal.

From around five months, youngsters put their energy into growing leg height, and the amount of food they have had is now insufficient to keep weight on their body and to grow long legs. Also they need fats and not high protein at this stage, because if they grow too tall, too quickly, they can develop panosteitis (colloquially known as growing pains). A mix of lamb and tripe is a ideal balance, as there is good protein in the lamb, low protein in the tripe, and both are high in fats.

BACTERIA AND PARASITES

One fear of feeding raw is the alleged increased risk of bacterial infection to both humans and dogs, particularly of salmonella, E. coli and campylobacter. Certainly raw meat for either human or dog that is not correctly prepared can be a health risk, but there have been no reported outbreaks of salmonella poisoning in humans or dogs from raw meat fed to dogs from 2006–2016. (Source: Centre Disease Control 2016.)

Conversely since 2009 there have been no fewer than 137 pet-food recalls for kibble infected with salmonella, E. coli, foreign objects, mould growth, and aflatoxin and mycotoxin contamination. (Source http://www.dogfoodadvisor.com/dog-food-recalls)

EVALUATING WEIGHT AND CONDITION

The Dobermann should be a sleek, muscular and elegant dog, not heavy or overweight. With his smooth coat it is easy to see if the Dobermann is carrying too much weight as he will feel lumpy and will not have a clean outline. One indicator is wrinkle over the base of the neck and the shoulder. When you run your hands down his back to the tail there should be no bump of fat pushed up before your hand. If he is underweight you will be able to feel and see his bones, particularly those on his spine, his pin-bones (the top of the pelvis), and his ribs. There should be a slight indent at the waist, but it should not be pinched in. Some show exhibitors keep their dogs heavier, at what they may call 'show weight', and some agility competitors keep theirs at what others would consider very underweight. However, working dogs in training and competition can't do a day's work if they are overweight.

As with any food, intake should be adjusted accordingly for increased exercise or work. Dogs will also burn more calories to keep warm in winter and fewer in summer.

If feeding kibble, don't religiously follow the feeding guide on the pack, because it is literally just a guide. Even dogs of the same age, height and weight will differ in their energy requirements depending on their individual metabolism, energy and activity rates. Learn to evaluate your dog's condition and weight on a daily or weekly basis, as comparing dogs to weight charts without considering the bone and build of the dog is meaningless.

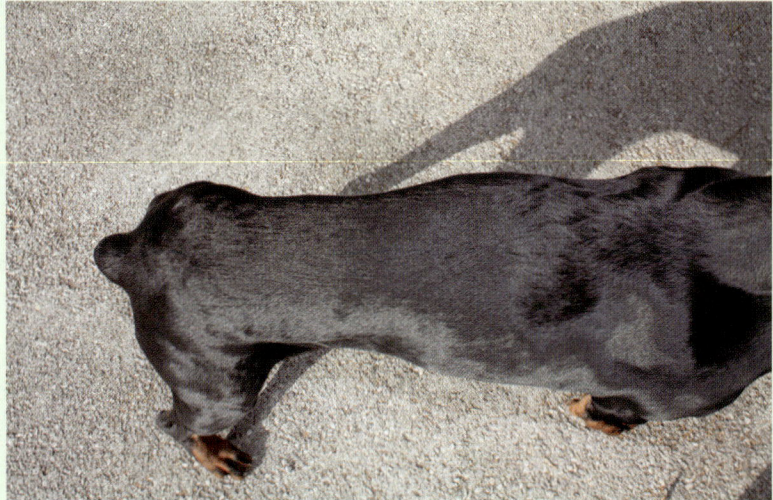

The indentations behind the shoulders and in the waist area of this dog indicate that he is far too thin. His owner had maintained him on the same weight of food that he had as a puppy, and did not account for his rapid growth as a young male.

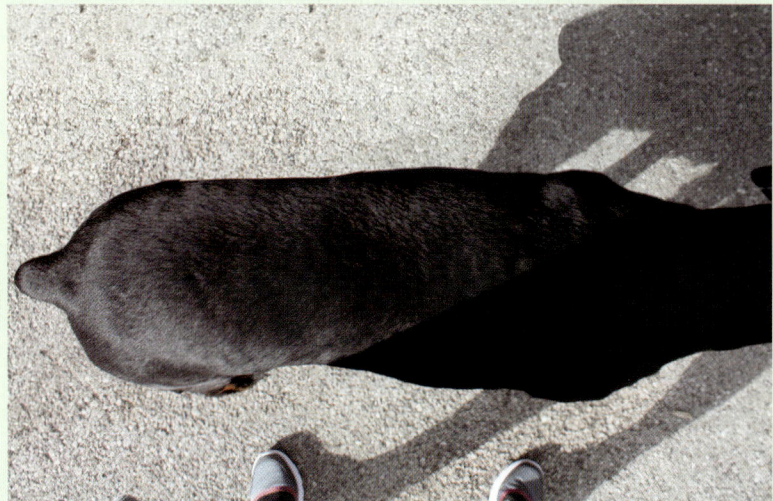

This bitch is at medium weight with a slight definition to her waist, but sufficient substance.

Organisms usually pass through the digestive system quite quickly, rarely getting the chance to establish in healthy dogs, and it is generally only in health-compromised dogs (and humans) that pathogens can become established to form unhealthy bowel flora. Raw-fed dogs are generally more resilient to pathogens due to their stronger stomach acid and digestive enzymes.

Regardless of diet, various studies have found that salmonella is present in around 40–60 per cent of healthy dogs (and 20 per cent of healthy cats), being part of their normal bowel flora. Salmonella organisms are naturally shed in faeces and saliva. E. coli is a natural resident of the human colon.

In 2015 UK health officials found an estimated 65 per cent of chicken on sale in supermarkets harboured campylobacter, which although it is killed by cooking, remains a potential source of infection on the work surface, knives and bowls, or on the hands of the cook. Raw meat fed to dogs should be deep frozen to kill some of the pathogens. Freezing kills campylobacter, but E. Coli and salmonella are merely inactived whilst the food is frozen. Processed muscle meat will contain fewer pathogens and protozoa than, for example, a wild rabbit, so requires a shorter period of freezing than the rabbit, which is better deep frozen for a couple of weeks; this will kill tapeworm larvae.

The FDA recommends that 'hands are washed thoroughly after handling either kibble or raw meat', as they are equally likely to carry salmonella and other bacteria. Take the same hygiene precautions when preparing food for human or dog consumption: use a separate work surface for dog and human meat to prevent cross contamination, disinfect work surfaces, utensils and bowls, and wear rubber gloves when handling raw meat. There is then no more risk of salmonella than if you feed kibble.

Stainless-steel or porcelain bowls are the best choice for food and water, as ceramic and plastic bowls are porous and allow bacteria to establish. Food and water bowls should be washed daily, as not only is it unpleasant to feed dogs from dirty bowls, but bacteria will thrive in the rim of bowls of standing water and any saliva left in the bowl.

Worming

Owners often ask if they should worm their dog more regularly if it is on a raw diet, and the basic answer is 'no', because worms are usually resident in the (GI) tracts of prey animals, and as guts are not generally fed to dogs or cats in food, there is little risk, if any, to them contracting worms through properly inspected meat. However, if the dog regularly catches his own food from the wild, then yes, he should be wormed more frequently, such as every three months, because he will acquire GI parasites from eating the faeces of other animals or the raw innards of any prey he catches. All raw meat should be deep frozen before use, and if you shoot or buy wild rabbits, put them in the deep freezer for a couple of weeks to kill the parasites.

Raw fish (complete) is a healthy addition to the dog's diet, but internal parasites can be an issue. Roundworms are often found in

Deep freeze the rabbit for a couple of weeks to kill tapeworm larvae. Defrost and feed raw and whole (jacket, claws and teeth).

wild salmon, but farmed salmon are regularly wormed through their diet. Tapeworms are sometimes found in the internal organs, digestive tract and body cavity particularly of large deep sea fish, so as with meat, deep freeze all fish to kill internal parasites.

WHY A NATURAL DIET IS BEST

The dog is an omnivore, capable of eating and digesting both flesh and vegetable: he is not an obligate carnivore like the cat, which must eat meat to survive (it requires taurine), and can live on a vegetarian diet. Nevertheless, the primary source of energy for the dog is glucose, and dogs are much more efficient at creating glucose from protein and fats than man. Furthermore the arguments against a largely carbohydrate diet are evidenced by key factors in the biology of the dog, namely the design of his teeth and jaw, the size of his liver and kidneys, the fact that there is no amylase in his saliva, and the risk of bloat when feeding kibble.

The Teeth and Jaw

Canine teeth are designed to tear flesh and crush bone: prey animals (and humans) such as ungulates, equines and bovines have flat surfaces to their incisors (front teeth), canines (fangs) and molars (back teeth) so they can crush plant matter by grinding it down; dogs do not have a single flat grinding tooth surface in their mouth, and their jaw is hinged for cutting and slicing – it can't move horizontally for grinding as does the jaw of the herbivore and true omnivore. Furthermore plant cell walls are composed of cellulose, which is resistant to digestive enzymes: herbivores overcome this by having an additional stomach chamber in which bacteria ferments cellulose, but dogs can only digest plant proteins if they are crushed by a prey animal (or machine), or cooked to make the proteins accessible.

The Liver and Kidneys

These organs are multi-functional. In the carnivore they are proportionally larger in comparison to body size (3–5 per cent) than those of omnivores (2–3 per cent) and herbivores (1.5 per cent).

One of the advantages of this is that carnivores are therefore better able to flush away the fifteen times more volume of uric acid (urea)/nitrogenous waste resulting from eating flesh than the waste resulting from a plant-based diet typical of the herbivore or omnivore. The dog's liver and kidneys are proportionally larger in comparison to his body size than those of omnivores, which indicates that the canid is designed specifically to eat primarily flesh.

Amylase and its Function

The herbivore and omnivore have the enzyme amylase in their saliva; amylase starts the process of breaking down starches and converting them to sugars, thus beginning the process of digestion. So when the herbivore chews its food, the food mixes with the enzyme-rich saliva and enters the stomach in a pre-digested state, broken down by as much as 75 per cent. This results in efficient nutrient absorption. However, canids do not have amylase in their saliva, and depend solely on the pancreas for the production of enzymes capable of digesting carbohydrate: this places an undue burden on the organ.

Risk of Bloat (GDV – Gastric Dilation-Volvulus)

It is of primary importance that Dobermanns on complete food are fed twice daily. All deep-chested breeds are at an increased risk of bloat (*see* Chapter 10, General Health and Welfare) because of the large volume of food needed per meal for adequate nutrition, and because the food swells once it is in the stomach.

The stomach wall is a muscle, and needs to work to stay elastic and 'fit'. Kibble is a solid mass of food that provides little exercise for the muscle wall of the stomach to work on, resulting in the muscles become weak and flaccid. A 2009 study at Purdue identified a number of feeding management and dietary factors that are believed to increase the risk of GDV; these include the following:

- Feeding just one large meal instead of the recommended two a day: this is definitely a contributory factor to bloat as it stretches the stomach wall, which progressively weakens

- Feeding only kibble, particularly those containing fat and corn among the first four ingredients
- Increased physical activity just before and just after eating
- Reduced water intake before and after eating
- Pre-soaking of dry food before feeding; this risk rose when foods with citric acid were moistened
- Having a first-generation relative with a history of GDV
- Having a fearful or nervous temperament; such a dog should always eat in a separate, quiet environment

Statistical evidence shows there is a decreased risk of bloat when more protein ingredients of animal origin are fed, and specifically more in the first four ingredients (that is, more protein and fewer carbohydrates are beneficial).

The Purdue study also identified that eating from a raised feeding bowl contributed to GDV. However, the opinion of this author is that the research was flawed because the majority of dogs involved in the study were Great Danes, whose owners normally fed them using raised feeding bowls. Hence a 'common factor' in a dog with GDV would be a raised feeding bowl stand.

TEMPTING THE POOR EATER

Poor eaters, especially hormonal young males, can refuse food for days on end – some owners often resort to hand feeding them. There is an old saying that no dog will starve itself to death, but trying for days to get a dog to eat can be hard to cope with, especially if you want to work or show your dog.

Leaving food down will never encourage a dog to eat it. Unless they eat within ten seconds, take the bowl straight back up.

Trying to tempt him with something tasty, and pleading with him to eat, will make the situation much worse. Dogs are opportunist feeders and scavengers, and being *offered* food goes completely against the natural order of things in the canine world. When off your food for whatever reason the last thing you can face is a big plate of food – though you might pick at a few crumbs, and this is how we start to change the dog's mind to get him eating again.

Once you are sure there is nothing physically wrong with the dog, the key is to get him begging for food. This can be done by switching on his natural seeking behaviour and his instincts to hunt, forage, chase and scavenge. He needs to earn his food; he doesn't get anything for nothing. But you will have to be patient because it's a slow process.

The first few days of this are tough on the owner, but not on the dog who isn't eating anyway. You now need to change everything about the way you have previously fed him – so don't feed him on time, don't call him for his food, and don't make eye contact when preparing food. He soon starts to realize it is *you* ignoring him, not the other way around, and when he eventually wants food he'll have to ask for it.

After a day of not feeding him, put his food bowl down empty. No calling him to come and eat, don't even look at him. He may look at it and walk away, or he may show interest, but either way pick it straight back up again. Do the same thing in the evening, and don't be tempted to relent! The next morning put the food bowl down empty again. If he is interested throw *just one* piece of food in the bowl or near it. Ideally the food should magically appear on the floor near him when he is looking the other way or sniffing around on the floor. We don't want him to see that the morsel is coming from you at this stage; if he sees you watching him hopefully, he'll switch off, so avoid eye contact.

If he doesn't go to eat it, pick it up immediately, put it in the bin, and try again later.

At mid-morning the next day (so, not at normal breakfast time), put the empty bowl down, again without looking at him or calling him for breakfast. He may go to it and sniff – if he walks away, don't try anything else, just leave it until that night, but if he looks interested in seeing if there is any food around, throw just one piece of food into it or near it, once again without him seeing it coming from you. He may be peckish by now, so whilst he is sniffing around throw another piece from the other direction. If he eats

CHEWS

Chewing is an essential biological function for the canid, which needs to keep the jaw, teeth and gums strong to dissect their prey. Although modern dogs don't often need to catch their own food, chewing relieves teething pain and keeps dogs occupied.

Rawhide sticks are a commonly bought product for dogs. When they moisten through chewing, they wrap around the teeth and help remove plaque build-up. Rawhide is made by chemically separating the outer layer of skin from the hide, which is then twisted into shapes, sometimes with flavours and colours added before being dried. The production process can leave some toxins (arsenic, formaldehyde and adhesives) on the product. Although products made in this way are banned in the US and the UK, many rawhide treats are imported into these countries from the Far East, where the process is widely used.

Throw away rawhide treats when there is only a small part of it left, as dogs can swallow small pieces, which they can choke on.

Nylabones are a tough nylon chew toy made in various shapes and sizes. They are not designed to be eaten.

A natural treat is a large whole fish head, which can be fed frozen in summer. Feed outside to avoid the house smelling like a fish market.

An investigation by the Humane Society International (US) found that some rawhide was made from the skin of dogs that had been inhumanely slaughtered in Thailand and China. To avoid your dog eating dog skin, ensure the product is made in countries with animal welfare laws (China has none).

179

it, repeat again with no more than just a couple more pieces, and *leave it at that*.

After the next mealtime is due (avoid routine) repeat the same procedure: empty bowl down, interested/sniffing dog, throw a piece down, and another. Hopefully his seeking drive is now switched on and this game becomes interesting. Keep this up for a few days, *slightly* increasing the food. Stop before he gets bored.

Your aim now is to get a signal from the dog, and a lip lick is just the trick. We feed our dogs in a wooden cabin alongside the house where we keep the dog kitchen, and taught one of our less non-eating males to give a signal of licking his lips before we went in there if he was going to eat. If we had a bitch in season and he wouldn't eat there wasn't even any point in opening the cabin door, but we knew when he would eat as he licked his lips.

This won't be an immediate fix, but it does go some way to at least having him eat something. Don't over-feed him, and remember always to keep him wondering where his next meal is coming from. Instead of feeding in a bowl at outine mealtimes, go out to lay a track with his food, or use it for training. Clicker training is excellent for this because the dog starts to expect food.

Show exhibitors sometimes have a problem with dogs who won't take bait (treats) in the ring, and bring boxes of various baits in case their dog goes off one sort. Naturally all dogs have a preference for certain foods, but playing the 'seek it out' game of swapping hands/hiding it around the legs/waiting for it, is much more exciting to a dog than having the food pushed into his mouth.

9 BREED-SPECIFIC HEALTHCARE

Dobermanns are generally healthy, and there are no diseases that affect just this breed. Their average lifespan is around nine-and-a-half years, and many reach the age of twelve, and over. The three most common causes of death are old age, cancer and heart failure.

Just twenty or thirty years ago there was barely any knowledge of inherited health conditions,

A fit and happy thirteen-year-old dog. Sam Walsh's Irish Ch. Samenco Hitman, Celtic winner 2006.

and breed books limited health topics to first aid and general care, but we are now much more aware of health issues. Specialist referral centres now cater for complex cases which years ago would have resulted in most dogs being put to sleep.

However, there is no more possibility of guaranteed health in dogs than there is in humans. Most prospective buyers try to find breeders whose dogs have had at least the bare minimum of health testing, but unless a gene marker (DNA test) exists for a disease, there can never be any such guarantee for any human, dog or bloodline.

In 2012 a television programme called *Pedigree Dogs Exposed (PDE)* condemned the breeding practices in many breeds on the basis that:

- inbreeding has destroyed vital genetic diversity and resulted in a serious disease burden in pedigree dogs
- selection for 'beauty' has led to conformational extremes that adversely impact health and welfare
- the Kennel Club/breeders have not done enough to tackle the problems, despite overwhelming evidence that breeding practices have been damaging to dogs

Fortunately Dobermanns were not on the targeted list of breeds, but the programme was far-reaching in its effects, and the breeding of all pedigree dogs came into public scrutiny.

Historically the Kennel Club had not interfered with breeders regarding health testing, but they subsequently tightened changes to the KC Assured Breeder Scheme (*see* Chapter 14), which required breeders to meet certain criteria on standards and health.

The following section investigates genetic (hereditary) disease and conditions.

GENETIC (HEREDITARY) DISEASES AND CONDITIONS

Dilated Cardiomyopathy (DCM)

DCM is one of the biggest concerns to the Dobermann worldwide today. It is a heart disease causing congestive heart failure and/or sudden death arrhythmia, particularly in middle-aged to older dogs. DCM is equally prevalent in Dobermanns in Europe, the USA and the UK.

DCM is seen in other large breeds, and is the most common cause for heart transplants in humans. DCM is inherited as an autosomal dominant trait (only one gene from one parent needs to be inherited in order for the trait to develop), but the variable expression of DCM may be caused by a combination of genetic, environmental and lifestyle factors, making it impossible to track. However, veterinary cardiologists and surgeons believe that Dobermanns have a more severe and rapidly progressive form of DCM than other breeds. The average survival for Dobermans treated for CHF caused by DCM is eighty to ninety days, while other breeds with the same condition survive on average for 280 days.

In congestive heart failure (CHF), the muscles of the left chamber (ventricle) of the heart become weak and lose their ability to contract normally. The left chamber enlarges, so that it does not pump oxygen-rich blood effectively around the body. Blood congests in vital organs such as the lungs, and latterly other parts of the body.

One of the first signs of CHF is a cough, which indicates the dog is trying to clear the retained fluid in the lungs. Less oxygen being delivered to the brain causes mental lethargy, and the paw and ear extremities become cold from poor circulation. Blood damming back throughout the body affects liver function, and as the kidneys are not being flushed through with fresh blood, toxins accumulate. Because the reduced oxygen supply fails to clear toxins from the muscles and organs, muscle wastage occurs.

DCM cannot be diagnosed by clinical examination, x-ray or by stethoscope unless the dog is already in failure; in fact once the symptoms become noticeable, the heart has already been in decline for some time. A weak pulse, irregular rhythm or murmur should be investigated further.

Tests to Monitor Heart Health

Echocardiogram (Doppler): With the dog remaining awake and lying flat, pulse monitors attached to the paws and body provide detailed recordings, measurements and images of the heart and blood flow.

Holter monitor: A twenty-four-hour recording of heart function. Adhesive pulse monitor pads are placed around the chest and secured in place with a flexible jacket. Data is uploaded and analysed.

Blood testing for Troponin levels: Troponin is a hormone released into the blood when the heart is damaged due to cardiac stress. In 2010 a team in Germany, led by Gerhard Wess, published research in the *Journal of Veterinary Internal Medicine* showing that raised cardiac Troponin I levels correlated well with the echocardiographic status of Dobermanns. There are two Troponin blood tests:

- NT-proBNP (brain neuro-peptide) measures heart-muscle wall stress. It is likely to be high in Dobermanns with abnormal echos and sub-clinical (not yet symptomatic) DCM. Levels are raised in Dobermanns with heart failure.
- High sensitivity Troponin 1 measures heart-muscle cell damage, which occurs in cardiac arrhythmias.

Tests should be viewed together to provide an overview of heart health.

Raised Troponin levels can also indicate various other diseases – for example, 32.2 per cent of human patients with viral or idiopathic acute pericarditis have elevated Troponin 1 levels, so dogs with raised levels should undergo further tests.

In 2014 a Kennel Club grant was approved to help fund research at Liverpool University headed by Jo Dukes-McEwan, aiming to prove that both tests used together are a reliable alternative to expensive yearly echo and holter tests.

DNA (Genetic Marker) PDK4 Gene

There was much excitement when the US geneticist Dr Kate Meurs at Washington State University identified one of the gene mutations responsible for inherited DCM in Dobermanns: the so named PDK4 gene located on canine chromosome 14, and developed in a DNA test in 2010.

In 2012 a panel* of international canine cardiac specialists concluded that the results of the study of 132 Doberman Pinschers (as it is named in the USA) of mostly American origin could not be replicated in a larger cohort of European origin. Their report states 'We found no evidence for an involvement of the PDK4 gene in the etiology of DCM.'

*Marta Owczarek-Lipska, Theresa-Bernadette, Mausberg, Hannah Stephenson, Joanna Dukes-McEwan, Gerhard Wess, and Tosso Leeb, Vetsuisse Faculty, Institute of Genetics, University of Bern.

Heart Failure (Sudden Death)

Arrhythmias (irregular rhythm) are one of the most common causes of human death in Western countries and are the cause of most sudden deaths in Dobermanns. The electrical impulses of the heart are the natural pacemaker initiating the action of the heart muscles to contract and pump blood throughout the body. When impulses travel through the heart in a disorganized pattern, the heart rhythms are thrown into chaos (arrhythmias) and the sudden drop in blood pressure causes weakness, fainting or death.

Just before sudden death the dog may appear to falter and lose its step. Death is immediate, and the dog does not appear to suffer pain or distress.

Not all arrhythmias are immediately life-threatening, but if they continue, they leave the otherwise smooth heart wall scarred. Further electrical pulses are disrupted, and the heart becomes progressively weaker. It is eventually unable to contract fully, and congestive heart failure can develop. The following conditions will cause heart failure:

- arrhythmia (irregular rhythm)
- tachycardia (heartbeat too rapid)
- bradycardia (heartbeat too slow)
- VPC ('Ventricular Premature Contraction')
- weakening of the upper chambers (atria)
- weakening of the lower chambers (ventricular)

Treatment/Management of DCM

There is no cure for DCM and the prognosis is always bleak, but early diagnosis and prompt medication extends the dog's lifespan. Without medication from the onset of symptoms of heart failure, Dobermanns typically live for an average of six weeks before becoming increasingly debilitated.

Dogs with a pre-clinical diagnosis of abnormalities may have between two to six years of good health with medication.

Any Dobermann that develops a cough should see a vet for a check-up. Whilst it may just be kennel cough, it is one of the first symptoms of congestive heart failure. Owners of any Dobermann with a heart condition should ask for a referral to a specialist canine cardiologist – otherwise it is like asking your GP to treat you for a serious heart condition.

von WILLEBRAND DISEASE (vWD)

von Willebrand's factor is a coagulant that binds injured blood vessels; with insufficient amounts of von Willebrand's factor blood fails to clot. vWD is the most commonly inherited bleeding disorder in dogs and humans, and is inherited as autosomal recessive or incompletely dominant. Affected dogs have two copies of the gene.

The disease was initially discovered in Dobermanns in the USA, and became established in the breed before anyone realized the depth of the problem. Testing was initially done by Elisa factor assay blood test to identify circulating von Willebrand's factor antibodies, but test results are affected by a dog being immune-suppressed, hormonally affected, or stressed. Later correlations between assay and DNA tests showed wide variability between the results.

In 1996 the US laboratory Vetgen identified and patented the gene mutation, providing a definitive gene marker status of Clear, Carrier or

von Willebrand Disease Breeding Combination Chart

	Clear Male	Carrier Male	Affected Male
Clear Female	***100 per cent Clear***	**50/50 Carrier/Clear**	**100 per cent Carrier**
Carrier Female	**50/50 Carrier/Clear**	*25/50/25 Clr/Carr/Affected*	*50/50 Carrier/Affected*
Affected Female	**100 per cent Carrier**	*50/50 Carrier/Affected*	100 per cent Affected

> * ***Ideal breeding pair: Puppies will not have the disease gene as either Carrier or Affected.***
> * **Breeding is safe: No Affected puppies will be produced. Some or all puppies will be Carriers.**
> * *High-risk breeding: Some puppies are likely to be Carriers and some puppies are likely to be Affected. Although there may be some Clear puppies from Carrier-to-Carrier matings, these breedings are not recommended.*
> * <u>Breeding is not recommended: all puppies will be genetically Affected.</u>

Affected. This simple buccal mouth swab (saliva) test is now the benchmark test for the disease.

Unlike severely Affected breeds, which can bleed spontaneously and severely for no apparent reason, vWD affects Dobermanns in the milder form of Type 1. Even Affected Dobermanns produce 10–20 per cent of normal von Willebrand's factor, which is generally enough to sustain the dog through general cuts and bruises. The difficulty in managing vWD Affected dogs is that any necessary surgical procedures carry higher risks than to animals that are not Affected, and some of the medication owners may wish to give, particularly in old age such as anti-arthritic drugs, cannot be tolerated by the Affected dog.

vWD Carriers do not suffer from the disorder in any way, and when mated to Clears, will only produce Clear or Carrier puppies. vWD Affected bitches are at risk of bleeding from potential caesarean, but a vWD Affected male can be used on a Clear bitch as the puppies will be only Carriers. These dogs can then be mated to Clears to produce 50/50 Clear or Carrier. As the number of Clear dogs increases, so the breeder has a wider selection of dogs, and more Clear to Clear matings can occur without loss to genetic diversity.

Nearly 16,000 Dobermanns have now been tested by Vetgen for type I vWD since November 1996. In July 1998, having tested over 2,070 Dobermans, Vetgen vWD statistics were:

Clear: 21.5 per cent
Carrier: 49.7 per cent
Affected: 28.8 per cent

Seven years later, a 2005 analysis of results showed a 2 per cent decrease in vWD Affected Dobermanns tested by Vetgen, with statistics as follows:

Clear: 25 per cent
Carrier: 49 per cent
Affected: 26 per cent

Eight years further on, in 2013, there was a nearly 8 per cent decrease in Affected dogs in the Vetgen vWD statistics:

Clear: 38.6 per cent
Carrier: 41.6 per cent
Affected: 19.8 per cent

The steady decline of Affected Dobermanns has been achieved by sensible breeders carefully avoiding producing Affected progeny whilst still using Carriers. Vetgen vWD total results to date are:

Clear: 4,880
Carrier: 7,512
Affected: 3,377

Note that recorded figures are mainly from US Dobermanns but also include UK and European Dobermanns.

UK KC figures show that just 4 per cent of the tested UK population are vWD Affected – possibly because we had advance warning of the disease from the US. Carrier status remains consistent with that of US Dobermanns.

Results submitted to the KC show that 1,197 UK Dobermanns have been vWD DNA tested (either by Vetgen, Finnzymes or Laboklin):

Clear: 51 per cent (618 dogs)
Carrier: 45 per cent (531 dogs)
Affected: 4 per cent (48 dogs)

The test is done by the owner swabbing the inside of the cheek with a small brush and, carefully ensuring it is kept otherwise uncontaminated, returning it to the laboratory. Test kits can be obtained directly from Vetgen (www.vetgen.com) or Laboklin (www.laboklin.co.uk), who are licensed by Vetgen as European agents for vWD DNA testing. The Kennel Club recognizes both.

As with most health testing, it is the show communities who have led advances in embracing health testing, and all good breeders now vWD test.

The rarer form of acquired vWD can develop due to autoimmune, hypothyroidism, and other disorders.

Eye Health (PHPV)

There are incidental reports of various eye anomalies in Dobermanns, as in any dog, but these are very uncommon. The main eye condition that can affect Dobermanns is persistent hyperplastic primary vitreous (PHPV). PHPV is a congenital (that is, present at birth) inherited eye condition. To break down the acronym:

Persistent: remaining
Hyperplastic: thickened/over-developed
Primary: present initially
Vitreous: thick, transparent substance that fills the centre of the eye

The membrane of blood vessels that help develop the eye in utero can leave threads of hazy old tissue strands over the eye, which cause varying degrees of sight impairment. It can affect one or both eyes.

Testing is by clinical examination, where the optometrist dilates the pupils to view the back of the eye. There is as yet no gene marker.

All other countries in the world use a grading system – Grade 1: least severe, to Grade 6: most severe. UK ophthalmologists may advise the owner of the grade or severity of the condition, but the UK system simply classes dogs as Affected or Clear, with no formal method of recording how badly Affected or not the dog may be. This unsatisfactory situation means that a Dobermann with a single small strand of primary vitreous remaining on one eye will be classified in the same category as a totally blind dog of Grade 6 (severely Affected).

The incidences of PHPV in Dobermanns in the UK are very low, and when Dobermanns are Affected, it is rarely over Grade 1 or 2. PHPV at lower grades is not a progressive disease. There is no requirement for further testing during the dog's life.

The BVA recommends that Affected dogs are removed from breeding; however, as this is a clinical test and not a genetic one, this is a dangerously idealistic recommendation for the breed, narrowing the gene pool unnecessarily. Nevertheless breeders should avoid mating two Affected dogs to reduce the occurrence and severity of the condition. If progeny are affected, this is rarely to any greater degree than the Affected parent.

CASE STUDY

In 2009–2012 a male Dobermann with a single strand of PHPV (less than Grade 1) in one eye was clinically examined and classed as PHPV Affected. He was used for breeding at stud on three Clear tested bitches. All twenty-seven puppies were clinically tested by the age of seven weeks, and all were tested Clear of PHPV.

PHPV Statistics

	Total Dobermanns examined recorded	PHPV Affected	Total Dobermanns KC registered – Breed Record Supplement	per cent Tested	per cent Affected of dogs tested
2008	34	1	1,871	1.8	2.9
2009	62	1	1,600	3.8	1.6
2010	87	3	1,678	5.2	3.4
2011	61	1	1,457	4.1	1.6
2012	76	1	1,346	5.6	1.3
2013	61	2	1,212	5	3.3

Puppies can be tested from two to three weeks, by which time the primary vitreous in a normal eye should have regressed. A more accurate diagnosis is obtained from six to eight weeks of age. Veterinary opticians test litters of puppies either at their home or in clinic.

In 2011, six litters were tested; three puppies in a litter of nine were PHPV Affected

In 2012, two litters were tested; five puppies in a litter of ten were PHPV Affected

In 2013, no litters were tested

There are no other eye conditions reported in Dobermanns in any sufficient number to raise concern. The BVA reports that for seventy-six Dobermanns tested in 2012 there were six cases of persistent pupilliary membrane, one nuclear cataract, one other cataract, two hyaloid remnants, and eight pigment on posterior capsules.

HIP DYSPLASIA (HD)

HD was first identified by Gerry Schnelle in 1935, and is one of the most common orthopaedic diseases in dogs. This general term means 'abnormal development of the hip joint'. A hip may be dysplastic for various reasons, and excess move-

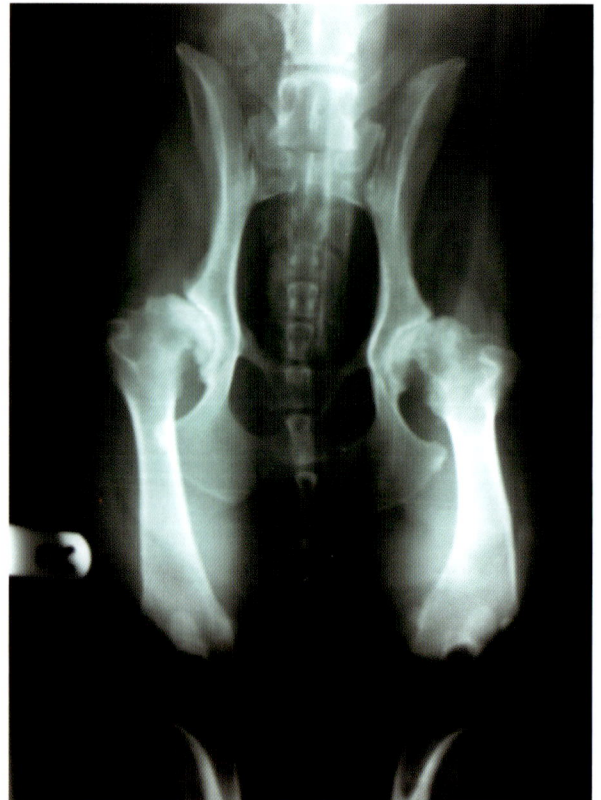

These hips are very poor. Despite the dog not being positioned straight, which skews the symmetry, the rough-edged 'ball' has no visible socket in which to sit. This dog had both hips replaced.

BRITISH VETERINARY ASSOCIATION/KENNEL CLUB HIP DYSPLASIA SCHEME

To: British Veterinary Association
7 Mansfield Street, London W1G 9NQ
Telephone: 020 7636 6541

06 - 61355

| THE ORIGINAL OF THIS |
| CERTIFICATE IS GREEN |

Owner's Declaration
(PLEASE COMPLETE USING BLOCK CAPITALS AND BLACK INK)

KC Registered Number: AG 0012 1.

KC Registered Name: ARITAUR NOMINATOR.

Breed: DOBERMANN   Sex: M.   Date of birth: 22/11/05.

Name of owner: HORGAN   Address: THE HEADMASTERS HOUSE,
COTTON COLLEGE, COTTON STAFFS.

Sire: INT, MULTI, FR CH. FIHIRAM ABIF ROYAL BELL.	PGS: EKO ROYAL BELL
	PGD: EBONI VON RESIDENSCHLOSS
Dam: NED CH. ARITAUR DOMINATRIX	MGS: RAMONBURG'S VALDO
	MGD: CRISLEA CENTREFOLD OF ARITAUR.

I hereby declare that (NB: DELETION OF ANY OF THESE ITEMS INVALIDATES THIS CERTIFICATE)
(a) The particulars above are correct and relate to the dog submitted today for radiographic examination
(b) This dog is a minimum of one year old and has not previously been scored under the scheme
(c) I give permission for a copy of the certificate to be sent to the geneticist retained by the breed society or other representative body
(d) I give permission for the results of the examination to be used at a future date for the purpose of statistical research
(e) I give permission for the results to be published and included on the relevant KC documents

Owner's signature ....   Date 12/12/06.

Submitting Veterinary Surgeon's Certificate (PLEASE COMPLETE USING BLOCK CAPITALS AND BLACK INK)

Microchip/tattoo number (if known):
985 200 77384

I certify that the radiograph relating to the dog identified above was taken on the following date 12/12/06 and in conformity with the provisions of the HD Scheme Procedure Notes

Veterinary surgeon submitting radiograph (BLOCK CAPITALS) PAUL LEWCOCK

Address BLENHEIM VETERINARY CENTRE BLENHEIM ROAD, AIRFIELD INDUSTRIAL ESTATE, ASHBOURNE DERBY. Post code DE6 1HA

Date 12/12/06   Signed ....   F/MRCVS

Please submit the correct fee for the radiograph to be processed (cheques payable to BVA.) For current fees contact BVA

CERTIFICATE OF SCORING

HIP JOINT	Score Range	Right	Left	
Norberg angle	0–6	O	O	**NB** The scores represent the opinion of the BVA appointed scrutineers for the radiograph submitted. The lower the score, the less evidence of hip dysplasia present. Please consult the current procedure notes and breed mean score sheet for relevant details (available from BVA)
Subluxation	0–6	1	1	
Cranial acetabular edge	0–6	2	2	
Dorsal acetabular edge	0–6	0	0	
Cranial effective acetabular rim	0–6			
Acetabular fossa	0–6			
Caudal acetabular edge	0–5			
Femoral head/neck exostosis	0–6			
Femoral head recontouring	0–6	✓	✓	
TOTALS (max possible 53 per column)		3	3	6

Total score (max possible 106)

WE HEREBY CERTIFY that the score of the radiograph submitted for the dog identified above was produced using the scoring criteria of the BVA/Kennel Club Hip Dysplasia Scheme

Date 16 JAN 2007

Signed .... F/MRCVS   Signed .... F/MRCVS   1/97

HD green form.

ment (laxity) in the hip causes friction in the joint. New bone is formed in an effort to stabilize the joint, but ligaments and tendons already strained from trying to maintain stability can't run smoothly over the new bone. The joint capsule may also become inflamed and thickened. HD usually affects both joints, but can sometimes be bilateral. (*Ref.:* Todhunter *et al* 1997.)

The British Veterinary College (BVA) has held a hip-scoring programme in collaboration with the Kennel Club for over forty years, and around 1,600 Dobermanns have been scored to date. Dogs must be over one year old. Examination is by x-ray at most vets.

The vet sends the image with the 'green form' to the BVA, where a panel of specialists measure and assign a score for various aspects of the hip. The score is then totalled and displayed, as, for example, 3:6 (9). The lower the score the better the hip, with the ideal being the unusual 0:0 (0).

The score sheet is then returned to the vet and owner, and a copy sent to the KC for their online health records.

Vets are now required to check and record the ID of dogs by microchip or tattoo, and all KC Assured Breeders must have their dog hip scored in order to register puppies.

Hip Dysplasia Registries
The registry of a population is compiled by calculating the middle 'median' hip score of the dogs it consists of. The mean score is the average,

The Middle 'Median' Score of the Population

Year	No. of Dogs	BMS (Mean)	Median	Range
1994	37	9.7	8	4–24
2008	587	10.2	9	0–58
2013	1,581	10.7	9.5	0–64

Comparisons with Other Hip Dysplasia Registries

BVA (UK)	FCI European	USA OFA	SV (Germany)
0–4 (no more than 3 per hip)	A–1	Excellent	Normal
5–10 (no more than 6 per hip)	A–2	Good	Normal
11–18	B–1	Fair	Normal
19–25	B–2	Borderline	Fast Normal
26–35	C	Mild	Noch Zugelassen
36–50	D	Moderate	Mittlere
51–106	E	Severe	Schwere

where all the totals of all the individual scores are added up and then divided by the number of dogs scored – but if the majority of dogs have low scores and just a couple have excessively high scores, the average score is skewed. Calculations are therefore adjusted to represent the middle 'median' score of the population.

In other countries the hip x-ray and assessment is taken in the same way, but the results are recorded slightly differently. The chart below gives approximate comparisons with other hip dysplasia registries.

PennHip Tests

PennHip was pioneered by Dr Gail Smith at the University of Pennsylvania, USA, hence the name 'Penn'. Dogs with loose hips and excessive laxity have an increased risk of developing HD compared to dogs with tighter hips and minimal hip laxity (looseness). Compared to other methods which test only on hip extension, PennHip tests the hip in three ways: under distraction, compression and extension.

Mike Guilliard introduced PennHip scoring to the UK in 2009. The test is more expensive than conventional x-rays for HD, but it is believed to be more accurate in predicting the likely onset of osteoarthritis. Unlike the UK system, where hips are compared to any other breed, PennHip ranks hips compared to others in the same breed: so for example a ranking of 30 per cent means the dog has tighter hips than 30 per cent of the dogs evaluated, while 70 per cent of the dogs evaluated have tighter hips than the dog. Another advantage of PennHip is that, rather than waiting a year, dogs can be tested from sixteen weeks, so the breeder can decide whether or not to keep him for further breeding.

The Cause of HD

The inheritance and development of hip dysplasia (HD) is unknown even in humans, where the condition is termed as 'developmental dysplasia of the hip' (DDH). One cause of DDH occurs when the human foetus is restricted in its movement in the womb or lies in an awkward position. Breech births may have a stretching effect on the liga-

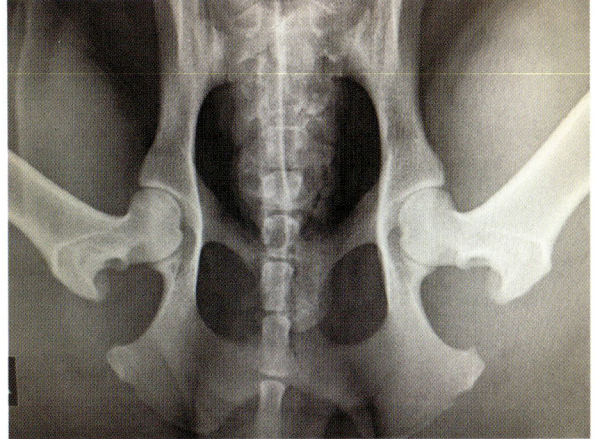

PennHip 1. MIKE GUILLIARD

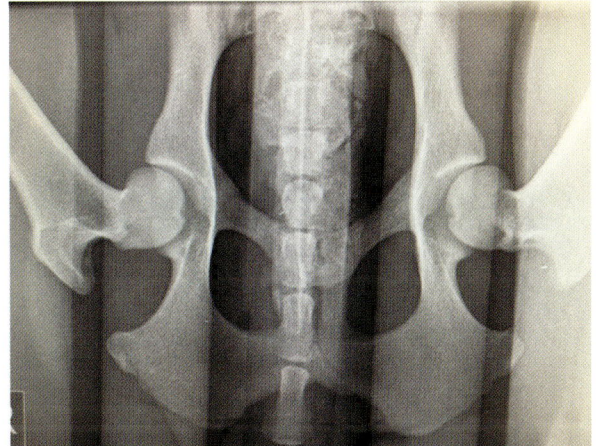

PennHip 2. MIKE GUILLIARD

ments, which later causes joint weakness and instability.

The underlying cause of HD is genetic, and according to research at Cornell University, there are 'at least two and possibly as many as twelve canine chromosomes that hold quantitative trait loci (QTL) for HD'. As offspring inherit normal and abnormal genes in multiple combinations, even siblings from two normal parents can be markedly different, with one being normal and the other severely dysplastic, due also to the variable expression of the condition. Some dogs with bad

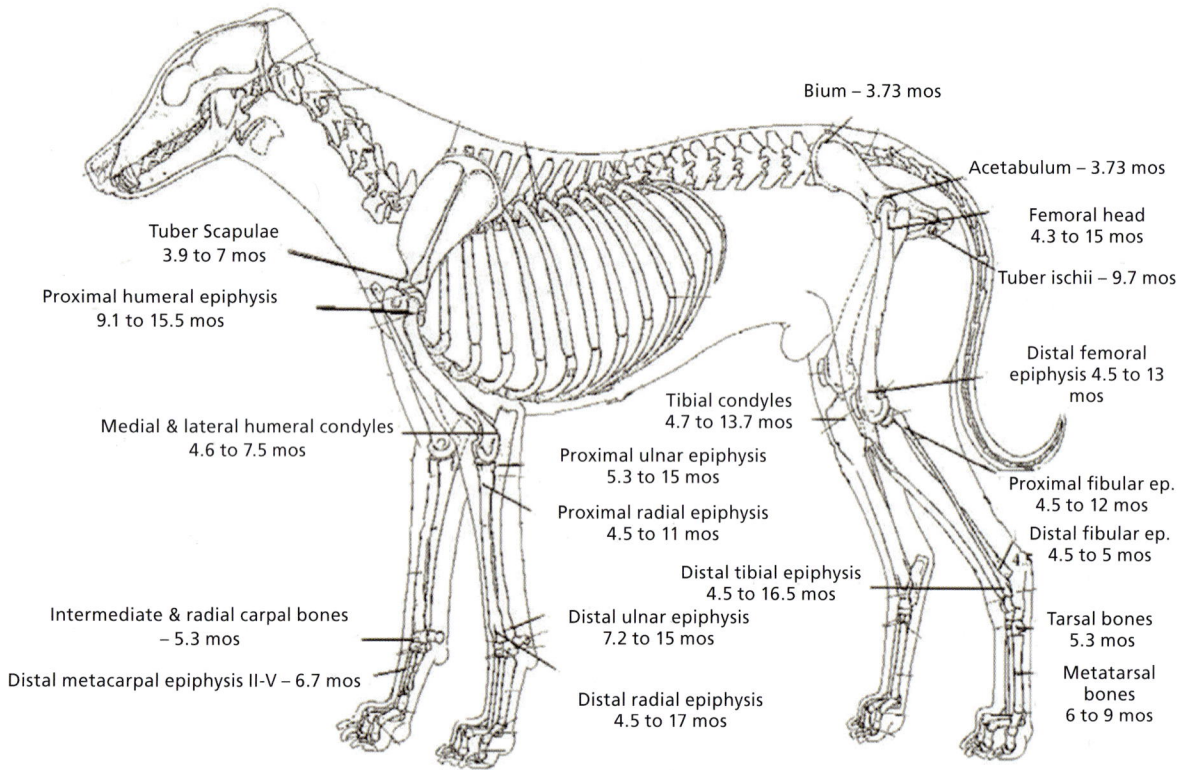

The ages at which the growth plates close, when the dog finally finishes growing.

hips cope well, whilst others are severely crippled by the effects of arthritis caused by excessive laxity.

Despite years of hip scoring across many breeds, excessively high scores occur as randomly as ever. Dogs with high scores sire progeny with 0:0 scores, and full siblings raised in the same home from generations of low-scoring dogs have vastly diverse scores.

The idealistic advice from the BVA to remove a dog from breeding 'unless it is well below the breed mean score' removes otherwise excellent dogs from breeding and minimizes the gene pool. (*See* inheritance above.)

The Effect of Hormones in Hip Health

Growth plates are areas of dense growing tissue at the end of the long bones (bones longer than wide in legs and arms), which solidify when growth is finished. The rapid growth period between four and seven months strains the already vulnerable surrounding ligaments, tendons and muscles. When immature dogs are castrated there is no hormonal signal to stop the lengthening of these long bones, so the dog grows far taller than he should, has finer bone, greater risk of osteoporosis, and a generally feminine appearance. Early neutering increases the risk of orthopaedic disorders such as HD and cranial ligament problems – but despite this, many vets encourage owners to have their dog castrated at this crucial growth stage.

A study by Gretel Torres de la Riva *et al.*, 2013, of early neutered males (less than twelve months) showed an incidence rate of later hip dysplasia of 10.3 per cent, more than double the incidence rate in intact males of 5.1 per cent. There was no increase in HD in early neutered bitches. This data is also supported by research finding that castrated male dogs were significantly more likely than entire dogs to have HD at an odds ratio of 1.21. (*Ref.:* University of Missouri (JAVMA) 2008.)

Being overweight has a big impact on the hip joint and general joint health. The amount of calories consumed, and when in life they are consumed, increases the risk of a dog genetically prone to HD developing the disease. This may explain the variable expression between siblings with significantly different scores.

Research in 2014 into gene mapping for hip dysplasia in a UK study of Labrador Retrievers found that no single chromosome explained more than 23 per cent of the genetic variance of the traits; there are multiple genetic components, but each has only a small to moderate impact. (*Ref.:* Sánchez-Molano *et al.*, Quantitative trait loci mapping for canine hip dysplasia, October 2014.)

The development of the KC's Estimated Breeding Values (EBV) programme calculates risk not just in the individual dog, but in all his relatives on a vertical and horizontal pedigree. With other known factors such as breed predisposition to HD, this aims to predict the outcome of progeny hip health. However, as of 2016, EBVs are not yet available for Dobermanns.

Genomic selection rather than clinical selection may be a future strategy for reducing HD.

Treatment for HD

Treatment varies individually in each dog. Not all dogs with clinically poor hips will demonstrate pain or abnormal gait, but for others it is a cripplingly painful condition. There are various surgical options, but operating on a two-year-old with joint problems is very different to that of a nine-year-old whose recovery will inevitably be impaired by his age.

Cruciate (Knee/Stifle Joint) Failure

Also known as cranial cruciate ligament disease (CCLD), anterior cruciate ligament damage (ACL), or CrCL injury.

There are four main ligaments in the knee, which run diagonally across the middle of the knee to hold the bones of the joint together and keep it stable. They prevent the shin bone (tibia) at the front of the knee from shifting forward relative to the femur, and also stop the stifle (knee) joint from over-extending or rotating by bracing it against unusual movement to keep it stable.

However, like a fraying rope, ligaments can suffer either a full or partial tear. Lameness can occur suddenly during exercise, with the dog suddenly holding up a hind leg, often with an accompanying yelp. If you suspect knee damage, see the vet, rather than carrying on hoping it will improve.

CrCL injury is responsible for most problems of instability in the dog knee. The knee becomes chronically painful and swollen, and joint instability leads to arthritis.

Instances of both HD and CrCL damage have increased significantly in the last forty years, and Dobermanns are particularly susceptible. CrCL injury occurs more in certain breeds and may well be hereditary. A 2008 study by Witsberger *et al* into the 'Prevalence of, and risk factors for, HD and CrCL injury in dogs' showed that early sterilization had a significant impact on these ligaments, particularly in the younger dog. Spayed dogs over four years old are nearly twice as likely to develop CrCL injury as entire dogs.

Other factors are general fitness and condition (namely obesity), and even smooth modern flooring; also insufficient warm-up before exercise contributes to the problem. However, injury can occur with even the best conditioned dog.

Surgical or Remedial Treatment for CrCL Repair

Vets prefer to operate on partial tears, because repair on a full rupture rarely leads to full recovery, and unstable knees will also develop arthritis. Various surgical options involve reducing bone height and angle to lessen the stretch on the ligament. Dogs are usually able to return to full exercise or work with little or no eventual lameness.

Whether or not the dog has surgery, he needs to undergo the same recovery programme of rest for around six weeks with limited lead walking to reduce inflammation, followed by at least three months of rehabilitation and physiotherapy, and *strictly* no free running for six months.

It is important to maintain strong supportive muscles around weak joints, but high impact games of throw and fetch with sudden stops, sprinting and spinning, can put exceptional strain on the joint and supporting structures. So don't be tempted to let the dog have even a little blast, or all that effort will be wasted.

Steady, structured exercise taken regularly in short sessions, rather than long weekend walks, keeping the knee straight, promotes equal weight-bearing across all joints and muscles. This is important with CrCL injury because 50 per cent of dogs will also need surgery on the opposite leg, which has been taking all the strain.

Hydrotherapy enables the dog to exercise without having to weight-bear, and mind games in the house provide relief from the boredom of limited exercise.

Maintain long-term joint supplements to relieve arthritis in the affected joint that has been caused by instability or injury.

The drugs Cartrophen and Adequan reduce pain from osteoarthritis by stimulating the body's production of cartilage, increasing synovial fluid and nutrition to the joint; these drugs are also anti-inflammatories. They can provide relief from pain and lameness for many months.

OTHER GENETIC CONDITIONS AND DISEASES

Cervical Spondylomyelopathy (CSM)

Also known as cervical vertebral instability (CVI). The nerves are compressed by the spinal column, resulting in neurologic dysfunction where the nerves send variable signals to the legs. 'Wobblers' is the common term for this condition. Symptoms are an uncoordinated gait on the dog's hind legs, particularly on slippery floors; he may carry his head lower to avoid pressure on the spinal cord, and may struggle to stand up after lying down. He may drag his feet when walking, and his nails may become scuffed as a result of his abnormal gait. As the condition worsens, his front legs may also buckle over. Dogs can deteriorate to the point where they become suddenly and acutely paralysed in all four legs.

CVI can develop from abnormality or injury, or because of general degenerative change. For whichever reason, vertebrae become misaligned or degrade, causing compression on the spinal cord. The term 'wobblers' covers the condition, not the cause. Either way it results in pain and neurological changes.

Large and long-necked breeds are predisposed to the condition. A US survey showed that approximately 5.5 per cent of Doberman Pinschers suffer from CVI. (Ref.: Ronaldo C. da Costa, Ohio State University.)

Even the most observant owner may be forgiven for attributing the signs of advancing wobblers simply to old age.

Definitive diagnosis is by CT or MRI scan with a myelogram (x-ray image taken after dye is injected around the spinal cord) to allow visualization of the compressed spinal cord. Surgery is necessary in the earlier stages of the condition, rather than waiting for the condition to worsen, otherwise the continued excessive movement of the neck causes irreversible damage, and surgery is then no longer an option.

A study of over 100 dogs at the Ohio State University College of Veterinary Medicine showed that 50 per cent of dogs with wobblers improve with medical management, and about 30 per cent remain stable. The condition worsens in the remaining 20 per cent. If the older dog's pain can be managed, it is probably not in his interest to proceed with surgery, as recovery is limited. Certainly the balance of pain versus life quality is a narrow one.

In the 1980s a group of Dobermanns in the UK were neck scored at Liverpool University Small Animal Teaching Hospital to try and identify a genetic link. Some dogs with low scores subsequently developed wobblers, and the progeny from some dogs which had later developed wobblers, had both low and high scores. Neck scoring is rarely done these days.

Head Tremors/Bobbing

Also known as 'idiopathic head tremors', or IHTS. This is an odd condition occasionally seen in some Dobermanns, where the head shakes or bobs.

Most dogs remain alert and responsive during an episode of head tremors, which on average lasts for five minutes, and with two episodes a day. The length of the period without head tremors ranges from one to 1,800 days, with the medi-

an being sixty days. The time between episodes of head tremors may last days or months. It is not considered a health condition, as there appear to be no ill effects to the dog either emotionally or physically. Tremors occur without any apparent triggers.

Although the owner worries, the dog does not suffer in any way, and is easily distracted during episodes. Despite its name this is not 'wobblers', nor is it related to it.

The Institute of Genetics at Bern, Switzerland, researched head bobbing and concluded that 'Head bobbing does not require any specific treatment, and most Dobermanns grow out of it, although some have head tremors throughout their lives. Head bobbing is definitely not related to epilepsy.'

Research has shown that out of 291 dogs of various breeds, most dogs with IHTS were purebreds (84 per cent), with bulldogs being the most commonly reported (37 per cent), followed by mixed breeds (16 per cent), Boxers (13 per cent), Labrador Retrievers (11 per cent), and Doberman Pinschers (8 per cent).

Liver Failure

Liver failure is also known as copper toxicosis, and chronic active hepatitis. Hepatitis refers to inflammation of the liver, and can be caused by, for example, infections and viruses.

When the liver fails, the blood becomes poisoned with the toxins that the organ has been unable to cleanse. The dog feels increasingly nauseous, and may be weak and depressed with low appetite, diarrhoea and weight loss. Liver-compromised dogs are usually extremely thirsty and drink copiously in an attempt to flush the liver clean; as a result they are often incontinent, with dark urine. Jaundice develops later.

Dobermanns can also suffer from the serious condition of chronic hepatitis – *aka* copper toxicosis – which usually presents from middle age onwards, developing acutely or progressively. Copper is an essential trace mineral for the growth, functioning and repair of bone, organs and connective tissue. Copper storage (copper toxicity) occurs when the liver fails to excrete the mineral, and becomes overloaded with it.

Cirrhosis (scar tissue) occurs, and the abnormal flow of bile causes further copper retention.

It is believed that these dogs are born with a faulty liver function and are storing copper from birth. By the time the copper has accumulated to such a degree that symptoms are noticeable (usually by middle age), significant liver damage has already occurred and the dog will require hepatic support for life.

Blood tests may reveal elevated levels of the liver enzyme ALT (Alanine Aminotransferase), which is released into the bloodstream when the liver is damaged or diseased, but correct diagnosis is only possible by a liver biopsy done under anaesthetic.

The condition in Dobermanns was first recognized in the early 1980s, although it is not known how widespread the disease actually is in the breed. In 2000, a USA-led group investigated cases of subclinical hepatitis in 106 randomly selected three-year-old Dobermanns: this revealed subclinical hepatitis in twenty-two dogs (nineteen females and three males). Foods that are excessively high in protein are indicated as having either a causal or contributory role.

Treatment of copper storage hepatopathy requires chelation therapy, which is a process of injections to remove metals from the body, and the drug Penicillimine to suppress the immune system reaction, which causes inflammation.

Managing the Liver-Sick Dog

Feeding the hepatic dog is crucial in managing the condition. The damaged liver must be treated gently and not be made to work too hard, so the diet should consist of easily digestible foods that are high in fat, and low in protein. It cannot break down raw meat in the way a properly functioning liver can, and the by-product of ammonia and nitrogen from the digestion of meat is particularly dangerous as these are excreted unfiltered into the bloodstream by the non-functioning liver.

Dietary copper should be reduced to 0.1mg copper/100kcal diet. If drinking water passes through copper pipes, it should be changed to softened water.

Milk thistle can be given at 1,000mg daily,

along with other liver drugs. Oral lactulose, a type of indigestible sugar, lowers the pH within the gut and reduces the absorption of ammonia. It also enables the rapid transit of faeces through the intestinal tract to reduce the amount of time that ammonia-producing bacteria can spend on it.

The condition has no cure, but it can be managed with a good diet and with liver medication drugs for life. (Courtesy Pauline Rose, 2014.)

Liver failure and its connection to DCM is an unresolved issue in the breed.

Lumps

Dobermanns are very prone to lumps and bumps, particularly in old age. Most are soft, smooth, benign fatty lumps, but there may be growths that are knotty, hard and immoveable. Broadly speaking, if you can get your fingers around and under a lump it is probably innocent, but any lump which appears suddenly, is discoloured, changes shape rapidly, or seems knotted and fixed with a root, should be examined. Some lumps can multiply rapidly when disturbed, so vets usually take a sample by fine needle aspiration to have skin cells analysed. It can then be decided whether to remove the lump or not.

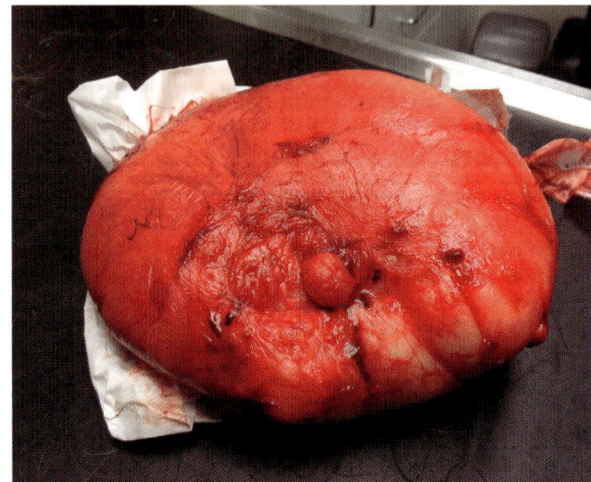

This benign tumour was removed from under the front shoulder of ten-year-old Darcy, as it impeded his movement. Dobermanns can often become quite lumpy as they grow older, but unless a lump causes problems it is better left alone.

Most fatty lumps are best left alone, though if the dog has one under the armpit, for example, it is probably best to remove it early, as a growth in that area can affect movement, and later on, when it is bigger, may cause him to walk awkwardly.

(*See* Chapter 9, General Health and Welfare, for more information on cancers.)

Thyroid Disease

Hypothyroidism (HypO means insufficient) describes the condition where an underactive thyroid gland (situated in the neck) causes inadequate levels of thyroid hormone (thyroxine) to be produced in the body. This can result in a variety of symptoms, which may include weight gain, general tiredness and fatigue, and feeling cold, so the dog seeks out a warm place to sleep. The skin is dry and thin and often has symmetrical alopecia on the loin, and darkening or thickening of the skin where hair loss has occurred. The hair will feel woolly and fragile and will break easily. Other common symptoms include adverse behaviours and poor concentration, and the heart rate may be unusually slow. Owners may have noticed their dog becoming 'fat and lazy'.

Hypothyroidism can have a big effect on behaviour, with previously happy family dogs becoming moody, sullen and aggressive. Thyroid dysfunction has been found in 62 per cent of aggressive dogs, 77 per cent seizuring dogs, 47 per cent fearful dogs and 31 per cent hyperactive dogs (*Ref.:* Jean Dodds DVM).

Hypothyroidism is the most common endocrine disorder in dogs, and is not uncommon in the Dobermann. Most dogs develop hypothyroidism between the ages of four and ten, and although both genders are equally affected, spayed females are at a higher risk than entire females. It is not known why hypothyroidism develops; dogs can be born with congenital thyroid gland failure, and there is a genetic link to dogs developing autoimmune hypothyroidism.

When the thyroid gland begins to fail it secretes the hormone erratically until the gland eventually fails completely. This fluctuation makes diagnosis difficult.

Blood tests can confirm diagnosis. Treatment is to take a daily pill of supplementary thyroxine for life to replace the missing hormone. Symptoms will quickly begin to reverse, and signs of improvement such as increased energy levels may be seen within a week.

Hyperthyroidism (HypEr = too much) is unusual in dogs.

Fertility in both genders is greatly affected by thyroid disease, and the world-renowned expert on canine hypothyroidism, Jean Dodds DVM, based in the USA, reports that an estimated 80 per cent of cases result from autoimmune thyroiditis, and that 'the heritable nature of the disorder poses significant genetic implications for breeding stock'.

LONGEVITY AS A MARKER OF HEALTH

Longevity in bloodlines is undoubtedly the best marker of health in the Dobermann. The USA has had a formal breed-club sponsored longevity program for many years, which is a great resource for breeders hoping to establish longevity as a breeding goal. In 2014 Georgie Kuhl in the UK developed a database to start the scheme in the UK. Some breed clubs have embraced the idea, and the website was launched in 2016. http://www.dobermannlongevityprogram.co.uk

References:
2002 IMHA Study by Carr, Panciera, Kidd at University of Wisconsin School of Veterinary Medicine

2005 IMHA by Weinkle, Center, Randolph, Barr and Erb at Cornell University, Ref.: Jean Dodds, DVM

10 GENERAL HEALTH AND WELFARE

These days when the most complicated and expensive treatments are available to dogs (at least for the insured), owners and vets usually overlook the old remedies that have served dogs and owners very well for years. Few vets will tell owners just to treat a small wound with saline for fear of a negligence claim if things worsen, and feel obliged to prescribe something, if only to make the client feel better. However, no medication is innocent, and unnecessary treatment damages the finely balanced immune system. The following life case shows the stress and damage, not to mention costs, that can be caused by inappropriate treatment.

LIFE CASE

Although their dog had never had fleas, his owners kept noticing all the adverts and thought they should use a 'spot on' medication for flea and tick treatment. A fortnight later the dog had lost a lot of hair around his neck and was scratching there. The vet prescribed a medicated shampoo to be used three times a week. This stripped the coat's natural protective oils and the dog scratched even more from his already irritated and now extra dry skin.

Suspecting a flea allergy, another application of 'spot on' flea treatment was prescribed. A week later the area was completely bald, and the dog bled from scratching. He then had steroid injections to reduce that inflammation, was prescribed 'hypo-allergenic food' – at £64 a bag! – and skin scrape tests were sent to America. He developed diarrhoea from the diet change, and the tests came back negative. He had to wear an Elizabethan collar to stop him scratching at his stitches, and was now thoroughly depressed. The next day he tore the protective collar off, scratched his stitches out, tore the wound and chewed himself frantically to relieve the itching.

Antibiotics were prescribed to try and reduce the skin irritation.

He was now bald across his front and shoulders, the shampoo stripped the natural oils from his skin and left it dry and flaky, and he had ballooned from the steroids. His stomach continued to be unsettled from the change of food, he needed the wound re-dressing constantly, and both dog and owner were stuck in a downward spiral of veterinary treatment, tests, medication and misery.

Finally the owners consulted a vet in another practice, who identified the cause of all these troubles as being the original flea treatment. The dog was taken off steroids and other medication (though he remained on antibiotics until his wounds healed), went back to his original food, and eventually made a full recovery.

Equally there are stories from owners whose homes have become besieged by fleas – but a trusted vet, and a good gut instinct for when something is wrong, is essential.

GENERAL HEALTH

Vaccination

The following abbreviations are used in this section:

WSAVA: World Small Animal Veterinary Association
BSAVA: British Small Animal Veterinary Association
AVMA: American Veterinary Medical Association
VMD: Veterinary Medicines Directorate

Vaccines Defined

Vaccines stimulate the body to produce pre-prepared antibodies to rapidly eliminate a future viral or bacterial invasion before it can cause damage.

Core vaccines are defined as those that protect dogs from severe life-threatening diseases caused by viruses that are found worldwide. These are distemper, canine adenovirus (CAV) and canine parvovirus (CPV). Non-core vaccines should be determined by locality/environmental exposure risk.

Dogs are usually vaccinated against the following:

Distemper (D) (CDV)	Canine distemper virus
Hepatitis (H) (ICH)	Infectious canine hepatitis
Adenovirus (A)	Canine adenovirus (CAV)
Parvovirus (P)	Canine parvovirus (CPV)
Para-influenza (Pi)	(CPiV)
Leptospirosis (L)	

Vaccines are usually given in a combined dose, grouped together under the acronyms DHPPi-L, DAPPi-L, DAPPvL2+CV, and so on. The numbers as in CPV2 or L2 or L4 denote which viral strains they cover. When a vaccine is administered, the small sticky label that is removed from the vaccine bottle and put on the vaccination card details exactly what has been given, the date, and the batch number.

Viruses against which Vaccines are Effective

Canine distemper virus (CDV): Attacks the respiratory, gastrointestinal and central nervous system. CDV is transmitted airborne, or through direct contact with fresh urine, blood and saliva. Some dogs may survive, but CDV is often fatal.

Canine parvovirus (CPV, aka parvo): Usually attacks the small intestine, causing inflammation. CPV is transmitted by direct contact from infected dogs or their contaminated faeces. The virus is resilient and very stable, surviving in the environment for many months. Puppies are most vulnerable. The virus can multiply rapidly in the heart causing inflammation (myocarditis). Sudden death or other heart failure is to be expected.

Infectious canine hepatitis: Targets the upper respiratory system, spreading to the liver and kidney. Initial infection can produce a hacking cough. Secondary infection develops into pneumonia. Healthy dogs may show just a raised temperature, and the disease may clear the organs in ten to fourteen days, but dogs with low immunity may suffer severe hepatitis, or die suddenly. Eye discoloration and inflammation is a classic sign due to the connection between liver and eye health.

Canine para-influenza virus (CPi) is one of the contagions associated with kennel cough (Bordetella Bronchiseptica). It is spread airborne and through contact with other infected dogs. Around forty agents cause kennel cough, but the vaccine only covers a couple of strains.

Canine Leptospirosis

Canine leptospirosis is a bacterial infection, not a virus, that can affect humans and other species. Rats are the main source of the disease, carrying the bacteria in their kidneys and shedding it in their urine. 60–75 per cent of UK cattle also carry leptospires.

Symptoms range from mild infection including digestive upset, fever and lethargy, to severe liver and kidney infection. In chronic cases jaundice develops from multiple organ failure. If identified early enough leptospirosis infection is usually quite easily treated by antibiotics, and even if the dog is in renal failure, antibiotics can rid the urinary tract of the organism.

The WSAVA (World Small Animal Veterinary Association) makes the following observations regarding vaccination against canine leptospirosis: it says that leptospirosis vaccines are 'associated with more adverse reactions than occur for any other optional vaccine', and 'vaccination should be restricted to geographical areas where a significant risk of exposure has been established'. Because the lepto vaccine lasts only a few months, it also states 'if the dog lives in a high risk area, more frequent vaccination of six to nine months is recommended'.

Despite not being recommended by the WSAVA as a 'core' vaccine, it is routinely given by vets. From 2014–2016, the VMD (Veterinary Medicines Directorate) received 2,000 reports of dogs having suspected adverse or fatal reactions to 'Lepto-4'.

In 2012, seventy-eight confirmed cases were reported in humans in the UK, mostly in sewage, water and farm workers, vets and butchers. In 90 per cent of human cases leptospirosis only causes mild flu-like symptoms. No commercially available vaccine for humans exists.

Thirteen leptospirosis cases were reported to the VMD in a twelve-month period from 2013 to 2014. All but one were in unvaccinated dogs; eight of the thirteen died.

Rabies: Vaccinations are not required for dogs resident in the UK, only for those travelling abroad.

VACCINATION AND THE LAW

There is no legal requirement in the UK to have any dog vaccinated. Only if the owner plans to board the dog in kennels will he need to be vaccinated. Check the policy of the boarding kennels.

Boosting

The frequency of boosting and the duration of immunity is one of the most hotly debated subjects in veterinary medicine today, and advice varies between vets. The BSAVA (British Small Animal Veterinary Association) says:

> The BSAVA strongly supports the concept that a thorough benefit/risk assessment on an individual case basis should be discussed with clients when deciding on the timing of vaccination and the use of particular vaccines for particular animals.
>
> BSAVA 2015

Vets rarely, if ever, undertake any risk-benefit analysis of the individual, ignoring directorates from every governing body.

Vaccines can confer lifelong immunity by storing antibody memory in the event of future exposure to disease. For a dog already with antibodies, 'boosting' is of no advantage as antibody memory cells block subsequent vaccines from working, so the new 'threat' is immediately neutralized. Therefore if memory cells exist, 'boosting' is of no benefit to immunity levels because the body is already primed for future attack. 'Boosting' is only of value to antibody-negative dogs, which is not known without an antibody (titre) test. But as long as owners and vets continue to believe vaccines are harmless, boosters will continue to be standard practice.

VETERINARY ASSOCIATION GUIDELINES

- AVMA guidelines: 'Unnecessary stimulation of the immune system does not necessarily result in enhanced disease resistance, and may increase the potential risk of post-vaccination adverse events.'
- WSAVA 2010 guidelines: 'Dogs that have responded to vaccination with MLV core vaccines maintain a solid immunity (immunological memory) for many years in the absence of any repeat vaccination.'
- WSAVA 2010 guidelines: 'Vaccines should not be given needlessly. Core vaccines should not be given any more frequently than every three years after the twelve-month booster injection following the puppy/kitten series, because the duration of immunity is many years and may be up to the lifetime of the pet.'

Puppy Vaccines

Maternally derived antibodies (MDA) comprise the natural passive immunity gifted to puppies from the colostrum-rich milk of their dam acquired in the first few hours after birth (*see* Chapter 14 that discusses breeding). MDA blocks and destroys any foreign object or toxin, including vaccines.

From around eight to twenty weeks the puppy has reduced MDA but does not yet have a full immune system. Vaccines are given during this period so the vaccine is accepted. Most vaccines used to be given at eight and twelve weeks, but some modern vaccines override MDA interference and are often given at seven weeks, which enables earlier socialization.

Vaccines do not take effect immediately because the antigens must be identified, responded to, and remembered by the immune system. Disease protection does not begin until at least five days after vaccination, and as long after as two weeks.

The WSAVA recommend a twelve-month booster to 'ensure immunity for dogs that may not have adequately responded to the primary puppy vaccination course'.

Vaccination Myths and Dangers

Alternatives to vaccination: Are unproven, as no trials have ever been conducted. No pharmaceutical company would fund research into something that could not be patented, such as plant medicine.

Options may include extending the duration of the conventional revaccination schedule, or antibody (titre) testing, which measures antibody levels in the blood. Antibodies may be generated by vaccination, or through natural exposure to disease from infection challenges.

Homoeopathic nosodes: Are condemned by the veterinary industry, which cites the lack of any scientific trials and data. But in post-hurricane flooding in Cuba 2007 leptospirosis exposure was prepared for with the use of homoeopathy. This successful Cuban Government health programme covered over 2.4 million people with two doses of homoeoprophylaxis.

The black and tan vaccination myth: Owners of Dobermanns may be told that because their dog is black and tan it is more susceptible to parvovirus and should receive a third booster at sixteen weeks of age. This claim originated in the USA in the 1980s, when some Rottweiler litters did not respond to their parvovirus vaccination. However, these breeds have no more non-responders to parvo vaccine than other breeds,

and research showed the vaccines themselves were never analysed for fault. No evidence exists for this claim.

Faeces eating: Puppies occasionally eat their own and their siblings' poo. Whilst this in itself is not a particular problem, a grave danger occurs when puppies are vaccinated, and then shed viruses in their faeces. The puppies have not yet produced antibodies to the particular threat of parvovirus, and when they eat the infected faeces, they develop the disease from the vaccine. Any breeder with puppies that eat poo should not vaccinate the litter, and puppies should not be vaccinated until they go to their new homes.

Adverse/allergic vaccine reactions: Can include facial swelling, anxiety, and restricted breathing (anaphylaxis). Neurological problems such as ataxia (uncoordinated gait) can occur even two weeks post vaccine. Granulomas (hard tissue formations) and sarcomas (aggressive locally invasive tumours) can form anywhere, but particularly at the site of injection. Death from vaccines is very rare, but is not unknown. Long-term vaccine effects are not always obvious. If the dog shakes or scratches his head following vaccination, consult the vet promptly. Respiratory irritation is sometimes seen with intranasal Bordetella (kennel cough) 'vaccine'.

It is normal that dogs and puppies may be slightly tired after their vaccines, but if they are limp and lethargic they should be rushed directly to the vet for assessment and therapy.

NEUTERING

One of the first suggestions made by a vet to owners when they take their new puppy for its first visit is that it should be neutered. This is perhaps largely a legacy from the days when there were many strays, and pregnancy and rescue rates were high.

The UK and the USA have the highest routine sterilization rates in the world: around 80 per cent of the UK dog population is neutered. However, those vets who advocate neutering rarely alert their clients to the physical and psychological advantages and, more importantly, the disadvantages of neutering.

Neutering Males

As with various species, including humans, young hormone-driven males can be difficult to manage, and the pressures of territorial and sexual dominance may tip over into defence aggression. If the dog is becoming defensive/aggressive, castration before he fights prevents 'learned' behaviour.

It is very cruel to keep highly sex-driven dogs intact. Their life revolves around finding bitches to mate, and they can barely function, let alone be trained. But not all male Dobermanns have a high sex drive, and many are quite content to socialize with other males, so for those dogs there is no benefit in castration. The only physical health advantage of neutering males is to prevent benign prostatic hyperplasia (prostate enlargement) in mature dogs, and testicular cancer. Although castration eliminates the risk of a dog developing testicular cancer, the statistical risk of testicular cancer in entire males is *just 1 per cent*, with only half those tumours being malignant. Castrated dogs have up to a four

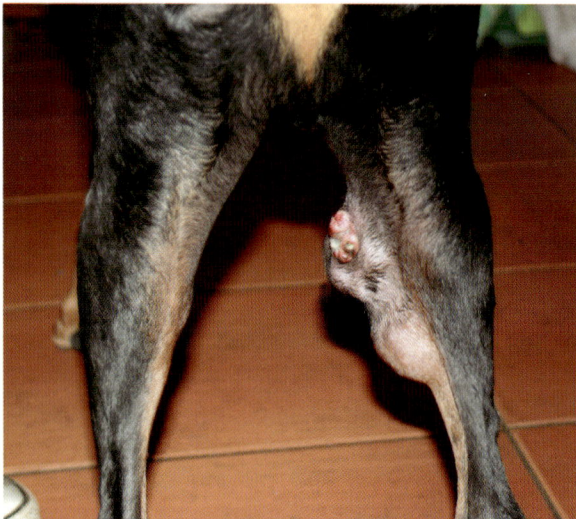

This lymphosarcoma began as a small wart-like lump and progressed rapidly to a large lump. It re-grew rapidly within eight weeks of the first operation to remove it.

times greater risk of developing prostate cancer than intact animals.

Data gathered from North American veterinary hospitals found that castration increases total malignant prostate cancer by eight times for some prostate cancers, and increases the most common type of bladder cancer by about four times.

Reduced oestrogen and testosterone affects the muscles, tendons and ligaments that hold bones and joints in place. This is especially important during growth-plate closure. Where normally the dog's hormones would cause the growth plates of his joints to close, so he matures in body, not height, early castration results in the plates staying open, and he continues to grow upwards, developing an immature body with a narrow chest and fine bone.

Joint disorders HD and CCL, and cancers, are significantly higher in both sexes if they were neutered either early or late compared with entire dogs. (*Ref.*: U.C. Davis, de la Riva, Hart *et al*, 2013.)

The risk of osteosarcoma (bone cancer) for dogs rises to one in four if a dog is castrated when he is under one year old, and more so in Dobermanns, as larger breeds are at increased risk of bone cancer.

Temporary chemical castration solutions of injection or implant are available to see if behaviour changes before committing to castration.

Neutering Females

Neutering females prevents all risk of pyometra (womb infection, see below) developing, and reduces the risk of mammary tumours developing. Mammary tumours are 25 per cent more common in unspayed bitches, or those spayed at over two years old. If a bitch is spayed before her first season the risk of her developing mammary tumours is 0.5 per cent. If she is spayed after her first season, the risk is 8 per cent, and after her second season it rises to 26 per cent.

Studies of 237 Rottweiler bitches which died at between 1.3 and 12.9 years found that those who had kept their ovaries until at least 4.5 years old had 37 per cent lower mortality than those whose ovaries were removed before that age.

Bitches who retained their ovaries up to the age of seven were three times more likely to achieve exceptionally long lives than bitches that kept their ovaries for the shortest period of time. Women whose ovaries are removed when they have a hysterectomy, statistically die younger than women whose ovaries are retained.

In 2012 the BSAVA stated that 'the evidence that neutering reduces the risk of mammary neoplasia, and the evidence that age at neutering has an effect, are judged to be weak and are not a sound basis for firm recommendations.' (*Ref.:* Beauvais *et al.*, Royal Veterinary College 2012.)

Incontinence is more common in large breeds weighing over 20kg and those spayed younger, occurring in between 11 per cent and 20 per cent of spayed bitches. The main cause is the deficiency of oestrogen, which causes weakness in the sphincter muscle.

Medications containing Estriol (Propalin© syrup or Incurin© tablets) restore oestrogen levels to improve urinary control. It is worth trying a 'loading' dose, and gradually reducing the amount or the administration frequency.

Oestrogen enables the body to metabolize fat loss, which is one reason why neutered dogs and bitches become fat despite food reduction. Oestrogen loss also leads to a soft, dry or thin coat, particularly between the back legs and belly.

Specific Care of the Bitch

Bitches have their first season when they are between six and twelve months old, and thereafter on average every six months. Some bitches may go with seven, eight or nine months between seasons. Coming into season she may be more alert and may guard more than usual. She will urinate frequently (marking), and groom herself.

Some bitches have a swollen vulva for a month or more before bleeding, others come in season almost overnight. A daily dab with tissue helps monitor the first day of her season. The season lasts for three weeks from the first blood being seen. The blood is initially pale, then darkens with a heavier blood flow. In the middle week the bitch is nearing ovulation and the blood pales again. Ovulation can occur at any time in this stage, but is usually around days eleven to thirteen. The bitch is now at her most fertile, and as semen can live for around five days, she must be kept apart from males prior to ovulation if it is not wanted to breed from her.

Some bitches have a 'silent' or 'dry' season where they do not bleed but still swell and ovulate. They are as fertile as bitches who bleed.

Phantom pregnancies increase the risk of mammary cancers, which are the second most common cancer in dogs after skin tumours.

Phantom Pregnancy

In a phantom pregnancy the bitch thinks she is pregnant and her body behaves accordingly. This evolutionary process creates general harmony in the pack when there are vulnerable puppies around, and enables other females to help care for puppies. Bitches often produce milk, and may huddle around imaginary toy or cushion puppies.

Keep her very lean and fit before she goes into her season, as she will convert any excess weight to milk. Counting from the first day of bleeding, she will ovulate on around day twelve, and if mated would conceive a day or so after that. Approximately three weeks later when there is slight swelling of the teats, give the homoeopathic remedy Urtica Urens 6c three times daily. If at four weeks of pseudo pregnancy the teats are getting larger, a prolactin inhibitor such as Galastop®, which is an oral solution, can be given.

Note that one of the active ingredients of Galastop® is cabergoline, and extended use past three or four days is likely to bring on a full season again. If you have a matronly bitch that you are not planning to breed, and which becomes depressed during phantoms, it may be fairer to spay her.

Pyometra

Pyometra is a life-threatening infection of the uterus whereby bacteria is trapped inside the uterus. Signs are an increased temperature, excessive thirst, diarrhoea, depression, lack of appetite, vomiting, and a foul-smelling discoloured discharge. The abnormal discharge in 'open cervix pyometra' at least gives a warning of the problem in time to treat with antibiotics. 'Closed-cervix pyometra' gives no warning as pus cannot drain out of the uterus. It cannot be stressed enough how life-threatening this condition can still be if not caught quickly enough.

Specific Care of the Male

Retained Testicles

The testicles originate up near the kidneys, and start to descend after mid-term gestation, entering the inguinal canal at around a week old. They usually fully descend into the scrotum by the time the puppy is six to eight weeks old, after which the canal starts to close. If a testicle has not yet descended by this time, it may not descend naturally. However, a testicle can 'hover' at the edge of the inguinal ring (just before the scrotal sac), withdrawing into the canal, and back out again. It is known for a testicle to descend even when a dog is a year old.

Some retained testicles develop tumours, but few are malignant. Most vets will recommend intra-abdominal castration of the retained testicle, which is the simplest solution to any concern regarding malignancy developing.

* Although a dog with a retained testicle is thirteen times more likely to develop a tumour of that testicle than entire dogs, only 1 per cent of entire dogs ever actually develops testicular tumours, with around 38 per cent of those being malignant. The actual risk of a dog developing cancer from a retained testicle is 6 per cent, compared to dogs with normally descended testicles.

Massaging the area down towards the scrotum may help, but unless you are sure (by scan or palpation) where the retained testicle is located, you will be working blind.

Enlarged Prostate

The prostate gland is located inside the rectum, where it secretes an enzyme-rich carrier liquid enabling seminal fluid to travel and survive on mating. Enlargement of the prostate gland (benign prostatic hyperplasia) usually only occurs in entire dogs, and around 80 per cent of dogs over five years old suffer from it. Prostate enlargement can be either benign or malignant. Symptoms may include blood in the urine or from the sheath. Dogs frequently need to urinate,

but struggle, and the condition can occasionally cause faecal impaction in the rectum, with flattened poo. The vet may treat the condition with an injection of chemical castration, and will perhaps scan if he can't feel the enlargement rectally. If malignant the dog may have the same symptoms but these will worsen, with weight loss, pain and depression.

Retired stud dogs can suffer from enlarged prostate glands, and although Tardak® may be useful in the short term, the dog shouldn't stay on regular medication, so castration may be the best remedy. For dogs at active stud, regular matings will relieve the condition temporarily, but semen may be contaminated with prostatic fluid. Visual examination shows this as dark and discoloured semen instead of a slightly opaque colour, and the dog may need antibiotics to clear infection.

WORMS AND WORMING

Five main types of worm affect dogs: heartworms, roundworms, hookworms, tapeworms and whipworms, and generally only roundworm and tapeworm in the UK. Puppies are born only with roundworms, which do not multiply or breed in the gut: numbers depend on how many eggs were ingested.

Dogs become infested with worms by eating meat, slugs/snails already carrying worm eggs or larvae, or being bitten by an intermediate host such as a mosquito or flea. Worms in low numbers are not a problem unless they migrate to erratic locations inside their host. Worms in the stomach steal a dog's nutrients, causing it to have low energy due to malabsorption and diarrhoea. In the heart and lungs they degrade the organ function. The dog can cope with an incredible volume of parasites, and show only subtle signs until infestation is advanced, but once they overload those organs they can be fatal.

Worm-infested dogs generally have a dull coat, skin irritation, and loss of hair and/or rashes. They may itch and rub their bottom on the ground, known as 'scooting'.

Worming only kills worms in the intestinal tract and not the encysted larvae, so a regular programme of worming every three to six months is necessary. Not all worming products cover all worms. Some products cover mites, mange, fleas and lice (MMFL).

Worming Naturally

The natural compound diatomaceous earth (DE, aka silica) is a fine powder made from the fossil-ized remains of a type of hard-shelled algae. DE is extremely drying and has microscopically sharp edges which pierce the outer protective coating of the parasite, absorbing oils and fats from their exoskeleton so they dehydrate and die. It also kills some worm eggs and larvae the same way. It must be food grade, not pool (filtration) grade, which is toxic. DE is also used on the garden, the

Worms Covered by Worming Products

	Roundworm	Tapeworm	Lungworm	Hookworm	Heartworm	MMFL
Milbemax	Y	Y	Y	Y	Y	
Panacur	Y	Y				
DrontalY	Y		Y			
Stronghold	Y			Y	Y	Y
Advocate	Y		Y	Y	Y	Y
Droncit	Y					
Endogard	Y	Y		Y		

Detailed and updated information is available on individual product packaging.

Worm Count Results

Date	Name	Dog Lungworm	Fox Lungworm	French Heartworm
10.5.15	Finton	None seen	None seen	None seen
10.5.15	Hugo	None seen	None seen	None seen
10.5.15	Darcy	None seen	None seen	None seen

Date	Name	Toxocara Species	Hookworm species	Other in sample
09.05.15	Finton	<20 epg	<20 epg	None seen
09.05.15	Darcy	<20 epg	<20 epg	None seen
09.05.15	Hugo	<20 epg	<20 epg	None seen

floor and on dog bedding to kill external parasites such as fleas and their eggs.

Whether using natural or chemical wormers, a worm count can ensure effective control of worms. Send a stool sample to www.wormcount.com where results are calculated as 'eggs per gram of faeces'.

Cross Contamination

Humans acquire worms from ingesting eggs from faecally infected material, such as poo from a dog with worms shedding eggs. Dog saliva does not in itself carry worm eggs, but if the dog had recently coughed, vomited or licked its anus, then transfer is possible. The main risk is to small children who often put dirty hands in their mouths.

Toxocara (roundworm) can infect humans. To a healthy adult with a good immune system this is of little consequence, but if a child is infected and the larvae ends up in a sensitive area such as the retina, this can cause blind spots and total blindness. Moorfields Eye Hospital in London deals with about twenty to thirty cases annually of roundworm larvae in the human eye.

ROUTINE CARE AND MANAGEMENT

Coat and Skin Care

Grooming the short, hard coat of the Dobermann is easy, and skin condition as a valuable indicator of health can be easily monitored. Even during the bi-annual seasonal moults the hair loss on a Dobermann is light and quite easy to manage. Regular brushing with a soft rubber brush will help to remove old dead hair.

The breed's single coat is one reason why the Dobermann should not live outdoors, as they simply can't keep warm enough (some other breeds also have an undercoat). Note that the use of coats in wet and freezing weather is kind for the thin-coated and elderly dog, but the modern tendency to use coats when they are not really necessary inhibits the dog's own coat from growing through properly, and is unhealthy. For inactive dogs a coat is kind, but dogs that exercise energetically will get very warm, even in freezing weather.

Dandruff on the back of the neck does not necessarily indicate a dry coat, but is often produced when the dog is over-stressed or excited, and it generally disappears when he settles.

Dogs should not be washed regularly as shampoo strips the natural protective oils from the coat and skin. If the dog rolls regularly in fox poo there is no option but to wash him, but use a medicated shampoo and rinse the coat very thoroughly afterwards. For rashes or unexplained itching, vets usually recommend a strongly medicated shampoo. However, this is harsh on the skin and upsets the ph balance, so unless a particular mite or bug has been identified, regular shampooing can do more harm than good.

Dental Care

Dental care for dogs is a huge industry, with toothbrushes, toothpaste and plastic chews replacing what a knotty raw bone does perfectly: satisfies the dog's need to chew, while the tendons, ligaments and small pieces of cartilage act as a natural dental floss.

The teeth of dogs fed on kibble (complete) feed often become scaled up at the gum margin, causing gum infection. Cleaning and removal must be done under anaesthetic as teeth and any pockets of gum disease must be examined thoroughly.

Teething

Most of the second teeth should be 'through' by the time the puppy is around sixteen weeks, and these continue to grow until the head has finished forming, at around eighteen months old. During heavy teething, the cartilage at the top of the ear sticks up and out, and the ears 'fly' instead of sitting neatly flat against the head.

During teething the feet go flat, as the extra demand of calcium and phosphorous required to grow strong teeth is taken from the bones, tendons and ligaments which support the feet.

Retained baby canines don't drop out when the adult canine comes through: the tooth becomes wedged in next to the adult canine and can take many months to dislodge. These can be removed under anaesthetic, but because they are small and soft in comparison to the strong adult canine tooth, they are unlikely to change

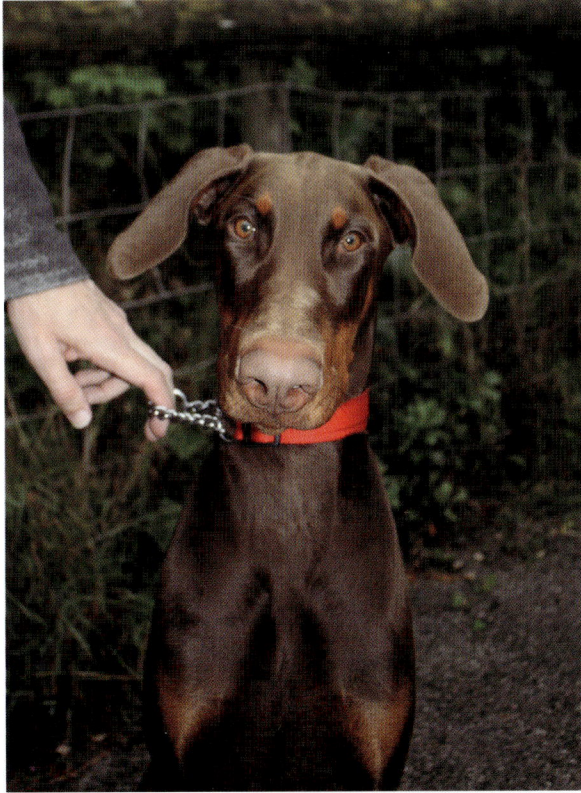

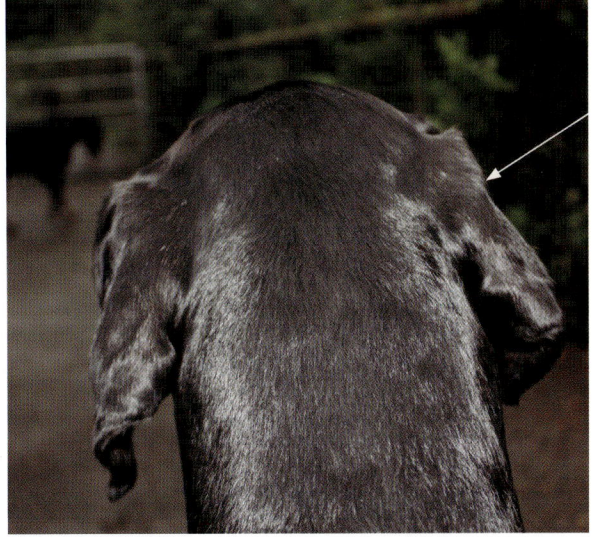

A normal ear, with ears lying close to the head and the fold in the centre line of the ear.

Five-month-old puppy Kobi is teething heavily and his ears are flying. The cartilage at the top of the ear can be massaged or taped lightly down from seven to twelve weeks. Get a breeder to show you, rather than trying on your own.

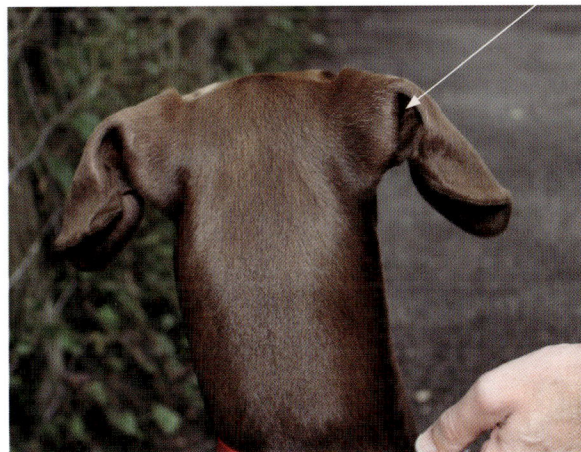

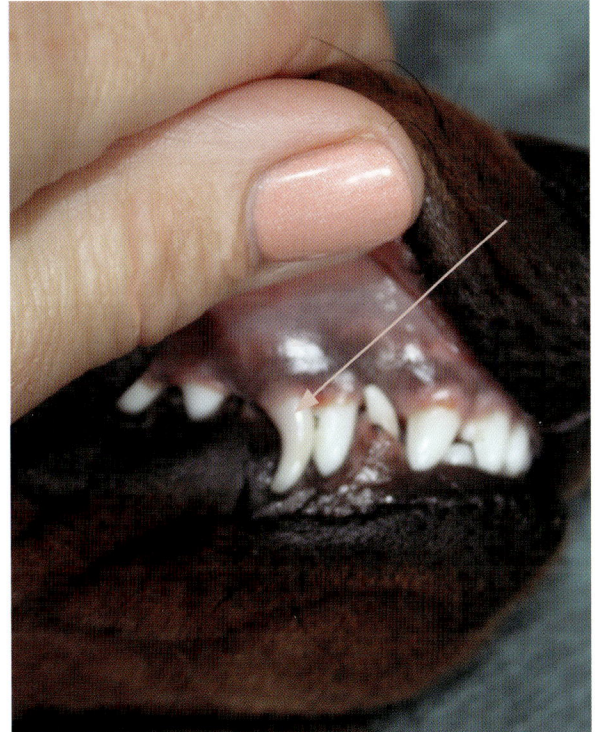

The fold/crease, normally in the middle of the ear, has folded at the back (aka a rose ear).

The first baby canine tooth is wedged behind the new adult canine tooth.

the growth pattern and development of the jaw. Feed a knotty bone such as lamb ribs to help dislodge them.

Ear Care

Ear infections are uncommon in Dobermanns as there is plenty of airflow around the outer ear. High carbohydrate diets can cause yeast overgrowth. Infected or cankerous ears will smell musty and metallic.

Cracked skin at the ear edges is caused by an autoimmune condition called 'cold agglutinin disease'. In reaction to cold temperatures, antibodies bind to red blood cells in the ear tips forming them into clumps (agglutination) and damaging the fragile membranes. It is not contagious, and only spreads locally. Keeping the ear tips warm in winter (try a stocking or scarf around the ears) will help. Severe cracking may be lasered or stitched.

Eye Care

Puppies often have an eye discharge when they are teething. If the discharge is discoloured, smells bad, or the dog is rubbing his eyes, *see the vet*. Only a vet should be dealing with eye problems, but if the eye needs flushing urgently, only use saline solution from a prepared solution, such as for contact lenses. *Never guess how much salt to put in water*. The sclera (white part of the eye) usually becomes discoloured due to age, but if it is otherwise discoloured it may indicate other illness, so consult a vet.

Nails and Feet

The foot of the Dobermann must be kept well cared for to maintain it in perfect working order. The breed standard calls for 'well arched, compact and cat-like feet with dark nails. Turning neither in nor out, with tough, hard pads.'

Flat feet may be inherited, and too much exercise on a puppy's soft bones will also result in flat feet (*see* Dental Care, Teething, above), but the main cause is long nails, which flatten the toes, preventing the foot arching as it is designed

The Dobermann has no common issues with eye problems, as the skin around the almond-shaped eye is tight to the ball.

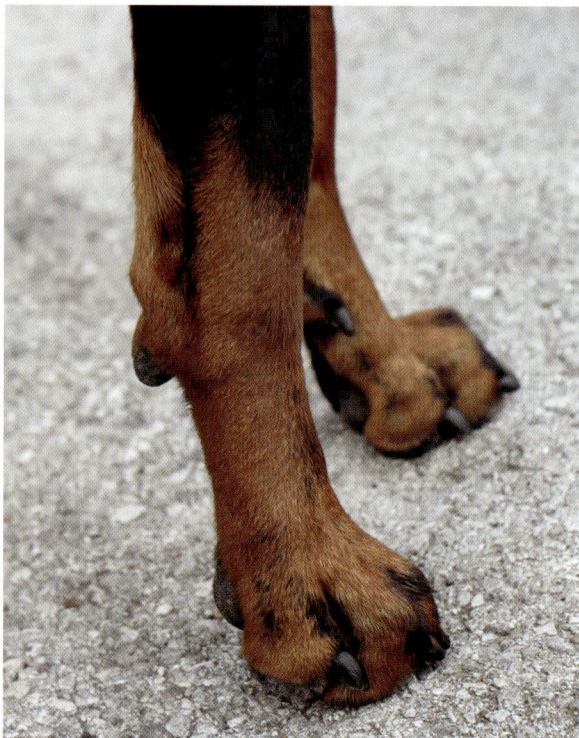

Good, cat-like feet. The cushioning provides impact support.

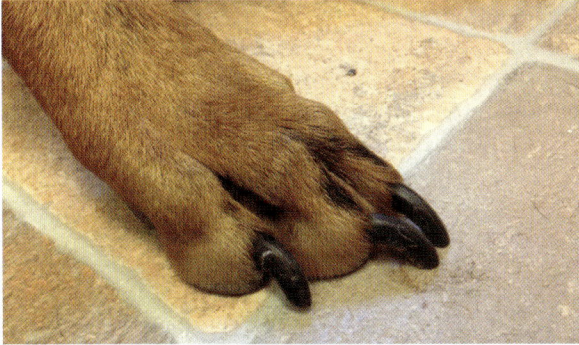

These very long nails cause flattened arches, with the nails pushing the toes apart and the foot back on its heel. GEORGIE KUHL

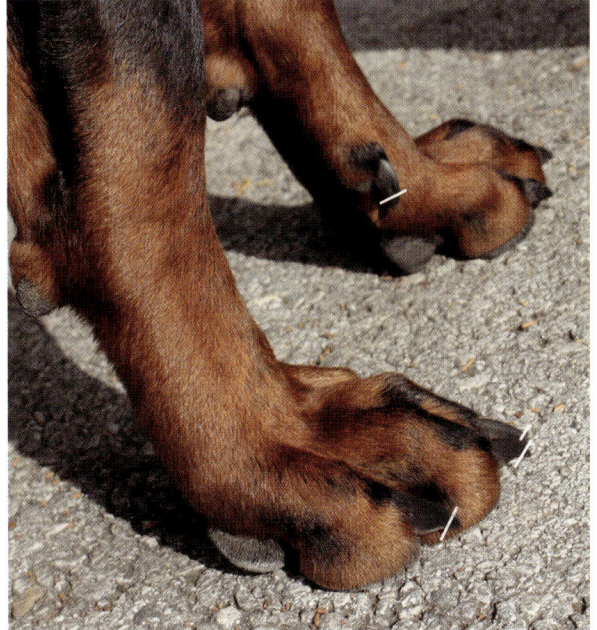

The white lines show where to cut the nail without catching the quick: just beyond the curve. Take these ends off weekly, and the quick will recede naturally.

Start clipping baby puppies with human nail clippers, then move on to the smaller toy dog clippers, and eventually the large size.

to do. Reduced cushioning provides no shock absorption for the joints. The alignment of the skeletal system is altered, leading to arthritis and joint pain.

Road walking may wear nails down a bit, but is rarely sufficient unless the dog has naturally short nails. Vets often don't understand cat-like feet in dogs, and tell owners that the length of the nails is fine when in fact they are far too long to keep the feet tight.

Owners often dread clipping nails because the nail is black and it is impossible to see where the quick (vein) ends. If the nail has grown very long, trim gradually until the chalky white area of dead keratin can be seen, or the softer area felt just before the pulp. This encourages the quick to recede without cutting it. A small nail grinder leaves a tidy finish, but can also catch the quick. Scissor-type clippers are more accurate than the guillotine type, as tiny slices can be taken off rather than one large chunk.

With baby puppies, start by using human nail clippers (not toe-nail clippers as they are too hard sprung), then as the puppy gets bigger, move on to small toy dog clippers, and eventually the large size.

Don't make the dog uncomfortable by lifting the leg too high. If you have previously caught the quick he will understandably hide and shake when the clippers come out. If you can't cut the nails yourself, take your dog weekly to a groomer who will usually trim the nails while you wait.

Even the best groomers occasionally nip the quick by accident, and nails bleed as profusely as ears. Keep some Styptic powder or potassium permanganate, which will stop bleeding very quickly, and apply it on to the bleeding nail. Otherwise drag the nail across the surface of a bar of soap to clog it up. Don't worry about a bit of bleeding: it is no worse than a cut finger. A treat will take the dog's mind off it.

Ticks and Their Removal

Ticks jump on dogs from grass or woodland, but unless you are in a high tick area (deer are particularly likely to carry ticks), regular preventative tick treatment is unnecessary. As the Dobermann is a short-coated breed it is usually sufficient to run your hands over your dog daily to feel for any ticks.

Never pull a tick straight out, as it is essential to remove the head, which will be buried under the skin of the dog. If the head stays inside the dog it can cause infection and lead to an abscess. Ideally use a proper tick remover to hold the head of the tick, and gently twist.

Note that some ticks, particularly in southern Europe, can carry serious and deadly diseases.

THE OLDER DOG

Caring for older dogs can be a difficult balance as they must be kept fit to maintain joints, but they mustn't overdo it. Old and infirm dogs will still want to walk with you way beyond their physical limits, so do regular short walks, rather than one long walk.

Body fat has a pro-inflammatory effect that increases pain, so it is best to keep the old dog on the lean side, to minimize strain, and consequently inflammation, to old joints. Keeping him warm and out of draughts with a hot water bottle or heat pad near the affected joints will be very welcome for relieving arthritic pain. Regular massage from owner and therapist keeps joints and muscle areas free and supple, thus helping to maintain mobility.

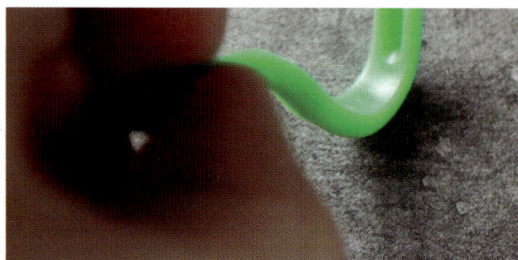

Slide the tines behind the neck of the tick – between the tick and the skin – and slowly twist. The tick releases its hold on the host and comes out alive, when it can quickly be killed and disposed of.

Mood improvement is one of the strongest painkillers available. The body produces endorphins (a group of hormones), which activate the brain's opiate receptors to provide an analgesic effect. And old dogs can still learn new tricks: keeping him mentally alert with interactive

Ned. Ch. Aritaur Dominatrix, EJSgrn02, enjoying the sunshine at twelve and a half years old.

Older dogs have difficulty regulating their temperature as their reduced mobility lowers their metabolism. But they still love to go out in the snow, so a warm coat on a cold day will be very welcome. Only use coats when dogs are slow-moving or static, not when they are exercising.

games is ideal for a dog whose exercise must be limited. (*See* Chapter 6, Working and Training, for ideas.)

Many natural remedies are valuable painkillers, but 'natural' doesn't necessarily mean they are all safe. When treating your dog, the vet should be made aware of any medication, whether natural or not.

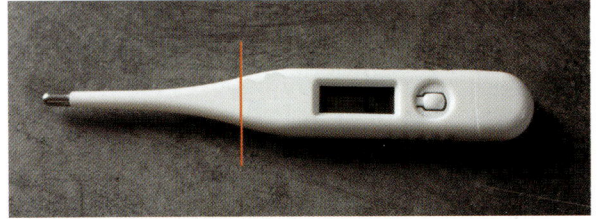

Insert in the rectum to the red line shown here, don't just push the tip in.

GENERAL HEALTH AWARENESS

Humans have become so reliant on modern diagnostics that we usually forget the old methods of identifying illness. Dogs can sniff out cancer cells and give advance notice of epilepsy in humans, but humans can also smell sickness. Swedish studies on humans show that the immune system responds to bacterial or viral invasion by giving off a general smell of sickness. The suggestion is that infection smells bad – metallic and sour – to provoke revulsion in other people and to repel them, thereby keeping them safe.

Everyone should keep a thermometer in their dog medicine kit bag, as this will give them a good indication of whether they are dealing with infection or not, and may save an unnecessary trip to the vet. A dog's normal temperature is 101–102°F (38–39°C).

WOUNDS AND HEALING

All wounds must be cleaned, but antiseptics kill both good and bad bacteria. As long as the body's immune system is generally healthy and infection does not take hold, nature can heal many of the deepest wounds. Most wounds can be effectively washed with saline, but it is essential to get the correct balance, as salt is abrasive on the skin. Keep a bottle of ready-made saline (such as for contact lenses) on the shelf. In an emergency bottled fresh water is better than nothing.

Creams and powders prevent air reaching the wound, but are good on closed skin. On open wounds use only sprays, liquids or light gels.

A 2014 study found 'moderate quality evidence that honey is more effective than antiseptic for healing wounds infected after surgical operations' (source: Jull, Cullum *et al*). Some vets now keep tubes of Manuka honey in stock, though its healing properties depend on how fresh it is – the old pot from the back of the cupboard is unlikely to be beneficial. Most dogs enjoy the taste of honey and lick it off unless it is covered.

Fibroblast cells create scar tissue, which grows like a mesh over a wound. On a clean cut wound they knit over smoothly, but over a wound with ragged edges the mesh will be very irregular, and hair from a destroyed hair shaft will not be able to grow back. Once the wound is fully healed, firmly massage in a cream or oil to keep the skin supple and break down the underlying mesh to allow a hair to break through. Natural oils are ideal, but it is more the process of the massage than the product used.

Under some wounds, a pocket of blood (haematoma), plasma serum (seroma), or air (crepitus) can form in body cavities, usually due to a big bump against the body. It is designed to be a healing and cushioning mechanism, and looks like a soft, floppy bag. Syringing fluid from it may reduce it sufficiently for the body to reabsorb the reduced volume more easily, but usually it just refills, and it can persist for months. 'Crepitus' describes the crinkling sounds and sensation of air trapped under a wound. Air is usually absorbed after a few hours, but otherwise may indicate an accumulation of gas caused by bacteria.

PUNCTURE WOUNDS

Dog bites from another dog (or other animal) that puncture the skin should be treated with antibiotics. If you can't get to the vet immediately, wash the worst of the dirt out of the wound with mild saline until you can get antibiotics.

Puncture wounds must be never be stitched closed as this prevents infection escaping. It will heal quickly from the inside out. Torn skin usually needs debriding – any ragged skin needs removing – so it can knit back together efficiently. Bandages should be used only if necessary, to help keep a surgically cleansed wound clean; air should be able to reach the wound, so they should be light and allow good ventilation.

With multiple bites from a prolonged fight or attack, the dog will be bruised and shocked. Lactic acid and adrenalin released into the muscles to aid fight or flight will now be causing them to seize up with a painful burning sensation. Keep him warm and quiet, and provide Metacam or some other anti-inflammatory for pain relief.

BANDAGING AND DRESSINGS

First and foremost, if you have never been taught how to apply a bandage to an animal, don't! A major cause of amputations in dogs is due to over-tight bandaging. Blood can't flow back out of the limb, which then swells to more than double its normal size. Without oxygen the blood and tissues rapidly start to necrotize, and amputation is the only option. To learn how to bandage in case of emergency or home care prescribed by a vet, ask the vet nurses to teach you.

When a dog chews at dressings and bandages, it usually indicates that he is bothered by something more than just having a dressing on. If he is constantly crying or trying to rip the bandage off, don't just put an Elizabethan collar on him, but check for infection or over-tight bandaging.

PAINKILLERS

Although 'human' drugs such as aspirin, paracetamol and anti-inflammatories have been tested for toxicity on dogs (through animal testing), they will not have been trialled as painkillers for them, and guessing a dosage and home administering at home is potentially dangerous. Keep to specific medication for dogs from a vet.

Corticosteroids are used in humans and animals to treat the pain and inflammation associated with osteoarthritis, but the side effects can be unwelcome (such as a reduction in muscle mass, which keeps the affected joint relatively stable).

Acupuncture is now practised in some veterinary surgeries and by other qualified animal health professionals, and can have impressive results, particularly with regard to pain relief and mobility.

VETERINARY TREATMENT AND INSURANCE

Pet care treatment today is equal to human medicine, and every condition known to dogs can be treated with unlimited funds. Specialist referrals are now very big business, and some practices have targets for their vets to promote their medical care plans, and referrals.

Insurance companies rarely cover re-existing conditions. Obviously if you didn't declare something the insurance company may quite rightly refuse to pay out, but you must challenge a company that you feel is acting unfairly. In ongoing disputes they may offer to refund all your premiums. That is usually the first settlement offer, but you may still decide to challenge for full payout if you feel you have a case.

Vaccination and insurance concerns some owners, who believe they must have their dogs fully vaccinated (annually if advised by the vet) in order for the dog to be insured. The small print misleadingly infers an insurance company would not pay out for an illness or injury if the dog is not vaccinated. This is false. If a condition is unrelated to vaccination, insurance companies know they would never be supported legally if they refused a claim. If you remain concerned, write to your insurance company to clarify the exact terms in the event of any illness unrelated to vaccination. Call handlers will generally only read out their terms without providing detailed information.

None of this advice is intended to be a substitute for veterinary attention in the case of a sick animal.

A TO Z OF MANAGING CONDITIONS AND INJURIES

Allergies

Allergies are an over-reaction of the immune system to an overwhelming event, and are manifested as rashes, rhinitis, vomiting, diarrhoea, collapse, and even death. Allergies may be acute or chronic, and can develop from pollens, diet, toxins (such as pesticides, household chemicals – plug-in or spray air fresheners – washing powders), vaccination, and fleas and ticks, or the treatment against them (contact or inhaled).

The areas affected sometimes give a clue as to the allergy. Grass allergies usually show as red spots of welts on the underbelly, inner legs and feet; food reactions may cause spots on the shoulders and back; while itchy, sore and swollen feet indicate yeast infections (excess starches and carbohydrates in the diet). A very unpleasant yeast is Pityrosporum, which causes the skin condition Malasezzia (often blamed on grain allergy). Yeast thrives on areas of warm, moist skin, so will target the ears, armpits, belly and feet. Symptoms are endless scratching of red and sore areas, and hair loss. Dogs may bottom scoot and chew their feet and legs. They may smell musty, and their skin becomes greasy and sweaty, and sometimes has a yellow tint. This condition may be treated with apple cider vinegar, see below.

Diet has a great impact on the immune system, with around 70 per cent of allergies originating in the gut. Similar to IBS in humans, we can all become intolerant to even good things if we take them to excess. Grain is often blamed for allergies, but moulds are the major aggravator. Clinical signs can show outwardly on the skin even if the allergen is inhaled (*see* Aflatoxins in Chapter 8, Nutrition and Feeding).

A huge industry of allergy panels, blood tests, skin biopsies and 'hypo-allergenic' dog foods now exists. Vets may suggest a skin scrape, or even a skin punch, when the dog is anaesthetized and a deep section of the skin is removed for examination. Most of these rarely show more than an allergy to house dust or grass pollen.

Treatment Options for Allergies

Acupuncture: Researchers in Germany found that acupuncture brought long-term benefits for human allergy sufferers, who were given acupuncture treatment for their symptoms.

Antihistamines: For mild allergies, antihistamines (such as for hay fever) are often recommended by vets. However, these are short-term fixes, and veterinary advice should be taken.

Apple cider vinegar (ACV): ACV is a wonderful old remedy for many health conditions, and particularly allergy control; it works by cleansing the gut and lymphatic system, and reducing mucus production. ACV can be used internally and externally. It is an ideal remedy against yeast, which hates acidic environments, so is effective against the very unpleasant yeast Pityrosporum, which causes the skin condition Malasezzia (often blamed on grain allergy). Add a couple of teaspoonfuls in the dog's drinking water, introducing it gradually until he is used to the taste. Also apply a solution to the sore areas: mix 50/50 ACV and purified (boiled) water, and apply with a sponge to the affected areas all over. Don't get liquid down the ear, but wipe a damp cotton pad of solution around the ear-hole. A lukewarm Epsom salt and ACV footbath is ideal for the feet: immerse them for five to ten minutes daily.

Barrier creams: For grass allergy, liberally apply a barrier cream (such as canola or coconut oil) to the stomach, inside the back legs and between the toes before going out.

Immunotherapy: This works by giving weekly injections of the substance to which the dog is allergic for many months, gradually decreasing to injecting bi-annually.

Lactobacillus: A long-term reduction in allergy was demonstrated in human test groups using Lactobacillus (probiotic) to reduce the incidence of atopic eczema. (*Ref.:* Furrie, E. PubMed.Gov.)

Laxative treatments: Cleanse the gut and bowel of residual fungal infections with gentle laxative treatments such as aloe vera, senna and Epsom salts. Dandelion root and milk thistle support the liver to clean the blood.

Quercetin: The natural flavonoid plant pigment Quercetin may help reduce histamine release and subsequent inflammation. Like most plant remedies, it is slow to work, and if the dog has a recurring seasonal allergy, start treatment a month or more before the allergy season.

Steroids: Although Elizabethan (plastic neck) collars and bandaging may stop the dog chewing himself, if he is suffering physically and mentally, steroids will at least get him comfortable in the short term. But it's a Catch 22 situation, because although steroids work quickly to suppress inflammation, they also suppress the immune system, leaving him vulnerable to infection and disease.

Anal Glands
The anal glands are two small sacs located one on each side of the anus just inside the body. Puppies often develop smelly anal glands but they clear themselves; however, if a vet expresses them unnecessarily, they will never self-regulate and may ultimately need removing, which is a painful operation. For kibble-fed dogs there is no roughage to express the glands. Charcoal biscuits and/or a raw juicy bone can help (though limit the time spent chewing).

Arthritis
Arthritis causes stiffness and inflammation and can occur at any age due to degenerative changes in the joints, or injury. The aim for arthritis treatment is to reduce inflammation, and many fish-oil products help with this. Generations of humans have taken cod liver oil, particularly in wintertime, and that or salmon oil is equally ideal for dogs. Omega 3, MSM, glucosamine and chondroitin are all used to treat arthritis by increasing the quantity and viscosity of joint fluid. Green-lipped mussel extract helps protect the cartilage and is a natural anti-inflammatory, as is Devil's Claw. Essential fatty acids (EFAs) have been used for many years to improve coat and skin condition, particularly for allergies, but more recently have been found to be very beneficial in controlling inflammation.

Ann Sread and Asia. The perfect combination of a sunny day and a canine physiotherapist to ease tight muscles and old joints.

Bites and Stings

If you can see the barb (wasps have straight stings, bees have barbed stings), flick it out of the body as a barb can continue to inject venom even after the bee has disengaged from the sting. If the dog has been stung on the face or in the mouth, it may prompt an anaphylactic shock reaction that may cause breathing difficulty and collapse. Don't make him walk, as an increase in the heart rate can disperse the poison further around the body. Keep him calm and lying quietly and call for help.

Bloat

Bloat (**GDV:** gastric dilation volvulus) is a serious, life-threatening event that can affect deep-chested breeds such as the Dobermann. For various reasons the stomach begins to expand with gas and fluid (dilation), and can rotate on itself. This action of rotation is called volvulus, and this can be a twist of 180 degrees to a full torsion of 360 degrees. Depending on the degree of twist, blood circulation to other organs, and especially the heart, is restricted and the pressure on the diaphragm makes it difficult for the dog to breathe.

Signs of bloat are an abnormally enlarged stomach, and unsuccessful attempts to belch or vomit. The dog may drool as he feels sick and nauseous, and will turn his head towards his stomach in distress, lying down in a sphinx-like position and sometimes taking short panting breaths. His gums will often be pale, dry and tacky to the touch.

As dilatation rapidly progresses, the sphincters (the constriction points at the beginning and end of the stomach) twist closed, preventing him belching or vomiting to release the gas. Without blood flow reaching the stomach, it quickly necrotizes. Full collapse and death is imminent unless a vet operates immediately to physically untwist the stomach.

Depending on the severity of the bloat and the length of time before surgery, the stomach may be so weakened that it re-twists, so the vet may stitch the stomach wall to the side of the abdomen in a procedure known as laparoscopic gastroplexy. Dogs that have suffered bloat and do not have this procedure have a recurrence rate of bloat of 70 per cent, and a mortality rate of 80 per cent.

Dogs that survive surgery may subsequently suffer shock, dehydration, bacterial septicaemia resulting from the degradation and perforation of the gut, and cardiac arrhythmias. The first twenty-four hours are critical. The survival rate of dogs after an emergency GDV operation is 70 per cent.

Bloat develops suddenly and without warning, often in middle-aged to older dogs that are often healthy and active. (*See also* Chapter 7, Nutrition and Feeding.)

Broken Tail

Broken tails are nowhere near as common as was predicted following the docking ban in 2007. However, if a tail is broken, it is difficult to mend and usually has to be removed.

Dogs with back pain may hunch up to avoid pressure on the spine, and a drooping, limp tail may indicate lower back or pelvic pain.

Echo had a full tail break halfway down. Surgery was successful, and a lightweight piece of pipe lagging kept it stable whilst it repaired.

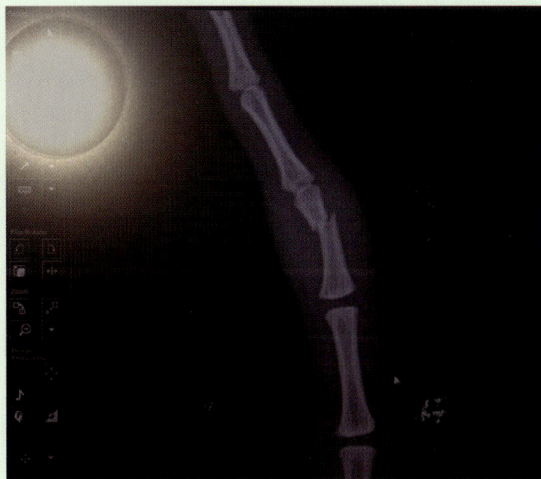

Bursa and Hygroma

When dogs lie down heavily, local injury and calluses can form on the elbow and hock joints, ranging from dry skin to large swellings of fluid. Kennel dogs repeatedly lying on hard surfaces may suffer elbow and hock irritation, but even the most pampered dog on a soft bed can develop a bursa. Initially the area becomes sore, and the skin becomes roughened, dry and crusty. Each time he lies down it is re-injured, and layers of dense fibrous tissue develop over the site, with more fissures occurring. Skin cracks can lead to bleeding and irritation. Elbow bursa (false bursa) can develop in old dogs.

If the area is red and weeping, this indicates that septic bursitis has developed, for which antibiotics are needed.

If the area is dry and cracked, clean it with a mildly medicated wash, then apply witch hazel and aloe vera gel or Vaseline to keep the area supple and prevent more fissures and cracks developing. Provide padded bedding for protection, and use an elbow pressure bandage. Some dogs throw themselves down on hard ground when they lie down, so encourage them on to a blanket or to lie down slowly.

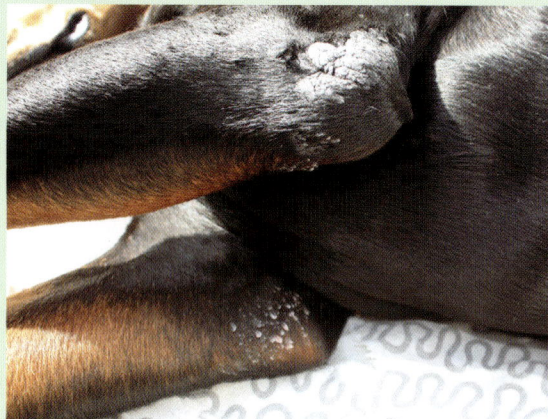

This dog rarely lay on a hard surface, but developed elbow bursa in his older years.

Cancer

Cancer is an ancient disease: tumours have been recorded in the remains of dinosaurs, and a reference to tumours of the breast exists on Egyptian papyrus written between 3000 and 1500BC. Cancers can develop as a result of constant exposure to toxins, idiopathically (for no known reason), or from a predisposition to the disease through genetic inheritance.

Benign tumours: May cause no imminent threat to life, but they can impinge on movement and general function.

Lymphoma (lymphosarcoma): A highly malignant tumour of the lymph system; it is the most common form of cancer in both humans and small animals. Lymphoma can occur anywhere in the body where there is lymph tissue. If left untreated, most dogs die within four to six weeks. With chemotherapy the average survival time for dogs is one year, with a quarter surviving two years.

Mast cell tumour (mastocytoma): Mast cells are the protective immune cells that provide rapid response to infection, injury or invasion by producing histamine and heparin for inflammation and wound healing. Mast cell tumours (MCT) can occur anywhere in the body, often being identified by an unusual bump just under the skin. They are notoriously difficult to follow.

Osteosarcoma: The most common type of bone cancer in dogs. Larger breeds are more prone to bone cancer, and there seems to be a genetic (inherited) factor. Primary osteosarcoma can be found in many sites, such as mammary tissue, organs and subcutaneous tissue, later developing in areas such as the

Seven-year-old Jedidah had been limping and licking his foreleg for some time, but due to a late diagnosis of osteosarcoma of the humerus (he had been treated instead for the lick sore he had created), the amputation and chemo were too late to be effective. He was pain free and happy but only lived for four-and-a-half months after the amputation. PETER WILLIAMS

shoulder, wrist and knee. It is extremely aggressive. In 90 per cent of cases by the time the tumour has become visible, the cancer cells have already spread into other parts of the dog's body (metastasized). Long-term prognosis is poor. Dogs receiving radiation and chemotherapy live on average up to seven months post diagnosis. A combination of surgery and chemotherapy gives an improved outlook, with a quarter of dogs surviving two years after diagnosis.

Chin Spots

Chin spots are acne-type spots that can bleed and become infected. They are easily cleared up without veterinary treatment or antibiotics. Keep the chin clean after eating, and apply a warm damp cloth to open the pores. Don't squeeze them, but tweezer out the compacted hairs to allow the pus to come out, and apply nappy rash cream two or three times daily.

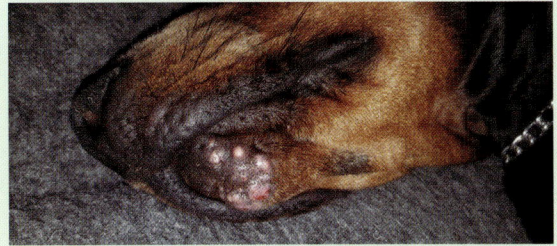

Chin spots can be treated with nappy rash cream. The old brand Antipeol® is hard to find but ideal.

Colour Dilute Alopecia (CDA)

CDA can affect dogs with dilute coat colours of blue or fawn, but it is not limited to either blue dogs or Dobermanns, and not all dilute-coloured dogs will develop it. Puppies have normal coats, but the adult coat can come through as very harsh textured and prone to breakage, sometimes with a recurrent infection of the hair follicles. Symmetrical alopecia (hair loss on both sides) is often mistaken for symptoms of hypothyroidism.

The underlying skin sometimes appears darker and mottled, and skin biopsies may show that the hair follicles are blocked with skin cells, broken hairs, keratin and melanin, causing what looks like large blackheads on the body. Blocked

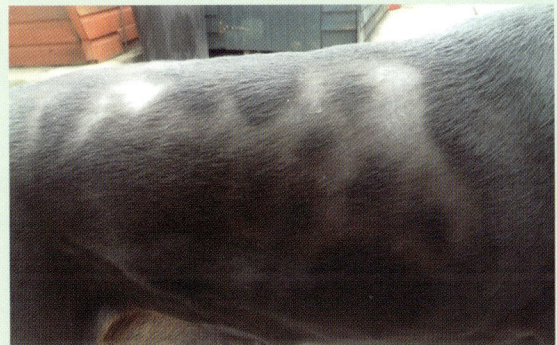

Colour dilute alopecia in a black and rust bitch whose coat quality began to thin and deteriorate from around three years of age. Both parents were black, but passed on the dilute gene.

215

hair follicles can develop a secondary infection, which may require antibiotics. The dog may become completely bald as he matures. The condition is unsightly, and affected dogs will obviously feel the cold, but it is not painful or life inhibiting.

A coat colour DNA test exists to help breeders identify whether a dog carries the dilute gene. Dogs can be tested by using buccal (mouth) swabs from Vetgen in the US, or Laboklin in the UK and Europe.

Coprophagia

Coprophagia is the eating of poo. It may be due to insufficient nutrients, minerals, enzymes and vitamins in their food, but even dogs fed on a raw, varied and balanced diet do it (perhaps to obtain any remaining enzymatic material). Dogs are scavengers and often eat things that are bad for them, but they don't necessarily have a deficiency. Feeding pineapple (natural or tinned) works for all but the most determined poo-eaters.

Coughing

Coughing could be a sign of something as simple as kennel cough, or as life-threatening as congestive heart failure. There could be a foreign object (*see* below), or the dog could have just scratched his throat. There is a different sound between an upper respiratory (tickly) cough, and a deep cough where the dog is trying to expel fluid from the lungs, but any Dobermann that is coughing should visit the vet to rule out the possibility of heart problems. A Troponin blood test is relatively cheap at around £30 to carry out (*see also* Chapter 8, Cardiomyopathy).

If it is just kennel cough or a sore throat, many owners use human cough medicine to ease the discomfort; pineapple juice is ideal for treating sore throats due to the anti-inflammatory enzymes of Bromelain. It also contains plenty of vitamin C to help boost the immune system.

Cracked Paw Pads

Cracked paw pads can develop from injury to the pad, contact with salt and anti-freeze from the roads in winter, or harsh cleaning products in the home such as bleach, or a diet deficient in minerals and oils. As the skin dries and splits, keratin hardens and grows over a crack to try and protect it. Hyperkeratosis (overgrowth of keratin) can lead to fissures in the snout and pads. Infections can develop and antibiotics may be needed, but early topical treatments can aid progression. Soaking the foot in a mild solution of Epsom salts (magnesium) is beneficial, and a zinc cream helps healing.

Cystitis

Cystitis is a bladder infection that is not uncommon in puppy bitches. Signs are frequent attempts to urinate, but with little urine coming out. The puppy or bitch will need antibiotics.

Foreign Objects

Foreign objects are impossible to determine without x-rays. Taking the dog's temperature should eliminate infection as a cause. If the dog is hunched over with an arched back this may indicate a blockage. As he tries to eliminate the foreign object or substance, he may develop sickness and diarrhoea, and will drink copious amounts of water. If his condition has reached this stage, take him to the vet rather than waiting for it to pass.

For a general upset stomach, kaolin is a trusted remedy. Most veterinary surgeries sell syringe kaolin solutions off the shelf. Note that Pepto-Bismol® and Imodium® can be toxic to dogs.

Hiccups (Hiccoughs)

Hiccups are as common in puppies as they are in children. They may result from having eaten too quickly, or from having a bit of gas in the stomach that presses against the diaphragm. Reverse or backward sneezing accompanied by plenty of snorting can be alarming, but is unlikely to be damaging. Foreign objects in the back of the nose may cause it, and dogs can sometimes do it so hard that it makes them retch.

Lameness

There are many causes of lameness; more commonly these might include a nail bed infection, a twisted ligament, a pulled shoulder muscle, or panosteitis (growing pains in young dogs, see below). Observing how the dog stands and walks will often show up the problem. Examine the nail beds for any heat, inflammation or redness: if the dog has stubbed the toe or nail, inflammation occurs, the temperature rises and infection thrives. Shine a torch on the toe in the dark to show up any glistening or moisture, which indicates infection.

Lick Sores

Lick sores commonly develop on the lower leg area, which is easily accessible. Initially the dog may have had an irritation on a certain site, and persists in licking it. Continued obsessive licking causes the skin to thicken around the edges, resulting in further irritation. Dogs left alone for long periods of time often develop obsessive behaviours through boredom, and the theory is that excessive licking stimulates endorphin (calming hormones) release. Giving them something else to chew helps to distract them, and may give the skin a chance to heal.

Treating the condition is virtually impossible as the dog rips off wraps and bandages, and creams and bad-tasting anti-lick spray are simply licked away. An umbrella collar will stop the dog licking, but it is miserable for a dog to have to wear one permanently. Besides, as soon as the collar is removed he either finds a new patch to lick or returns to the original site. Anti-bacterial neoprene leg wraps may be useful, and silver colloidal cream helps the skin to heal.

Obesity

Fat dogs are either fed too much, fed incorrectly, don't exercise enough, or have a medical condition. Owners often excuse their fat dog by claiming 'he is big boned' or 'he is all muscle'. However, Dobermanns are not meant to be heavy Molosser types like a big Rottweiler, but should be lithe, muscular and agile, with the skin fitting firmly around the frame. Useful indicators of excess weight are wrinkles around the shoulders, the waistline and the croup (just before the tail).

Poos are a useful way to monitor weight: large poos indicate the dog is eating too much, foamy poos indicate a gas problem, and small poos indicate everything is being absorbed. If the ribs are too easily felt, more food can be given. Males tend to weigh around 40kg, and females 27–36kg.

Occiput Damage

The occiput is the lump at the highest point of the skull at the very back

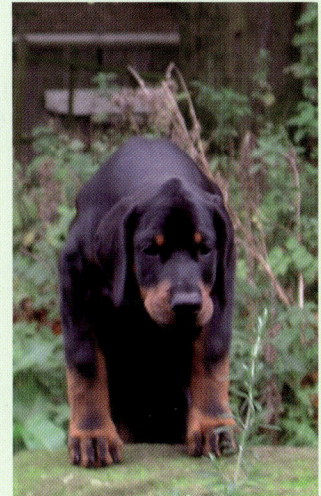

A lump on Tess's head.

of the head, resembling a pterodactyl-shape head. Any bump to the head here causes a big swelling, as the cushioning to protect the brain against injury cannot go inside the skull or it would result in pressure on the brain. Like any bruise, it should reduce in a few weeks.

Panosteitis

Otherwise known as 'growing pains', this painful lameness is a symptom of growth: it will pass without any lasting effect, and is best controlled nutritionally. At around five to eleven months of age the growth plates in the long bones are creating new bone, which causes inflammation. The front legs are usually affected, but the pain may shift around. Pup may be very miserable, refusing to move from his bed. Although full exercise won't harm him, it will create more inflammation and pain; besides, at this age his bones and joints are not yet fully formed, so he should not be exercising hard anyway. He will also be teething.

When examining a lame young dog, the sensible vet would suspect panosteitis, rather than jumping to a diagnosis of hip dysplasia or worse.

For treatment of the condition, reduce the protein levels in the dog's food immediately in order to slow down his growth rate. Although food changes should usually be gradual, over four to five days, getting him pain free quickly is more important than avoiding any digestive upset. For complete (kibble) feeders, buy a very low protein food (watch the additives), while for raw feeders, stop protein-rich meats and go straight on to tripe, which is high in fats and low in protein. Within a couple of days pup should feel happier, but you should expect a recurrence of panosteitis during future growth stages. Limit exercise to short, steady walks on a lead, and play 'brain games' to keep him occupied. Painkillers and anti-inflammatories can help, and a hot water bottle or heated blanket, and giving him leg rubs, will ease the deep aching.

Scars

To reduce the effect of a scar, use Vaseline or vitamin E oil. Massage firmly into the scar and reapply twice daily to keep the skin supple, otherwise hair can't grow through the toughened skin, and the scar will be permanent.

Upset Stomach

For a general upset stomach, kaolin is a trusted remedy. Most veterinary surgeries sell syringe kaolin solutions off the shelf. Note that Pepto-Bismol® and Imodium® can be toxic to dogs.

11 THE BREED STANDARD

A breed standard is the blueprint for the appearance and characteristics of a breed, and differentiates one breed from another in type and function. It lays out the physiological diagram of bones, muscles, shape and colour, and although it has more bias towards the physical traits, the mentality of the breed is also outlined. Whilst few Dobermanns in the UK still work for their original purpose, they should at least look and be capable of doing the job for which they were bred, which is to be a guardian for their owner and family.

European breeders and clubs require Dobermanns to show that their working ability is taken seriously, and that in this they are a dog of value to the breed. In many countries a dog cannot become a champion without passing a working test. The ultimate title of IDC (International Dobermann Club) Sieger is not possible without a ZTP, the 'fit for breeding' test, and a full working title is required before a dog can become an international champion. The UK and American Dobermann, on the other hand, is not required to work in order to be titled.

Although the Dobermann was derived from a terrier (Pinscher), it is not designed to go to ground to rats, nor is it a draft animal designed to pull carts: the Dobermann is a guarding breed, and as such it must be capable of great speed in order to catch an intruder, and strong enough to bring him down. And although they are very sociable dogs, they are meant to be a deterrent: thus we do not want an intruder looking over the garden fence and being welcomed by a Dobermann with a 'sweet face' – we want him to be faced with a guard dog's impenetrable stare that will deter him from entering without our permission. Without these traits we may as well breed Dobermanns with the character of a Labrador.

Any breed needs to be fit for the purpose for which he was bred in both mind and body.

DOBERMANNS WORLDWIDE

There are essentially four different general 'strains' of Dobermann in the world: the UK show lines, the USA show lines, the European show lines, and the European working lines. The true working-line breeder rarely, if ever, integrates their breeding with show-line breeding, even if those show-line dogs work at the highest level.

Sandy Machado's Joker Gaïano de La Villa Valiano ZTP 1A V.

DEFINING TYPE, STYLE AND STRAIN

Type distinguishes one breed from another: terrier type, gundog type. The word 'type' is often used incorrectly to describe the difference between, for instance, an American Dobermann over a European-style Dobermann – but they are the same, being a 'Dobermann type'. What differs is the style, or strain.

Because the free movement of bloodlines was restricted by quarantine regulations, UK dogs developed a style that was quite distinctive from the original European and USA styles. Because there were fewer imports, in the 1970s and 1980s lines became increasingly in-bred. Bodies became more rounded, with longer and softer backs, and legs became shorter. Heads were often heavy in the back-skull, muzzles were snipey, and under-jaws weak.

Following the relaxation of quarantine laws in 2000, the breed was influenced by prepotent imported stud dogs, and shape started to change once again. Bodies became more compact, and the substance of head bone improved, particularly in the foreface.

There are no weight specifications for Dobermanns in the UK or American breed standards. The FCI (Fédération Cynologique International) breed standard provides a weight guide for the Dobermann for males of around 40–45kg, and for females of around 32–35kg.

Breed style differs markedly across Europe, though Dobermanns throughout Europe generally all have a firm backline and deep rust markings.

In eastern Europe: Males having the biggest frame and bone size. Dogs are shown at a heavy weight (50kg), and can sometimes verge on the Molosser in style. Although some eastern European females have enough substance to dwarf some of the lighter UK and US males, they still retain great elegance.

Dutch breeders: Prefer substantial dogs, although they are not as heavy as those from Russia and the Balkans; they are often high on the leg.

Italian Dobermanns: Are renowned for beautiful heads. Their character can be very high drive.

The American and Canadian Dobermann: Elegant, with a long clean head; they are generally shown cropped and docked, which adds to their look of nobility. The breed in the USA suffered for a long time from a very straight front and a very over-angulated rear, but this problem has now been largely remedied. The body is generally deep, and the loins are usually short. Many American dogs have pale markings. Owners in America and the UK generally prefer a dog with a softer character than the European Dobermann, and in these countries to some extent the tough spirit of the Dobermann has been sacrificed for an easier dog to live with.

Australia and New Zealand: Dobermanns in these countries are based predominantly on American-bred Dobermanns.

The Far East/Asian countries: Based much of their breeding on old Dutch lines, and recently some prominent eastern European kennels, with some Italian breeding. These are medium-weight, not over-sized dogs, and have strength with elegance. One of the most prominent breeders in Indonesia is Andi Hudono, whose Harmonic Dobermanns are based largely on vom Franckenhorst dogs.

Int., Multi Ch. Zordan Zewi del Citone, IDC Sgr 07, WW 08, AIAD Sgr 08, IPO3. GIOTA

BIS, BISS Am. Gr. Ch. Dabney's Phenomenon. Bred and owned by John and Linda Krukar.

South Africa: Had many Dutch imports and some early Dizown dogs in the late 1970s. Most dogs are now of Italian and eastern European lines.

INTERNATIONAL KENNEL CLUBS AND ORGANIZATIONS

The pedigree Dobermann (or Doberman Pinscher, as it is named in the USA) is governed throughout the world by three main authorities:

• The UK Kennel Club governs England, Wales, Scotland and Northern Ireland
• The FCI (Fédération Cynologique International) governs kennel clubs over five world regions: Europe (including Southern Ireland), the Americas and the Caribbean, Asia and the Pacific, the Middle East and Africa
• The USA has two kennel clubs: the AKC (American Kennel Club), and the UKC (United Kennel Club)

Kennel clubs worldwide have reciprocal arrangements to enable the registration, exhibition and exchange of dogs and pedigrees internationally.

Breed clubs in each country report directly to their country's kennel clubs.

There are three official breed standards for the Dobermann: the UK; America and Canada; and the Rest of the World FCI (Fédération Cynologique International). Each describes essentially the same breed of dog, but with slight variations in different regions.

THE CROPPING AND DOCKING OF TAILS AND EARS

Ear cropping has not been allowed in the UK since 1899, after King Edward VII wrote to the Kennel Club to express his dislike of the practice; subsequently an order was made to ban it.

The first mainland European country to ban ear cropping was Switzerland in 1981, and tail docking in 1988. Finland was next for both procedures in 1996, followed by other Nordic and Scandic countries, then Germany with a ban in 1988. Ear cropping has now been banned in many parts of northern Europe, but is still permitted in Russia, some Eastern European countries, the Far East and America. It is illegal in some states of Canada, but still permitted in the USA.

The European Convention for the Protection of Pet Animals required all EU member states to ban docking, and this was accepted by Scotland and Wales in 2006, England in 2007, and Ireland in 2014.

A traditionally cropped and docked Dobermann meeting the future look of the breed.

UK BREED STANDARD

Reproduced with the kind permission of the Kennel Club.

General Appearance and Demeanour

Medium size, muscular and elegant, with well set body. Of proud carriage, compact and tough. Capable of great speed.

Dobermanns need to be athletic and light enough to be capable of great speed, yet substantial enough to 'bring an assailant down'. Elegant should not mean wispy or fine boned. Both sexes are required to work to the same standard, regardless of gender.

Libby skeleton. KORIFEY DOBERMANNS

Characteristics

Intelligent and firm of character, loyal and obedient.

Temperament

Bold and alert. Shyness or viciousness very highly undesirable.

It is quite natural for males to display sexual rivalry against other males, and this is not deemed to be vicious behaviour.

Head and Skull

In proportion to body. Long, well filled out under eyes and clean cut, with good depth of muzzle. Seen from above and side, resembles an elongated blunt wedge. Upper part of head flat and free from wrinkle. Top of skull flat, slight stop; muzzle line extending parallel to top line of skull. Cheeks flat, lips tight. Nose solid black in black dogs, solid dark brown in brown dogs, solid dark grey in blue dogs and light brown in fawn dogs. Head out of balance in proportion to body, dish-faced, snipy or cheeky very highly undesirable.

This young female has a good wedge-shaped head that is well filled under the eyes, a characteristic that hopefully she will retain. Puppies often have correctly filled wedge heads, but as the head elongates, the fill under the eye is often lost.

A common fault is lack of muzzle substance and length, as too short a muzzle results in a triangle rather than a wedge. It is not possible to have an elongated blunt wedge with a short muzzle. The wedge is seen both from above and from the side. Viewed from the front, the head should widen gradually towards the base of the ears in an unbroken line. Sufficient fill under the eye is necessary to avoid a pinched-in foreface. The muzzle must be wide enough to accommodate full dentition; too sharp a wedge would result in a snipey muzzle. A short foreface spoils the elegant line of the head, but too long a head is also incorrect.

The Zygomatic arch (cheekbone) sits under the eyes. Prominent zygomas cause pronounced cheeks and prevent a clean line from the back of the head through to the foreface.

Wide and heavy back skulls are a major fault. The neck has to become wider and more muscular to carry a wider load, and both require heavy shoulders for support. The more loaded the shoulders, the less elegant the dog becomes, and less capable of the great speed required of the breed.

Although the skull must be flat, growing youngsters have a pronounced occiput (the pterodactyl-like lump on the back of the head). A domed skull with a slope off the back of the skull is concealed by erect cropped ears. Parallel head planes are

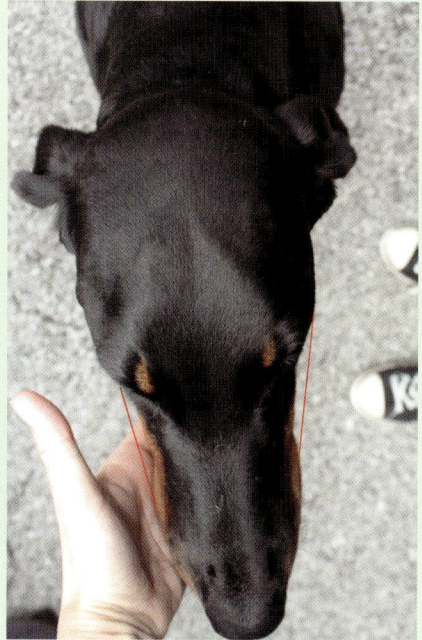

Although the length of the foreface to skull is correct, this head lacks fill under the eyes to provide the true wedge head (rarely seen in adult dogs anywhere in the world these days due to the desire for the longer head). A useful exercise for any owner/breeder who thinks their dog has a correct wedge head is to view it from above and draw a line like this from the zygoma (cheekbone) to the muzzle.

This female has parallel head planes, a flat skull and a long muzzle without weakness.

Unfortunately it is not uncommon to see such badly angled head planes.

essential. Note that young dogs may have head planes that are not parallel until the head is fully finished at around twenty months.

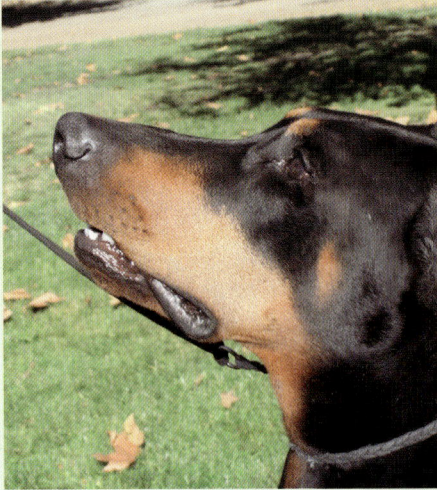

This adult male's lip is caught on his teeth, and it shows his very weak underjaw, which had been concealed by deep upper lips. His lower lips (flews/jowls) are also excessively loose.

This female has a masculine 'block' head without elegance. Her head length is good with nearly parallel head planes, but she has a shallow stop and is very deep in the foreface, with a slight drop over the nose. Her underjaw is very substantial but her lips are loose.

Loose lower lips (alias 'flews' or 'jowls') give a saggy, unclean look to the face. Young dogs may be slightly loose around the lips until the muzzle lengthens, which will effectively tighten excess skin.

Ned. Ch. Aritaur Dominatrix EJSgrn (Ger. VDH Ch. Ramonburg's Valdo x Crislea Centrefold of Aritaur). Top Brood Working Group 2007.

The Eyes

Almond-shaped, not round, moderately deep set, not prominent, with lively, alert expression. Iris of uniform colour, ranging from medium to darkest brown in black dogs, the darker shade being more desirable. In browns, blues or fawns, colour of iris blends with that of markings, but not of lighter hue than markings; light eyes in black dogs highly undesirable.

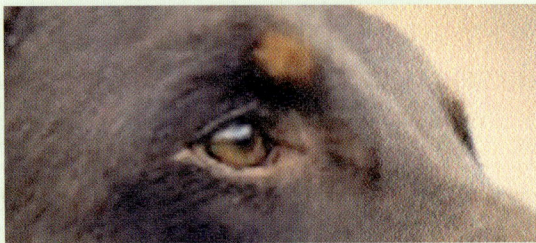

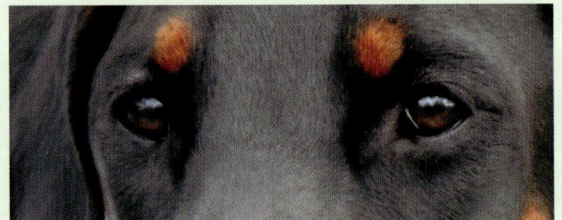

Correct almond eye shape and colour on a black and a brown Dobermann.

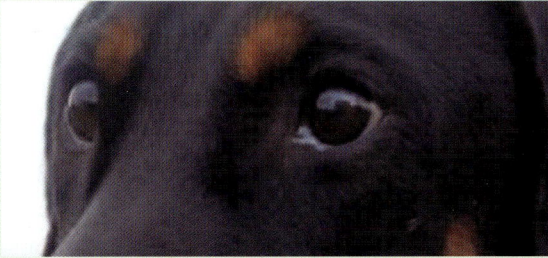

This female has a prominent round eye, giving a startled expression.

Light eyes in a black dog is one of the few points in the UK breed standard referred to as highly undesirable (other faults being simply 'undesirable'). Browns escape such harsh criticism, despite some having eyes verging on yellow, which is a very unpleasant fault.

The UK standard omits reference made by the FCI standard that 'baldness around the rim of the eye is highly undesirable'. This baldness, sometimes referred to as a monocle (as in spectacles), is more easily seen in brown dogs, and along with light eyes, greatly spoils the expression of the Dobermann.

This dog has a deeply pronounced stop. The 'stop' is the point between the eyes, forehead and nose, and it determines the eye shape on a dog: too deep will result in a round eye shape, and too shallow will result in too tight an eye. Consider the round eyes of a Bulldog, with his deep stop, as compared to a Bull Terrier with no stop and slanted eyes. This dog also has a domed skull, and his head planes are not parallel as he is slightly dish-faced.

The Ears

Small, neat, set high on head. Normally dropped, but may be erect.

This low earset does not give the required alert expression.

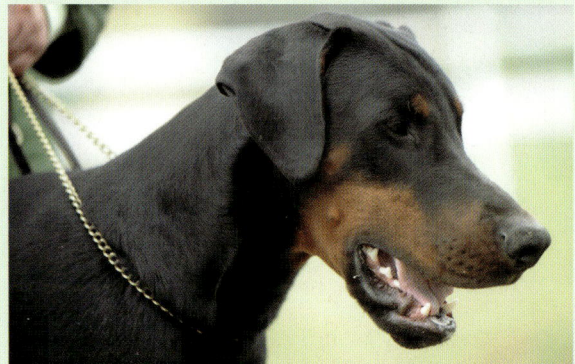

Correct earset. The ears are not carried above the skull line, but the set is higher on the head. Int, Est. Ch. Helios Diathos Diathos de La Villa Valiano (It. Ch., AIAD Sgr, IDC Sgr, IDC JSgr Pathos Delle Querce Nere Pathos Delle Querce Nere x Diaspora Fedone de La Villa Valiano). FRANCK HAYMANN

'High on the head' does not mean that the ear is carried high or erect, although if the ear is carried above the skull line, it is not a fault. It means the set begins high on the head. Large and pendulous ears are not uncommon, probably due to the fact that breeders of traditionally cropped dogs have not had to concentrate on maintaining small ear size, and the real ear size is an unknown factor.

Mouth

Well developed, solid and strong with complete dentition and a perfect, regular and complete scissor bite, i.e. upper teeth closely overlapping lower teeth and set square to the jaws. Evenly placed teeth. Undershot, overshot or badly arranged teeth highly undesirable.

(*See* section on dentition at the end of this chapter, where full details are given.)

Neck

Fairly long and lean, carried with considerable nobility; slightly convex and in proportion to shape of dog. Region of nape very muscular. Dewlap and loose skin undesirable.

For any running breed the neck must be long and elegant, though it must be of the same breadth to carry the head; an elegant neck cannot carry a wide, heavy head. Thick necks are suitable for draft animals.

Forequarters

Shoulder blade and upper arm meet at an angle of 90 degrees. Shoulder blade and upper arm approximately equal in length. Short upper arm relative to shoulder blade highly undesirable. Legs seen from front and side, perfectly straight and parallel to each other from elbow to pastern; muscled and sinewy, with round bone in proportion to body structure. Standing or gaiting, elbow lies close to brisket.

Ch Jojavik Molly Mobster JW, ShCM (Ch Krieger's The Wizard Of Oz JW X Ch/LUX Ch Jojavik Gangsters Moll JW). This female is square, with legs well set under her compact body; she has well balanced front and rear angulation. For ideal counter-balance and support, the forelegs fall vertically from the top of the withers to the floor through the elbow to the feet. JOJAVIK DOBERMANNS

An eleven-month-old female who is too straight in both front and rear angulation. This is a difficult age at which to assess the future angulation of a dog, as angles can change. In this case her brisket (chest depth) later drops to meet her elbows, but angulation this straight, at this age, won't improve.

The UK and AKC standard requires a right-angle return of 90 degrees at the angle between the shoulder and upper arm, whilst the FCI standard requires a wider angle of 105–110 degrees. The shoulder determines reach (how far ahead the dog can reach on the move).

If the whole front assembly is too far forward in the body, the backline is left unsupported.

Body

Square, height measured vertically from ground to highest point at withers equal to length from forechest to rear projection of upper thigh. Forechest well developed. Back short and firm, with strong, straight topline sloping slightly from withers to croup; bitches may be slightly longer to loin. Ribs deep and well sprung, reaching to elbow. Belly fairly well tucked up. Long, weak, or roach backs highly undesirable.

Some UK-bred dogs went through a period of having very prominent buxom forechests. This is not 'room for heart or lungs' as is often claimed – the heart is not situated in front of the forelegs – it is just flab. This flatters the inexperienced eye into thinking the dog is strong and powerful up front. In fact excess fat hampers a dog's speed, which is a requirement of the breed.

The European dog often has deeper and flatter sides to the chest, with no spring of rib, but he still has sufficient lung capacity for endurance work.

The Dobermann should not be barrel-chested nor slab/flat-sided on the ribs, although the latter is probably the lesser of two evils as the dog will track cleanly on the move, and does not have to swing his legs round an over-sprung chest.

Hindquarters

Legs parallel to each other and moderately wide apart. Pelvis falling away from spinal column at an angle of about 30 degrees. Croup well filled out. Hindquarters well developed and muscular; long, well bent stifle; hocks turning neither in nor out. When standing, hock to heel perpendicular to the ground.

Power comes from the dog's rear end, which needs good muscular development throughout the hindquarters, with strong hams (buttocks) and thighs.

'30 degrees' refers to the angle of the pelvis. This should *never* be a visible drop, as the standard also requires the croup to be well filled, and to be a smooth continuation of the spine into the tail.

A 'long, well bent stifle' is unspecified in relation to other angles. It must be well angled enough to provide so-called rotary drive on the move, but not so long

This female has an exaggerated, high tuck-up/underline, from her deep brisket to her high, pinched-in waist. A small, weak waist means the dog cannot brace their torso in protection, and it is easier to 'flip' him off the sleeve/man. This female has a perfectly straight topline: it is clean from the neck over the shoulders, and slopes gently to an immaculate croup and tailset. (Note that 'straight' topline never means level to the ground.) Newfords One Vision (Ch. Amazon Talk of The Devil x Emrichme Belgium at Newford). KUHL

227

that the hind feet are way out behind the dog and too much stress is placed on the hocks. Balance to the front is essential.

Feet

Well arched, compact, and cat-like, turning neither in nor out. Long, flat, deviating feet and/or weak pasterns highly undesirable.

Well-rounded feet provide cushioning for impact, which is impossible with a flat foot. Nails must be short in order not to impede the action of the foot or turn the toes or leg out.

Pasterns should not be ramrod straight as they provide part of the cushioning between the foot and the leg, and some give or spring is essential to absorb shock from impact.

Tail

Previously customarily docked.
Docked: Docked at 1st or 2nd joint. Appears to be a continuation of spine without material drop.
Undocked: Appears to be a continuation of spine without material drop, kink or deformity. May be raised and carried freely when the dog is moving or standing.

The tail has become one of the most contentious issues since docking was banned, and focus on the tail is disproportionate to all the other aspects of a dog.

The tail *set* determines tail *carriage*. A tail curled tightly over the back is considered by many to be unattractive. If the tail set is correct as a continuation of the spine, the tail will usually curve over the back. Note the difference between 'curve' and 'curl'. A high 'set on' tailset usually results in a spitz-type or utility-type curl. Guarding breeds will naturally elevate their tails when alert, and the new FCI standard describes what most would accept as the ideal: 'The tail is left natural and is ideally carried high in a slight curve.'

Continuation of the spine through a clean croup to the tail. Aritaur Unique (Aritaur Nominator BH x Ch. Aritaur A Little More Soba).

When dogs are alert or moving, they will carry their tail higher over the back in a scimitar shape. This dog is being moved in a clockwise circle, which is why he appears to be over-reaching. Newfords Moves Like Jagger At Calonmac. (Tevro D'Vine Last Heir at Wintablizard x Emcrichme Belgium at Newford). KUHL

Dobermann breed clubs in the UK have sensibly decided to maintain the 'interim breed standard' on tails. It is far too early in the development of this traditionally docked breed to specifically detail how the undocked tail should be carried.

Gait/Movement

Elastic, free, balanced and vigorous, with good reach in forequarters and driving power in hindquarters. When trotting, should have strong rear drive, with apparent rotary motion of hindquarters. Rear and front legs thrown neither in nor out. Back remains strong and firm.

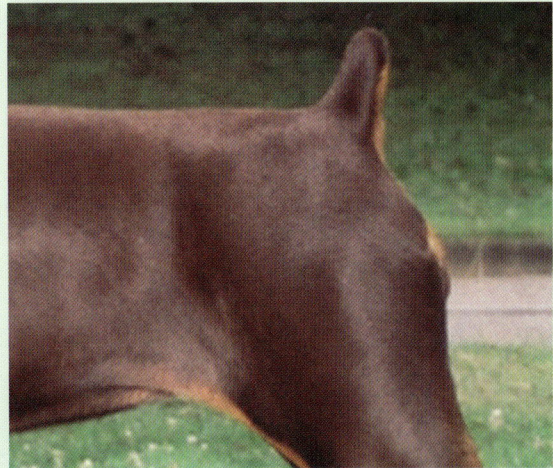

Whether docked or undocked, a 'gay', or high set-on tailset is not a continuation of the spine. This tailset in fact stops abruptly where the spine meets the tail. The tail carriage following the angle of a gay tailset would be upright, and the tail would probably curl tightly.

The 'rotary action of the hindquarters' describes the circular motion of the legs, in the same way as a wheel turns providing efficient propulsion.

*The most essential factor in any construction is the balance between parts. The dog that is straight in both front and rear will move more efficiently than the dog with a perfect front and straight rear, and vice versa.

A straight front and over-angulated rear means the propulsion generated from rotary rear drive is producing more energy than he can use. His straight shoulder limits his forelegs reaching forwards as normal, and to avoid his hind legs knocking into the front legs, he will either move wide, twist/crab, over-reach, or lift his front legs up (hackney).

For maximum efficiency the hind foot lands in the print of the forefoot that has already left the ground. If the hind foot goes past that point the dog is over-reaching. Note that a dog in a suspended trot – that is, with all four feet off the ground – may appear to be over-reaching, but because the front foot has already left the ground, there will be no collision.

'Reach' – which is how far the foreleg can stretch forwards when moving – is determined by the angle of the shoulder layback. A straight shoulder inhibits reach. BE, NL Ch. Grafmax Louis Armstrong ShCM RL1Ex. (Int, Lux Ch. Aritaur Histabraq SchH3 x Cosajora Nina Simone.)

Coat

Smooth, short, hard, thick and close-lying. Imperceptible undercoat on neck permissible. Hair forming a ridge on back of neck and/or along spine highly undesirable.

The coat varies in thickness, but must never be wavy or woolly.

Colour

Definite black, brown, blue or fawn (Isabella) only, with rust red markings. Markings to be sharply defined, appearing above each eye, on muzzle, throat and forechest, on all legs and feet, and below tail. White markings of any kind are highly undesirable.

Muddy, merged, faded markings are to be avoided. Lighter coat colours remove the element of surprise in guarding work.

A ridge on the neck is a major fault, but a ridge on the nose is not a fault. This young female also has a very good, clean wedge head, well filled under the eye with flat cheeks.

There are few fawn or blue Dobermanns in the UK, but they are more common in the USA. The top winning fawn bitch John and Linda Krukar's Am./Can. Ch., MACH, Royal Future JP Sakura of Dabney. STANDARD IMAGE PHOTOGRAPHY

Sharply defined dark rust markings on a dog and bitch. The penny or thumbprint markings can be seen on the side of the cheek and the front of the chest. Markings are often merged on puppies, and then separate as the dog matures.

Size

Ideal height at withers: dogs: 69cm (27in); bitches: 65cm (25½in). Considerable deviation from this ideal is undesirable.

With no specifications as to exactly what 'considerable deviation' means, the judge uses their own judgement regarding the quality of the animal.

Ch. Aritaur Cardinal Red at Jodaseen ShCM (Int, Lux Ch. Aritaur Histabraq SchH3 x Leibwache Honey Hustler to Aritaur). A standard sized male.
KEVIN WEST

Ch. Supeta's Spells Trouble JW, ShCM (Ch., Lux Ch. Supeta's Ozzy Osbourne JW, UK Breed Record Holder x Supetas Witchqueen JW, ShCM)

Dogs are not generally penalized for being rather taller or smaller than the standard dictates. 27in males will look comparatively small to the other exhibits these days, but they are the correct sized dogs.

The height of puppies is completely irrelevant. Some lines grow tall at first and mature later; others grow as perfect replicas of their adult form.

Faults

Any departure from the foregoing points should be considered a fault, and the seriousness with which the fault should be regarded should be in exact proportion to its degree and its effect upon the health and welfare of the dog and on the dog's ability to perform its traditional work.

Note

Male animals should have two apparently normal testicles fully descended into the scrotum.

Unlike FCI standards, the UK Kennel Club breed standard for Dobermanns has no disqualifying faults, so dogs cannot be dismissed from judging if, for instance, they have missing teeth or are of a colour not recognized by the UK standard.

FCI BREED STANDARD

Reproduced with kind permission of the Fédération Cynologique International (FCI).
(Valid from 01/08/2016): FCI-Standard No. 143 - DOBERMANN FCI-St. No. 143

Int. Multi Ch. Pride of Russia Ruslana, IDC JSgrn (Int, Multi Ch Oksamit de Grande Vinko, IPO3, Korung x Int, Multi Ch. Pride of Russia Dolce Vita)
ANNA VIUGINOVA

The Dobermann Breed
The Dobermann breed requires a medium-sized, powerful, muscular dog. Despite his substance he shall be elegant and noble, which will be evident in his bodyline. He must be exceptionally suitable as a companion, protection and working dog, and also as a family dog.

General Appearance
The Dobermann is of medium size, strong and muscularly built. Through the elegant lines of its body, its proud stature, and its expression of determination, it conforms to the ideal picture of dog.

Important Proportions
The body of the Dobermann appears to be almost square, particularly in males. The length of the body measured from the tip of breast to the point of the buttock shall not be more than 5 per cent longer than the height from the withers to the ground in males, and 10 per cent in females.

Behaviour Temperament
The disposition of the Dobermann is friendly and calm; very devoted to the family. Medium tempera-

ment and medium sharpness (alertness) is desired. A medium threshold of irritation is required with a good contact to the owner. Easy to train, the Dobermann enjoys working, and shall have good working ability, courage and hardness. The particular values of self-confidence and intrepidness are required, and also adaptability and attention to fit the social environment.

Head
Cranial Region
Strong and in proportion to the body. Seen from the top the head is shaped in the form of a blunt wedge. Viewed from the front, the crown line shall be almost level and not dropping off to the ears. The muzzle line extends almost straight to the top line of the skull that falls, gently rounded, into the neckline. The superciliary ridge is well developed without protruding. The forehead furrow is still visible. The occiput shall not be conspicuous. Seen from the front and the top, the sides of the head must not bulge. The slight bulge between the rear of the upper jawbone and the cheekbone shall be in harmony with the total length of the head. The head muscles shall be well developed.

Stop: Shall be slight but visibly developed.

Facial Region
Nose: Nostrils well developed, more broad than round, with large openings without overall protrusion. Black – in black dogs; in brown dogs, corresponding lighter shades.

Muzzle: The muzzle must be in the right proportion with the upper head, and must be strongly developed. The muzzle shall have depth. The mouth opening shall be wide, reaching to the molars. A good muzzle width must also be present on the upper and lower incisor area.

Lips: They shall be tight and lie close to the jaw, that will ensure a tight closure of the mouth. The pigment of the gum to be dark; in brown dogs a corresponding lighter shade.

Jaws/teeth: Powerful broad upper and lower jaw, scissor bite, forty-two teeth correctly placed and normal size. (*See* Dentition below.)

Eyes: Medium-sized, oval and dark in colour. Lighter shades are permitted for brown dogs. Close-lying eyelids. Eyelids shall be covered with hair.

Ears: The ears are left natural and of an appropriate size; they are set on either side at the highest point of the skull and are ideally lying close to the cheeks.

Neck
The neck must have a good length and be in proportion to the body and the head. It is dry and muscular. Its outline rises gradually and is softly curved. Its carriage is upright and shows much nobility.

Body
Withers: Shall be pronounced in height and length, especially in males, and thereby determine the slope of the topline from the withers to the croup.

Back: Short and firm, of good width and well muscled.

Loin: Of good width and well muscled. The female can be slightly longer in loin because of the required space for suckling offspring.

Croup: It shall fall slightly, hardly perceptible from sacrum to the root of the tail, and appears well rounded, being neither straight nor noticeably sloping, of good width and well muscled.

Chest: Length and depth of chest must be in the right proportion to the body length. The depth with slightly arched ribs should be approximately 50 per cent the height of the dog at the withers. The chest has got a good width with especially well developed forechest.

Underline and belly: From the bottom of the breastbone to the pelvis the underline is noticeably tucked up.

Tail
The tail is left natural and is ideally carried high in a slight curve.

Limbs
Forequarters
General appearance: The front legs as seen from all sides are almost straight, vertical to the ground and strongly developed.

Shoulder: The shoulder blade lies close against the chest, and both sides of the shoulder-blade edge are well muscled and reach over the top of the thoracic vertebra, slanting as much as possible and well set back. The angle to the horizontal is approximately 50 per cent.

Upper arm: Good length, well muscled.

Elbow: Close in, not turned out.

Forearm: Strong and straight. Well muscled. Length in harmony with the whole body.

Carpus (wrist): Strong.

Metacarpus (pastern): Bones strong. Straight seen from the front. Seen from the side, only slightly sloping.

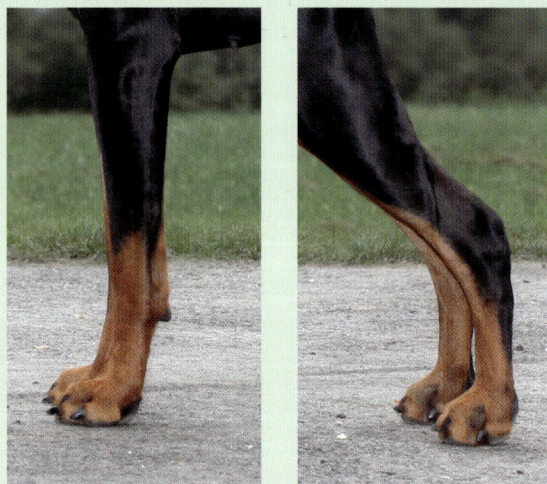

British and American exhibitors pay great attention to breeding and maintaining good feet. European exhibitors tend to leave the nails much longer and consequently the feet are sometimes poor.

Forefeet: The feet are short and tight. The toes are arched towards the top (cat like). Nails short black.

Hindquarters
General appearance: Seen from the rear, the Dobermann looks, because of his well-developed pelvic

muscles in hips and croup, wide and rounded off. The muscles running from the pelvis towards the thigh and lower thigh result in good width development, as well as in the thigh area, in the knee joint area and at the lower thigh. The strong hind legs are straight and stand parallel.

Thigh: Good length and width, well muscled. Good angulation to the hip joint. Angulation to the horizontal approximately between 80°–85°.

Stifle (knee): The knee joint is strong and is formed by the thigh and lower thigh as well as the knee cap.

Lower thigh: Medium length and in harmony with the total length of the hindquarter.

Hock joint: Medium strength and parallel. The lower thigh is joined to the metatarsal at the hock joint.

Metatarsus (rear pastern): It is short and stands vertical to the ground.

Hind feet: Like the forefeet, the toes of the hind feet are short, arched and closed. Nails short, black.

Gait Movement
The gait is of special importance to both the working ability as well as the exterior appearance. The gait is elastic, elegant, agile, free and ground-covering. The forelegs reach out as far as possible. The hindquarter gives far-reaching and necessary elastic drive. The foreleg of one side and the hind leg of the other side move forward at the same time. There should be good stability of the back, the ligaments and the joints.

Skin
The skin fits closely all over and has good pigmentation.

Coat
Hair: The hair is short, hard and dense. It lies tight and smooth and is equally distributed over the whole surface. Undercoat is not allowed.

Colour: The Dobermann is bred in two colour varieties: black or brown with rust red, clearly defined and clear markings (tan markings). Tan markings are on the muzzle as a spot on the cheeks and the top of the eyebrow; on the throat; two spots on the forechest; on the metacarpus, metatarsus and feet; on the inner side of the hind thigh; on the forearms and under the tail.

Size and Weight
Height at the withers: Males: 68–72cm
Females: 63–68cm

Medium size desirable
Weight: Males: about 40–45kg
Females: about 32–35kg

Faults

Any departure from the foregoing points should be considered a fault, and the seriousness with which the fault should be regarded should be in exact proportion to its degree and its effect upon the health and welfare of the dog and its ability to perform its traditional work.

Lack of sexual dimorphism; little substance; too light; too heavy; too leggy; weak bones.

Head too heavy, too narrow, too short, too long, too much or too little stop; ram's nose, bad slope of the top line of the skull; weak lower jaw; round or slit eyes; light eye; cheeks too heavy; loose flews; eyes too open or too deep set; ear set too high or too low; open mouth angle.

Back not straight; sway back; roach back; insufficient depth or width of chest; tail set too low; sloping croup; too little or too much tuck-up.

Too little angulation in forequarters; hindquarters with too little or too much angulation; loose elbow; feet too close together or too wide apart; cow hocks, spread hocks; open or soft paws, crooked toes; pale nails.

Tan markings too light or not sharply defined; smudged markings; mask too dark; big black spot on the legs; chest markings hardly visible or too large; hair long, soft, curly or dull. Thin coat; bald patches.

Deviation of size up to 2cm from the standard should result in a lowering of the quality grading.

Gait that is not harmonious, in particular pacing.

Disqualifying Faults

Aggressive or overly shy dogs.

Any dog clearly showing physical or behavioural abnormalities shall be disqualified.

Yellow eyes (bird of prey eye); different coloured eyes.

Overshot – level bite; undershot; missing teeth according to the formula.

White spots. Visible undercoat.

Dogs that deviate more than 2cm over or under the standard.

NB: Male animals should have two apparently normal testicles fully descended into the scrotum. Only functionally and clinically healthy dogs, with breed typical conformation should be used for breeding.

AMERICAN KENNEL CLUB BREED STANDARD

Reproduced with kind permission of the American Kennel Club (AKC)

General Appearance

The appearance is that of a dog of medium size, with a body that is square. Compactly built, muscular and powerful, for great endurance and speed. Elegant in appearance, of proud carriage, reflecting great nobility and temperament. Energetic, watchful, determined, alert, fearless, loyal and obedient.

Size, Proportion, Substance

Height at the withers: Dogs 26–28in, ideal about 27½in; bitches 24–26in, ideal about 25½in. The height, measured vertically from the ground to the highest point of the withers, equalling the length measured horizontally from the forechest to the rear projection of the upper thigh. Length of head, neck and legs in proportion to length and depth of body.

MBIS, MBISS, Am. Gr. Ch. Protocols Veni Vedi Vici, Westminster BOB. Protocols Veni Vedi Vici (Ch Foxfire's All Star x BISS CH Protocol's American Dream). Owned and handled by Jocelyn Mullins.
GAY GLAZBROOK

Head

Long and dry, resembling a blunt wedge in both frontal and profile views. When seen from the front, the head widens gradually toward the base of the ears in a practically unbroken line. Eyes almond shaped, moderately deep set, with vigorous, energetic expression. Iris, of uniform color, ranging from medium to darkest brown in black dogs; in reds, blues, and fawns the color of the iris blends with that of the markings, the darkest shade being preferable in every case. Ears normally cropped and carried erect. The upper attachment of the ear, when held erect, is on a level with the top of the skull.

Top of skull flat, turning with slight stop to bridge of muzzle, with muzzle line extending parallel to top line of skull. Cheeks flat and muscular. Nose solid black on black dogs, dark brown on red ones, dark grey on blue ones, dark tan on fawns. Lips lying close to jaws. Jaws full and powerful, well filled under the eyes.

Teeth strongly developed and white. Lower incisors upright and touching inside of upper incisors true scissors bite. 42 correctly placed teeth, 22 in the lower, 20 in the upper jaw. Distemper teeth shall not be penalized. Disqualifying Faults: Overshot more than $3/16$ of an inch. Undershot more than $1/8$ of an inch. Four or more missing teeth.

Neck, Topline, Body

Neck proudly carried, well muscled and dry. Well arched, with nape of neck widening gradually toward body. Length of neck proportioned to body and head. Withers pronounced and forming the highest point of the body. Back short, firm, of sufficient width, and muscular at the loins, extending in a straight line from withers to the slightly rounded croup.

Chest broad with forechest well defined. Ribs well sprung from the spine, but flattened in lower end to permit elbow clearance. Brisket reaching deep to the elbow. Belly well tucked up, extending in a curved line from the brisket. Loins wide and muscled. Hips broad and in proportion to body, breadth of hips being approximately equal to breadth of body at rib cage and shoulders. Tail docked at approximately second joint, appears to be a continuation of the spine, and is carried only slightly above the horizontal when the dog is alert.

Forequarters
Shoulder blade sloping forward and downward at a 45-degree angle to the ground meets the upper arm at an angle of 90 degrees. Length of shoulder blade and upper arm are equal. Height from elbow to withers approximately equals height from ground to elbow. Legs seen from front and side, perfectly straight and parallel to each other from elbow to pastern; muscled and sinewy, with heavy bone. In normal pose and when gaiting, the elbows lie close to the brisket. Pasterns firm and almost perpendicular to the ground. Dewclaws may be removed. Feet well arched, compact, and catlike, turning neither in nor out.

Hindquarters
The angulation of the hindquarters balances that of the forequarters. Hip Bone falls away from spinal column at an angle of about 30 degrees, producing a slightly rounded, well filled-out croup. Upper Shanks at right angles to the hip bones, are long, wide, and well muscled on both sides of thigh, with clearly defined stifles. Upper and lower shanks are of equal length. While the dog is at rest, hock to heel is perpendicular to the ground. Viewed from the rear, the legs are straight, parallel to each other, and wide enough apart to fit in with a properly built body. Dewclaws, if any, are generally removed. Cat feet as on front legs, turning neither in nor out.

Coat
Smooth-haired, short, hard, thick and close lying. Invisible gray undercoat on neck permissible.

GENERAL DENTITION

The 'standard dentition formula' for dogs is forty-two teeth: twenty upper and twenty-two lower, and for the Dobermann a scissor bite is required. Dentition is taken very seriously in the Dobermann.

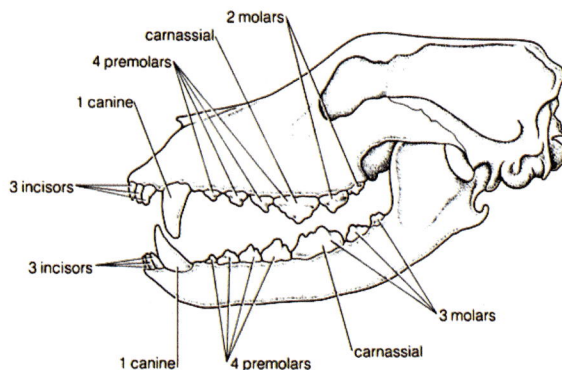

Diagram of skull and dentition reproduced by kind permission of Trevor Turner, BVetMed, MRCVS.

Color and Markings
Allowed Colors: Black, red, blue, and fawn (Isabella).
Markings: Rust, sharply defined, appearing above each eye and on muzzle, throat and forechest, on all legs and feet, and below tail. White patch on chest, not exceeding ½ square inch, permissible.
Disqualifying Fault: Dogs not of an allowed color.

Gait
Free, balanced and vigorous, with good reach in the forequarters and good driving power in the hindquarters. When trotting, there is strong rear-action drive. Each rear leg moves in line with the foreleg on the same side. Rear and front legs are thrown neither in nor out. Back remains strong and firm. When moving at a fast trot, a properly built dog will single-track.

Temperament
Energetic, watchful, determined, alert, fearless, loyal and obedient. The judge shall dismiss from the ring any shy or vicious Doberman.

Shyness: A dog shall be judged fundamentally three fractions if, refusing to stand for examination, it shrinks away from the judge; if it fears an approach from the rear; if it shies at sudden and unusual noises to a marked degree.

Viciousness: A dog that attacks or attempts to attack either the judge or its handler, is definitely vicious. An aggressive or belligerent attitude towards other dogs shall not be deemed viciousness.

Faults
The foregoing description is that of the ideal Doberman Pinscher. Any deviation from the above described dog must be penalized to the extent of the deviation.

Disqualifications
Overshot more than $3/16$ of an inch, undershot more than $1/8$ of an inch. Four or more missing teeth. Dogs not of an allowed color.

A scissor bite describes the tight closure such as the two blades on a pair of scissors: that is, the upper (maxillary) dentition upper teeth close tightly over the lower (mandibular) dentition lower teeth.

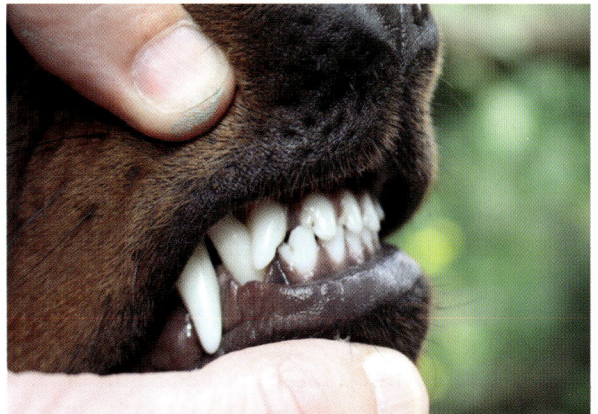

Correct scissor bite, where the upper front teeth (incisors) tightly overlap the lower incisors.

There are four types of teeth, each having different functions:

The incisors: Smaller front teeth, used for cutting and nibbling food, scooping, picking up objects and grooming. There are six upper incisors and six lower incisors (twelve in total). The lower two centre incisors occasionally sit lower in the gum and can converge.

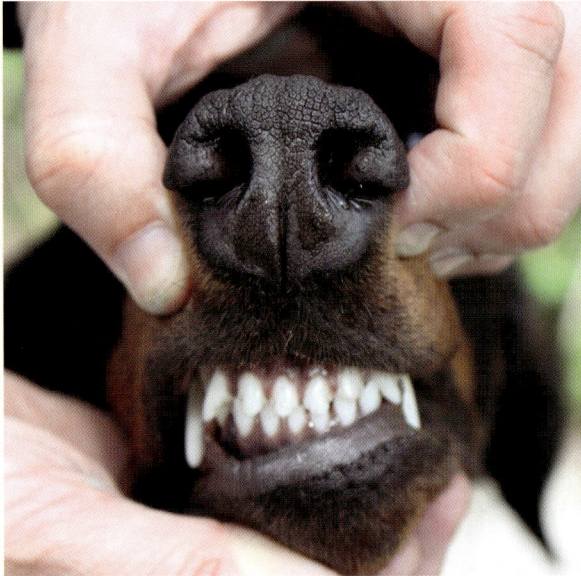

Full and correct incisor and canine dentition.

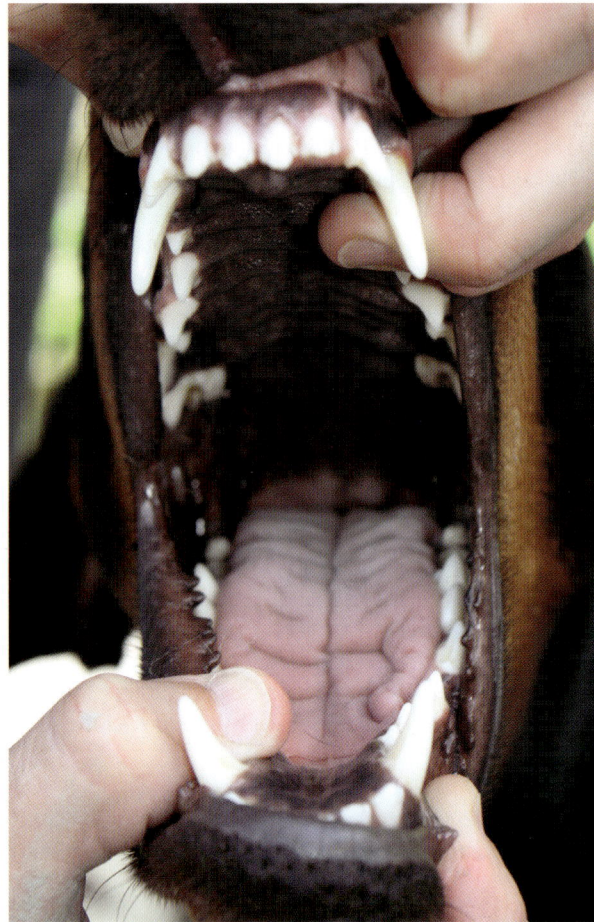

Full and complete dentition at the back of the mouth.

The canines: Fangs, that hold and tear food, prey and opponents. There are two upper and two lower canines on each side of the jaw (four in total), and the lower canines sit just in front of the upper canines set.

The premolars: Behind the canines are the premolars (P1, P2, P3, P4), which shear, cut, hold and break food into small pieces. There are four upper and four lower on each side of the jaw (sixteen in total).

The molars: The large back teeth used for chewing and grinding large food items into small pieces. There are three molars on each side on the bottom jaw, and two molars on each side on the top jaw: thus four upper, six lower (ten molars in total).

The first teeth are twenty-eight baby (deciduous) teeth, which first erupt at about three to four weeks of age. Puppies do not have any molars or a P1. The adult teeth begin to emerge at about three to four months of age.

The upper and lower jaws grow at different rates, often leaving a gap between the upper and lower front teeth, resulting in either an under-bite (undershot) or over-bite (overshot). It is unusual for an under-bite to correct itself, but a slight over-bite may end up forming a scissor bite in adulthood.

A full set of baby teeth does not indicate that a full set of adult teeth will grow, and a missing baby incisor or canine does not mean that an adult tooth will not come through correctly – but it is less likely that it will.

European dogs with their larger heads, stronger jaws and usually longer muzzles generally have larger teeth than their UK and European counterparts.

A missing tooth, or a level or wry bite that disqualifies a dog in Europe often goes unnoticed in the UK. The American (AKC) standard allows up to four missing teeth, the United Kennel Club (USA), allows none. UK judges are free to exercise their own judgement over the severity of the fault.

Dogs with missing teeth may still do their job, and are not affected in eating, drinking or holding objects. However, the more a fault is ignored, the more it becomes established. Fewer teeth eventually affect the shape of the head in that the jaw becomes smaller as it does not need to accommodate as many teeth, the jaw muscles are weaker as they do not need to work as much, and the muscle's anchor point behind the occiput does not need to be strongly pronounced, so diminishes…and on it goes.

European breeders allow no missing teeth for breeding or show, and as dogs with missing teeth cannot be titled, no one wants to use them for breeding.

There is no restriction on breeding from dogs with missing teeth in the UK or America, since the inheritance of missing teeth in breeding cannot be predicted.

Missing PM1

In 2013 the committee of the FCI Breeding Commission confirmed that the PM1 is 'an evolutionary deteriorating structure and the dogs do not really need it'. They also stated, 'however, the other permanent teeth, especially other premolars, are developing from the common dental lamina, and when missing, it is almost exclusively inherited'. The recommendation was that a missing PM1 should be considered an evolutionary relic that is disappearing gradually in dogs and should not be regarded as a disqualifying fault or fault that prevents the dog's use for breeding.

The proposal was approved by both the FCI Standards Commission and the FCI General Committee in November 2014, and a change to the new FCI Model Dentition Standard published in December 2014 reads as follows:

> **Jaws/Teeth:** Shape of jaw, number and properties of teeth, position of the incisors, bite (scissors or pincer bite), over or undershot mouth.

> **Recommendation:** lack of PM1 and M3 is scientifically proved as an evolutionary and not a hereditary trait, hence no longer considered as a disqualifying fault. (General Committee, Amsterdam, November 2014.) The information will be sent to all Commission members and will be spread to the Kennel Clubs.

Although this information does appear on the FCI website, judges and exhibitors remain largely unaware of the recommendation, and even in 2016, dogs were still being penalized in Europe for missing P1s.

DIAGRAMS OF ANGULATION

In all standards for the breed, the body of the Dobermann is required to be square. This has led to various diagrams of the Dobermann being made with a square box and lines drawn on, in an effort to follow the skeletal outline of the dog. Some are idealistic and incorrectly drawn using imaginary points of the whole dog, including muscle and fat points. Other lines on diagrams attempt to squash the hind legs within the virtual box shape by shortening and bending the femur (the thigh bone). *No breed standard has ever required the entire dog including hind legs to fit inside this virtual box shape.*

If you want to measure your dog in real life or from a photo, don't just follow where you think the lines should go or impose imaginary lines, but feel the bone joints and take your lines from those points.

The height of the Dobermann should be 50/50

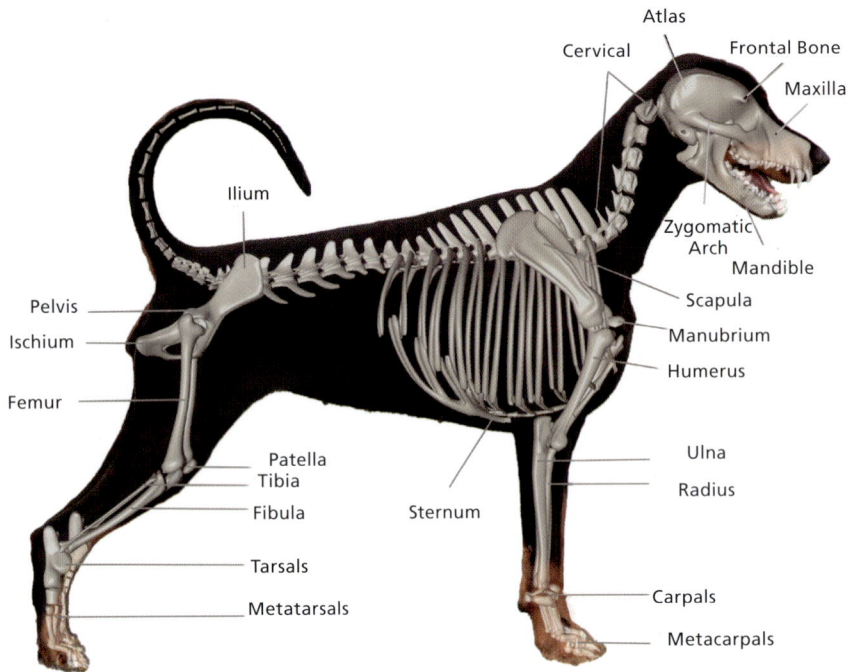

Skeleton courtesy of Parkes Productions Ltd from an original image of Aritaur Enchante. KORIFEY

Atlas
Cervical
Frontal Bone
Maxilla
Ilium
Zygomatic Arch
Mandible
Scapula
Pelvis
Manubrium
Ischium
Humerus
Femur
Patella
Tibia
Ulna
Fibula
Radius
Sternum
Tarsals
Metatarsals
Carpals
Metacarpals

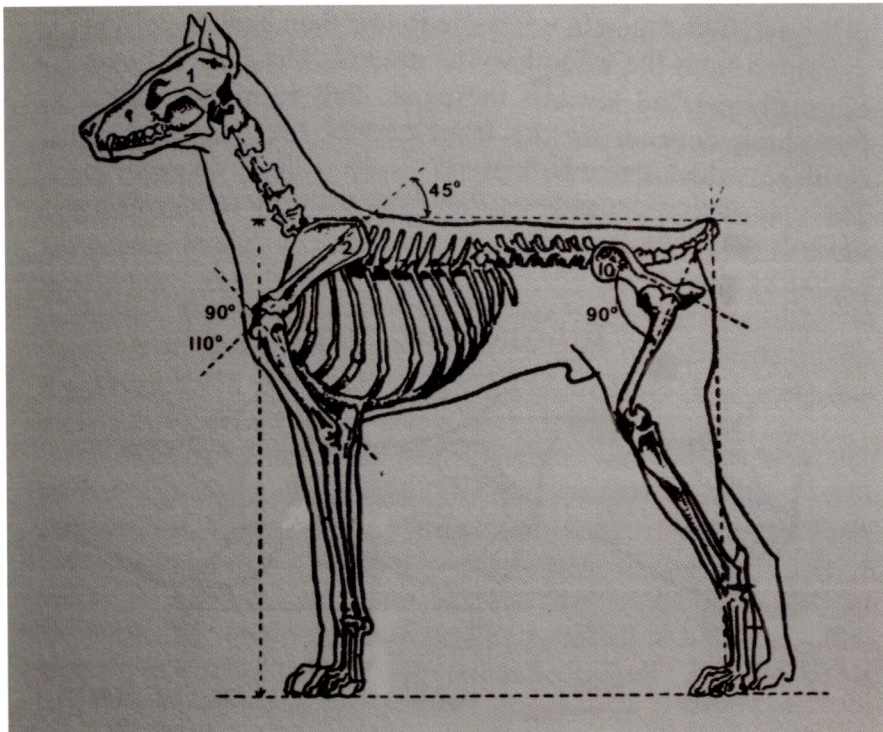

An incorrectly drawn image of a Dobermann. To fit both body and legs within a square, the illustrator has angled the femur (thigh bone) steeply under the body (perhaps to try to meet the AKC requirement for 'Upper Shanks at right angles to the hip bones', which is not required or even mentioned in the other breed standards). Getting a 90-degree return from a 30-degree hip angle would, in real life, result in the knee being inserted half way up the thigh, as can be seen in this diagram. This diagram also shows the topline to be horizontal, and the dog in this diagram has no rear angulation to provide rotary action.

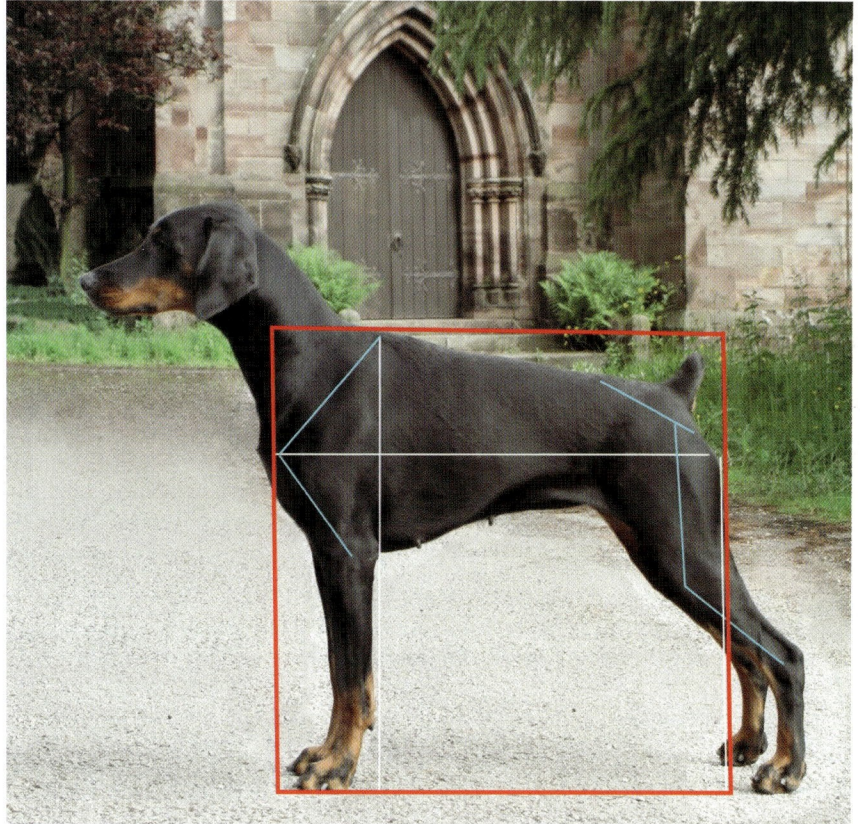

A square Dobermann, with lines applied to demonstrate approximate angulation, measured from the manubrian to the ischium, and from the highest point of the withers (the top of the shoulder) to the floor. Aritaur Tarantella, 2 CCs, (Int, Multi Ch. Tom-Dober Hagi x Ned Ch. Aritaur Dominatrix EJsgrn).

from the floor to the elbow, and from the brisket to the top of the shoulder.

The chest area between the points of shoulder and upper arm junction is called the pro-sternum. It is the flat band of bone that holds the ribs together at the front. The foremost and uppermost bone of the pro-sternum is the manubrium bone (alias point of breastbone, point of forechest). Measure from that point to the ischium (rear point of the pelvic bone). These two points are important landmarks as they remain stationary on the body regardless of musculature or fat, which are not included in the conformational measurements of a dog.

Diagrams and terminology may help illustrate the basic structure of a dog, but they are of relatively little benefit in evaluating the living dog. The skeletal, neurological, muscular and locomotive system, combined with sound mentality, dynamic character, great energy, and good conditioning all combine to capture the essence of the Dobermann.

12 SHOWING THE DOBERMANN

Dog showing is often seen as a silly beauty pageant for dogs that serves no purpose other than to satisfy owners' egos. But despite the pageantry, showing plays an important role in maintaining breed standards and promoting the breeding of excellent dogs. Only by comparing our dogs against those bred by others can we expect to continually improve the dogs we have.

Despite endless criticism from the anti-pedigree world, perhaps an unexpected benefit originating from showing is that every single advance in health testing has been initiated and driven by the show community. Breeders outside the show or working community remain largely unaware of the health of the breed.

Being involved in the showing environment teaches us a great deal about our breeds and dogs in general, and many new exhibitors who come into showing often go on to become successful breeders of the future.

The Dobermann needs to be as close to their humans as they can get, and having 'show dogs' doesn't mean anything has to change. Although the terminology for breeders is that they have 'a kennel', there are barely any in the UK who keep their Dobermanns in outside kennels, and most breeder/exhibitors keep around two to ten dogs as pets in the home. Dogs that enjoy showing get hugely over-excited on show days and can't wait to get in the ring. Dogs that don't enjoy the ring and look miserable about it simply aren't shown.

CHOOSING A PUPPY FOR SHOW

If you are a newcomer to showing the pick of the litter may not be available to you, but if you can prove you are serious by visiting shows and sorting out ring-craft places before your puppy is born, this will encourage the breeder to sell you a good quality puppy. Your puppy will carry their good name, so they will want to make sure that you will represent them successfully. All breeders are wise to the buyer who begs for the pick of the litter promising to show, but who never even goes to training class. Buyers think they will get a better quality puppy

Summer showing at a breed club championship show.

244

Ch. Liason Latanya (Ch. Amazon El Torro JW × Janzins Fire Cracker at Liason), BOB Crufts 2012. Bred and shown by Alison Swain, owned by Mr and Mrs Underwood. CLIVE EVANS

The future UK Breed Record Holder Ch. Supeta's Ozzy Osbourne JW at nine weeks.

that way, whereas the difference between the shoulder placement or eye colour on another puppy is so minor that only the expert would ever notice it. There are many other good quality pups available, but it is deceitful to take the best puppy and not show.

As you will not be experienced at choosing a puppy you have to rely on the guidance of your breeder, so it is essential to choose a breeder with quality history. If you have a good eye and basic knowledge of construction you will be able to see the quality of a good puppy.

There is no right or wrong choice between the puppy with the quality head but poorer angulation, and the puppy with light eyes but with excellent topline. In these cases it often comes down to that special something, the indefinable air of quality of the puppy with the 'wow, look at me' character. Judges aren't just looking for a

good-looking dog, they are looking for a Dobermann shining with health and with great attitude, who is justifiably proud of himself. There are many champions who, despite their faults, set the ring alight when they walk in. Equally there are text-book perfect puppies without an ounce of 'show-off' about them who are better suited to the sofa.

The basics of what to select when choosing a show puppy are correct teeth, and testicles on a male. If the latter are not in place at seven to eight weeks they are unlikely to come. Although the inguinal canal doesn't fully close in large breeds such as the Dobermann until around six months, it is a big risk to take a super puppy whose testicle(s) haven't fully descended.

The lower and upper jaws grow at different rates, and we can sometimes find to our horror that the future world-beating puppy with the perfect scissor bite as a baby has developed a level bite, or even worse is undershot. If the bite is level at around four months it may end up as a correct scissor bite by the time the upper jaw has finished growing, but if it is even slightly undershot, it is unlikely that the upper jaw will grow fast enough for it to finish correctly.

At seven to eight weeks the Dobermann is quite similar to its finished appearance as an adult.

Eight-week-old future champion Supeta Spells Trouble JW, holding great promise for the future.

Ch. Supeta Spells Trouble JW. Twelve CCs to date, runner-up top Dobermann 2015, Group 1 SKC, BCC and BOB Crufts 2015. KORIFEY DOBERMANNS

Heads are not finished fully until eighteen months old, when the teeth and jaw are fully set and head planes usually level out. In very 'down-faced' puppies, where the foreface is tilted downwards and is not parallel to the top of the skull, the foreface rarely ends up fully parallel.

Choosing a puppy to show is a matter of experience, skill, chance and good luck. If it were easy to predict how puppies will turn out, all the top breeders would have faultless dogs – but there is no such thing as a perfect dog, so we acknowledge the faults we have in our dogs (whilst trying to hide them in the show-ring) and aim to correct them when we come to breed.

'What you see is what you get' is true only so far as rearing the puppy goes. Many breeders have been disappointed when their home-bred puppy that is sibling to a champion, does not mature to its full potential. If you want to make the best of your show-prospect puppy, you must follow the guidance of the breeder as regards correct exercise, feeding and training, which are equally determining factors to future success.

PREPARING YOUR DOG FOR SHOWING

Short-coated breeds need very little preparation apart from keeping the nails neat and short, as you should anyway. Very few Dobermann exhibitors bath their dogs regularly, and they will rarely do so just before a show as this will strip the natural oils out of the coat and it can come up quite scurfy the following day. Unless the dog has rolled in something or has ingrained dirt in his coat, a brush over with a soft brush or rubber grooming glove should take the old hairs out.

Exhibitors may use a wet wipe to take any dust off the coat. However, take note of the KC regulations, which state: 'No substance which alters the natural colour, texture or body of the coat may be present in the dog's coat for any purpose, at any time, during the show.'

The show dog must obviously be in generally excellent condition, as any normal dog should. He should be well toned and in peak fitness with bright, clear eyes. Although it is a beauty contest, this is a working breed, and judges accept the inevitable scratches, scars and scrapes.

It is now common and normal to see dewclaws left on show dogs; the UK and the US are the only countries in which they are routinely removed shortly after birth. Any judge remarking on it should be reminded of the more important things to concentrate on.

Never present a dog with dirty teeth to a judge.

Ready for assessment.

TRAINING FOR SHOWING

Training for showing essentially requires the dog to stand still for presentation, inspection of his teeth and general examination by the judge, and to trot steadily round the ring alongside you so his movement can be assessed.

Ring-craft classes help you and your dog get used to the routine and procedure in a show ring.

New exhibitors are often anxious if their dog is unsettled, perhaps throws himself on his back in the middle of the ring, which they would find humiliating in front of ringside spectators. However, dogs fidget for many reasons: perhaps you are over-stretching his back feet, perhaps he is having a bad growing pain day, or just can't concentrate from all the excitement of the other dogs. Other exhibitors will always help someone struggling. Don't lose patience with your dog, as he may then come to hate showing, and no one will like your bad attitude.

A well-trained puppy may be impressive, but if it comes at the expense of joyful puppyhood it isn't worth it.

The two main ways of teaching the dog to show are positioning (stacking) by hand, and the free stand, and it is worthwhile teaching both methods.

Puppies are normally trained to stand on the table at the breeder's home from around five

Puppy at six weeks on the table for the first time. Puppies are usually assessed for show at around seven weeks.

weeks of age to get them used to being stacked up. Use a soft cheese squashed in the palm of your right hand, and hold it at the puppy's head height so he licks it off. Keeping the right hand still keeps the head in the same position whilst the left hand adjusts the feet.

Lift pup on and off the table gently and slowly. Don't try and achieve perfection at the start, just let him have a good time learning to stand, and finish on a high note.

Using a mirror to stack puppy in front helps you improve positions, or ask a friend to video it for you so you can see what needs improving.

Train for *no more* than a few minutes twice a day, and keep it fun. At this stage it is about muscle memory, and if you make him hold his position for long periods it will make him miserable, and may make him 'switch off' showing completely.

After a few weeks the next stage from licking is to start using solid food, such as a piece of cheese, as the 'treat'. Make the treat delivery promptly – anticipate that he will move, and treat before he does. Gradually increase the duration of waiting time to two or three seconds as he learns to wait for his treat. It is no different to training the 'sit' or 'down', except that you need to keep adjusting his legs.

Teaching the puppy to free stand, where he stands correctly naturally and is not positioned, demonstrates the dog's balance without the handler needing to adjust anything.

Hand stacking gives a very smart presentation, but the more you adjust a dog by picking up and placing his legs, the more he will slump. Manhandled dogs usually feel, and look, flat and dull. No one likes being pulled and prodded around, so get the dog to do half the work of the stand himself by walking into it, so that all you have to do is just tweak a leg here or there.

Training for a free stand is just like training for any other position in that when the dog takes a particular position, you give a verbal cue and/or click, and reward. When he stands and presents in

Puppy at eleven weeks. By this time you will have moved her to the floor. Ideally the back foot to the hock should be perpendicular, but don't push her too fast to get perfection at this age.

Puppy is now five months old and has learned to wait for her food. During this time he must also learn to tolerate being gone over by a judge, and to having his teeth examined. It is critical to be very gentle, and literally just lift the lips on young pups as they have sore gums from teething. Having someone heavy handed on their mouth is off-putting to any puppy. Only let gentle, confident and experienced people anywhere near your puppy at this time.

If you find your puppy swings out his back end when you stand him, stack him up against a fence line so he can't swing out.

Free standing. Billy Henderson with Ch.Ilr. Ch. Aritaur Hipnotique, who was shown this way to all her wins.

Shown in the American style, Linda Krukar with BIS, BISS Am. Gr. Ch. Dabney's Phenomenon (Am Ch. Eastwick's Meadow Monster X Ch. Dabney's I Can't Wait), sire of Ch. Korifey Black Diamond.

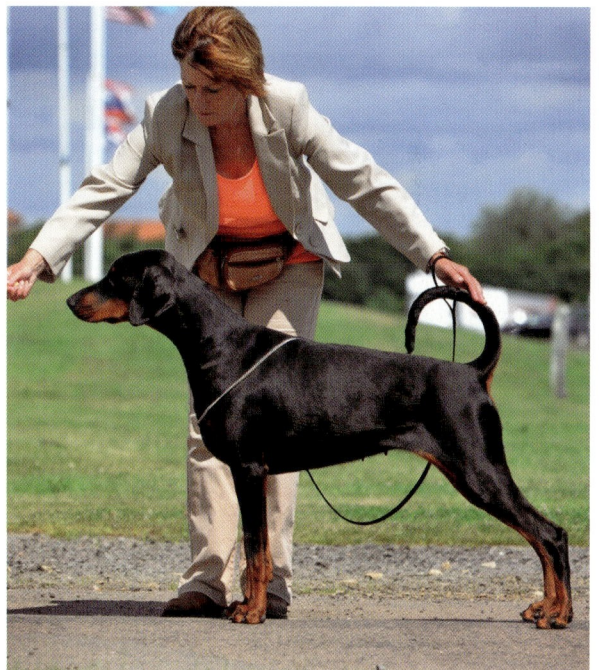

Lita and Tim Lainchbury's Ashlain Trypiti, (Ch. Jasprico Jazz Master Flash JW ShCM x Ashlain Kazaviti JW ShCM)
KORIFEY DOBERMANNS

249

front of you with his front feet parallel, promptly give the verbal cue 'stand', click and reward. Progress by repeating this just once or twice a day, and he will start to offer you the behaviour by standing in front of you hoping for a treat.

Practise a variety of handling styles for the dog: it may look better with you standing in front, or pulling into the lead. Handlers usually stay kneeling down beside a young pup so they can reposition him if he moves.

Don't worry about precise foot placement if your dog looks miserable or bored. Attitude and keen expression are the key factors that should tip the balance between your dog and those of your competitors. A judge may remark that a bouncy puppy needs ring-training, but that pup will be a better prospect in the long term than the over-trained puppy who is taken to ring-craft training twice weekly, shown both days at a weekend, and kept standing in position too long.

Years ago all handlers stood up to present their dogs on the end of a long lead, and the practice of kneeling down beside the dog and baiting him into position became a trend in the early 1990s. Baiting with food was originally used to encourage a keen expression from the dog, but its over-use draws criticism particularly from all breed judges, who may forgive puppies needing bait, but not adults.

When waiting in line in the class don't keep your dog in show position all the time, but keep him amused – use it as time to teach him free standing, as that way he keeps looking fresh in case the judge turns round and notices him.

SHOWING THE DOG MOVING

Dobermanns are shown moving at a fast, active trot. This pace is not about going as fast as possible with the legs flying out: the trot should be active and extended but controlled and balanced. The dog is shown moving on the left of the handler, and trots either at his side or a little ahead of him.

Karen King's Ch. Nerak American Dream in the group ring.

JUDGING

Judging starts with all exhibitors standing in line with their dogs for a group assessment. The judge may ask all dogs to be moved collectively once or twice around the ring. You then go forward to stand your dog for individual assessment by the judge, who asks you to move the dog around usually in a triangle, straight up and down, usually with a free stand in front of them. Handler and dog then return to stand in line. Once all the dogs in the class have been assessed, the judge selects the dogs he feels most fits the breed standard, and places them accordingly from first to fifth place.

SHOWING IN EUROPE

Some UK exhibitors enjoy showing in Europe where dogs are often double-handled: the handler stands behind the dog, and the owner or helper attracts the dog's attention with a ball or food so he pulls into the lead, thus achieving a dynamic pose.

Ch., Lux. Ch. Amazon Russian Romance (Int., Multi Ch. Grand Mollis Armani × Ch. Amazon She Will Be Loved JW) is shown in both UK handling style, and double-handled as in Europe.
ANNA LOPAREVA

Slow down round corners otherwise you will be leaning over the dog (as if cornering on a bike), and the dog will also lower himself to go round the corner, which will make him look squashed. Corners should be rounded rather than taken at a tight right-angle.

The dog doesn't have to run closely to heel. If you move your left arm slightly away from your body so the dog is moving more freely it looks more impressive than the dog trotting closely to heel. If your dog is pulling to the side, use your voice to encourage him to move more with you.

Your touch on the lead should be feather light, especially if the lead is carried just behind the ears: it is often positioned here to give more control and direction, rather than at the base of the neck where all the strength of the dog is concentrated.

FINDING AND ENTERING SHOWS

There are four types of show held around the British Isles, ranging from the local village show to Crufts. All pedigree dogs entering shows must be registered with the Kennel Club. Dogs to be shown in Southern Ireland must be separately registered with the Irish KC.

Fun dog shows: Not KC licensed; no pre-entry is required. They are often held alongside country fairs.

Companion shows: KC licensed; no pre-entry is required. These used to be called exemption shows, and were often held alongside country fairs. They are open to all pedigree dogs and various breeds, which are judged against each other.

Limit shows: KC licensed, and pre-entry is required. Open to club members and their pedigree dogs; classes are for one breed, or mixed.

General open shows: KC licensed, and pre-entry is required. There are separate breed classes for many different breeds, or AV classes, if not otherwise scheduled (Any Variety Not Separately Classified – AVNSC). Average Dobermann entry may be between one and twenty dogs. In a Dobermann Breed Club open show the entry is around forty to sixty dogs.

Championship Show Judging List 2016

SHOW	DATE	DOGS / BITCHES
Boston	Thu 18/01	Margaret Young
Manchester (Stafford)	Sat 17/01	Dr Ronald James
CRUFTS (NEC – Birmingham)	Sat 12/03	Sue Brassington
South East Dobe Club	Sun 20/03	Wendy McColl
Working & Pastoral Breeds Wales (Builth Wells)	Sat 16/04	Christine Parker
West of England LKS (Malvern)	Sun 24/04	Lita Lainchbury
National (Birmingham)	Fri 06/05	John Purnell
Scottish Kennel Club (Edinburgh)	Fri 20/05	Elaine Turnbull
Dobermann Club (Hertfordshire)	Sat 28/05	Elaine Drennan / Victoria Ingram
Bath	Sun 29/05	Sue Searle
Southern Counties (Newbury)	Sat 04/06	Stuart Mallard
Three Counties (Malvern)	Fri 10/06	Robin Newhouse
Border Union (Kelso)	Sat 18/06	Hazel Leggett
North of England Dobe Club (Warrington)	Sat 25/06	Billy Henderson
Blackpool	Sun 26/06	Richard Kinsey
Windsor	Thur 30/06	Chris Hollands
East of England (Peterborough)	Sat 09/07	Keith Baldwin
National Working & Pastoral Breeds (Malvern)	Sat 16/07	Jay Horgan
Leeds	Fri 22/07	Wendy Meikle
NE Co's Dobe Club (Tyne & Wear)	Sat 23/07	Hans vd Burge
Paignton	Mon 08/08	Jackie Ingram
Bournemouth	Sat 13/08	Bridgette Bodle
Welsh KC (Builth Wells)	Sat 20/08	Liz Cartledge
Scottish Dobe Club	Sat 27/08	Richard Meredith
Scottish Kennel Club (Edinburgh)	Sun 28/08	Steve Waldie
City of Birmingham (Warwick)	Sat 03/09	Derek Smith
Richmond (Guildford)	Sat 10/09	Jane Brock
Darlington (no CC's)	Sat 17/09	Ian Rimmer
NI Dobe Club	Sat 27/09	Rita Hughan
Belfast	Sun 25/09	Kevin Young
Driffield	Thu 29/09	Peter Forshaw
Welsh Dobe Club (South Wales)	Sun 02/10	Marion Sargent/ Roger James
South Wales (Chepstow)	Sun 09/10	Peter Greenaway
Birmingham Dobe Club (Birmingham)	Sat 23/10	Diane Smith / Martin Horgan
Midland Counties (Stafford)	Thur 27/10	Anne Ingram
Working & Pastoral Breeds Scotland (Edinburgh)	Sat 05/11	Lynn Glass
Midland Dobe Club (Derbyshire)	Sun 13/11	Graham Hunt / Mel Merchant
South West Dobe Club (Gloucestershire)	Sat 19/11	Yvonne Bevans/Geoff Duffield
LKA (no CC's) (NEC – Birmingham)	Sat 10/12	Alison Swain

Crufts 2017 Dave Anderson, Crufts 2018 Roberta Wright

Judges are a mixture of breed specialists and what are known as 'all-rounders' – those whose main breed is not the Dobermann, but who have passed the necessary exams to judge the breed.

General championship shows: KC licensed, pre-entry required. There are separate breed classes for many different breeds. The standard is high as dogs can qualify for Crufts. Entries range from fifty to 150 Dobermanns.

Dobermann Breed Club championship shows: These range from fifty to 150 dogs.

The table opposite lists all the UK Dobermann club and General Championship shows. Dates change slightly each year, but are listed for reference.

For many years the UK has had two weekly newspapers called *Dog World and Our Dogs*, which provide regular news, show results and critiques, breed notes, classified adverts and forthcoming show announcements, but in mid 2017 *Dog World* ceased trading, so now *Our Dogs* is the only weekly publication for show news. Adverts will give the contact details for the society secretary, who will send out an entry form.

For shows requiring pre-entry, paper entry forms are available from the society secretaries, or they can be entered online through the websites of Fosse Data, Higham Press.

Exhibitors register on the websites and can find forthcoming shows. The closing date for paper entries is around five to six weeks before the show date, while online dates may be as late as three weeks before the show. Some societies send out passes in the post, while others are available to print from the online websites at home by the exhibitor. Passes are not needed for entry to open shows or breed club shows.

What Class to Enter

Shows have different classes for males, females, puppies and adults. These range according to age and prior wins, and are listed on every show schedule.

Unless you are trying to gain points for a particular competition, such as the Junior Warrant, just enter one class at a championship show. Although it may seem a long way to go for just one class, it is far better to enjoy it than risk the dog getting bored because he must stand in line for long periods – and no one puts an immature puppy against a champion adult in open.

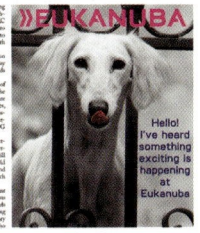

The front cover of Dog World, *which in this issue featured Ch. Jojavik Midnight Express winning Best In Show at Three Counties Championship Show 2016 with handler Josh Henderson for Jojavik Dobermanns.*

To become a champion, the dog must become 'Best Dog' or 'Best Bitch' (at a championship show) over all the other Dobermanns of his/her sex, and then be awarded the Challenge Certificate (aka the CC or 'the ticket'). This must happen from three separate judges.

The European system is similar to the UK in that four or five CACs (the equivalent of CCs) are required to become a champion. Entries at even the international shows (the equivalent to our championship shows) may average twenty dogs. The annual World Show attracts around 100 to 150 dogs. The biggest Dobermann show in the world is the annual International Dobermann Club – the IDC – show, which attracts around 600

Class of black females at the International Dobermann Club (IDC). JOE BLOOGS PHOTOS

for the following year. This is obviously a great accolade, as everyone wants to show their dog at the most prestigious dog show in the world. See current KC regulations for qualification criteria.

WHAT TO WEAR

There is no dress code for UK dog shows except to look smart and wear sensible shoes in which you can run properly. Although showing is all about the dogs, it is a bit of an anachronism to present a beautifully prepared and conditioned dog and then to show him off wearing old trainers and dirty jeans.

to 700 Dobermanns. The working competitions of the IDC are held separately, and both events are a Mecca for the serious breed enthusiast who is interested in incorporating new blood to their breeding.

Avoid black clothes when showing a black dog, as the dog's outline won't be seen clearly against your trousers. Keep clothing close fitting, with no pieces flapping against the dog. All the UK summer shows are outside, and although there is always wet weather tenting for the outdoor shows, handlers often show in wellington boots if the ground is rain sodden.

Qualifying for Crufts

Dogs that win first, second and third in certain classes at championship shows qualify for Crufts

In America all lady handlers wear skirts or dresses, and the men sharp suits. In Europe, on the other hand, everyone wears jeans, and anyone dressing up to show their dog, even at the biggest event, looks very conspicuous.

It. Ch. Pocho di Prisconte (It. Ch. Nemo di Prisconte × Ully di Prisconte) IDC Sieger 2014, AIAD Champion, ZTP 1A.

SHOWING RESTRICTIONS FOR DOCKED DOGS

Docking is now banned in the UK and Southern Ireland. Legally docked dogs from Europe may be shown at UK shows that do not charge an entrance fee for the general public, such as breed club shows. This is government legislation and not a KC rule. Some championship shows dropped the entrance fee to allow docked dogs to compete, but large shows such as Crufts rely heavily on entrance fees from the public and it is unlikely that this will change.

Ruth Robinson with her Remesca's Reet Petite (Ch. Aritaur Cardinal Red at Jodaseen ShCM, × Ch. Remesca What Eva). Light-coloured clothing compliments a dark dog. TANYA PILGRIM

DOG SHOW ETIQUETTE

In any subjective sport or hobby there will be unfairness, and as much as there are good and fair judges there will be poor and crooked judges. It may take a while in showing to get to recognize the names of judges you respect. Also new exhibitors may be quite shocked to hear other exhibitors predicting the result because person A used person B's dog at stud, or person X gave person Y the ticket last time they judged. The easy answer for a poor loser is to blame the judge rather than to look honestly at their own dogs. There are some 'bent judges', but there are more honest ones.

If you really want to learn about the breed, rather than just showing for a first place rosette, watch other dogs and handlers, and which dogs the judge is placing. It may become clear that the judge may prefer a different style of dog to yours, or if you have asked a straight-talking friend how your dog went, or to video it for you, you may realize that your dog moved really badly and didn't deserve to be placed.

Exhibitors and judges should not have conversations with each other, or critique dogs verbally in the ring. Some judges may take time later to talk with the exhibitor, but they are not obliged to do so. Remember the judge may have been on their feet all day and needs a rest, rather than being held to account by a disgruntled exhibitor. Judges are contracted to submit a critique to the dog press detailing their assessment of the first and second placed dog.

Show careers for dogs often end well before they can go into the veteran class aged seven years, but in recent years a number of dogs have won CCs and been made up into champions in veteran. In 2014 Ch./Ir. Ch. Aritaur Tomahawk Marillium became a champion at seven and a half years, and Judith Balshaw's Ch. Janzins Jamelia JW ShCM, bred by Peter and Janet Forshaw, won three of her ten CCs as a veteran, with one just short of her tenth birthday.

Another big winner in veteran was Ch. Supeta's Wicked Wizard at Sonakint, owned by Eloise Atkinson and Sue and Pete Mycroft, who had a great show career with ten CCs, and who won seventeen Best Veteran in Shows.

Marion and Bill Mulholland's Ch./Ir. Ch. Aritaur Tomahawk Marillium (Int., Multi Ch. Tom Dober Hagi × Ned Ch. Aritaur Dominatrix, EJSgrn02) won his last CC from the veteran class.

13 JUDGING THE DOBERMANN

If you have spent some years showing and studying the breed, it may be time for you to take the next step: to judge the Dobermann.

To demonstrate your understanding of the breed standard you will need to attend breed seminars and take judging exams on the basic points of the dog, on its conformation and movement, and on the rules and regulations. You will also need to learn how to steward (the steward's role is to assist the judges and as ring manager) to gain procedural experience. Seminars and exams are held by breed clubs, show societies and clubs, and notifications on them will be in the weekly dog papers, on club websites and on social media groups. Ask your local society if you can steward

Lynne and Sam Jones' Ch. Korifey Black Diamond (Am. Gr. Ch. Dabney's Phenomenon × Ch., Lux. Ch. Amazon Russian Romance) winning one of her many BPIs. Judged by breed specialist Von Cox.

alongside someone experienced. If you are seen to have a genuine interest and knowledge of the breed, you may be invited to judge at a general open show, starting off with three classes for your first appointment.

There are ten UK Dobermann breed clubs in the UK (*see box*), and until 2014 they were all grouped together under the umbrella organization of the Dobermann Breed Council (DBC); however, due to political differences, too many clubs left the DBC for it to be able to continue, and in 2014 it was dissolved. Some of the clubs group together, so if you are on the judging list of one club you will be on the list for that group of clubs.

Judging criteria for each club vary slightly; these can be found on their websites, or will be provided by the club secretary.

After some years of judging at open show level, you may be invited to judge a club show, and provided you have judged sufficient dogs, you can eventually apply to award CCs.

UK DOBERMANN BREED CLUBS

The South West Dobermann Club (SWDC)

The South East Dobermann Club (SEDC)

The Midland Dobermann Club (MDC)

North of England Dobermann Club (NEDC)

Birmingham and District Dobermann Club (BDDC)

The Dobermann Club

Welsh Dobermann Club (WDC)

North Eastern Counties Dobermann Society (NECDS)

Scottish Dobermann Club (SDC)

Northern Ireland Dobermann Club (NIDC).

PROCEDURES AND RING MANAGEMENT

A good steward is invaluable in looking after you, as judge, and keeping the ring running to your requirements. However, although your steward will assist you, this is your undertaking: your ring to manage, your dogs to judge, and your documents to sign, so it is essential that you learn the rules and procedures. First-time judges will always be helped by an experienced steward, so don't feel embarrassed to mention that this is your first time judging.

It is important to look professional when judging, but comfort is also essential. Long scarves and neck ties can dangle in the dog's face, and puppies especially can be put off by judges wearing hats. Low-heeled shoes are necessary from both a comfort and safety aspect; stepping backwards and inadvertently treading on a dog's foot or owner behind you is one thing in flat shoes, but a high heel into a dog's foot could end their show career.

On arrival at the show, report to the secretary's table where you will be given a judging 'book' by the society, which details the number of entries you have in each class. Once you have checked your book, go over to your ring in good time to introduce yourself to the steward and review your ring.

The best way to learn both how to judge, and how not to, is to watch experienced judges and see how they manage their ring and assess the dogs presented to them. On the day it is up to you whether you start all your classes by seeing all the exhibits in movement, or by going straight to the individual judging; just maintain your routine in subsequent classes so that all exhibitors have an equal chance to show their dogs.

Judging is a serious undertaking, but no one wants a miserable judge, so it is equally important to be relaxed and to enjoy yourself, and to give everyone a pleasant day. Some of your newer exhibitors will be as nervous as you are, so put them at ease with a smile.

Your time spent studying the breed standard, watching dogs in and out of the ring, and the seminars you have attended, will help you to realize how much you do know when you run your hands over each dog.

Timing and Routine of Judging

At open shows these days you may have an entry of between ten and twenty dogs to judge, split across three to five classes. This provides enough time to appraise each dog sufficiently. At a championship show Kennel Club guidelines state that the judge should endeavour to judge around thirty dogs an hour, which equates to just two minutes per dog. This includes checking ring numbers as they come in, assessing the dogs on stand and move, short-listing, placing, signing the judging book, writing critiques on the first two, and any lunch break the judge may be lucky to have.

TECHNIQUE IN ASSESSING A DOG

Readers may be familiar with the original 'horse whisperer' Monty Roberts, who teaches that how we approach a horse is fundamental in gaining its trust. It is similar with dogs, and studies have shown that a dog's pulse rate increases when it is approached head on directly, but remains level when it is approached in a curve or from a 45-degree angle. Thus it is best not to approach a dog head on or from behind; also do not approach him either swiftly, or too slowly (which to the dog appears as a stalking manoeuvre), and avoid making eye contact with the dog. Politely greet the exhibitor, which relaxes everyone, including the dog.

Occasionally a dog may back off when you approach it or attempt to go over it, which is upsetting to the handler and yourself, as well as the dog. You may decide that a Dobermann that backs off in this way lacks the required character for breed type, and this assessment is your prerogative. Certainly a mature animal should be expected to stand firm and confident, but there can be many reasons why a youngster backs off – perhaps a heavy-handed judge has upset him at ringcraft class, or if it is a bitch, she may be coming in season and worried about someone touching her rear. Most judges will give a little time to help a dog and handler overcome the issue without any pressure – but judges are always under a time constraint, and shows are not ringcraft classes.

Approaching with hands outstretched to examine the head and teeth is particularly confrontational to any dog. Perhaps such dogs shouldn't be in the show ring, but why put a dog into a defence position in the first place? It is wholly inappropriate to put a dog under pressure in the show-ring to test its character. Dogs are trained not to respond to such threats in the ring, and it puts them in conflict with their training. Save the character tests for the working field.

Similarly judging conformation is not a character test, and there is no purpose in subjecting a dog to being touched all over for the sake of it. Physically going over a dog is something you will have been taught how to do at seminars, or you will have asked an experienced friend to show you the best way to proceed in this – but think about why you are actually touching the dog. With a short-coated breed such as the Dobermann there is no question of artfully trimming a lustrous coat in order to hide faults of conformation, and the dog's condition will show on the move, so there is actually no need to touch a short-haired dog all over its legs and body. Some judges are far less hands on and will only touch the dog to examine teeth and testicles.

Checking the head planes and the tidiness of the lip line.

Avoid looming over the dog, and touch him with firm, but not hard hands. To check entirely on males, run your hand down their back and between their hind legs, rather than suddenly placing a hand on their testicles and making them jump.

If a youngster is nervous of being gone over, sometimes getting him to move helps to relax him. Tension in a dog may have physiological origins, in that fear, stress and excitement lead to the release of adrenalin, which in excess can cause a build-up of lactic acid in the muscles, resulting in the muscles seizing up; movement helps to disperse the lactic acid.

In Summary
When judging do not:

- approach or touch a dog from the rear, and especially not a guarding breed
- pick up a Dobermann's feet: the colour of the pad is irrelevant, and cat-like feet can be seen without handling them
- stare into a dog's eyes
- loom over the dog when going over him
- put your head close to the dog's mouth to check dentition; if you can't see properly, wear glasses
- look up the lead to see the handler

ASSESSING CONFORMATION

The Head and Mouth
Check the head from both the top and the side. This gives you the basic form of the head – the wedge, the length of the skull to foreface, depth of stop, and whether the planes are parallel or not.

Judging the mouth may well distinguish the breed specialist from the all-rounder, who in a cursory glance will inevitably fail to see any missing teeth or wry bites. It is an insult to a working breed to ignore the mouth, and woe betide the breed specialist who misses faulty dentition, but how a judge places a dog with incorrect dentition in competition is his personal decision. In Europe not one missing tooth is tolerated, while in America up to four missing are permitted (although it may be more, as judges have only a cursory check). Judges in the UK are encouraged to be diligent about correct dentition (as required in the standard), and to penalize faulty dentition accordingly.

Be careful not to pull the dog's head up too high to check his dentition, as that will be uncomfortable for him – but equally important is not to position your face so it is level with the dog's face, especially with guarding breeds. Also, be careful not to cover the dog's eyes with your hand as you examine his teeth and jaw.

In Europe dogs are presented in a sit so the judge can open the mouth wide to check the molars; this makes it much more comfortable for both dog and judge. When you are checking the mouth you are also looking at the jaw shape and alignment, the scissor bite, and the number and position of the incisors.

You don't need to physically count the teeth (unless you want to), but you should learn what to look for in the mouth by examining your own dog's dentition and that of your friends' dogs so you become familiar with its structure.

Few outside mainland Europe would eliminate a dog with one missing tooth that is otherwise outstanding. However, the line has to be drawn somewhere, because if a problem is continually ignored and those dogs are bred from, it will risk being perpetuated until there is not one single dog in a community with complete dentition. (*See* the section on dentition in Chapter 11.)

Construction and Angulation

Construction can be correct in terms of angles but a structure may be in the wrong place. For example, if a dog's entire front assembly is too far forward, this can make him look long. In fact it is an optical illusion because just more of his ribbing is exposed. However, his topline will be unsupported and will not hold firm on the move. The dog appearing to lack forechest may have just as much as another dog, but because his front assembly is further forward, it conceals his forechest.

When dogs pull into the lead, the angulation between shoulder and upper arm, and thigh and stifle will tighten under tension. However, don't be fooled by what appears to be superb angulation on dogs pulling into the lead as they are shown in Europe.

Two important aspects of front assembly are the 'lay-back' of the shoulder, and the 'lay over'. Lay-back refers to the angle of the shoulder blade when seen from the side of the dog, and this angle determines how far the dog can

Checking the dog has full and correct dentition.

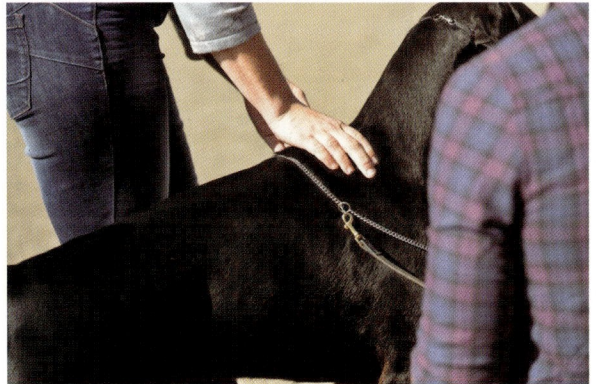

Judges usually start at the head and move down the neck to feel the placement of the shoulders.

Double handling with the dog pulling into the lead, tightens up/creates more bend at the joints of front and rear angulation.

'reach' the leg in front of itself on the move to cover good distance. The lay-over refers to how closely fitting the shoulder blade is around the top of the frame. Loose shoulders will result in the whole front having a loose fit, so be prepared to see some 'wagging elbows' on the move.

ASSESSING MOVEMENT

Balance is fundamental in all aspects because if it is out of symmetry the dog will not flow correctly on the move either in side gait or tracking. Consider the dog who is quite straight in his shoulder and upper arm, but who is over-angulated behind. His reach will be limited (determined by the straight shoulder angle), but the propulsion from his back end will push him along faster than his front can reach, so unless he is longer than the square required of the Dobermann, he will either twist sideways (sidewind/crab), move wide with the rear legs stepping inside a wide moving front, or high step (hackney) in order to avoid the inevitable foot collision of over-reaching. The dog that is both straight in front and straight behind will be limited in his front reach and lacking rotary action at the back, but he is balanced.

Clever handlers can often hide conformation faults on the stack but conformation faults usually give themselves away when the dog is on the move. It is always a disappointment when a dog that looks a picture standing, moves really badly – though as you become more experienced you will be able to go over a dog on the stand and

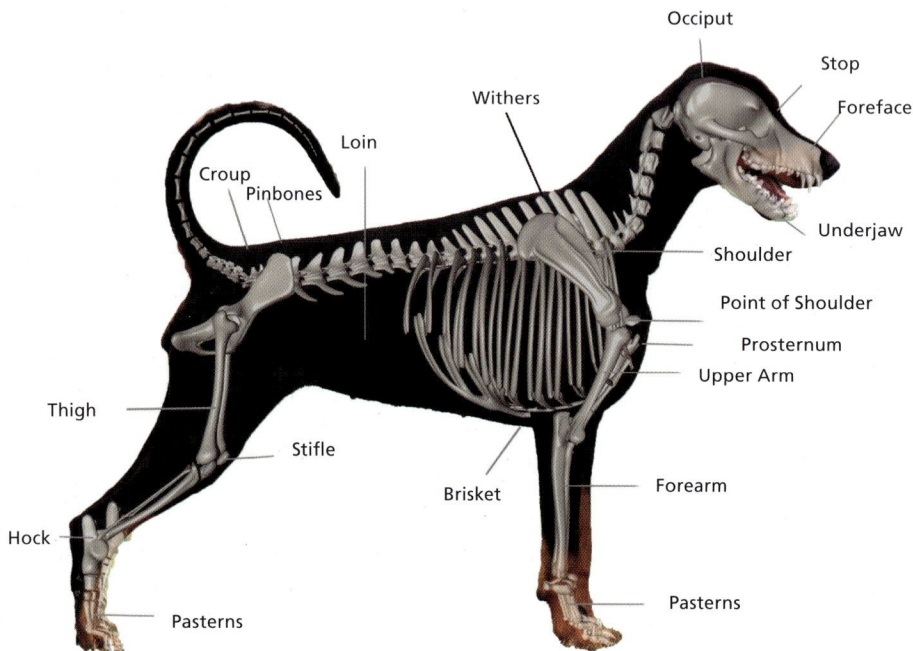

Common names for the bones and points of importance. KORIFEY

know in advance how he will move. The following conformational faults will result in irregularities in movement:

- Barrel-shaped ribs interfere with the swing of the foreleg, which has to come out and round the wide ribs so he will come at you wide in front. A dog with a pigeon chest will probably toe in, as will the dog whose whole front assembly is too far forward
- Weak hocks indicate rear over-angulation
- A high wither (shoulder) with a break before the topline (that is, not one continuous line) results in the back not holding firm on the move

In a poorly constructed dog (or a young dog that is still growing), the hind feet may strike the front feet (overreach), and to avoid foot interference the dog twists his body sideways and moves sideways, 'crabbing' along.

Triona Ni-She's Fiastra Wot A Thriller at Ruholfia Irish Junior Ch. '11, Celtic JW'11. (Int., Multi, It. Ch. Pathos del Querce Nere IDC JgdSgr'05, IDC Sgr'06, AIAD Sgr'07, IPO 1 × Lux, Ned. Ch. Keyala's Wot A Dream). Bred by Debbie Gamble. Here with co-breeder/handler Dean Gartan-Spires, shown at an active but steady pace to show off her balanced movement with excellent reach and drive.

Dogs moved at a fast active trot may appear to be over-reaching, but as a fast trot (also called a flying or suspended trot) results in a moment of suspension where all feet are off the ground, the forward movement coupled with the momentary suspension allows for foot clearance.

This is why watching the dog moving straight up and down is important. Just watching a flashy side gait may not show that the dog is twisting to avoid foot collision, or pinning it, or toeing in. The dog should move away cleanly with no deviation, without flipping in or out on the pasterns, or toeing in, or dropping the hocks.

Single Tracking, Convergence or Toeing In

The term 'single tracking' often confuses people, but it is just a natural way of walking or trotting at speed to conserve energy.

Consider the construction of the body and the legs, which are placed under the body at each corner. If at a trot the legs fall straight down without any convergence, there would be imbalance because whilst there is just one leg (of a front or rear pair) on the ground at any one time, the body will move slightly in the opposite direction to balance itself – if just the front right leg is on the ground, the back end of the dog will pitch slightly to the left. A perfect example of this is the bulldog, with his pitch and rolling gait and no convergence. When humans stand, our legs fall in a nearly straight line from our hips to the floor. When we walk, our legs converge towards each other (unless we are bow-legged), and our feet are closer together near the ankles than they are at the hip. In dogs it is more easily seen in faster trotting, where the legs converge to the centre line under the dog's body.

In single tracking the legs remain in a straight line from the shoulder to the foot on the move. In toeing in the dog's legs curve towards each other on the move, and if they are really bow-legged the legs may brush and knock against each other.

In dogs that 'toe in', the feet land with the pressure on the outside of the carpal joint (wrist).

In practice you will probably not see much single tracking in the show ring due to a lack of ring space and the generally slower gaiting, but it is still something to be aware of so you don't confuse it with toeing in.

There is no mention of single tracking in the UK or FCI breed standard, although the US references it by stating 'When moving at a fast trot, a properly built dog will single track'.

Each breed or group of dogs has a unique or particular style of gait, and many people worldwide are rightly concerned over what is disparagingly termed 'generic dog show movement'. This refers to very different breeds moving in the same fashion, as a Cocker Spaniel moving like an Afghan Hound, moving like a Golden Retriever, or terrier, or utility breed. Keep uppermost in your mind that the Dobermann is a working breed, not a fancy prancer.

Seminars and reading the breed standard can teach you the names of bones and what correct angulation should look like, but more importantly it is how bones correspond with each other, and what specific construction actually means in terms of movement. A short upper arm will usually produce toeing in. A straight shoulder will limit reach. Prospective judges should sit and watch dogs to learn for themselves, or ask someone they respect to mentor them.

One of the best explanations of canine locomotion is by the world-respected Rachel Page-Elliot, author of *Dogsteps*, which is an invaluable source of information in understanding canine anatomy and movement.

Don't let theory overcome the practical, and get so wrapped up in measuring angles that you forget that the most 'honest' dog stands in front of you. If you are getting stressed, or under time pressure, take a moment, and return with a fresh eye. Sometimes that moment of clarity will reveal what you are looking for.

FINAL ASSESSMENTS

Clever Handling versus the Honest Dog

There are some clever and experienced handlers who know what their dog's faults are and how to hide them. If the dog is wearing an American collar (a fine cord placed around the neck at the highest point behind the ears and under the jaw) you might suspect it has a lot of loose skin under the chin – so you can ask the handler to undo the collar, which will reveal how bad it is. The exhibitor can always replace it to move the dog.

Clever handlers can lift up a wide-moving dog so the lower front assembly converges and straightens up the dog on approach. To reveal this, ask the handler to show him on a loose lead to show his natural movement. You may ask the handler to free-stand their dog so you can evaluate it naturally.

Others who know their dog's faults will deliberately not come back in a straight line to you.

Between assessing each dog and waiting for the next dog to stack up, take a moment to cast your eyes around the dogs waiting in line. A dog may be shown topped and tailed for a reason, as it is long cast with a weak topline, but the handler relaxing in line may have forgotten to keep it presented.

The Tylers' Chancepixies Angelena (Int., Multi Ch. Grand Mollis Armani × Chancepixies Serenity) winning the Reserve Bitch CC at Midland Dobermann Club championship show from breed specialist judge Karen Barlow.

Weighing Up Faults and Merits

Although we all try to make judging objective, there is always going to be individual preference or dislike for particular merits or faults in dogs. Some judges may dislike wide or weak heads but may forgive paler markings; others may not tolerate unparallel head planes but will forgive untidy movement.

Although judges may focus on particular aspects of the breed, look at the whole dog and try not to be a fault judge. You may be presented with a dog which has a high shoulder, saggy back and set-on tail, and another with a roach back and low croup. Another exhibit may be very tall with extremely straight angulation, a roach back and rounded croup. This dog won't be able to move much faster than his fat friend.

Although no dog is perfect, we can find virtues in all dogs that have reached a good degree of showing. There are many dogs that have not reached the heights of stardom perhaps because they are with a novice or poor handler, so although it is difficult, try to look beyond just the beautifully handled dog.

Nothing can prepare you for the quandary you face between the dog with an excellent head which could hold an attacker firmly but whose body is so badly made that he couldn't run to catch him, and the dog with such a weak under-jaw that he couldn't hold a feather but who has text book angulation. Neither fits the breed standard perfectly, so it will come down to the movement or perhaps the panache and presence of a dog, which is equally as important as the right conformation. But always ask yourself – is this dog capable of doing the job for which it is bred?

Judging Different Styles

Wherever you are judging, you will encounter dogs that look different to others in their class. This is why it is important that all dogs should be judged against the breed standard and not against each other, because as long the dog conforms to type, it is irrelevant whether it is an American, English or European bred dog.

The expectation that a line-up should resemble dogs of a particular style, as was the case when there were 300 or more dogs in the ring, is now unrealistic with around only 100 dogs at many championship shows. Judges today don't have the luxury of choosing from a great depth of similar styles, and have to select their winners from what may be very different styles of dog.

Although you may believe that a particular style of dog more closely fits your interpretation of the standard than others, choosing a dog from each class simply because it looks like all the other class winners is a very poor judging method.

Furthermore, don't make the mistake of dismissing the 'odd dog out', as you may be eliminating the most excellent dog in favour of the majority of mediocre dogs. The 27in male may look out of place being the smallest dog in a line-up of tall dogs, but he may most closely fit the breed standard.

Breed specialist Judge Steve Waldie judging Tracy Feeney's Ch. Stormhold Enigma from Diego JW ShCM (Italo Elite House, Imp Pol x Diego's Temptation with Stormhold), handled by Hollie Kavanagh.

263

OBSERVING THE FORMALITIES

Unlike some overseas systems, most UK judges still both breed and show, and this crossover of roles can sometimes cause friction between friends. One of the most common fall-outs occurs when judges don't place their friends' dogs. Some 'friends' will also try to influence you against another dog, and you must have the courage and conviction to reject their efforts and tell them that when they are judging they can do what they want, but you are quite confident in your own judging. No real friend would expect you to compromise your integrity for them, and just because you get on, doesn't mean you have to like their dog or opinion.

Never address exhibitors by their first names in the ring, but keep to 'Sir' and 'Madam', which keeps everything impersonal, as it should be. It is quite fashionable nowadays to see exhibitors give judges a great display of hugs and kisses when they win. Imagine how that looks to other exhibitors – that you just gave your best friend a good win. Keep professional by holding your hand out to shake theirs. You can always hug later.

Most judges are happy to explain their findings to the exhibitor after judging, although you are under no obligation to do so. If an exhibitor challenges you after judging, being annoyed that their dog didn't win under you, you may tell them that you will be providing details of findings in your critiques which they can read in the weekly dog papers in due course, or you may decide to tell them why you made your decision. If they don't accept that, there is little you can do about it.

Your job is to judge the breed, not to promote yourself by doing favours for friends. Sadly this means you should accept that after judging there will probably be people whom you thought were friends, whose friendship you will lose. You can mitigate this to some extent by warning them in advance that if they expect you to be 'bent' in their favour, they will be disappointed, and perhaps they shouldn't enter if you are the judge if they can't take your decision. However, you must not ignore a dog just because it belongs to a friend. Favours may gain the friendship or influence of one person, but you will lose the respect of the community, earn the reputation of being a bent or incompetent judge, and have to live with the fact that you did more for yourself than for the breed.

THE WRITTEN CRITIQUE

Judges in the UK must supply written critiques on the first and second placed dog at limited, open and championship shows to the weekly dog press: *Our Dogs*.

Your critique is your personal view, and reflects how you see the dogs. You may therefore want to avoid it being too over-flowery about how you have loved the dog since you helped whelp him, and both his parents were great favourites of yours. You are not judging pedigrees or friends, you are judging to service the Dobermann, and that is all. In the words of Peggy Adamson: 'Above all have integrity. Integrity cannot be taught or learned; you either have it or you don't.'

IN SUMMARY

When judging, *do not*:
- call exhibitors by their first name
- stand chatting to exhibitors before you judge, or pet their dogs. No need to pretend you don't know them, but a good morning to everyone is quite sufficient
- do favours for friends, or penalize them
- travel with friends to the same show and then judge their dog

14 BREEDING, PREGNANCY, WHELPING AND REARING

BREEDING

It is hoped that the breeder will form his opinion of the dogs to use for breeding purposes from the analysis of bloodlines and proper breeding methods, and not from such considerations as whether a stud dog is a German Sieger or an American Champion.

Philipp Gruenig

Many years ago most pedigree dog breeders bred frequently, and through their many litters studied the positive and negative values of their stock. They learned how the phenotype (looks) of their dogs might marry in a combination, and importantly what the genotype (genes) of the dog produced – what the hidden merits and faults of the dog's pedigree were.

A contented dam with her newly born puppies. Ch. Tronjheim Belladonna From Jojavik JW ShCM. Top Brood Bitch 2014, 2015, 2016. JOJAVIK DOBERMANNS

Most dog breeders today are considered 'hobby breeders', keeping and breeding a small number of dogs in the family home. This is much more suitable for the Dobermann than being in a kennel, but it makes it difficult to identify the particular merits and faults of a breeding line.

Without competition in ring or field the breeder may suffer from 'kennel blindness', whereby they see no fault in their dogs and are therefore unable to choose a suitable breeding partner. We all start as novices, so seek advice from a successful mentor, whose knowledge and experience will guide you in your quest to breed quality Dobermanns.

The practice of appointing 'breed wardens' (Zuchtwart) originated in Germany. Wardens were usually retired breeders or judges appointed by breed clubs to guide novice breeders. They assessed the bitch and helped plan breeding combinations, and visited each litter by the time the pups were three days old to check their health and that of the dam, and their living quarters. Deformed or mismarked puppies would usually be culled (painlessly by a vet or professional by the eleventh day at the latest), and if there were too many puppies for the dam, a foster bitch would usually be found for her. The wardens would later tattoo the puppies and evaluate them, and advise which should be kept for show, work and breeding. Any puppy considered substandard would not be issued with a breeding pedigree.

Culling is very rarely practised now, and the idea fills most breeders with horror, but breeding then was about producing dogs that were truly fit for purpose, and there was no role for a dog that might have been unable to do its job. Far better, it was thought, to maintain the vigour of the breed rather than dilute it with dogs of poor quality, or worse, to have unwanted dogs filling up the dog pounds.

RISKS AND COSTS OF BREEDING

The only way to get rich by breeding is to do it commercially and without care for the dogs. Even with a large litter there are no wealthy breeders – but for most people the fulfilment of raising quality puppies is worth the expense.

Breeding is never without risk to the bitch, and even the most experienced breeders can suffer fatalities of both bitches and puppies. Anyone who thinks that a bitch should have one litter 'because it's good for her' should not be breeding.

Pet insurance policies don't cover breeding conditions, so having funds before breeding is essential for emergencies. Unless you have made alternative arrangements, payment for a proven stud dog is due for the service (mating), not for pregnancy confirmation or live puppies born. If your bitch does not become pregnant, loses the litter through infection or trauma, or, even worse, dies, the stud dog owner is still entitled to payment.

Even before you take your bitch to be mated, the facilities that you will need to provide for a bitch and her puppies are a main consideration, especially for a large litter. Puppies cannot live in a small pen or room, as they need fresh air and space in which to develop. And if the breeder has a regular job, who will be at home to feed the bitch and puppies for their required four daily meals? Food can't be left down for them to help themselves all day.

For a winter litter the puppies will not be hardy enough to play outside, so a spacious room with waterproof flooring is essential. Thick plastic, grey camping groundsheet over the entire floor will prevent leaks. Hygienic puppy quarters reduce disease and infection – and potential buyers don't want to see dirty puppies in a small, filthy pen.

Planning how to sell the puppies is important even prior to mating. Good buyers will wait for quality litters, but be wary of buyers who expect to buy 'off the shelf'.

The best chance of successful sales is to register your puppies promptly with the Kennel Club, who will provide potential owners with a list of breeders with registered puppies. Puppies whose parents are of sound character, and with good health test results, are always appealing, and if the parents have show or work titles it will make your litter even more so.

However, even once you have sold the litter, there will probably be at least one owner who decides at some stage that they no longer want the dog they bought from you as a puppy. If you have no room for him and the owners want him gone, he could end up in rescue kennels – so unless you want that on your conscience, you must plan for returnees. The show and work communities co-operate well to save dogs going into rescue, and breeders who don't look after their own are very badly regarded.

A litter of strong, healthy puppies – but when the bitch was carrying her second litter a year later, disaster struck in the seventh week of pregnancy: she developed autoimmune haemolytic anaemia, and despite emergency care and blood transfusions, she died along with her unborn puppies.

THE KENNEL CLUB ASSURED BREEDER SCHEME

The Assured Breeder Scheme (ABS) provides a register of inspected quality breeders who must follow relevant breed health screening recommendations and maintain high standards of raising puppies. In 2013 the scheme was recognized by the United Kingdom Accreditation Service (UKAS), and all ABS members are inspected by a KC inspector. Full details of the scheme can be found on The Kennel Club website.

BREEDING FOR GOOD HEALTH

British breeders lagged behind the European and US breeders for many years, but perplexingly for the idealist, despite their generations of health testing, the health of the European or US Dobermann is no better than that of the British Dobermann. Apart from the DNA von Willebrand's disease (vWD) test, it is impossible to predict the outcome of hip, eye and heart health. All other tests are *clinical* only.

The BVA idealistically advises breeders not to use dogs without perfect health results. Simultaneously we are warned against diminishing the gene pool by the over-use of popular sires and line-breeding. No perfect dog with perfect ancestry exists, and eliminating an otherwise excellent dog for one undesirable health fault will eventually bring other faults to the surface – for example, excluding vWD Affected males and Carriers of both genders from breeding would result in a loss of 60 per cent of the available gene pool.

The following conditions can be tested against:

Dilated cardiomyopathy (DCM): Available tests are by echo-cardiograph (Doppler), or the Troponin blood test, currently undergoing trials in the breed.

Hip dysplasia: Although the BVA suggests that 'breeders should choose breeding stock with hip scores below the breed median score', there are many Dobermanns with scores well above this who should not be excluded from breeding. The importance in any health scheme is in avoiding mating high scoring dogs, or those with high scoring ancestry together.

PHPV: This is an inherited condition, but the test only reflects the clinical status of the dog, not what he/she will produce. Clear parents can produce affected progeny, and vice versa. Mildly affected dogs should still be included in breeding as long as it is to a clear opposite line.

All health testing in pedigree dogs has come from the show community, and breed clubs rec-ommend the following breed specific tests (mandatory for ABS members): hip score, von Willebrands disease (vWD), eye testing for PHPV.

Although the KC requires dogs to be *tested* before breeding, there is currently no minimum standard of any health results required to register litters even for ABS members.

Any stud dog in the show or working community today will have at least the minimum level of health tests. Their owners usually decline poor quality or non health-tested bitches for mating as the negative impact of any low quality progeny can ruin the dog's reputation.

PLANNING THE LITTER

Choosing the Stud Dog

Your choice of stud dog should be based entirely on the merits and faults of your bitch regarding health, character and conformation, and how the pedigrees complement each other. Researching pedigrees and considering combinations are skills that will set you apart from the breeder who randomly chooses a dog perhaps on location, or who owns it himself.

The diligent breeder studies the stud dog's phenotype, genotype, pedigree, and what he has produced to various bitches. All beings repeat their characteristics in their descendants, but many traits are hidden. The way a dog is bred – whether he is in-bred or out-crossed – often has more bearing on his progeny than how he looks himself. For example, both parents may have dark eyes, but if there are other dogs that are light-eyed on both sides, some of the resulting progeny will have light eyes.

Breeding from a Suitable Bitch

Although bitches reach sexual maturity from six to eight months, Dobermann bitches under the age of two years old are not sufficiently mature in mind or body to be bred from.

Each season saturates the uterus with progesterone, decreasing reproductive fitness and making it progressively more difficult for the bitch to conceive and maintain a pregnancy. Waiting until the bitch is five years old or older for a first litter also increases the risks of a difficult whelp-

A promising eight-week-old puppy.

ing, as the pelvis hardens with age, and the risk of pyometra (womb infection) rises significantly after the age of six years. Breeding at this age if the bitch has already had a litter is not an issue, but breeding much past seven years places a greater risk on her.

The Kennel Club will not accept an application to register a litter when the dam:

- has already whelped four litters
- was under one year old at the time of mating
- has already had two litters delivered by cae-sarean section
- is over eight at the time of whelping

The gestation period of a bitch is sixty-three days, and puppies go to their new homes at around eight weeks.

OESTRUS AND OVULATION

The bitch's season lasts for around twenty-one days (three weeks), with ovulation generally in the second week.

Proestrus marks the start of the season, when oestrogen levels rise and eggs in the ovaries start to mature. The vulva swells and becomes soft and spongy, and dabbing it daily with a tissue enables you to mark the first day of the bitch's season, as you will clearly see the first specks of blood; when she is showing these signs she is described as being 'on heat'. Proestrus generally lasts for around nine days, but can last many more. Males are attracted to her, but she will not be ready to mate until ovulation.

The next stage is oestrus, when the colour of the blood specks now turns paler. Just prior to ovulation there is a significant increase in luteinizing hormone (LH). The LH surge may occur at any time from three to twenty-eight days after the first signs of heat; the average is ten days. Around forty-eight hours after the LH surge, follicle-stimulating hormone (FSH) triggers the ovaries to release the eggs, which then take thirty-six to forty-eight hours to mature for conception.

Some bitches will flirt and stand to the male to encourage him to mate her, but conception can only happen once the eggs have 'dropped' and matured. If you are mating your bitch you should start to test for progesterone from around day

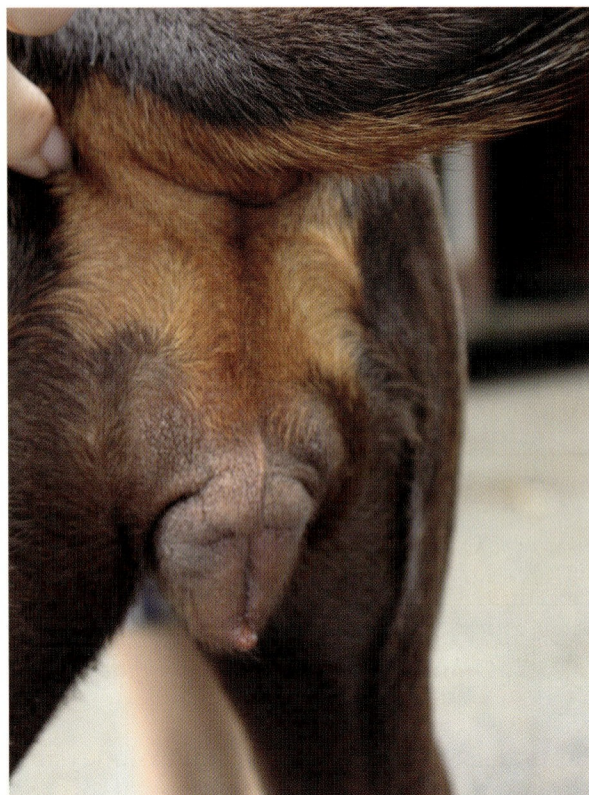

Some bitches have a very small vulva even when they are ready for mating. Although this bitch's vulva was very swollen and she stood from day twelve, she was progesterone tested and only eventually mated on day twenty-four of her season.

seven of her cycle, so it is important to know the day she first bled. Guessing when ovulation occurs can result in bitches being force mated (raped) to fit in with an expected routine. Progesterone testing is a small price to pay to save on a long journey and to ensure a successful and comfortable mating.

Experienced breeders often rely on instinctive 'stockmanship', and most bitches ovulate around eleven to thirteen days after the start of proestrus. This can vary greatly, so many breeders now take advantage of modern cytology.

Testing For Ovulation

Guide Dogs for the Blind, which is the biggest breeding organization in the UK, analysed the success rate of pregnancy in 100 of their bitches and found that from fifty matings judged by stockmanship, 78 per cent became pregnant, compared to those determined by cytology results, where 92 per cent became pregnant.

Qualitative progesterone analysis: This procedure accurately determines ovulation and the optimal mating day, thus increasing the chances of successful conception with a good-sized litter. Veterinary diagnostic laboratories accurately measure the progesterone in the blood to predict whether the bitch has ovulated, is just about to ovulate, or if she is not ready, and to re-test.

Using a sample kit directly from the laboratory, the breeder takes the bitch to their local vet for a blood sample to be taken, which the breeder then sends by guaranteed next day delivery. Do not let the vet persuade you that their in-house test is sufficient, as it will not be as accurate as an outside laboratory.

Results are reported in either nmol/l or ng/ml (depending on the lab), but the breeder does not need to be concerned about this, as the lab or vet will simply advise them of the best mating day.

Premate 'traffic light' testing: The in-house vet test: a chemical agent is added to the blood sample, which changes colour according to the levels of progesterone in the blood. The tester visually

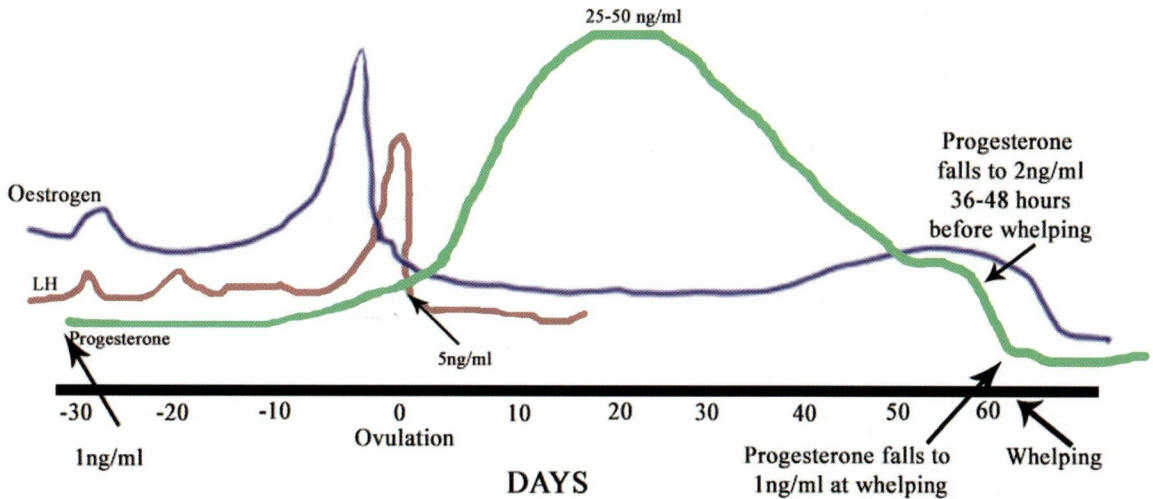

Progesterone gradually rises above base levels (under <1.5 nmol/L) prior to the LH surge. When the LH surge occurs, progesterone may reach 6 to 12 nmol/L. Ovulation generally occurs when the level of progesterone exceeds 10 nmol/L, and ideal mating dates are then advised accordingly.

compares the colour on the strip to a chart on which is displayed varying colours according to the levels of progesterone. If the sample is left for any time, or a slightly different volume of reagent is used, results will be distorted.

Vaginal swabbing: This procedure examines the cells high up in the vaginal wall under a microscope for changes in form. Nearing ovulation the epithelial (structural) cells change. Increased oestrogen leads to capillary breakage, and red blood cells leak through the uterine epithelial cells. The nucleic centre of the cell diminishes and the cell edges become cornified (flattened). Swabbing is only accurate if analysed over a number of days, ideally from as early as day four of the season, and the swabs compared against each other. Cells must be taken high up towards the cervix to gain a true reading, rather than swabbing the old degraded cells lower in the vagina.

Saliva testing: As oestrogen increases, so does the concentration of electrolytes (salinity) in the saliva. This shows as crystal 'ferning' patterns,

ADDITIONAL FACTS

- The ovulation day of 40 per cent of bitches varies by up to eight days from one season to another
- A bitch is born with all the eggs she will ever need
- Semen is viable for up to five days
- Small puppies are more likely to have been attached to poorer areas on the uterus, rather than being a late conceived puppy

indicating that ovulation is imminent. Ferning is seen around three to five days before ovulation.

Ovulation pads: These pads consist of small slips of fabric on a plastic strip which are inserted just inside the bitch's vulva. Like the in-house test strips at the vets, they react to the levels of lutenizing hormone in the vaginal fluid produced with different colour ranges. Strips can be affected by urine and other fluids.

THE MATING PROCESS

Note that all bitches have a resident population of bacteria in the vagina, so routine bacteriological swabbing of bitches prior to mating is unnecessary as it is not a sterile site and only normal bacteria will be recovered. Antibiotics kill beneficial bacteria as well as any 'bad' bacteria, and routine treatment use of antibiotics prior to mating can do more harm than good.

The natural mating process is detailed in Chapter 14, The Stud Dog.

Artificial Insemination (AI)

Artificial insemination with either frozen or chilled semen is now commonplace, and means that breeders can use dogs that otherwise would not be accessible to them.

Canine reproduction vets can be found in most regions, and they will manage the collection and processing of the semen, inseminating the bitch, or sending semen overseas. Semen is collected and analysed for volume, count, motility and any deformities. Using a teaser bitch, the dog mounts the bitch but instead of allowing the dog to enter the bitch, the handler will hold the dog's penis and divert the semen into a sterile bag.

The collection is placed in a buffer solution (which protects the semen during the chilling or freezing process), and stored in straws.

Semen can be chilled for use within seventy-two hours, or frozen. Chilled semen is more motile on thawing, and produces statistically larger litters. However, it only lasts for seventy-two hours, so for overseas use, tight preparations are needed for collection, processing, shipping and customs clearance, or all can be lost.

Frozen semen can be imported well ahead of time and stored at the facility where the bitch will be inseminated.

Bitches can be artificially inseminated either trans-cervically (intra-uterine) with a fibre-optic endoscope through the vagina, depositing the semen high up into the uterus, or by surgical implantation directly into the uterus, which requires a general anaesthetic. The Royal College of Veterinary Surgeons, and the Kennel Club following their guidance, do not approve surgical AI procedures except in exceptional situations.

Dual sire: This is the mating or insemination of a bitch to two males. This provides more genetic diversity for a gene pool in one single pregnancy. Dual siring has been commonplace in the USA for many years, and is now permitted by the UK Kennel Club without prior permission.

After Mating

Shortly after a successful mating you should notice that the vulva 'closes down', and the bitch refuses any further advances from males, including her mate. However, she will still be fertile for some days, so be vigilant that no other dog mates her accidentally, as you don't want to have to abort the litter, having paid a big stud fee for the dog you chose. Bitches that have not conceived, on the other hand, may often be keen to continue mating.

PREGNANCY

An early sign of pregnancy is that the bitch tends to become emotionally softer and crave affection more than usual. In the wild, this state encourages the other pack members to feel well disposed to her, and to support her and her future puppies.

At around week three you will notice tiny physical changes: her vulva will not have returned to its pre-season size, and will have remained slightly enlarged and soft. These could be signs of a phantom pregnancy developing, but in a genuine pregnancy her teats will soon gradually change, becoming softer and slightly pink in colour; this 'pinking up' does not happen in a phantom pregnancy.

Experienced hands can palpate the bitch to find out if she is pregnant, but it is impossible to determine accurate numbers in a large litter.

Ultrasound scanning can be done at around four weeks. Most vets will not tell you how many puppies the bitch is carrying; however, dog-scanning professionals operate in most regions, at usually half the price of a vet scan, and they will quickly tell you whether she is expecting two or ten puppies – though they usually stop count-

RECORD KEEPING

Record keeping is essential in breeding matters, and in case the stud dog owner does not have one, you should take with you the KC litter registration form: Form 1, known as 'the green form'. Once the mating is complete and you have paid for the stud dog's service, the stud dog owner should sign the form as proof that the mating took place, and that you have their permission to register puppies by the dog. Whether or not you register your litter online, you should always obtain a signed green form. You may also be asked to sign a stud dog owner's contract.

Do not expect to receive the signed green form until you have paid for the stud services.

ing at over eleven, as the puppies are too tightly packed for accurate definition on the ultrasound. Sexing is not possible.

Gender distribution is as follows:

X = female chromosome
Y = male chromosome
XX = female pup
XY = male pup

The male contributes X and Y, and the female contributes X and X. The male makes equal amounts of X and Y sperm. Once inseminated, it is purely down to chance which of the Y sperm find an X to make a male, and which of the X sperm find an X to make a female.

The bitch does not have a single womb, but has two uterine horns (tubes). After conception the embryos implant at spaces along the tubes where individual placentas form to support each puppy.

CARE OF THE PREGNANT BITCH

Although it is tempting to wrap a pregnant bitch in cotton wool and confine her to lead walks only, it is important that she still runs and keeps fit so as to maintain deep and supportive core muscles. However, you should stop other dogs 'playing rough' around her, particularly around day sixteen of gestation when the embryos are implanting in the uterus and developing their individual foetal sac. We will cycle for a few miles and our bitches trot alongside us, up until the fifth or sixth week of pregnancy; they will indicate when they want to start slowing down.

Feeding the pregnant bitch depends on how many puppies she is carrying, which is why a scan is useful. A couple of weeks after mating, bitches usually become ravenous for food, even stealing and begging. Resisting this emotional onslaught is unbearable, but we must, because the tiny embryos make no nutritional demands on her body until they are at least five weeks, so at this stage we would be over-feeding her. Fit bitches usually whelp quickly and efficiently, delivering strong, healthy puppies. Overweight bitches take ages to push puppies out due to low muscle tone. You pay a large bill for a caesarean, which is why you should resist her pleading eyes in those early weeks. To stave off hunger pangs give her fresh carrots or similar to chew.

At week six – the beginning of the third trimester, and final stage of gestation – the cartilage in

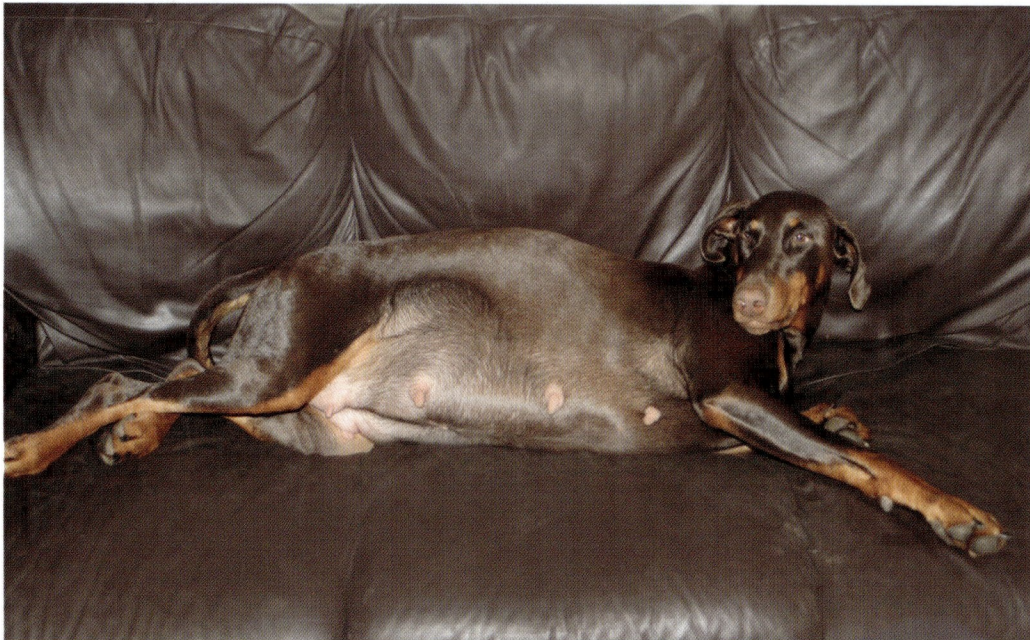

A heavily pregnant bitch relaxing after an hour of normal road walking and free-running exercise. Bitches naturally slow down and indicate how much exercise they can do.

ADDITIONAL FACTS

- Less than 30 per cent of foetal development occurs in the first four or five weeks, with three-quarters of growth occurring in the final third of gestation
- The average bitch will gain anywhere from 15–25 per cent of her pre-breeding weight prior to whelping (Burger, 1993)
- Energy requirements for pregnant bitches are between 30–60 per cent of her pre-breeding requirements, depending on the litter size (Romsos *et al*, 1981; Debraekeleer *et al*, 2010)
- Bitches may have morning sickness and go off their food for a short time

the foetus starts to mineralize and solidify into its skeletal formation. The nutritional demands on the bitch now increase, so the volume and quality of her food must be adjusted accordingly. Although under-nutrition of a pregnant bitch will not lead to conformational abnormalities in the puppies, it can result in low birth and brain weights.

Never feed calcium supplement during pregnancy, as this predisposes the bitch to primary uterine inertia (*see* Potential Whelping Problems below), where the suppression of the parathyroid gland inhibits the mobilization of calcium at whelping time – there is so much calcium already present that there is no signal to produce extra calcium when it is needed.

With a good quality kibble there is no need to change or supplement the bitch's diet until the sixth week of pregnancy. From six weeks introduce a couple of ounces of puppy food per meal. Don't change her entirely on to puppy food as this would be unnecessarily high in protein; equally a high volume of food is unwise as it encourages premature mammary development and she will risk developing mastitis. She will then need antibiotics to fight infection before the pups are even born.

If you feed a natural raw (BARF) diet, it is probably quite broad-based already. With a basic raw diet such beef/lamb/tripe, start to include high protein foods such as eggs, chicken and fish. The bitch needs nutritional bone from, say, a chicken carcass, but if she is carrying a big litter she may struggle with the volume, so split the carcass over a couple of meals, or feed the bone pre-ground. Don't feed heavy recreational bones in late pregnancy with a big litter as her digestive organs are already squashed and she can become constipated.

By nine weeks she should be having around 50 per cent extra food on top of her normal pre-pregnancy intake. If she is carrying a big litter, this should be split into three or four meals as she won't be able to fit in her required nutrition over just two meals.

There is no graph or chart to consult, as every litter is different, but her poo consistency and mammary development will give you an idea of how she is doing.

WORMS AND WORMING BEFORE AND DURING PREGNANCY

Puppies only have roundworms, which they acquire directly from the bitch; they do not acquire tapeworms or other worms as pups. It is estimated that 70 per cent of puppies are already infected with roundworm at time of birth. Roundworms mature rapidly and rob nutrition from the pup, so a good worming regime for dam and pups is vital, as a heavy worm burden can be fatal if not treated.

Roundworm larvae go through the cycle of development within the host. Larvae that have been dormant in the bitch reactivate when the bitch becomes pregnant, and migrate through the placenta to the lungs of the fetal pups. When the puppies are born, the puppies cough up the larvae and swallow them, hence their migration to the intestines. Additional worm transfer comes via the milk when they are suckling.

Only specific wormers are licensed for use in pregnant bitches, so take veterinary advice on a safe product. Different drug companies vary in the ages at which their worming products should be used, but worming of puppies is generally done at around at two to three weeks, then at five, eight and twelve weeks of age, and then monthly until they are six months old. Most breeders worm the bitch routinely, and then worm in conjunction with the puppies until they are weaned.

VACCINATION OF THE DAM AND IMMUNITY OF THE PUPPIES

For puppies to acquire immunity from canine diseases they must acquire antibody protection; from the dam this is called 'passive immunity' or 'maternally derived antibodies'. If the bitch is up to date with her vaccines, she will not necessarily require a 'booster' to increase her levels of antibodies. Vaccinating suppresses the immune system and she needs to go into pregnancy as healthy as possible. If the breeder realizes after mating that the bitch is 'overdue' vaccinations, it is unlikely to cause a problem. Vaccinations are now known to last a great deal longer than previously claimed, and although some (killed adjuvant) vaccines are licensed for use in expectant bitches, few breeders or vets would vaccinate a pregnant bitch. (Read more on vaccinating puppies in Chapter 9, General Health and Welfare.)

WHELPING

The bitch's due date is normally sixty-three days from the date of conception, but puppies can be safely born a week early, as their lungs are fully developed by then. Pregnancy should not exceed sixty-three days, which is why progesterone testing with a qualitative test is so important, so you know exactly when ovulation took place.

Ensure in advance that your vet will come out, and what their out-of-hours terms are, because if your bitch is in trouble you will not want to be arguing with an on-call vet, or trying to find a late night emergency vet.

You will need to have the following equipment ready in preparation for whelping:

- High-sided whelping box, twice the size of the bitch, so a 3 × 4ft box for a large litter. The sides should be 2ft high. Ideally whelping boxes are made of PVC: wooden boxes are difficult to clean so must be binned after use. We use high-sided fencing around three sides with a canopy/tent to maintain temperature and exclude draughts. Provide a small lip to keep the puppies in, but which allows the dam to jump in and out easily herself
- A raised bed in the room, where she can rest without being mobbed for milk
- Portable adjustable radiator
- Room thermometer; wall chart thermometers are available online
- Thermometer: take the bitch's temperature morning and evening for advance notice of whelping
- A large rubber sheet for the room floor and under the whelping box to prevent fluids leaking through
- New and washed vetbed, a non-slip rubber-backed one and a plain-backed one. Vetbed has a one-way barrier so moisture and urine pass through, leaving the top layer dry for the animal to lie on
- Towels and old sheets for absorbency and scratching up
- New and washed face-flannel cloths for holding on to slippery newborns
- Calcium – liquid calcium (for its fast absorption rate) with vitamin D to aid the absorption of the calcium
- Puppy milk. Avoid the brands (even the expensive ones) with high salt and sugar contents. Also colostrum replacer
- 1ml syringes and latex (make-up) sponges for supplementing puppy milk
- Scissors, surgically clean, for cutting the umbilical cord if necessary
- Surgical spirit or sterilizing wipes for cleaning the scissors between each whelp

• PAPER PEN & STOP WATCH

- Dopram V for reviving weak/not-breathing puppies
- Surgical latex gloves in case puppy is stuck and you need to feel inside
- Note-pad and pen for noting contractions, birth times and placenta
- Vet telephone number – and secondary vet number in case of emergency
- An experienced breeder friend on standby to come and help you

The Whelping Box
Set the box up somewhere private, quiet and warm, never in a thoroughfare or where other dogs can access. The bitch must be able to relax in the knowledge that no other dogs or strangers will come near. A spare bedroom is private, and the temperature is easy to maintain. A conservatory is unsuitable for newborns as the temperature fluctuates widely.

A few days before the bitch is due, encourage her to get accustomed to her box. She may consider it a dark cave at first, and may not like it, so pull any top covers back. Don't push her or force her in, or she won't feel safe to have her pups there.

We use two pieces of vetbed, one with the ribbed rubber backing underneath, then another one on top for padding. Give the bitch towels to pull, tear and dig into when she's whelping.

Temperature
The temperature of the room and that of the puppies is critical, as newborn puppies have

Whelping box with a low lip at the front. Remove this by the time the puppies are two weeks old, so they can come out to defecate outside the box. A cover over the box (in this case made from a stretchy sofa cover) maintains warmth and humidity in the box and gives it a den-like feel. In winter it could be covered over at the front as well to keep out draughts. After a week or so she will want to rest from suckling, but still stay close to her pups, so make her a bed outside the box.

immature shivering and panting responses and can't regulate their own body temperatures. Maintaining a normal body temperature (96–97°F) during the first three weeks of life has to be done for them.

Pre-warm the whelping room to around 90°F to receive the puppies. Newborns need to be dried promptly and kept warm or they quickly lose the energy to suckle, and any fluid on the lungs quickly develops to pneumonia.

Stifling heat causes dehydration and is as dangerous as puppies getting too cold. Bitches can overheat when they have to lie under a heat lamp to suckle the pups; a portable radiator in the room keeps a more ambient temperature. Heat pads must be made specifically for animals. If the pups are spread around the box, it is too hot; if they are all curled in a heap, they are too cool.

With your whelping room set up, the waiting begins. Whilst there are indicators of pending labour at this stage, there are many different scenarios that can occur.

TIMELINE OF LABOUR

Clear or slightly opaque mucus some days before whelping is due is normal, but if it is discoloured or smells bad, take the bitch to the vet promptly as it could indicate an infection or a dead puppy.

Take her temperature regularly before her due date, as twenty-four to forty-eight hours before whelping, her progesterone levels drop and correspondingly her temperature drops from 37.7°C to 36.6°C (101.5°F to 98°F). The vulva, which has remained large and soft throughout pregnancy, will lose any firmness and become even softer, almost like a small bag of water, when whelping is imminent. As her pelvis expands you may see all, or just some, of the following indications that whelping is imminent:

Stage 1:
- Her belly will become rock solid
- She will groom herself
- Her eyes may stare and show some pain – the pupils will dilate

The bitch's temperature will drop twenty-four to forty-eight hours before whelping.

- She may refuse to eat
- She will have frequent poos and wees, straining to 'clear out' loose motions

Stage 2, pre-labour:
As she comes closer to delivery she may display the following behaviour:

- Digging
- Shivering
- Panting
- Staring at her rear end
- Licking her vulva and belly excessively
- Mild uterine contractions

The time lapse between the start of the first mild contractions to the first puppy being born can be around two hours, but as long as she is not having very strong contractions without producing anything during this time, you can relax with her. Note the times and strength of the contractions. There will be periods of both activity and sleeping.

The contractions will become progressively stronger and more frequent. Rub her lower back gently to provide some pain relief, and hold the sheet down for her to tear to help her cope with the contractions. Shortly before the first pup is born, you will see a shiny dark bubble emerge, which at first you will think is a puppy's head. This allantoic sac is full of amniotic fluid to lubricate the birth canal, and indicates the start of labour proper.

Stage 3, labour:
When the puppies are ready to be born the bitch will go into labour:

- Contractions will be stronger and more frequent

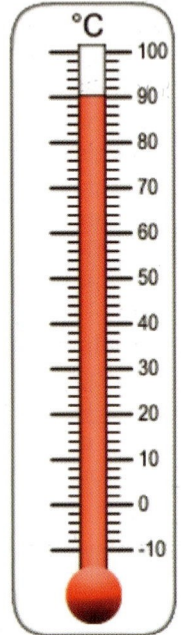

PRINT PAGE

- She will stand or sit up as if she is defecating
- She will be shivering
- Her waters will break
- She will grunt and push along with the contractions
- Finally the puppy arrives

The bitch is usually quite capable of whelping by herself, but with a large puppy half in and half out of the vulva, you can help her deliver it: hold the puppy with a clean, soft cloth and gently ease the puppy down towards the bitch's belly, not upwards. Your hold should be gentle, and should go along with the bitch's own contractions. Do not pull against her for fear of tearing or rupturing her – and absolutely *never* pull a puppy by the legs or tail. Horror stories exist about limbs being broken or tails being pulled off.

If the puppy is past the pelvis it will soon be born, and a few deep pushes from the bitch will finally push it out.

Once the pup slides out, give the dam a chance to break the sac; however, if it is her first litter she may not know what to do, so you could tear the sac at the puppy's head with your fingernails. Using a clean dry cloth, promptly wipe the mucus from the puppy's mouth, holding him face down. Rub him vigorously between hand towels to encourage the first breath. The dam usually tries to quickly eat the placenta and umbilical cord, so to stop her biting too deeply and causing a small umbilical hernia, squeeze the cord tightly between your fingers about 1–1.5in away from the belly. The remaining cord and stump will wither away by the following day.

If he has come out of his sac within the bitch, he may be congested, with a rattling chest indicating fluid on his lungs. It is vital that the airway is clear, as this can easily progress to fatal pneumonia. Gently turn him up (to the standing position) to enlarge the lungs, then tip his head down. Hold his body supporting his head and neck, then *gently* swing him head down between your knees: there should be no 'G force' pressure on his body, so do not swing hard, and never by holding the hind legs. Clear any expelled fluid from his nose and mouth, and keep rubbing him frequently to encourage a big gasp and a healthy

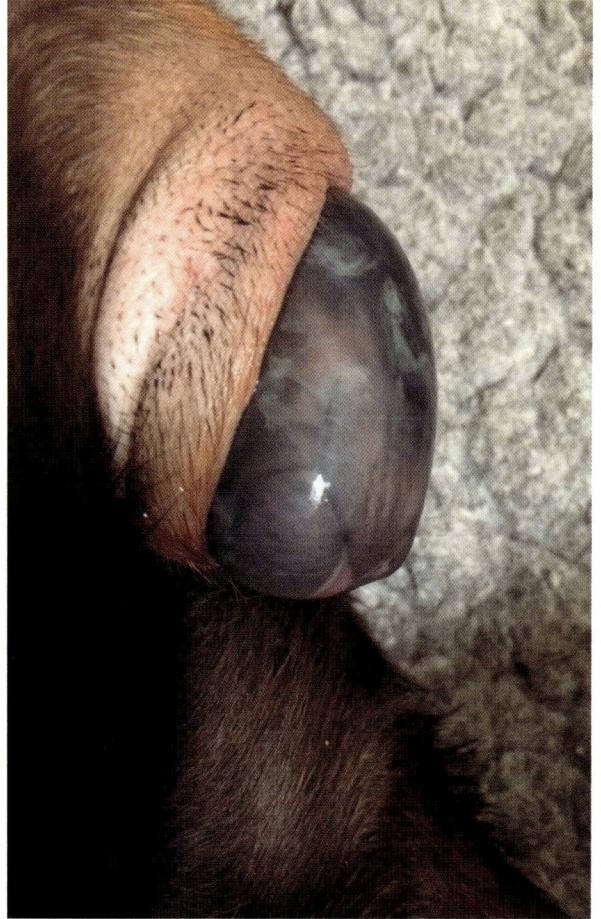

A normal presentation: a puppy coming head first still within the sac. CARL WESTFIELD

Placenta (the afterbirth). A highly valuable, nutrient-rich protein for the bitch to eat.

cry. Let him recover from the ordeal of his birth before expecting him to feed, but monitor him closely and keep him very warm.

A dark or green discharge before a pup arrives indicates that the placenta has detached from the uterine wall, so it is vital that the puppy is born quickly as it will be deprived of oxygen. A yellow discharge before a puppy is born indicates that the amniotic sac has broken, and the puppy needs to be born within thirty minutes of this happening if he is to survive.

DELIVERY OF THE PUPPIES

Although there is no specific time period between puppies, maiden bitches whelp at an average of thirty minutes between pups, and mature bitches average forty minutes. A bitch in weak muscular condition whelps at average intervals of sixty minutes, which is why she should be in prime condition before pregnancy to give both dam and puppies a better chance of survival.

Contractions for the next puppy may begin almost immediately following the last puppy, or up to three hours later. If the bitch is relaxed, help the first puppy on to the teat and ensure he feeds well. Most puppies crawl to the teat and suckle vigorously, but don't worry if a puppy is slower to suckle, especially if he has endured a long, slow labour.

If the bitch is sleeping calmly after producing puppies, don't wake her to try and get things going: she will wake up naturally when the next contractions start coming, and will have regained energy with a good sleep. If she has continued contractions with no visible puppy, try a walk to the garden (move her puppies to the other side of the box to make her get up), an Oxytocin injection, and/or some oral liquid calcium. If that still doesn't produce a puppy, consult a vet or breeding professional.

Contractions begin when the puppy is detached and is being pushed down the uterine horn, therefore the longer contractions go on with no puppy being produced, the more likely it is that the pup is no longer moving or will be in trouble when it comes out.

Oxytocin is a naturally occurring hormone in mammals stimulating uterine contractions and increasing maternal bonding and milk production. It is produced from puppies suckling, or via an injectable liquid drug from vets. VET ONLY

If the bitch is tired or weak after a long labour, injected Oxytocin may be used to expel retained puppies or placentas. The effects are very rapid, and puppies are often born soon after administration. Vets never allow inexperienced owners to administer Oxytocin as it is very dangerous if given incorrectly. If administered before the cervix is fully open, the puppies will be pushed down the uterus, can't exit and will be killed – probably along with the bitch; and too much may result in premature placenta detachment causing stillborn puppies.

An alternative is 'feathering', which stimulates deep uterine contractions. With a sterile glove, insert a finger inside the bitch's vagina and curl back around inside her pointing up towards the tail. When you very lightly stroke or massage the roof of the vagina you will feel how this stimulates deep contractions. As with Oxytocin this must never be done until the cervix is fully open.

Note the time of each event: contractions (deep or shallow), puppy born, gender, colour and weight and if a placenta was expelled. You will be so busy caring for the dam and newborns that you won't remember such potentially important details unless you log them.

Bitches rarely eat at the start of whelping, but as labour progresses, she may appreciate some water and/or puppy formula with an addition of liquid calcium. This is an easily absorbed energy boost. During a long whelping you could offer her some easily digestible food such as slightly cooked chicken or scrambled eggs, though she will probably decline it. If she has eaten many placentas she won't need it, and food isn't at the top of the agenda when giving birth.

It is not uncommon for the breeder to presume the bitch has finished, and to find an extra puppy in the nest in the morning.

POTENTIAL WHELPING PROBLEMS

The Dobermann tends to have few complications in pregnancy, but this section describes potential whelping problems, and how to deal with them.

Malpresentations

Malpresentations occur when a puppy is in the birth canal but is twisted in some way. Using a surgical glove, feel inside the bitch to find if there is a puppy at the rim of the pelvis. You may be able to feel the pads or nails with your fingers, and work out what is where. By hooking a finger around where he is stuck and turning his position, you may be able to help ease him out. If you can't feel anything, assume he is still in the birth canal and is on his way. Mal- presentations rarely correct themselves, so if he is stuck there don't waste time and effort.

Never use Oxytocin in this situation because pressure from above will force the puppy against the pelvic rim. Encourage the bitch to sit up, and to go outside for a wee to shift the puppy's position. If that doesn't work and despite the bitch continuing hard contractions, phone the vet for help, as time is tight, especially with breech births, and a caesarean may be needed. However, many breeders have been on their way to the vet to hear the cry of a healthy puppy being born on the back seat.

Uterine Inertia

Inertia means lack of motion, action or inactivity. The two main causes of uterine inertia are primary inertia, which can occur despite a temperature/progesterone drop, but when low Oxytocin levels do not initiate labour; and secondary inertia, which occurs where puppies are already born, but labour stops for no apparent reason with more puppies still inside.

Sometimes in very large litters the surround-

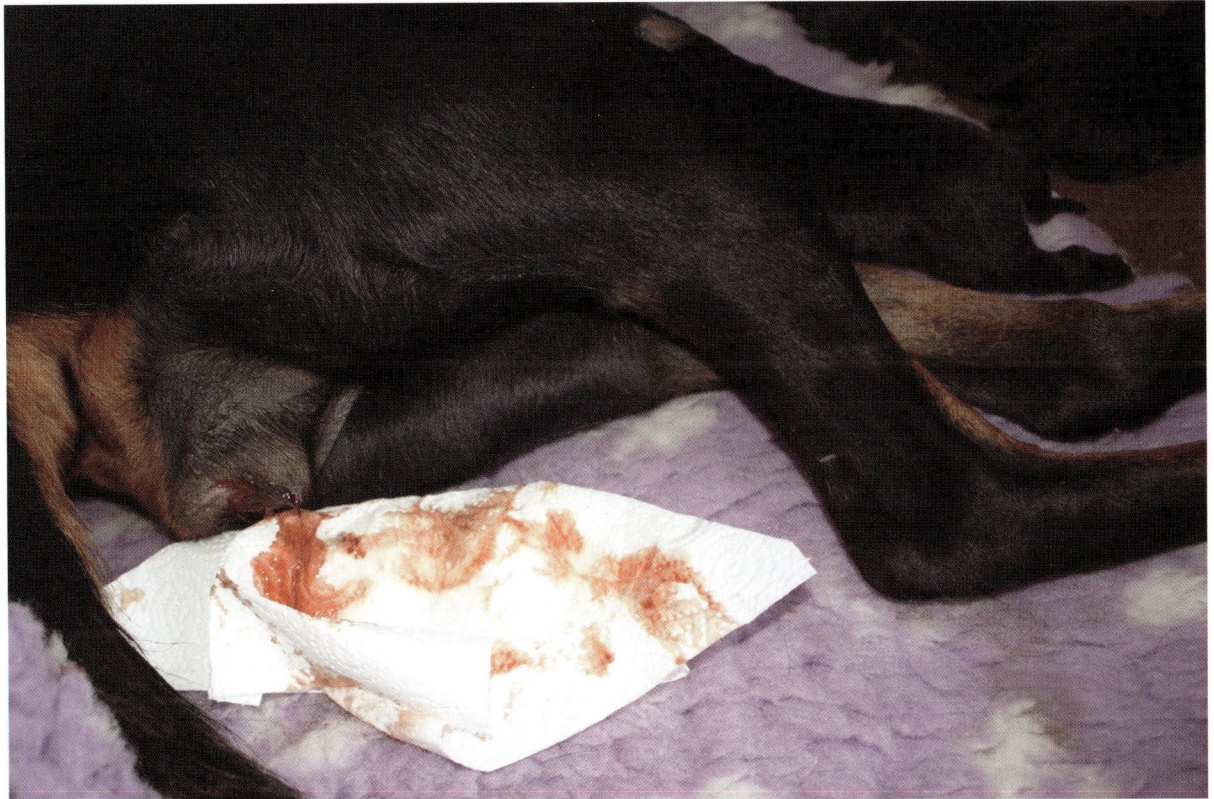

Bitches normally discharge heavily after whelping, and even up to twelve weeks following a large litter. Even with all placentas expelled, there will still be debris that needs to come out. Place tissue under her to monitor the colour. If it smells bad, she will need antibiotics.

ing muscles of the uterus are so stretched and expanded that they can't contract. If a bitch had inertia on a previous litter, she may well develop it on subsequent litters.

Immediate veterinary attention for a caesarean is necessary.

Retained Placentas

In a healthy dam a retained placenta will generally break down and be discharged of its own accord. If you are seeing a vet after a bitch has whelped her litter, have the important information they may need, such as the number of retained placentas and the times of the births.

Discharge

A discharge of a medium dark colour after whelping is normal, and the dam will usually have strands of discharge in her urine. If the discharge smells at all, you must take her to the vet promp-tly in case she has an infection – *see* Pyometra.

Pyometra

Pyometra is a potentially deadly infection of the uterus caused by trapped bacteria following a season, or from a retained placenta, or a dead puppy. Signs are high temperature, excessive thirst, sickness, diarrhoea, depression, and loss of appetite. With 'open' pyometra, where the infection is able to come out, there will be a foul smelly discharge.

The dam will urgently need antibiotics, and born pups may also become sick from any toxins that have seeped into the bloodstream and then into the milk. The bitch will die if not treated

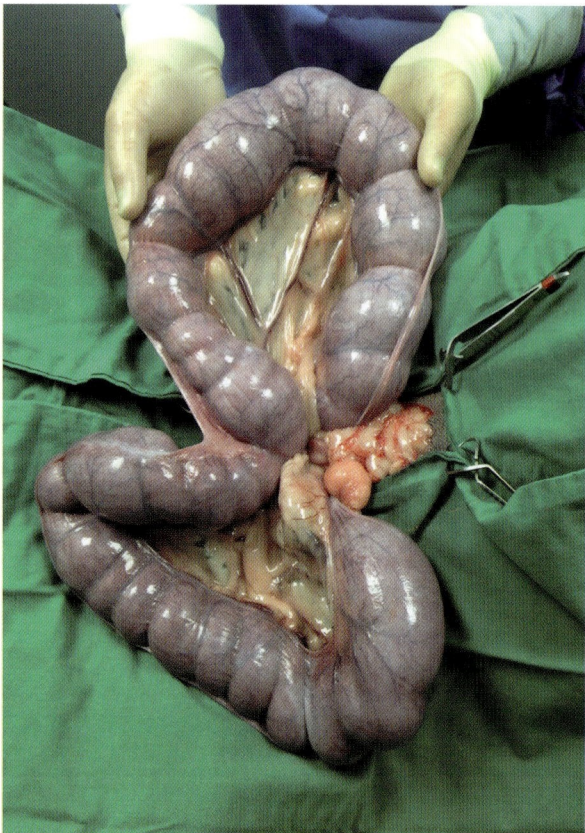

Uterine horns full of pus. Pyometra at this level will usually kill the bitch when the toxins leak into the bloodstream.

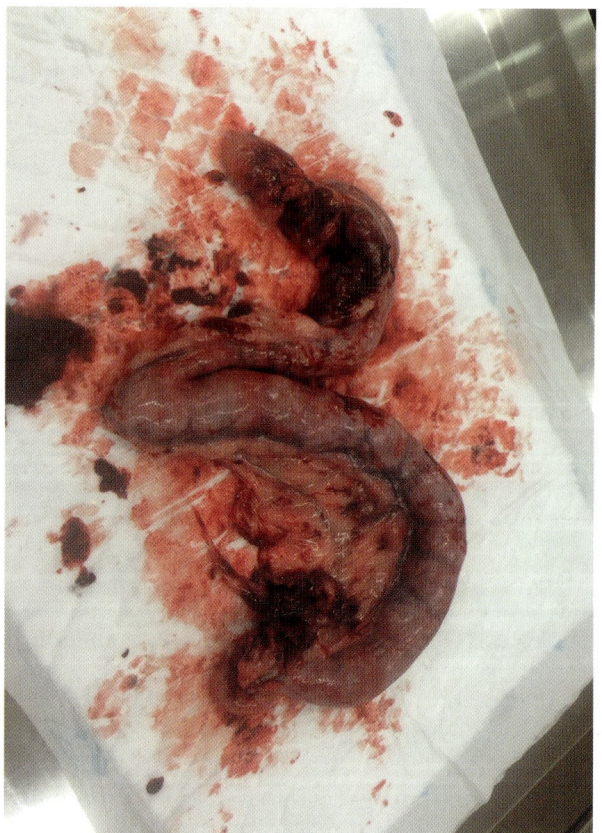

A pyometra that had already broken down the uterus. PAUL LEWCOCK, BLENHEIM VETS

immediately by surgery to clear and flush out the uterus. If she is pregnant she will inevitably lose the litter.

Mastitis

Mastitis is severe inflammation and infection of the breast, which can kill the bitch if untreated. It usually occurs when the dam has excess milk and the puppies are not drawing off a particular teat, which then engorges with milk. It starts as a hot, hard and lumpy breast with milk backing up into folds. The teat becomes blocked and infection sets in, with pus literally bursting out of the side of the breast, creating a large cavity.

Breast examinations are vital for the lactating bitch. If you feel any heat or hardness, hot towels will ease the pain, but most important is to get antibiotics for her promptly. Cut back immediately on highly nutritious foods to give the milk a chance to diminish slightly. If the puppies have been suckling on the teat they may have diarrhoea and cramps, and they, too, may need antibiotics. Prevent them from suckling on the affected teat until it is cleared.

Mastitis occurs less as the puppies grow older and draw off greater volumes of milk. Be careful what you feed the bitch: there is a fine balance between feeding for sufficient good quality milk, and making the milk supply too copious.

Caesarean (C-Section)

For any bitch, especially a first-time dam, it can be alarming to wake up to find puppies around her belly, and she may reject them. Some things can make a big difference to how well she accepts her puppies. Ideally she needs to go through all the routine behaviours of licking and cleaning herself in preparation for puppies, as this stimulates the production in her body of endorphins (the 'feel-good' hormone) and Oxytocin.

Her clean vulva also means that there are none of the natural birthing smells to stimulate her. Tell the vets not to dispose of the placentas but to keep them in plastic bags. Before she comes around, rub the placentas around her hind legs, vulva, and the puppies, strategically placing a pup next to a placenta, so when she goes to lick herself she will find the placenta – which hopefully she will eat, and will miraculously find a 'new-born' puppy there.

Eclampsia (Milk Fever)

Eclampsia can happen before whelping, though it more often appears in the first three weeks after delivery. It is caused by a drop in calcium levels, usually following too high a dose of supplemented calcium. Symptoms include glassy eyes, nervousness, whining, muscle twitching, fast heartbeat and shivering.

Critical Puppies

Around 70 per cent of apparently stillbirth puppies are actually born alive, but are so anoxic they die straightaway. This is mainly because the whelping takes too long, and the placenta detaches prematurely, resulting in a lack of oxygen. These puppies are floppy in comparison to a live and kicking newborn, and rarely revive, but where there is a tiny heartbeat, however slow and weak, you may have a chance to help the puppy survive if you act quickly.

If the puppy doesn't take his first gasp when the sack and mucus have been cleared from his head and mouth, support his head, place him between two hand-towels, and rub him vigorously. If taking the puppy away distresses the dam, work on him in the box at her level, or distract her and take him out of the room. If he is not gasping for breath the problem will be his low or lack of heartbeat, so you must stimulate him to get the heart going, and breathe for him. To do this, put your mouth over his nose and mouth, making sure his body, head and neck are well extended in order to have a clear passage for the air to go in. Carefully and slowly blow just a small amount into the tiny lungs to slightly elevate the chest, as in normal breathing. Repeat this every five seconds, whilst still rubbing. With your fingers on each side of the tiny ribcage, very gently press together in rapid strokes.

Dealing with a dead puppy: This is upsetting for everyone, but your feelings are secondary to the bitch, who needs protecting from distress. Distract her whilst you take the pup away until you decide whether you will bury it or take it to the vet for them to dispose of.

A Tiny but Viable Puppy

Sometimes a tiny and apparently under-developed puppy is born. In a large litter, space is at a premium, and some embryos implant on the uterine wall where others may squash them, or perhaps at a place scarred from previous pregnancies, so the placenta struggles to provide sufficient nutrients.

Correct temperature is vital for survival, but whilst he must be kept warm, the temptation is

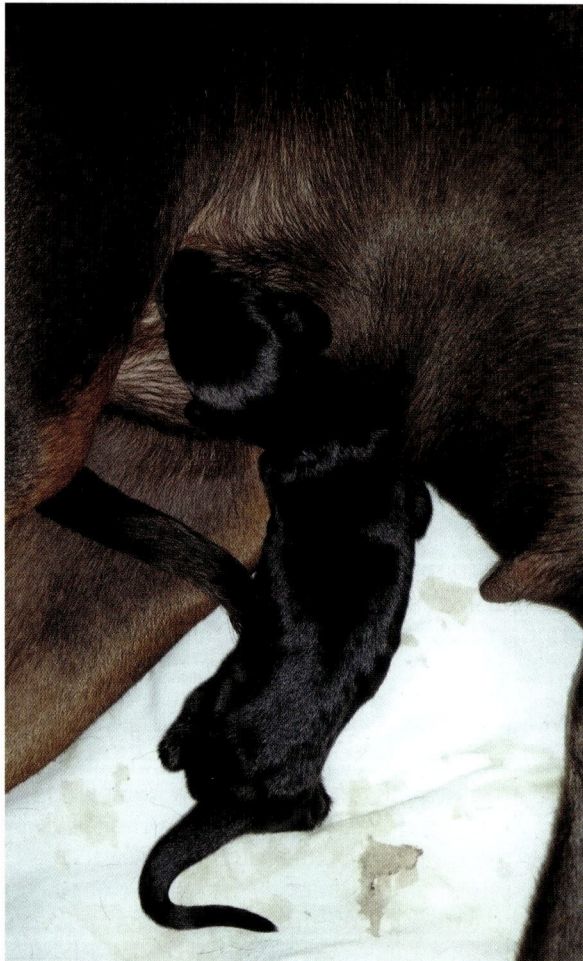

Despite intensive care from the breeder, these tiny puppies often die some days after birth. However, some do make it, and the key to survival is generally down to the first few hours of life.

to keep pups too hot. They then become dehydrated, which is as bad as being too cold. For a weak puppy who can't suckle and needs to be bottle fed, express some of the first colostrum milk from the dam to support his immune system, and top him up with formula. Seek professional help regarding keeping the puppy going.

AFTER DELIVERY

When whelping has ended and the bitch is clear inside, she will finally relax and sleep deeply. If the bitch was scanned by an experienced operator who detected seven puppies you can be fairly confident that she will have finished after seven have been born; otherwise you can only rely on gut instinct to determine whether she has finished or not.

The dam may continue to dig, experience contractions and pant after whelping to eliminate placenta debris. Light contractions may be expected for a day or so, but straining with deep contractions may indicate a retained puppy or larger debris, so consult the vet. Continue to take her temperature regularly. It will be a little high anyway due to the warmth of the room and the pups around her.

The dam may 'hunch' around her new litter in her instinctive drive to protect them. This normal behaviour stops in a few days once she relaxes, but it makes it difficult for the puppies to get to her teats and feed from her, especially if she has been out to the garden and has rushed back to huddle tightly round them. They may start shrieking because she is rolling them around, which will only aggravate her unsettled state. She may also have stomach cramps, which will cause her to curl up even more. With a large litter, encourage her to stretch out and relax so you can bring out her teats, which will have been stuck underneath her, so that all the puppies can feed. Teach her this stretching 'exercise' before she whelps.

You may need to keep a close eye on the puppies if the new mother is digging up her bedding and scratching around to get comfortable or make a nest – they may get thrown around, or covered under the bedding and risk being trodden on. She may not realize she is lying on a puppy, but if you are nearby, with any luck you will hear its muffled cries, and will be able to move the bitch in time to save it. Experienced breeders sleep close to the whelping box for the first few days and nights to safeguard the puppies.

REARING

Now your puppies are safely on the ground it is important to monitor their temperature and feeding to ensure their steady development.

The Importance of Colostrum

Puppies need antibodies for immunity, which initially they acquire from the dam (this is known as passive immunity) through her first milk, or colostrum. Without colostrum puppies are vulnerable to infection and disease. Colostrum lines the gut with a protective layer, aiding gut development. It is packed with large antibody molecules (immunoglobulin), vitamins and nutrients. These antibody molecules are usually too large to pass through the puppy's intestinal wall to provide immune response ability in other areas of the body, but in the first few hours after birth the

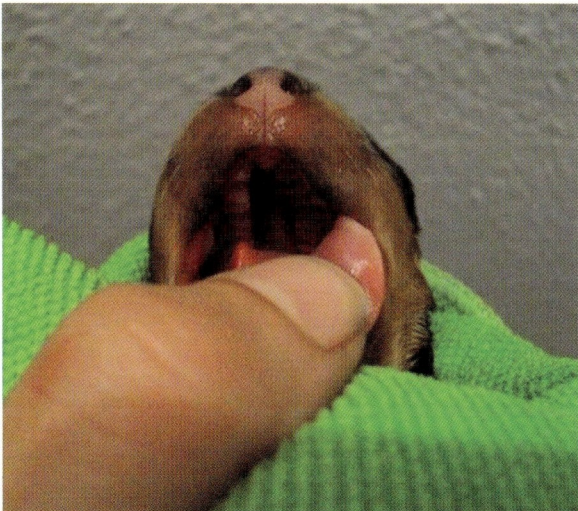

A cleft palate: the hole in the roof of the mouth can be seen. This prevents the puppy being able to latch on to the teat with any suction. Sadly there is no hope for this puppy, which must be put to sleep.
MARINE FREMY

gut is very porous to enable the large molecules to pass through the wall. 'Gut closure' begins just hours after birth, and colostrum is produced for only about twenty-four hours, so by the time the pups are twelve hours old there is very little absorption of immunoglobulin.

Colostrum also has a mild laxative effect to clear out the waste of dead blood cells. The first sticky puppy poo (meconium) is produced within a few hours of the puppy being born and suckling well.

It is important to check that each puppy has suckled to get a good level of passive immunity. However, just because puppies suckle vigorously doesn't necessarily mean they are receiving milk. The milk may not be fully let down, or the puppy could have a cleft palate (a hole in the roof of the mouth), so weigh each puppy at birth and monitor individual progress closely.

FADING PUPPY SYNDROME

Puppies may fade and die within a few days, or in the first weeks after birth. This terrible situation can be due to a variety of factors, but may be caused by the lungs not having cleared fully. During its descent down the birth canal the puppy is exposed to the normal viruses and bacteria that inhabit all healthy creatures. The umbilical cord and nasal/oral cavities provide ideal conditions in which bacteria can thrive, so whilst our whelping environment may be immaculately clean, we can never completely shield the puppy.

Puppies that have suckled plenty of valuable colostrum within twelve hours can usually fight off infection, but for a puppy with low antibody levels, just a small margin of the critical environmental conditions can result in death. Receiving colostrum late or not at all, and poor quality colostrum, are primary causes of neonatal deaths in newborns of all species.

Losing her puppies can be a terrible blow to the bitch, who will be desperately anxious when they are taken away. In this awful event it is recommended that once she has had time to assess that her puppies have died, you remove all puppy materials such as the whelping box and blankets, and keep her occupied by going on walks, playing with her, and generally trying to keep her mind off the loss of her pups.

The alternative option if she is full of milk and pining for her puppies, is that you could offer her as a surrogate mother for orphaned puppies. Most Dobermann bitches are wonderful dams and will accept other puppies as their own, though obviously great care needs to be taken, especially in the first forty-eight hours, that she does not reject and attack them. If she is a very kind and naturally maternal bitch, she could probably go happily to another breeder's home, or you may have the litter at your home.

There are some excellent online support groups, and also one on Facebook, that will rapidly swing into action to put owners of bitches in milk in contact with owners of orphaned puppies.

HAND REARING ORPHANED PUPPIES

A general rule of thumb is that a puppy needs to consume around 1ml of milk per oz of bodyweight every two to three hours. A new-born Dobermann puppy averages 1lb (16oz) in weight, which equals around 16ml of milk formula per meal. Feeding two to three hours day and night for two weeks is physically and mentally exhausting, but if puppies are to survive it is the only option. You should have a supply of quality replacement milk in the house ready for such an emergency, and should also be prepared for emergency hand rearing with tiny bottles and teats, and/or small syringes. A great method developed in recent years is the use of cosmetic sponges for puppies to suckle through (*see* online videos).

Puppies can't defecate and urinate on their own for their first two weeks of life, and stimulating them to do this is fundamental to their care. Using a piece of moist cotton wool or tissue, gently rub this over the anal and genital regions of the puppy to mimic the stimulation of the dam licking. Do this prior to, or during feeding, not after.

The temperature of the room and box is critical, as there is no dam for puppies to snuggle up to, and particularly for singleton puppies it is important that they have the regular stimula-

tion of being turned, rubbed and moved as they would be by their mother and siblings. It may be best to find a foster mother as soon as possible for the puppies.

RAISING THE LITTER TO EIGHT WEEKS

Post whelping care for the dam is essential. Continue to take her temperature for a week post whelping to monitor possible infection. Her temperature dropped before she went into labour and now it should have returned to normal at around 101°F. You can factor in a slightly higher temperature due to the heat in the room, but above 102°F is not normal and you must have her checked promptly by a vet.

In the past, many breeders would routinely give their bitches a course of penicillin after whelping, but this practice has generally fallen out of favour as vets try to limit the extent to which antibiotics are used routinely. Another practice was to give the dam a teaspoon of dark beer to stimulate milk production, as this is very rich in iron, and the dam will have used up her own iron supply during labour.

As a first-time breeder you will quite probably

The quick will only grow to the length of the nail, so it is good practice to cut the nails right back when the puppies are two to three days old: this will keep their nails short for life, and the puppies are too young to notice if you cut close to the quick. At this age the nails are very soft and will just flick off without you having to apply any pressure. Refer to Chapter 9, General Health and Welfare, for guidance on nail clipping.

have been alert and wakeful throughout the whole whelping process; this in itself will make you tired, and you may have been without sleep for as much as two or three days and nights. It is therefore essential that someone takes over from you to allow you to sleep, as nodding off even for five minutes could cost the life of a puppy.

For the first two weeks of their lives there is little you will need to do with the puppies except check their weight, make sure they are not too warm or too cold, change their bedding, and give their nails a very short trim in the first few days. If the litter is very large, split them for feeding, rotating them so that those that were the last to feed this time, are the first to feed next time.

In the first few days the room temperature should be around 90°F (32°C). For the second week it can be lowered to around 80–85°F (26°C–29°C), and from the fourth week and thereafter it can be lowered to around 75°F (23°C).

Don't wash the bedding with too much detergent as this can irritate soft baby skin. Add a few drops of germicidal solution for killing bugs on nappies, such as Napisan® or Milton®, and always give bedding an extra rinse cycle. Keep three or four pieces of vetbed so you have one in the box, one drying, and one or two clean and ready to use.

FEEDING THE DAM DURING/POST WHELPING

Each dam is different in their food requirements immediately post whelping; some will eat raven-

At around two to three weeks puppies need the freedom to explore their new space. With the front of the whelping box open, make sure they are not sleeping in a draught.

ously, while others may refuse food – but don't worry if she doesn't want to eat in the first couple of days as she will have eaten the puppies' placentas, which are nutritionally rich (her faeces will be very dark and tarry from this) and she won't need more food. A warm drink of puppy milk with honey and an egg beaten into it is usually welcome.

After whelping she can be given 50/50 adult food and puppy food. Her food needs to be higher than normal in all elements – fats, proteins and carbohydrates – and she will enjoy some puppy milk and fresh eggs as an energy boost. Her energy requirements increase following whelping and into lactation, peaking at approximately three to five weeks. At this point her food intake can be between two to four times the adult maintenance requirement (*ref.* Ontko and Phillips, 1958; Burger, 1993).

With a big litter, provide her with sufficient nutritious food four to five times a day so she can produce quality milk, but which is not too high in volume or protein – this will encourage a huge, cow-like udder, which could lead to mastitis or loose poos. Over-rich milk will also give the puppies colic, symptoms of which include crying and grumbling, and diarrhoea. Gentle rubbing and patting on the back, as with a baby, will soothe the pup. Reduce the protein in the bitch's diet immediately and increase carbohydrates. Keep an eye on the volume and consistency of poo from the dam and the puppies: if she has insufficient milk the poos of both dam and pups will be small and hard, indicating that she and the pups may be under-nourished. Large, foam-like poos indicate over-feeding.

For the first week she won't leave the box much, but as time goes by the puppies don't need her there permanently, and she must be able to escape when she doesn't want to feed them. Provide her with a bed or sofa just outside the pen so she can keep an eye on her pups without being hassled by them for milk.

At around eighteen days the puppies will start to come to the front of the box to wee and poo, and it is important that at this stage they are given more freedom – if they are kept shut in their nesting box they will have no choice but to pee and poo in there. This not only means dirty puppies and bedding, but they will habitually dirty their beds when they go to their new homes.

With the front panel of the puppy box down, pups will initially soil at the entrance of the box, but gradually they will soil further out. Use old sheets, towels or newspaper. Some breeders use wood shavings contained in a boxed area, as these quickly absorb moisture.

WEANING THE PUPPIES

Weaning should not be a fast process, but a gradual transition to solid food. Offer the puppies solids from nineteen to twenty-one days, or a few days earlier if the bitch has a large litter draining her of milk and energy. Feed puppies before they suckle, or they will fill up with mum's milk and ignore the solids. Some breeders feed kibble, some feed kibble and tripe mixed, and others feed just a raw diet.

Start with a few ounces of food between them. Soften kibble in a little water, mash it to a porridge, and serve with half a pint of hot puppy milk. The puppies will initially lap up the milk, then chew any solids that remain at the bottom. Slightly warmed tripe or minced beef can also be mixed with puppy milk if required. Let the dam in to clear up when they have finished.

Do not feed ordinary cow's milk. Dogs can't break down the enzymes in cow's milk and it isn't nutritious enough for them.

Just one meal a day for a couple of days is sufficient, then two meals a day. A week later meals may be up to ¾–1oz each per meal, plus the puppy milk. Increase this slowly if the puppies are still looking hungry for food, but cut back if their poos become loose. By four weeks they should be on four meals a day.

Puppies sometimes over-eat and sick up semi-digested milk, which looks like curd/cottage cheese. They usually perk up quickly once they have sicked it up. They can also get colic from over-eating, with a bloated hard tummy from trapped wind, and foamy diarrhoea. A tummy/back rub to wind them like a baby will ease their discomfort, and they are usually fine in twenty-

Older puppies may enjoy tearing a whole chicken carcass between them. Chicken wings may be gulped down whole, especially if puppy thinks the others will steal it. GEORGIE KUHL

four hours. If it continues, a vet may give an antibiotic injection just in case, a painkiller, and/or an anti-inflammatory injection.

Feeding the Dam during Weaning

Once the pups are on three meals a day, gradually decrease the dam's food intake to reduce milk production. The balance can be tricky because you need to keep weight and condition on her as she will be feeding them for around another week, but they are now getting their nutrition from solids and are just comfort suckling. She doesn't want to be hurt by the pups scrabbling for her teats, so if she is trying to avoid them when she goes in, don't chastise her for reprimanding older puppies if they try to suckle, and let her out. She won't hurt them, but they must learn respect for her and other dogs. A good

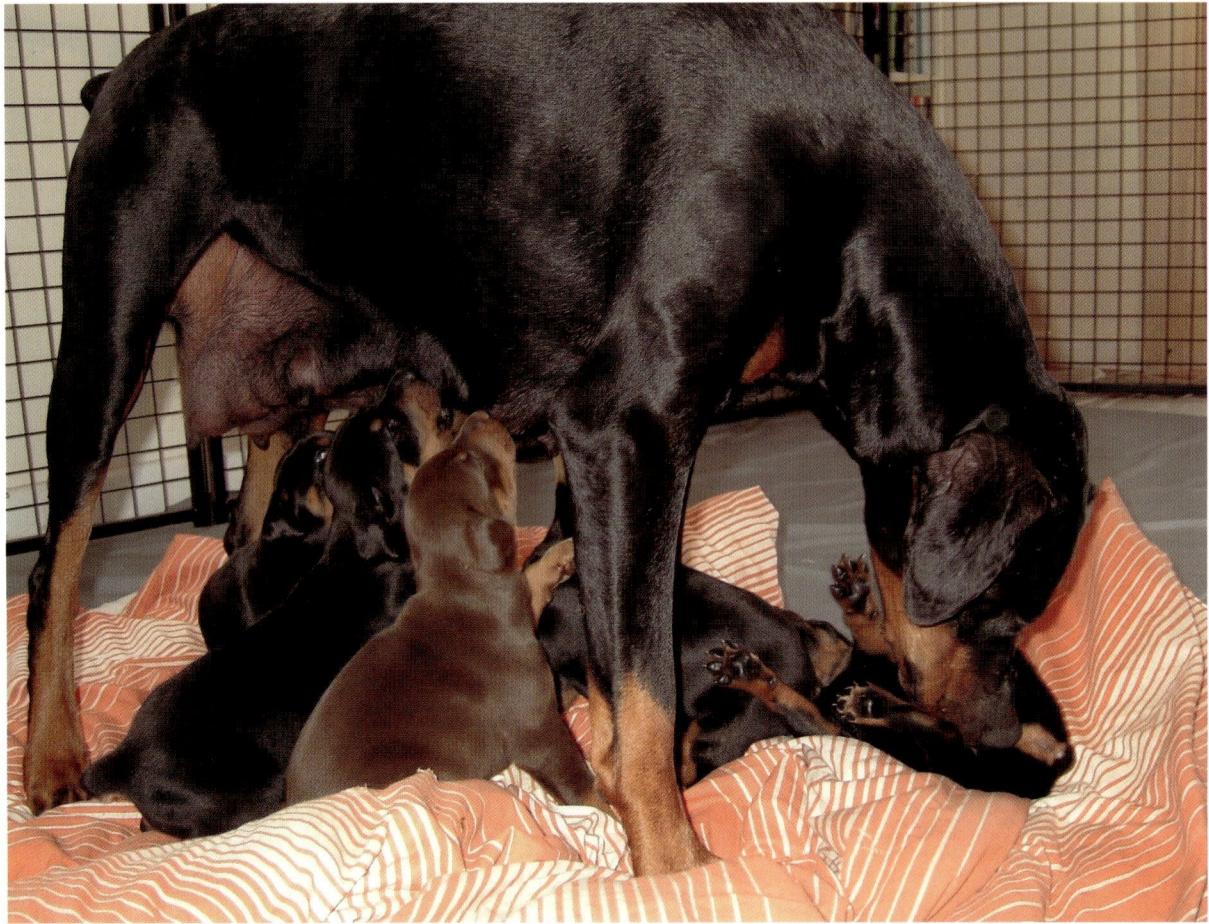

It is hard to get a bitch back in the show ring if her puppies keep drinking like this from her.

dam knows far better than you, how to correct her puppies.

If you plan to show her again, wean the puppies off by four to five weeks as they will pull her teats down, and no amount of hard work afterwards will get them back up. Most bitches dry up quite well after the first couple of full days away from their puppies, but you can use a prolactin inhibitor such as Galastop (no sneaky suckles from the pups!).

More maternal bitches still enjoy feeding their pups up to seven or eight weeks, and even continue to clean up after them for weeks, but most dams stop cleaning up after their puppies once they move on to solids.

From four to five weeks if the weather is good, puppies can start to go outside, which helps with early house training. As they wee outside, tell them 'do your business': this early conditioning stays with them, and the new owner will appreciate your efforts.

MEETING AND ASSESSING PUPPY BUYERS

Quality bred puppies whose parents are thoroughly health checked will always be in demand, and you will soon identify who is suitable as the owner of one of your puppies and who to decline. Try to meet prospective owners before

Older puppies can be fed in separate bowls. This feeding-bowl system is called the Weanafeeda. The partitions mean that each puppy gets a good and fair portion of food instead of having to fight for it, or eating too much, too fast.

your bitch has her puppies, so you can keep a provisional reservation list before they are born. If you do take a deposit at this stage, note that it is legally binding, and gives you no scope if you change your mind about someone.

No one should be allowed in the home before the puppies are three weeks of age, and this applies to friends, family or prospective buyers. Bitches with new-borns do not want anyone coming to visit their puppies, even just to peer round the door. It is disrespectful and unkind to a bitch, who needs security and privacy, to have to endure people coming to peer in at her puppies or touch them. Breeders who allow this care more about entertaining their friends than the welfare of their bitch.

After three weeks she will be more relaxed about her puppies, and will accept quiet visitors. Ensure they have not been to see any other litters that day, and that they remove shoes to minimize the risk of infection. Introduce the visitors to the dam in another room before you go to see the puppies. This allows her and you to get to know the visitors, and you can also see how the potential owners react to other adult Dobermanns. Young children may only visit the puppy room if they are well behaved and quiet. (If the parents can't control their children, they are unlikely to control their dog.) When the dam is comfortable with them, let her lead them in to see the pups. For tiny pups, limit the time of the visit: it is essential to have the best interests of the dam at heart, and not the buyers.

Entertaining puppies and humans. We are always wary of the visitors who sit on a chair and don't get down to interact with the puppies. Who doesn't want to cuddle puppies?

Never be embarrassed to ask even very direct questions, as it is your puppy's future you must be concerned with, not whether you upset someone by being personal. Informal chatting will reveal who will be home during the day with the dog, what sort of exercise they enjoy, what rooms he will have access to, their views on children and dogs together.

Good buyers want to be asked questions, as they appreciate the care and dedication you obviously show. Today's buyer is usually well informed and keen to ensure that their future pedigree puppy is free of inherited diseases. Health tests are now an important factor in the buyers' choice of breeder, and although future health is impossible to predict, the breeder should ensure that they are breeding from healthy dogs. In some Scandinavian countries, terms of sale are mandatory upon the breeder under consumer protection rights, and the purchase price of the dog must be refunded to the buyer if it is found to suffer from any genetic disease. This will inevitably occur at some stage in the UK, so all breeders should ensure they do not expose

REGISTERING THE LITTER

Applying to the Kennel Club for an affix ('kennel' name) may take some weeks to put in place, especially if your first few name choices are rejected, so you should submit your application to the Kennel Club before you mate your bitch.

You may register your litter using either the green Litter Registration Form 1 (see photograph above), or online by pre-registering for an online account with the Kennel Club. Note that you are still required to have the green form to confirm that the mating has taken place, and the stud fee has been paid.

The KC online registration system has various colour choices available. Although Dobermanns are commonly referred to as black and tan, the registration terminology is usually black and rust, brown and rust, and so on.

themselves to possible future litigation. Be open and prepared to show the health result documents to visitors so they know you have done your best to breed healthy dogs.

It is regrettable but necessary to safeguard your bitch and puppies from theft, as there are now many cases of whole litters and the dam being stolen, and puppies taken by thieves posing as buyers. If you are alone in the home and meeting potential buyers, ask a neighbour or friend to join you for company. If you are giving your home address to potential buyers, it is only fair to ask for theirs in return, and to check them out before they visit. The electoral roll proves that people live where they say they do, and Google Earth shows that the person who claims to live in a rose-covered cottage actually lives in a tower block. Be very careful what puppy information you put on social media, and who you and your family tell that you have puppies at home. Word can get round very fast, and not always in the right way.

SENDING PUPPIES TO THEIR NEW HOMES

It is a Kennel Club requirement that a buyer receives a pedigree and registration papers upon purchase, or as soon as possible. Breeders may place breeding endorsements R, and export endorsements X, on the registration documents of a puppy. Breeding endorsements may be applied to prevent the breeding of under-age animals or those without health testing.

An export endorsement does not stop the dog being taken abroad on holiday, but prevents him being registered with an overseas kennel club, so his value is negligible. Although it is rare for a UK Dobermann to be exported to the Far East, for example, it is not somewhere a good breeder would want their Dobe puppy to end up.

Both breeder and buyer should sign a written agreement regarding the terms of sale, and any endorsement. The breeder cannot then place endorsements and breeding terms post sale, and the buyer can't claim they weren't aware of the restrictions or terms of purchase. Contracts and breeding terms often become the subject of arbitration when breeder and buyer latterly disagree on terms. Without a clear written contract to show that the new buyer agreed to the endorsements, the Kennel Club cannot support the breeder.

From 1 April 2016 it became a legal requirement in the UK to micro-chip all dogs, both new puppies and existing dogs. Breeders are now required to be registered as the first owner.

Specific pet insurance companies offer breeders the facility to insure puppies free of charge for four to five weeks in the hope the new owner continues the policy with them.

Some breeders have a vet check and first

Vet check of the litter, and first vaccination at home.

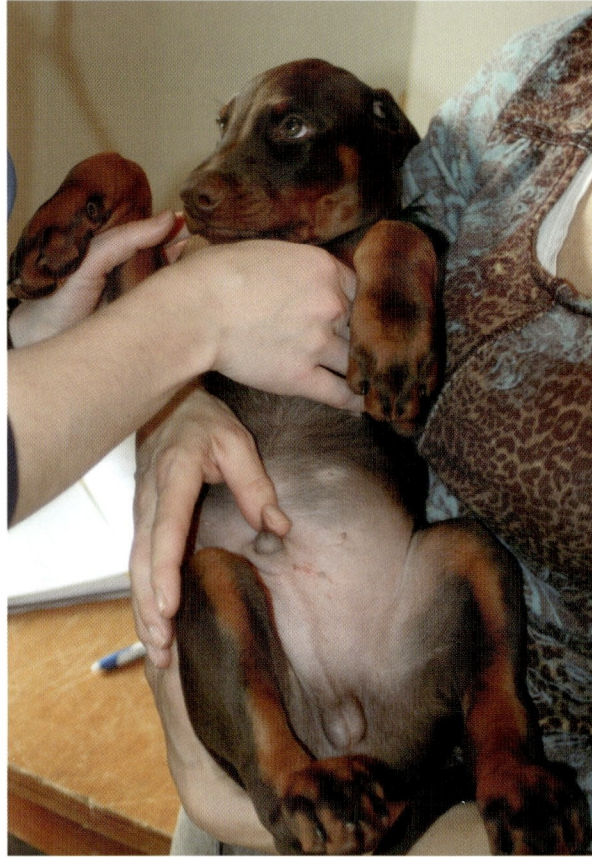

vaccination done before pups leave for their new homes.

Puppy Packs

Puppy packs vary greatly. Some breeders provide a well organized booklet with the microchip, registration, insurance documents, comfort blanket, feeding guide and food supply. Others supply just basic documentation. Puppies should go to their new homes with at least a small food supply to last them for about a week to avoid upsetting their stomachs, and to encourage new owners to stay on quality food. Having gone to the trouble to raise excellent puppies, don't let all that dedication be ruined by a bag of cheap supermarket food.

Keeping in touch with new owners is always rather unreliable, but at least you can let them know you are always there for support if needed, and to check the puppies are all thriving from the great start you gave them.

15 THE STUD DOG

As the owner of a stud dog it is just as incumbent on you to ensure that you are contributing responsibly to the Dobermann population as it is on the owner of a bitch. Allowing your dog to be used at stud is something that you should consider carefully, and if a good reputation is important to you, be careful which bitches come to your dog.

Checking out the owners of the bitch should be as important as if you were selling someone a puppy. You would ask similar questions: do they know what they are doing, are they in it just for the money, do they have a waiting list, and how/where do they plan to advertise the puppies? Whereabouts in the home will the bitch be whelping, and what health tests has she had? Her owners should bring her down for you to meet her (and them to meet you, of course) before she is due for mating so you can review her suitability. Don't expect 'Love Story' between the dog and bitch on any initial meeting: they will feel very differently about each other when she is in season.

You may be embarrassed to ask intrusive questions, but nothing is more heartbreaking than seeing filthy puppies sired by your dog, kept in a cold outdoor kennel, or being attacked by the dam because she has an unsound character and insufficient milk supply from lack of food. As no one wants to buy the skinny, wormy, fearful pups, they are eventually sold at a knock-down price to some awful puppy farmer who breeds from the bitches at one year old. Decline anyone who isn't completely open with you, and if you feel something isn't right, check them out further.

If progeny from your dog develop a health problem, terrible characters, or look awful, word very quickly gets out, and no matter how good your dog is, he will be blamed. It is unfair, but everyone forgets the bitch had 50 per cent input into the litter, so if you value your dog be fussy about whom you allow to use him, because he will be judged by his progeny.

PREPARATIONS FOR MATING

If you are taking money for stud services, be professional and do your research. Ask to accompany breeder friends to learn how matings are done so you can provide the very best service to visiting bitches, and be sure to treat both dog and bitch with the utmost respect.

New owners will need advice on progesterone testing to determine ovulation (see Breeding, Chapter 14). It is a waste of time for everyone if she is way off ovulating, especially if the owners have a long journey.

On their way to you, and before they arrive, ask the bitch owners not to stop to allow the bitch to wee, so that she will urinate in your yard. It will excite the dog greatly to smell her urine, and you can determine from that if she is ready for mating. Let her have a break to relax and get to know her surroundings before introducing her to the dog.

Novice bitch owners are often anxious about the mating process, and want a chance for the dogs to 'fall in love' with each other. In the wild, the dog would be expected to demonstrate to the bitch how fit he is, but visiting bitch owners with a long journey ahead may not have hours to watch foreplay.

Most dogs stand at stud at their own homes, especially for the first few matings until they become confident in their work. Some dogs are complete naturals and will mate anywhere.

Experienced breeders and stud dog owners who know how their dogs work, assess the bitch to determine whether she will be receptive, or is too overwhelmed by the attentions of the male to allow him near her. If she is nervous, let her play in a separate fenced area until she relaxes, and where on the other side of the fence, the proficient stud dog may flirt and flatter her until she accepts him. Some stud owners allow no foreplay at all, some allow a little. It is always nice to get a natural mating, but don't let the two exhaust themselves by running around, or put either at risk of being bitten.

A bitch that has ovulated and is ready for mating will usually be eager to mate. If she sits to avoid being mounted you can't be sure she is ready without having done a progesterone test.

As your dog becomes proficient as a stud dog, he will start to decline bitches who are not ready to be mated – that is, if she has not ovulated or has gone over. The novice dog may have a sniff and get excited but either doesn't know what to do, or humps her head or side. The experienced owner guides him gently, giving him time to learn to mount correctly.

After the bitch squeals and jumps around to make the dog prove himself, he stops to sniff her urine, and she may start to approach him. Soon after she can be held to allow him to mount her. The bitch should be held firmly to prevent injuries from her spinning around.

THE MATING PROCESS

When the two are ready to mate, the handler of the bitch stands by her head to stop her turning,

The bitch is enjoying the dog chasing her.

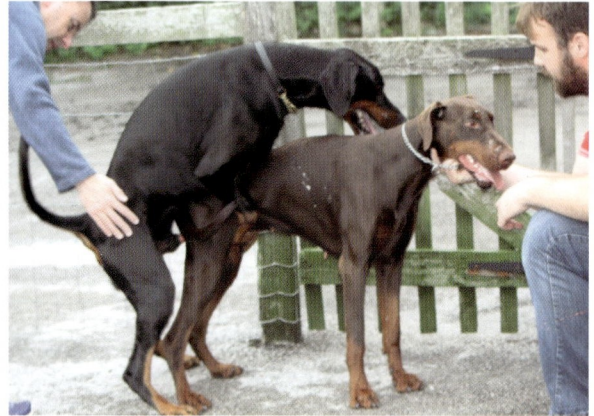

The owner of the bitch knows she is very receptive to the male, hence the light hold on her collar.

but avoids getting in the way of the dog mounting her. A height difference between them can make the mating a bit more difficult, but experienced dogs usually manage.

When the dog enters the bitch it is sometimes painful, especially for a maiden bitch, so be careful she doesn't whip round on him. He thrusts vigorously for a short time, and treads the ground.

After a few moments rest, he then turns himself or the handler will turn him.

One of his forelegs will come back over the bitch, and he will then put his front feet on the

Having entered the bitch, the dog now treads back and forth for a while until his bulbus glandis enlarges inside her to hold them together. He then stops moving.

ground on one side of her. The hind leg follows the direction he has turned in, and goes over her back to further tie them. As he turns, a bitch may find this uncomfortable so the handler should hold her firmly.

Take a note of the time, because a mating on the correct day often takes longer, and if you are doing two matings a couple of days apart, you will want to know on which day she may have conceived.

Once they are facing in opposite directions they will start to pull against each other. They don't have to be held rigidly together, and moving a little is natural, but avoid them turning right round

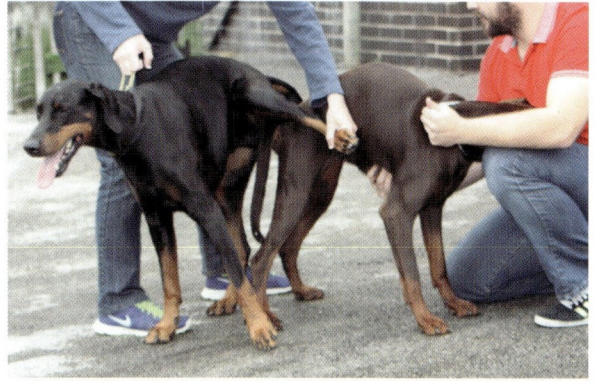

His hind leg now goes over her back; his penis is now turned 180 degrees.

The dog now stops treading and prepares to turn. Note his slumped forelegs no longer grasping hold of the bitch.

Now they are tied, and will remain like this until the bitch relaxes and the bulbus glandis reduces in size.

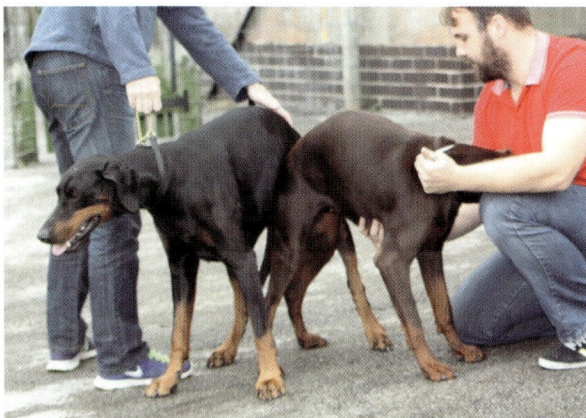

He now dismounts from the bitch, deciding himself which way he wants to turn, in this case clockwise

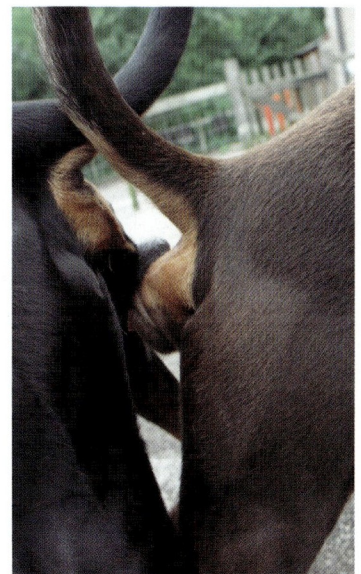

It can be seen how the dog's bulbus glandis is enlarged inside the bitch. His penis is turned back 180 degrees on himself, to lock them together.

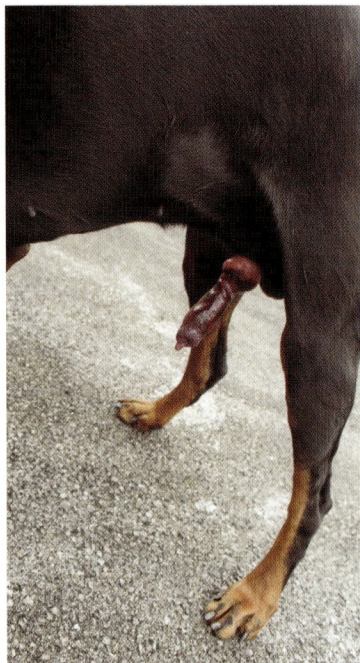

After mating the dog needs a few moments of quiet for his penis to withdraw into his sheath, so don't let the bitch bother him, and put him in a quiet place in the house. Keep the bitch walking around, and don't let her wee at this stage. She can then go back in the car where often she will be quite delighted with herself.

to sniff or lick each other. If the bitch has worn a muzzle for the mating (it must be a wide basket muzzle to allow her to pant openly), it may be removed once she relaxes, as long as the handler keeps a hold of her.

In a good mating, if you put your hand against the bitch's abdomen you can feel her abdominal muscles drawing the seminal fluid up into the vagina.

Refusal to Mate

The reasons for a stud dog refusing to mate are most obviously that the bitch has missed ovulation either way. Refusal on second mating may indicate that she has now gone over. Don't force the issue: they are telling you her season is finished, and she has started to close down.

An aggressive bitch can put off an inexperienced stud dog, so stud owners sometimes offer a free first mating to a steady experienced bitch to give their dog confidence.

If the dog and bitch live together, the dog is sometimes reluctant to mate her because of over familiarity, particularly if she is a strong 'dominant' bitch. If it is a mating you really want to happen, you may be better going to a local

reproduction specialist for their help to collect and inseminate.

The dog may be carrying an injury, and back pain is another reason why dogs won't mount. He could have a sheath cut or infection; also an enlarged or infected prostate can cause such discomfort that even the libido of an over-excited stud dog is dampened with the pain (though ironically a mating would usually provide relief). Experienced owners may collect semen from a dog and artificially inseminate – but don't even think about trying it if you don't know what you are doing. Hopefully he simply needs a poo, and once that is out he'll be raring to go!

Age of stud dog use: Although puppies can show mounting behaviours from five or six weeks, they do not produce semen at this age. Dogs produce viable sperm from around five months of age. Although it would not damage the young male to be used this young, most breeders would wish to carry out some health testing on the dog before he is used. Hips cannot be done in the UK until the dog is a year old (in the US it is two years of age).

Frequency of stud dog use: Each time a dog is used, not all his reserve of sperm is used. The most important features of semen are numbers of sperm, percentage of normal, and sperm motility. Provided he is willing and not sore, the dog could be used twice in one day, or a few days in a row. Sperm live for two to five days (this will be lower in an older male), whereas the egg takes two to three days to mature following ovulation and only lives eighteen to twenty-four hours. The aim in breeding is to have these two meet at the optimum time.

TERMS OF MATING

Stud services are an issue that can cause disagreements and bad feelings, so be very clear (preferably in a written agreement) as to your conditions.

There are no strict terms for stud dog use, as both owners come to their own agreement, but there are a couple of standard points to be considered for both owners. First, a stud owner pro-

STUD DOG CONTRACT

Between the owner of the stud dog, Mr and Mrs Smith
Address, telephone number, email

And the owner(s) of the bitch, Mrs Bloggs
Address, telephone number, email

Kennel Club Registered Name of dog   **Dobers Fred Astaire**

KC registration number: AB00032672   **Microchip 977200007571893**

Kennel Club Registered Name of bitch

KC registration number: **Microchip**

The stud owner confirms that to the best of their knowledge the stud dog is both fertile and in good health. The stud owner gives no warranties regarding the birth of any puppies arising from the mating(s) covered by this contract.

The stud dog has undergone the following health tests (copies attached):

Hip score   8:4 (12)
PHPV (Eye)   Clear
Von Willebrands Disease (vWD)   Carrier
Cardio Echo normal 05/11/2013, Cardio Echo normal 06/11/2014, Troponin 1 normal 04/08/2016, Troponin Probnp normal 04/08/2016.

The stud owner confirms they have seen the bitch's health test results.

The bitch owner will pay the stud owner the sum of £750 for the stud service on _____ dates of mating.

OR.... specify the detail of any other arrangement for the stud service, for example choice of puppy, or payment on confirmation of pregnancy payment on sale of the first puppy.

The stud owner will sign and provide a copy of the Litter Registration Form 1 to the owner of the bitch to confirm the date of the mating, and will provide any other information regarding the mating that the Kennel Club may require within seven days of a written request to do so.

In the event of the bitch not conceiving [stud owner to insert their own conditions, eg repeat mating free of charge] [set square brackets]

I confirm that the contents of this contract are accurate to the best of my/our knowledge.

Owner(s) of Stud Dog _____   **Dated** _____

I confirm that I have read and understand the detail and meaning of this contract prior to the mating, and fully understand its purpose and reason.

Owner(s) of Bitch _____   **Dated** _____

vides the service of stud work for his dog, which is not a guarantee of puppies. Provided your dog has already sired puppies or has puppies due, he is then proven at stud.

A bitch may not become pregnant for various reasons: it may be the wrong mating day, or she is barren, or an infection has killed the semen or embryos. This isn't the responsibility of the owner of a proven stud dog. However, the primary objective is to secure a good and healthy litter for the bitch owner, so most stud owners are flexible when it comes to money and repeat matings. If, for example, the bitch didn't take and is now too old to mate again, most stud owners would transfer the mating to another bitch – they are not obliged to do so, but after all, they have already had a generous stud fee from the bitch owner.

The usual payment method is a flat fee ranging from around £500 to £1,000, depending on the quality and titles of the dog, and whether he has previously produced top quality progeny. Some bitch owners may offer a puppy in return for a mating, but most stud dog owners prefer a straight stud fee. Some creative stud fees, such as a payment per puppy, offers a bonus for multiple puppies – but equally, nothing for none.

Owners may waive a fee until the bitch is in whelp or has puppies, at which stage they will sign the green litter registration document – Form 1 (*see* Breeding, Chapter 14) – and give it to the owner of the bitch upon payment for stud services. Even if the owner of the bitch plans to register the puppies online, they are still required to have a signed copy of the litter registration document as proof of mating and your consent to registration.

Whatever the arrangement, only hand the form over when you have been paid, as you will no recourse otherwise than to privately prosecute if the bitch owner defaults on payment. The Kennel Club cannot get involved.

Stud owners under the Kennel Club Assured Breeder Scheme are required to use a Stud Dog Contract (see sidebar). Similar templates are downloadable from the Kennel Club.

Keeping your stud dog in good condition for mating is no different to how he would be normally kept, with the exception of particular attention to a regular health check of his sheath and testicles. Some stud owners insist on a vaginal swab of visiting bitches prior to their mating to ensure they are clear of any transmittable diseases that can affect both dog and bitch. If your dog is used regularly at stud you may decide to have a periodic sheath swab analysed to make sure he isn't carrying anything that could impact on his health, the health of future bitches, and his value as a stud dog.

If a proven stud dog starts to miss to bitches you should have his semen evaluated and a general health test done. Older dogs can increasingly suffer from benign prostatic hyperplasia (prostate enlargement) or prostatic infection, which will kill his semen. (*See* Prostate Gland in Chapter 10, General Health and Welfare.)

16 GENETICS

This section is not full of complicated genetic sequences and algorithms, not least because the author has no claim to be a geneticist, and there are many far more detailed books on genetics than can be covered here. Nonetheless a basic knowledge of genetics (inheritance) is necessary if you want to be a successful breeder, and not one whose choice of stud dog is dictated by how much winning it has done, or who owns it.

Most breeders are generally only concerned with colour inheritance, and physical and mental trait inheritance, but perhaps the most fundamental thing to know about breeding is that crossing tall to small will not result in medium: it will result in some tall, some small, and some medium, and behind each, hidden genes will lie. Knowledge of the dog's ancestry is necessary to at least have an idea how the puppies will turn out (except when nature plays with our best laid plans).

LAWS OF INHERITANCE (MENDELIAN INHERITANCE)

Gregor Johann Mendel, 1822–1884, was an Austrian biologist who developed the major principles of genetic inheritance, and challenged the previously held belief that genetic combinations work by blending traits together – that if your father was tall and your mother was short, you would be of an average height.

In his famous experiments with sweet peas, Mendel demonstrated his first principle of uniformity when he cross-pollinated one purebred plant with another and produced offspring that looked like either one of the parent plants and not a blend of the two; for example when he crossbred green peas and yellow peas, the progeny had yellow seeds, but green seeds had not vanished; they re-appeared in the next generation in a ratio of three yellow seeded plants to one green-seeded plant 3:1. The traits of the parents were not directly blended but were inherited as 'packets of information'.

Furthermore, if the progeny of purebred plants crosses looked like only one of the parents with regard to a specific trait, Mendel called that expressed parental trait the 'dominant trait'.

Verifying Purity

Mendel experimented with his plants for two years, cross fertilizing pollens to ensure their features were constant in each generation. This verification of purity confirmed which combinations produced particular offspring. When Mendel determined consistency in subsequent generations, he then considered them purebred, or in modern terminology, homozygous.

COLOUR INHERITANCE

We instinctively visualize the Dobermann as a black dog marked with deep tan (rust) points on the head and body. The black/tan colour-

The 'traditional' colour of black and rust. Also referred to as black and tan, or simply black. Ch. Amazon Russian Ice JW. KORIFEY DOBERMANNS

TERMINOLOGY

homozygous: Having two copies of the same gene. All genes are inherited in pairs, one pair from each parent. If the pair of inherited genes from both parents is identical, the pair is called homozygous. Thus Dobermann × Dobermann = Dobermann progeny, or healthy gene × healthy gene = healthy progeny, or diseased gene × diseased gene = diseased progeny.

heterozygous: Having non-matching genes, i.e. Dobermann × Labrador = Doberador, or diseased gene × healthy gene = carrier progeny.

genotype: Genetic composition determining particular characteristics (phenotype) of an individual.

phenotype: Physical appearance determined by the genotype.

allele: Genes determine traits, features, vision, hearing, character. Variations of genes are called alleles, which lead to different traits and are either dominant or recessive.

polygenic: Two or more genes: poly = many. Also termed 'multi-factorial inheritance'. Identifying specific traits is difficult because it is the cumulative effect of several different genes, which do not follow typical dominant and recessive patterns.

dominant and recessive genes: If a trait (or disease) tends to be directly passed from parent to child, then the chances are it is a dominant one. If a trait skips generations or pops up out of nowhere, then the chances are it is recessive.

autosomal dominant: A dominant trait is by definition, always present in the offspring, and therefore an individual only needs to inherit the gene from one parent in order for the trait to develop. At least one of the parents will have the trait.

autosomal recessive: For a trait to develop, two copies of an abnormal gene must be present. The parents will be carriers of the trait, but they won't exhibit the trait because they have only one copy of the gene which is recessive to the normal counterpart gene. Autosomal recessive single-gene diseases often skip one or more generations, which makes tracking traits difficult.

If both parents carry a trait, there is a 25 per cent chance of the offspring inheriting both abnormal genes, and consequently developing the disease. There is a 50 per cent chance of offspring inheriting only one abnormal gene and of being a carrier, and a 25 per cent chance of offspring inheriting both normal genes. The inheritance of von Willebrands disease is a good example of this. (* *See* vWD inheritance chart in Chapter 9, Breed Specific Healthcare.)

locus: the position of a gene, or other notable sequence, on a chromosome.

variable penetrance: In a group of individuals with a particular genetic condition, those who do not exhibit from the condition are said to have variable (incomplete or reduced) penetrance. This may result from various genetic, environmental and lifestyle influences, and makes it challenging for geneticists to determine an individual's risk of passing on a genetic condition to future generations.

COI (Coefficient of In-Breeding): Calculates the percentage of genes passed down from a common ancestor. Each parent passes on around 50 per cent of their genes to their progeny, a grandparent passes on 25 per cent, a great-grandparent 12.5 per cent, and so on. Each time an ancestor appears in the pedigree, its frequency of occurrence is measured as a percentage of density of genes.

Brown and rust, also referred to as brown and tan, chocolate or liver (in the USA), or simply brown. Ch. Jojavik Constanzia JW, ShCM. JOJAVIK DOBERMANNS

Aspen has a deep colour and a full coat for a blue. Owned by Serena Henderson.

This fawn Dobermann bitch Am./ Can. Ch. MACH 5 Royal Future JP Sakura of Dabney, RN MXS2 MJG2 XF T2B, is No. 1 USA Agility Doberman 2016 at eight and a half years old, a remarkable achievement for her age and the popularity of the sport in the USA. STEWART EVENT IMAGES (note: the small spots on the image are raindrops).

ing is the dominant colour of the breed, but the Dobermann is also well known in brown/tan (in America known as liver, or chocolate), and more unusually in blue/tan, and fawn/tan.

The inheritance of colour in the Dobermann is based on a straightforward dominant and recessive pair of genes for black/tan, and brown/tan, with blues, and fawns (Isabella) being dilutions of black and brown respectively. Basic scientific nomenclature in genetics displays a dominant gene with a capital letter, and a recessive gene with a lower case letter. Thus:

Black is denoted by B
Brown is denoted by b

Each parent Dobermann contributes either a black gene or a brown gene to its offspring. BB Dobermanns always contribute a B gene, bb Dobermanns always contribute a b gene, and Bb Dobermanns can contribute one or the other, with a 50 per cent probability of each.

BB: The dog carries two black genes, and is both physically and genetically what we call 'dominant black'. It cannot produce brown offspring.

Bb: The dog carries one (dominant) black gene and one (recessive) brown gene. The dog is physically black but can produce brown puppies.

bb: The dog has two brown genes (recessive). The dog is physically brown and does not carry black, therefore can only produce brown puppies.

Each parent contributes to each pup one gene for colour and another gene for intensity of colour.

Dilution

Dilute genes determine the intensity of colour, but only a few Dobermanns carry the dilute gene. Dilute colours are recessive and are denoted by lower-case letters:

Blue (dilute of black) is denoted by **d**
Fawn (dilute of brown) is denoted by **b**
Lack of blue dilution is denoted by **D**
Lack of fawn dilution is denoted by **B**

As dilution is a recessive trait, two of these recessive genes must be present in order to produce a blue- or fawn-coloured dog.

A dog carrying no dilution factor for either blue or fawn is denoted as DD.

A dog that is Dd will be black or brown but can produce dilution for blue or fawn.

#1 black dog – genotype BBDD: Can only produce black offspring, i.e. dominant black.

#2 black dog – genotype BBDd: Can produce black and blue offspring. Carries a recessive dilution gene for blue, but doesn't carry a brown gene so cannot produce fawn.

#3 black dog – genotype BbDD: Can produce black and brown offspring. Carries both colours, but DD means it carries no dilute genes.

#4 black dog – genotype BbDd: Carries both colours Bb, and the dilute gene Dd, so can produce all four colours: black, brown, blue and fawn.

#5 blue dog – genotype BBdd: Can produce blacks and blues only.

#6 blue dog – genotype Bbdd: Can produce all four colours: blacks, browns, blues and fawns.

#7 brown dog – genotype bbDD: Being brown this dog carries the recessive brown gene, cannot produce blacks, and does not produce dilution.

#8 brown dog – genotype bbDd: This brown can produce dilution of fawn (but not blue, as it does not carry the dominant black gene which dilutes to blue).

#9 fawn dog – genotype bbdd: With two recessive gene pairs, this dog can produce brown, and the dd dilute of fawn.

In practical terms, for example, if a dominant black dog carrying the blue gene is mated to a brown bitch that does not carry the blue gene the litter will only produce black puppies. However, the puppies will carry the brown gene and the blue gene, and if subsequently mated to a dog carrying brown or blue, can produce either colour.

The first recorded fawn was born in Germany in 1912, and although European breeders generally dislike colours, Gruenig knew they were inevitable and natural, writing:

> ...it is indeed a matter of regret that the various breed organizations will not tolerate this beautiful Fawn colour. Our Dobermann could only profit by permitting this colour to assume its rightful place in the spectrum of the breed.

It is odd, therefore, that Gruenig was so disparaging of another unusual but naturally occurring colour in the breed: melanism, which produces a pure black dog without markings. Melanin is a dark pigmentation that colours the skin and/or hair black. Albinism is a condition in which there is a full absence of melanin, which colours the skin, hair and eyes. It is certainly worth reading Gruenig's *The Dobermann* for an in-depth consideration of the early study of colour inheritance in the breed.

The first fawn Dobermann shown in the UK was Twinglo The Silver Wraith of Roanoke, bred by Derrick and Marion D'Cruze, and owned and handled by Jimmy Richardson.

Colour Dilute Alopecia

This condition develops in fawn or blue dogs, and is sometimes seen in black or brown dogs carrying dilute colours. The coat of puppies and young dogs is thick and lustrous, but with maturity becomes progressively more coarse, dry, thin and patchy. The lighter the coat colour, the earlier the deterioration in coat quality. Bacterial infections may occur, usually on the backline where hair follicles become impacted from not being able to grow through the thickened skin. This keratosis can be treated with antibiotics, but the hair of the affected area is very slow to grow again, if it does so at all. (*See* Chapter 9, 'Colour Dilute Alopecia' in the last 'A–Z' section.)

WHITE DOBERMANNS

The first recorded case of a so-called white Dobermann was in the USA in November 1976 when a white-coloured bitch puppy was born from black and tan parents (Rasputin VI and dam Dynamo Humm). All the other puppies in the litter were normal black and tan. The puppy was named Padula's Queen Shebah, and had pale blue eyes, and a pink nose, and pink eye rims, pads and membranes; where tan markings would normally be, there was a cream colour. Being the first white Dobermann, the AKC had no system by which to register this colour, but Padula's Queen Shebah finally gained AKC registration in 1978.

Shebah was bred to a dominant black male, and produced fourteen black and tan pups. She was later mated to one of her sons and produced two white male pups by him. Sheba's son was then bred to his litter sister, and produced two white bitch puppies. This extremely high level of in-breeding has fixed the albino trait.

White Dobermanns are not dilute colour: they have an absence of melanin, which leaves them nearly without pigment. The true albino has a complete absence of colour (although the nose and eyes appear pink, this is due to the blood vessels). The white Dobermann has a cream-coloured coat and usually blue eyes: this is termed partial albinism, or with albinistic traits. Interestingly the coat on the white Dobermann is usually quite dense. There is currently no gene marker to identify white Dobermanns, and normal-coloured dogs carry the gene. The albino mutation is not related to the dilute genes of blue and fawn, and therefore cannot be bred by continued in-breeding of either colour.

The Doberman Pinscher Club of America (DPCA) claim through their research (from hav-

---

COAT THICKNESS

Thickness of coat ranges from black and tans with the thickest adult coat, at a reported 100 hairs per square inch, brown and tans with 80 hairs psi, blues with 60 hairs psi, and fawns with the thinnest coat density at 55 hairs psi.

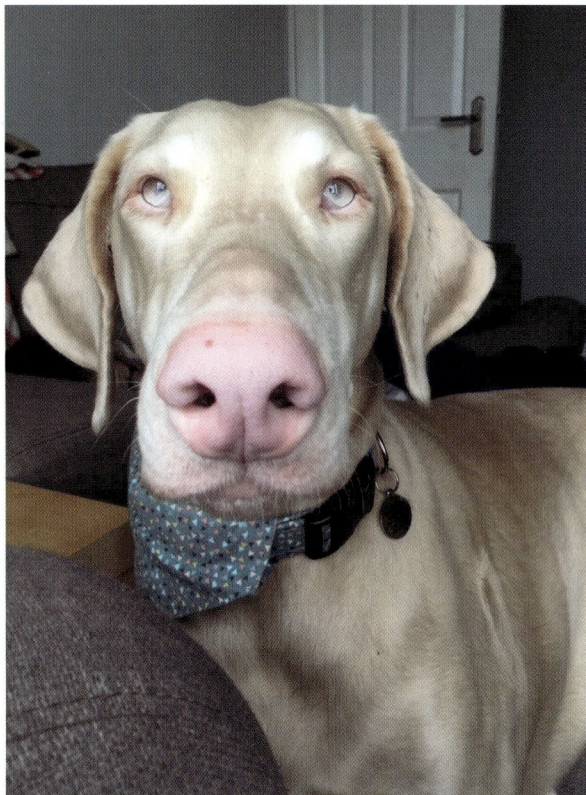

Nena, descendant of Sheba. Rescued and owned by Louise Lawson.

ing purchased two white Dobermanns) that albinistic dogs are photophobic (sensitive to sunlight), have vision problems resulting from abnormal development of the retina, are prone to skin cancer and skin lesions, and are susceptible to skin damage from the sun. The proponents of the white Dobermann counter that there are no such problems with their dogs, and that they function as normally as any other dog.

In 1982 the DPCA successfully petitioned the American Kennel Club (AKC) to prevent white Dobermanns being shown by amending the breed standard to include a disqualifying clause 'dogs not of an allowed colour'.

Breeders also feared they could mix their bloodlines with a white, if a dog carrying the white gene was unknowingly used in breeding, so the AKC introduced registration of white Dobermanns with the letter 'Z' denoting their

status. The DPCA were unsuccessful in requesting that the AKC impose breeding restrictions on the white Dobermanns.

The first white Dobermann in the UK was Phantom's Flaxen Lass CGC, born in 1997 (Krystal Palace's Cameo Dam × Phantom's Starlight TT CGC), who was imported in whelp by a breeder with a kennel name of Dobenar, who were already breeding for colours. The UK has no disqualifying clauses in any UK breed standard, and whites have been shown in the UK on a couple of occasions.

Following requests from the Dobermann Breed Council, the Kennel Club here also initiated a registry tracking system to enable breeders to avoid white Dobermanns in their breeding. Over a twenty-year period there are now around 531 Dobermanns in the UK with white ancestry (carrying the white gene).

BREEDING METHODS

The idea of purebred pedigree dogs is that they should breed true to type –that is, Mendel's verification of purity. When one breed is mated with another of the same breed, the progeny will have uniform characteristics and will resemble that particular breed (homozygosity). Selective breeding is done to fix a desired feature by mating dogs within a closely related line, although it can also expose undesirable recessive genes.

All Dobermanns will be related to one another at some place in their pedigree, and the terminology of 'in-breeding' and 'line-breeding' differ from each other only in terms of degree.

In-Breeding

In-breeding is the breeding together of two very closely related dogs, such as father/daughter, mother/son, brother/sister. The COI of these incestuous matings is 25 per cent, and they were banned by the Kennel Club in March 2009. Notably COIs in excess of 25 per cent can be made through continual close breeding throughout the pedigree.

In-breeding greatly increases uniformity (homozygosity) expression in litters, and therefore increases the chances of both beneficial and detrimental recessive genes meeting through creating homozygous recessive offspring (doubling up). In-breeding cannot create a problem which does not exist, but if a faulty gene exists on both sides of the pedigree, it significantly doubles the chances of the progeny developing that fault (expression), especially if in-breeding is continued over subsequent generations. A breeder may not realize they have missing teeth or light eyes in their line until they in-breed and these faults come to the surface. It is obviously of great importance, therefore, that only the very best examples of the resulting progeny from in-bred dogs *without those undesirable traits* should go on for breeding.

This is what happens when a rare or hidden faulty gene is passed through both the sire and dam. If you are to in-breed, be very careful that you know your stock extremely well.

Line-breeding

Line-breeding is the breeding together of two dogs that are related to each other, but to a lesser degree than in-breeding. Line-breeding aims to concentrate the genes of a specific ancestor or ancestors through their frequent appearance in a pedigree.

Genes from common ancestors on both the sire and dam sides of the pedigree have a better chance of pairing up (expression) in the resultant pups than when paired with genes from other individuals, which may mask or alter their effects.

Line-breeding may produce an excellent puppy, but if those qualities are not present in any of the ancestors he has been line-bred on, he may not breed true.

Ancestors much past the third generation (grandparents) generally have little direct impact on the phenotype of an individual, but that does depend on how they were bred, because whilst an influential individual may not appear in a five-generation pedigree, if they appear three or four times behind that, they obviously contribute a large proportion of the genes to the pedigree.

Line-breeding is still very commonplace in the UK, although grandfather/grand-daughter matings are rarely done now. Provided the breeder knows which physical and/or mental traits they

want to maintain, and which they want to eliminate, line-breeding can be a very effective way to produce dogs of outstanding quality and type if done sensibly and with dogs that are not already tightly line-bred.

A breeder with a tightly in-bred bitch may, quite sensibly, decide to out-breed to gain some of what is termed 'hybrid vigour'.

Out-Breeding

Out-breeding is the combining of two dogs with unrelated genes from different ancestors (heterozygosity). This results in wider gene diversity within each dog by increasing so-called hybrid vigour. It is quite common to produce an excellent quality dog from an out-bred litter, but with their low in-breeding coefficient they may not reliably pass on those good traits to their progeny, so after out-breeding, breeders often breed back to dogs in their original pedigree to increase homozygosity in an attempt to maintain the newly acquired traits.

Although Victor van Roveline was ostensibly an out-bred dog with a very low COI of 2.1 per cent, study of his pedigree shows he is line-bred on siblings Lucifer and Lema van Roveline. Vito's prepotency* is well evidenced by the 'stamp' he put on his progeny.

* Prepotent is the term used to describe a being which has great hereditary powers and influence in transmitting its hereditary characteristics to its offspring. The term is usually reserved to describe stud dogs, but it may equally be used to describe the hereditary powers of a great brood bitch.

The Disadvantages of In-Breeding

The statement that 'in-breeding causes health problems' is far too limiting, because if a line does not carry a specific defect it cannot be created. The issue is, however, that individuals who carry recessive (hidden) deleterious genes do not suffer clinical effects, but in a small population with close relatives continually mating with each other, there is a higher chance of those dogs matching up and producing two copies of the same recessive deleterious gene in the offspring, who will then suffer from a previously hidden condition.

With continued generations of in-bred dogs, the parents will become increasingly similar genetically, and this lack of new genetic material will ultimately result in what is termed an 'in-breeding depression'. The symptoms of in-breeding depression may be very subtle, and are often blamed on diet and other environmental factors. However, over time it progresses to a general loss of substance, lowered fitness, an increase in illnesses and less resistance to disease, auto-immune disease, a reduction in fertility and rates of conception, and an earlier average age of death in a line or in the general breed population.

As an island the UK was effectively cut off from access to dogs in mainland Europe for many years, and imported dogs had to go through six months quarantine. Although there were some notable imports to the UK, there was a profound and continued level of in-breeding, with COIs of 30 per cent or greater not being uncommon. Line-breeding became the mantra of breeders, and such was the devotion to this system that breeders were line-breeding just because a pedigree 'tied in', even if the dog that was being tied in was of poor quality.

READING A PEDIGREE

Pedigrees are usually shown with four or five generations of ancestry. At the top of the pedigree will be your dog's name with his date of birth, his breeder, and sometimes other information such as his sex, colour, KC registration number and perhaps the breeder's contact details.

IN SUMMARY

- In-breeding doubles up on merits but also on faults.
- In zoo and captive breeding programmes, studies on forty captive populations belonging to thirty-eight species showed an average increase in mortality of 33 per cent for in-bred matings (Ralls *et al.*, 1988).

Pedigrees always have the male line displayed on the upper part of the sheet, and females on the lower half. In the first top left-hand box you will find the sire of the dog, and in the first bottom left-hand box is the dam. From the sire's box you then look right to see his parents, which are your dog's grandparents, and in turn each grandparent will show their parents, which are your puppy's great-grandparents and in the fifth generation GGG grandparents.

The correct terminology for breeding is that puppies are sired *by a dog* and are *out of* a bitch.

Dogs are always listed above the line and before bitches in pedigrees, reference and adverts.

An interesting pedigree is not one that just lists the dogs' names, but one that declares some details regarding the dogs: their colour, titles and the major wins of their ancestors, their health test results, and perhaps their own date of birth and death. It is not possible to include all those details in the standard five-generation pedigree because of lack of space, but those names can be researched online for further information.

Championship titles are traditionally denoted in red type. Be aware that if you are choosing a sire in England, there will be far fewer championship titles in his pedigree than in the rest of the world, as it is far harder to title a dog in the UK. You would still expect to see some modicum of success at shows, but class wins and even BIS awards are not traditionally detailed on the pedigree.

If you are breeding for working or agility homes, you will attract more buyers if your dog's pedigree contains a history of dogs with working, agility or obedience titles.

BREEDING GOALS

When evaluating your breeding goals, remember that you will not change style or fix features in a single generation. Many thousands of genes interact to control individual features and variations of style within a breed, so the more information you can obtain on how certain traits have been transmitted by your dog's ancestors, the more successful you will be if you think more than one generation ahead.

In 2011 the Kennel Club introduced publicly accessible online programmes called Mate Select to provide breeders with information about the health of individual dogs and potential combinations in mating. These include Health Test Results Finder, Estimated Breeding Values, and Individual Breed In-breeding Coefficients, Mating In-breeding Coefficients, and Individual In-breeding Coefficients.

Wright's Coefficient of In-Breeding (COI) was devised by the American geneticist Sewall Wright in 1921 as a means of calculating the level of genetic uniformity (density of genes) in a pedigree. A complete outcross (based on no pedigree correlation) may have a COI of 0 per cent, and a highly in-bred dog could have a COI of over 40 per cent. From a general gene-pool health perspective, the lower the COI the better, and breed clubs in some countries do not approve matings over a particular percentage, usually around 12 per cent, for that reason. It is worth noting that in British law, cousins are allowed to marry, and their children have a COI of 6.25 per cent, which in itself is a reasonably low COI and is unlikely to produce expression of any deleterious traits.

The difference in COI between four and six generation pedigrees can vary greatly, and the more generations that are available, the more accurate the calculation of COI will be. Calculations can only work if it is known how tightly a dog is bred, and omitting two highly in-bred and related dogs even in the eighth generation or over, will show a considerably lower COI for the dog than he actually has. The COI on Mate Select is calculated using all the electronically held pedigree by the Kennel Club, typically going back to the late 1970s/early 1980s. Beyond about twenty generations COI is not expected to increase further, as the genetic variants are thought to have become 'fixed' within a population.

COI can help prevent the novice breeder from breeding too tightly, but the information is of little benefit unless you are informed about the dogs on which the calculations are based. A hypothetical mating may show that the combination of mates you are considering would give a COI of 15 per cent against the average COI for Kennel Club registered Dobermanns of 5.2 per cent (2016), but you may feel that the character, health and physical attributes of the combination outweigh the data of the higher COI.

FURTHER COI INFORMATION

The COI calculator provides you with a percentage score: the lower the percentage, the lower the degree of inbreeding. Therefore in-breeding coefficients may appear as follows:

- 0 per cent indicates a dog that comes from two unrelated parents, based on all available pedigree information
- 12.5 per cent would equate to the genetic equivalent of a dog produced from a grandfather to granddaughter mating
- 25 per cent would equate to the genetic equivalent of a dog produced from a father to daughter mating
- In-breeding can be accumulative, so if it has occurred to a significant degree over several generations, the in-breeding coefficient may exceed 25 per cent

See more at http://www.thekennelclub.org.uk/services/public/mateselect/breed/Default.aspx?id=5121#sthash.UMkWFU7b.dpuf

A high COI may not be clinically expressed (evident), which may mean that the recessive gene is not one of great importance – but it may also mean that it has not yet found an opportunity to express itself and is stored up for the future. In most cases the positive and negative effects of inbreeding are not apparent at less than 20 per cent, and there are examples of isolated herds of cattle and other species which despite having had a high COI for many years, continue to thrive with high levels of vigour.

As an example, Gino Gomez del Citone, born in 1997, was a prolific winner and producer. He sired over 500 progeny and his descendants are in most countries in the world. He became IDC Sieger, DV Sieger, and his work record was equally as outstanding, with SchH3 and Angekort 1A. Gino was the result of an incest mating, as his sire and dam were littermates. He had a very high COI of 30 per cent, and each parent had a COI of 9.3021 per cent. (Information kindly provided by www.dobermannpedigrees.nl.)

Mathematical equations and programmes can be useful to the novice breeder, and may be used as a reference for experienced breeders, but they must not be used as a stand-alone mechanism for deciding which mating combination to put together. Consider, for example, a hypothetical mating that offers a pleasingly low COI, but the grandparents both died young, had poor conformation and unsound characters. COIs are just one tool to assist the breeder who has already done the majority of their work.

Breeding is not a science to which algorithms and formulas should be applied. Should that ever become the case, the skills of research and imagination that make a great breeder would be lost to history.

GLOSSARY

Bite – the alignment of the teeth

Brushing hocks – hocks brush together on the move

Close coupled – short in loin

Coupling – area between last rib and pelvis, aka loin

Cow hocked – hocks turning in towards each other (like knock knees)

Crabbing – moving at an angle. Hind feet moving to one side of forefeet, aka side-winding.

Crest – arch at the top of the neck just behind the ears

Croup – from the uppermost point of the pelvis to the tail

Crossing over – front legs turn inwards on the move and cross over in front of each other, aka knitting

Cryptorchid – male with neither testicle visible

Cushion – full upper lips

Dewlap – excess skin under the throat

Dish-faced – the nose is higher at the nostrils than at the point between the eyes.

Domed-skull – the upper skull line is dome shaped and not level as it should be

Down-faced – the nasal bone inclines downwards towards the tip of the nose and is not parallel with the upper skull line

Drop-nosed – a drop from behind the start of the nostril line to the front of the nostril

Dry head – free from wrinkle

Dry lips – clean, tight lip line

Dry neck – clean, tight neck line

Elbowing out – elbows do not stay close to the body on the move

Ewe neck – neck curves upwards with over-developed muscles under neck line stronger than neck muscles on top of neck

Flews – loose hanging lips

Floating rib – 13th rib unattached to other ribs, and appears to float

Foreface – from eyes forward to nose, the muzzle

French front – feet turned out, pasterns close, out at elbows, aka Chippendale front

Gay tail – tail carried high set on, at right angle to the back

Hackney action – front legs picked up in high stepping motion, caused by straight angled front

Hare-foot – long flat foot

Haw – inner membrane at corner of the eye

Hocks well let down – hocks close to ground, short rear pastern

Knuckling over – pastern joint doesn't lock firm on the stand, often found on straight angled dogs

Layback – shoulder lays back at angle of 45 degrees/oblique angle

Loaded shoulders – over-muscled or heavy with fat on shoulders

Leggy – too long in leg in comparison with body depth

Level back – topline parallel to ground instead of having required gentle slope

Level on the move – topline does not bounce, sag or roach when dog moves (because the shoulders drop down on the move, the normal incline of the back from withers to croup levels on the move)

Level bite – front teeth meet together instead of as a scissor bite, aka even bite

Monorchid – male with only one testicle visible

Moving close – hind legs move close together, not single tracking

Occiput – protrusion at the top and back of the head

Occlusion – the meeting of the front teeth (upper and lower)

Over reaching – faulty movement; rear feet either collide with front feet or side-step to avoid collision

Pigeon-chested – protruding breastbone and lacking in fill underneath

Pigeon-toed – feet point inwards to each other, aka ten to two

Pinning in – legs bend inwards on the move

Ridge – section of hair growing opposite to the direction of the rest

Roach back – convex arch over the back carried high

Roman nose – top of muzzle curved

Scissor bite – upper teeth very slightly overlap the lower teeth (like scissors)

Slab sided – flat ribs with no spring or roundness

Snatching hocks – as hock passes a point on its upward motion there is a sharp snatch that causes the rear pastern to drop in under the body

Snipey – a narrow muzzle ending in a sharp point

Spectacles – pale or absent hair around the eyes

Sternum – breast bone

Straight in front – insufficient lay back of shoulder

Straight behind – insufficient turn of stifle (knee joint)

Sway back – concave arch on the back, carried low, aka saddle back

Throaty – excess skin under the throat

Thumb marks – the two tan prints on either cheek; also refers to black markings on feet

Tied at elbows – elbows too tightly adhered to ribcage

Tuck up – shape of the underline

Vent – tan hair markings under the tail

Wry mouth – lower and upper jaw out of alignment with each other

FURTHER INFORMATION

Chapter 2:
For info regarding breeds in the UK most commonly known for bite injuries:

https://www.avma.org/KB/Resources/LiteratureReviews/Pages/The-Role-of-Breed-in-Dog-Bite-Risk-and-Prevention.aspx

Chapter 3:

REGISTERED BREED RESCUE ORGANIZATIONS

Most of the organizations given below are national rescue/re-homing organizations, while some network with other organizations.

Dobermann Rehoming Association http://dobermannrehome.co.uk

Surrey-based national network: Mrs Chris Omar, tel. 01276 855326

Dobermann Rescue www.dobermann-rescue.co.uk

Two main centres:
Hilbrae Kennels in Telford: Val Griffiths, tel. 01952 4094740

Cranfield Kennels in Wickford, Essex: Mr and Mrs Gibbins, tel. 01268 733353

Dobermann Trust dogs@dobermanntrust.org.uk

Yorkshire-based national network, tel. 0330 111 4466

FOND – Friends of Northern Dobermanns www.fondofdobermanns.org.uk

Scottish-based national network, Pam Hall, tel. 01346 532227

Dobermann Welfare	National network
Sue Garner Kent	01895 253578
Sue James Wales	01685 844362
Diane Steane Middlesex	01895 833153
Evelyn Sengendo Scotland	01294 272184

Dobermann Rescue UK and Europe (DRUE)
Zara Hayes National/International 07712 647795
Liz Price National/International 07810 827367

Dobermanns in Need
Hampshire-based covering the south. Val McDonald and Mark Durrant, tel. 01243 542545

Some breed club websites have rescue details of dogs in their regions that need re-homing.

Birmingham and District Dobermann Club

Midland Dobermann Club

North East Counties Dobermann Society

North of England Dobermann Club

Northern Ireland Dobermann Club

South East of England Dobermann Club

South West of England Dobermann Club

The Dobermann Club

Welsh Dobermann Club

RECOMMENDED READING

Breed books

Gruenig, Philipp, *The Dobermann Pinscher* (Orange Judd Publishing Co., 1959, translated into English by Maximillian von Hoegen, 1939) Also published as *The Doberman Pinscher* for the USA market. Comprehensive reference to breeding and pedigree development of the Dobermann

Ladd, Mark, *Dobermanns* (The Crowood Press, 1989) Mark Ladd also produced a series of three volumes of Dobermann Champions of the UK

Richardson, Jimmy, *Dobermanns Today* (Ringpress, 1995)

The Complete Doberman Pinscher (Howell). A collection of topics by noted breed authorities, including Gerda Umlauff, daughter of Peter Umlauff, breeder, owner and President of the National Dobermann Pinscher Club.

Training and Psychology

Aloff, Brenda, *Practical Management, Prevention, and Behaviour Modification* (Dogwise, 2002). The author has written other useful books which are highly recommended.

Booth, Sheila, and Dildei, Gottfried *Schutzhund Obedience: Training in Drive* (Podium Publications, 1992)

Fogle, Bruce, *The Dog's Mind* (Turner Pubishing Co.,1992)

Hallgren, Anders, *Stress, Anxiety and Aggression in Dogs* (Cadmos Books, 2013)

Rugaas, Turid, *On Talking Terms with Dogs: Calming Signals* (Dogwise Publishing, 2005) Highly recommended.

Volhard, Jack and Wendy, *Dog Training for Dummies* (Wiley, 2001). Don't be insulted by the title; this book enables readers to understand basic and advanced drives, and how the owner/trainer can manipulate those drives for best advantage in both training, and management of dogs including 'problem' animals. The focus is on how changing our human behaviour changes the dogs' behaviour. http://www.volhard.com

For sport trainers, Ivan Balabanov series of online video tutorials are an asset for the trainer who wants to improve their relationship with the working dog.

http://malinois.com/obedience-without-conflict/

Breeding

Bloomfield, Samantha, *The Manual of Puppy Hand Rearing: The Complete Practical Guide* (Bloomfield Scully Ltd., 2013). Recommended reading on hand-rearing puppies.

Evans, J.M., and White, Kay, *The Book of the Bitch* (Henston, 1994)

Jackson, Frank, *Dog Breeding: The Theory and The Practice'* (The Crowood Press, 2000)

INDEX